THE NEW LATIN AMERICAN LEFT

Critical Currents in
Latin American Perspective

Ronald H. Chilcote, Series Editor

THE NEW LATIN AMERICAN LEFT

Cracks in the Empire

Edited by
Jeffery R. Webber and Barry Carr

ROWMAN & LITTLEFIELD PUBLISHERS, INC.
Lanham • Boulder • New York • Toronto • Plymouth, UK

Published by Rowman & Littlefield Publishers, Inc.
A wholly owned subsidary of The Rowman & Littlefield Publishing Group, Inc.
4501 Forbes Boulevard, Suite 200, Lanham, Maryland 20706
www.rowman.com

10 Thornbury Road, Plymouth PL6 7PP, United Kingdom

British Library Cataloguing in Publication Information Available

Library of Congress Cataloging-in-Publication Data
The new Latin American left : cracks in the empire / edited by Jeffery R. Webber and Barry Carr.
     pages cm. — (Critical currents in Latin American perspective series)
  Includes bibliographical references and index.
  ISBN 978-0-7425-5757-4 (hardback) — ISBN 978-0-7425-5758-1 (paper) — ISBN 978-0-7425-5759-8 (electronic)
  1. Social movements—Latin America. 2. Social change—Latin America. 3. Social conflict—Latin America. 4. Latin America—Politics and government. I. Webber, Jeffery R. II. Carr, Barry.
  HN110.5.A8N49 2013
  303.48'4—dc23

                                                                                    2012027849

Printed in the United States of America

Contents

1

Introduction

The Latin American Left in Theory and Practice

Jeffery R. Webber and Barry Carr

AFTER THE 1980S DEBT CRISIS and the parallel neoliberal assault across Latin America, the last decade has witnessed a resurgence of leftist movements and governments in the region (Petras and Veltmeyer, 2005, 2009). As imperial wars were waged in other areas of the world, Latin America served as a beacon of hope for the Left, a site of resistance. Latin American peasant, worker, and indigenous radicalism seemed to restore radical reform and, in some cases, revolution to the vocabulary. At the same time, center-left governments assumed power in Argentina, Chile, Uruguay, Brazil, Nicaragua, El Salvador, and, most recently, Peru, continuing the neoliberal capitalist projects that preceded them, if in modified forms. The possibilities and limitations of the Hugo Chávez, Evo Morales, and Rafael Correa governments in Venezuela, Bolivia, and Ecuador raise fundamental questions concerning the plausibility of advancing a twenty-first-century socialist model against the model of global capitalism.

This volume—bringing together political scientists, historians, sociologists, and economists—provides an assessment of the state of the Left in Latin America. In part I, our authors address the central thematic issues of the period in question, while in part II the focus on a number of nationally based case studies. Our authors address some fundamental questions: What role is there for state power in current left political projects? What might revolution look like in the twenty-first century? What forms do class struggles take in today's context? What are the dynamics of center-left governments? How do indigenous struggles relate to left politics? What is the role of gender in revolutionary and populist movements? How has the American empire reacted to the resurgence of the Latin American Left? What have been the advances and what obstacles remain in building a counter-hegemonic regional bloc of anti-imperialist peoples and states in Latin America? As the diversity of perspectives developed in this volume illustrates, our authors reflect the broad methodological and theoretical positions held by Latin Americanist scholars. They also try to avoid the uncritical celebration of the "pink tide" phenomenon that has dominated much writing.

In the early 1990s, the Latin American Left had reached its nadir of the twentieth century (Carr and Ellner, 1993; Chilcote, 2003). Anyone who had predicted then that less than a decade later the region would witness a resurgence in extra-parliamentary radicalism, a tide of electoral victories for left and center-left parties, and a renewal of debates around socialism and the future of anticapitalism would have been subjected to ridicule. The brutal bureaucratic authoritarian regimes in the Southern Cone during the 1960s and 1970s, and the Central American counterinsurgencies of the early 1980s, wiped out much of the Left in these areas. The 1980s debt crisis ushered in a quarter century of neoliberal restructuring that saw labor unions and working-class power decline sharply. The fall of the Soviet Union and its client states in Eastern Europe, the subsequent isolation of Cuba, and the electoral demise of the Sandinistas in Nicaragua in 1990 made any talk of a viable socialism appear hopelessly romantic.[1] Many social movements retreated into localized concerns at the neighborhood and community levels, as the objective of conquering power on the national stage seemed far beyond reach. Nongovernmental organizations, progressive intellectuals, and most left parties in Latin America turned sharply to the right, accepting the basic presuppositions of the Washington Consensus as the new parameters for reasonable debate and policy proposal.

Economic growth over the course of the 1980s and 1990s—the core neoliberal epoch of Latin America's "silent revolution"—included a modest boom (1991–1997), positioned between "the lost decade" of the 1980s and the "lost half-decade" between 1997 and 2002. The neoliberal policy era progressed through the "deep recession" of 1982–1983, the "false dawn" of a temporary and meager recovery in positive per capita growth from 1984 to 1987, the increasing depth and breadth of neoliberal policy implementation between 1988 and 1991, and a thorough attempt to consolidate the model throughout the 1990s and early 2000s in the midst of increasing contradictions and crises—the Mexican Peso Crisis in 1994–1995, Brazil's financial breakdown in 1998 in the wake of the Asian and Russian crises, and, most dramatically, the Argentine collapse, which reached its apex in December 2001.

Following twenty years of debt rescheduling, the region's total debt was approximately $725 billion U.S. by 2002, twice the figure at the onset of the debt crisis. Poverty rates between 1980 and 2002 increased from 40.5 percent of the population in 1980 to 44 percent in 2002. In absolute figures, this translated into an increase of 84 million poor people, from 136 million in 1980 to 220 million in 2002 (Damián and Boltvinik, 2006: 145). Latin America continued to be the most unequal part of the world, such that in 2003 the top 10 percent of the population earned 48 percent of all income (Reygadas, 2006: 122). A brief uptick in growth occurred beginning in 2003 as a result of high commodity prices, but the onset of the global financial crisis beginning in 2007 slowed down growth, albeit unevenly, throughout Latin America (Aguiar de Medeiros, 2009: 132). It is now widely understood that during "the twenty-five years of the Washington Consensus, the Latin American economies have experienced their worst quarter century since the catastrophic second quarter of the nineteenth century" (Coatsworth, 2005: 137). Measured by gross domestic product per capita, life expectancy, and literacy in the twentieth century, Latin America performed best between 1940 and 1980, the era of import-substitution industrialization (ISI). In the region's six largest economies, annual GDP growth in the ISI period was over four-and-a-half times greater than between 1980 and 2000, the years of orthodox neoliberalism (Love, 2005: 107).

Surveying the political landscape today, the balance of social forces has clearly shifted quite dramatically since the early 1990s. Social contradictions of the neoliberal model generated a series of crises in the closing years of the 1990s and opening moments of the current decade. Popular uprisings overthrew heads of state in Argentina, Bolivia, Ecuador, and elsewhere as rural and urban insurrection across the region began to challenge the impunity with which the ruling classes and imperialism had set the economic and political agenda. This popular discontent with neoliberalism also manifested itself through the ballot box, beginning with the election of Hugo Chávez in Venezuela in 1998 and culminating most recently in the March 2009 election of Mauricio Funes in El Salvador and the June 2011 election of Ollanta Humala. However, alongside the relatively hopeful if contradictory Bolivarian Revolution in Venezuela, the so-called pink tide has also included the governments of Luiz Ignácio Lula da Silva in Brazil and now Dilma Rouseff, Michelle Bachelet in Chile (until the right-wing candidate Sebastián Piñera won the presidential elections of early 2010), Néstor Kirchner (and now Cristina Fernández de Kirchner) in Argentina, and Tabaré Vázquez (and now José Mujica) in Uruguay, among other self-proclaimed leftists. These governments tend to speak out against neoliberalism while in practice enacting only "mild redistributive programmes respectful of prevailing property relations" and have proved capable of pushing "forward a new wave of capitalist globalisation with greater credibility than their orthodox neoliberal predecessors" (Robinson, 2008: 292).

In these mildly reformist cases, there has been only modest redistribution of income or wealth, much less a challenge to capitalist social-property relations.

The ultimate trajectory of the pink tide depends on the Left's capacities to counter right-wing oppositions and ongoing imperialist meddling in the sovereign affairs of Latin American nations; just as crucial, though, will be the course of the battle between different currents within the Left seeking to gain hegemony over the anti-neoliberal bloc. Latin America "has moved into an historic conjuncture in which the struggle among social and political forces could push the new resistance politics into mildly social democratic and populist outcomes," William I. Robinson points out, "or into more fundamental, potentially revolutionary ones." Results "will depend considerably on the configuration of class and social forces in each country and the extent to which regional and global configurations of these forces open up new space and push such governments in distinct directions" (2007: 148).

Between a Radical Left and an *Izquierda Permitida*

The Left, for the purposes of this volume, is broadly defined to encompass social movement, party, and regime modalities. We understand the Left to include regimes, political parties, and social movements that challenge, in different ways and to different degrees, neoliberal capitalism, imperialism, and class exploitation, as well as oppose sexual, gender, class, ethnic, and racial oppressions. A number of scholars have pointed out the specificities and multiplicities of the different lefts that have emerged within the generalized regional tide of the last decade (Ramírez Gallegos, 2006). Our theoretical framework seeks to take account of the particularities of each country's social formation and historical complexity without succumbing to mere empirical description of endless varieties.

Classifying and describing the forces of the Left in Latin America has become increasingly difficult. For a start, many of the political party formations that currently make up the pink tide have little if any imbrication in the history of the left wing as it has developed over the past half century. This is the case, for example, of Rafael Correa in Ecuador and to a large degree of Hugo Chávez in Venezuela and Ollanta Humala in Peru. Where, one might ask, should we place the president of Paraguay, Fernando Lugo, a former Catholic bishop with no prior history of involvement in left-wing politics other than a rhetorical commitment to "the poor." In other cases, governments that are sustained by familiar left-wing formations suggest a pattern of continuities that is somewhat exaggerated. The Frente Sandinista de Liberación Nacional (Sandinista National Liberation Front, FSLN) in Nicaragua (under President

Daniel Ortega), for example, has moved a long way from the revolutionary stance that the Sandinistas exemplified in the 1970s and 1980s. In Mexico, the largest party of the Left, the Partido de la Revolución Democrática (Party of the Democratic Revolution, PRD), has increasingly become a reservoir of disaffected elements or refugees from centrist and even conservative parties.

Nevertheless, it is useful, we argue, to situate contemporary Latin American lefts theoretically along a continuum between two ideal types: a radical Left, on the one hand, and an *izquierda permitida*, on the other. This is the driving theme tying together the various theoretical and case-study chapters. Which currents of the revitalization of Latin American radicalism represent a significant challenge to neoliberalism, imperialism, and even potentially capitalism itself? Which, in other words, constitute a radical alternative? And which components of the same resurgence represent a transition to an *izquierda permitida*, or "authorized Left"? Our use of the term *izquierda permitida* draws on Charles Hale's theorization of the notion of *indio permitido* in the era of neoliberal multiculturalism in Latin America. Hale used this term to describe the way in which neoliberal states in the 1990s adopted a language of cultural recognition of indigenous people and even enacted modest reforms in the area of indigenous rights; at the same time, these states set strict predetermined limits to the extent of reform. Neoliberal multiculturalism in this way divided and domesticated indigenous movements through selective co-optation. In particular, the era of the *indio permitido* has meant that cultural rights are to be enjoyed on the implicit condition that indigenous movements will not challenge foundational neoliberal economic policies. Indigenous movements that have submitted more or less to the framework of neoliberal multiculturalism fall into Hale's category *indio permitido*, or "authorized Indian" (Hale 1996, 2002, 2004, 2006).

Adapting this theoretical framework to the context of the Latin American Left, the authors of this volume explore the varied experiences of the ostensibly left regimes, political parties, and social movements of different countries in terms of how closely they adhere to the notion of *izquierda permitida* and ask whether they represent the mature realization of, or at least a potential transition toward, a more radical Left. The *izquierda permitida* signals deep continuities with neoliberal capitalism and adapts easily to U.S. imperial strategies. In its regime form, it seeks to divide and co-opt radical left social movements and parties. The radical Left, on the other hand, offers fundamental challenges to empire, neoliberalism, and capitalism.

The radical Left works to overturn capitalist class rule and capitalist states in Latin America through the activity and struggle of the popular classes and oppressed peoples themselves. It envisions a transition toward democratic social coordination of the economy and the construction of a development model in which human needs are prioritized above the needs of capital.

The radical Left fights for communal ownership of economic and natural resources. It pushes for worker and community control of workplaces and neighborhoods. The radical Left sees liberal capitalist democracy as a limited expression of popular sovereignty and seeks instead to expand democratic rule through all political, social, economic, and private spheres of life. It is anti-imperialist, seeking the regional liberation of Latin America and the Caribbean and challenging the imperial pretensions of the American empire, as well as those of its emergent rivals active in the region. This is quite distinct from earlier versions of state capitalism or nationalist populism in Latin American twentieth-century history, which sought merely state ownership of the means of production in strategic economic sectors and state allocation of resources.

The radical Left described here is an ideal type, a vision of society toward which increasing numbers of Latin Americans hope to transition out of existing capitalism through processes of struggle. No new economic system drops from the sky, Michael Lebowitz (2006: 61) points out. Rather than dropping from the sky or emerging pristine and complete from the conceptions of intellectuals, new productive forces and relations of production emerge within and in opposition to the existing society. One implication is that the new society can never be fully formed at the beginning. Initially, that new society must build upon elements of the old society. The radical Left indigenous social movements that arose in Bolivia between 2000 and 2005, and the radical socialist flanks of the *Chavista* movement in Venezuela, are arguably those social forces that most closely approximate the outlook of the radical Left described above.

Perhaps the best analytical starting point for an understanding of the *izquierda permitida* ideal type, the radical Left's antipode, is what Jorge Castañeda, a former leftist, describes approvingly as the "reconstructed, formerly radical left." The reconstructed governments of Chile under Michelle Bachelet (until her recent electoral defeat to right-wing Sebastián Piñera), Uruguay under Tabaré Vázquez (and now José Mujica), and Brazil under Lula (and now Rouseff), for example, stress "social policy—education, anti-poverty programs, health care, housing—but within a more or less orthodox market framework." When the parties of the *izquierda permitida* have come to office in recent years, their "economic policies have been remarkably similar to those of [their neoliberal] predecessors" (Castañeda, 2006: 35). As we have seen, in the final years of the 1990s and the outset of the 2000s, the region entered into a steep recession that fundamentally brought into question the legitimacy of neoliberalism as a development model and gave birth to myriad social explosions and popular struggles. The paradigmatic political parties and regimes of the new *izquierda permitida* are one expression of a reconstitution of neoliberalism in a new form.

In terms of its economic program, the *izquierda permitida* has been deeply influenced by the turn from classical structuralism to neostructuralism within the United Nations Economic Commission for Latin America and the Caribbean (ECLAC). Over the course of the second half of the 1990s and early 2000s, neostructuralism moved from the margins to the center of political influence in the region by challenging certain assumptions of the market dogmatism characteristic of orthodox neoliberalism while rebuking simultaneously the core presuppositions of classical structuralism. Post-Pinochet Chile became the poster child of neostructuralism throughout the 1990s. In this way it became a prototype for the *izquierda permitida*. Neostructuralism was also deeply influential in the "Buenos Aires Consensus," which came out of a June 1999 convention of the Socialist International and eventually became the model of political economy for Lula's Brazil, Kirchner's Argentina, Vázquez's Uruguay, and arguably the governments formed recently by formerly guerrilla parties in Nicaragua, El Salvador, and Guatemala (for a different view, see the chapter by Héctor Perla Jr., Marco Mojica, and Jared Bibler in this volume).

The areas of conceptual innovation at the heart of neostructuralism revolve around systemic competitiveness, technical progress, proactive labor flexibility, and virtuous circles. In an effort to distinguish itself from orthodox neoliberalism, neostructuralism in Latin America rejects the notion that markets and competition are the exclusive channels for social and economic interaction, and replace the basic neoclassical notion of comparative advantage with *systemic competitiveness*. By this, neostructuralists essentially mean "that what compete[s] in the world market [are] not *commodities* per se but *entire social systems*" (Leiva, 2008: 4). While granting that the market will remain the central organizing force in society, neostructuralists stress that the competitiveness of the entire system depends upon effective and thoroughgoing state intervention in infrastructure (technology, energy, transport), education, finance, labor-management relations, and the general relationships between public and private spheres in a way that orthodox neoliberal theory cannot grasp (Leiva, 2008: 4). The proponents of this paradigm, Greig Charnock (2009: 67) points out, "reject the market fundamentalism of the 1980s and early 1990s, represented by structural adjustment and shock therapy, and with these many of the assumptions about what the untrammelled free market can achieve." They call for a second generation of institutional shifts in state policies. These shifts will require a greater role for state engineering. States must fashion institutions that promote policy stability, adaptability, and coherence and coordination of markets. The institutions must be of high quality and embody "public regardedness" rather than personalistic clientelism.

Whereas orthodox neoliberals in the 1970s and 1980s saw the state's basic function as lubricating the dynamism of the market through the protection of property rights, contract enforcement, information collection, and strictly de-limited social provision for the destitute, neostructuralism "assigns the state an important auxiliary role in the search for international competitiveness," blending economic policy on various levels "with political intervention to construct a broad social consensus" (Leiva, 2008: 9–10). The state is to stimu-late and enhance market-based initiatives, selectively intervene in productive sectors of the economy, and supplement the invisible hand of the market with nonmarket forms of social, political, and economic coordination. Latin American neostructuralism sees modest and temporary state intervention as essential for encouraging a larger share of manufactured and valued-added exports into a country's export profile.

Proponents of the *izquierda permitida* model emphasize the necessity of "a configuration of class forces that can induce a capitalist class to accept a smaller share of the surplus in exchange for legitimacy, political and social peace, and high productivity." At the same time, "the influential organizations of the economic elites must be convinced that subordinate classes will not threaten private property." The orientation of the new *izquierda permitida* is to "pragmatically strive to reconcile liberty, equity, and community with the demands of a market economy" (Sandbrook, Edelman, Heller, and Teichman, 2006). The restructuring of neoliberalism in the direction of an *izquierda per-mitida* may offer "an alternative that combines representative democracy with a market economy and state initiatives to reduce inequalities and promote social citizenship" (Roberts, 2008: 87). The regimes of the *izquierda permitida* introduce targeted antipoverty programs, subsidies for small- and medium-sized businesses, increases in royalty regimes for multinational corporations operating in the natural-resource sectors, and joint private-public ventures between the state and foreign capital. These changes do not signify any change in underlying social inequalities of the neoliberal class system. They retain fiscal and monetary austerity, co-opt radical extra-parliamentary movements, and pursue "social pacts" between the ruling classes and the working class and the peasantry predicated on keeping wages down.

Constituent Parts of the New Balance of Forces

Within this overarching analytical framework, this volume takes up a series of issues that are critical for understanding the new balances of forces in con-temporary Latin America. Particularly important are the themes of socialist strategy, diversity of revolutionary subjects (labor, peasants, women, and indigenous movements), imperialism, and the still-unfolding turbulence of the global economic crisis since 2007.

In terms of socialist strategy, an old debate on the Left has reemerged that turns on the maturity of the productive forces in the region and whether or not they are sufficiently advanced—in terms of the presence of resources, technologies, and skills—to realistically initiate an anticapitalist transformation immediately. Traditionally, as Claudio Katz points out in his contribution to this volume, the Left has offered two different responses to this conundrum. On the one hand, there are those, following more or less the classical Communist Party lines of the region, who insist on a stagist theory of revolutionary transformation, including the necessity of a prolonged period of progressive capitalism prior to any socialist transition in order to allow for the necessary maturing of productive forces. The alternative response has been to argue for the immediate initiation of a socialist transition adapted to the particular weaknesses in productive capacities in different countries of the region.

Arguably the most influential rearticulation of the stagist thesis can be found in the work of Bolivian Marxist and current vice president in the Evo Morales administration Álvaro García Linera. In his expansive writings and lectures on what he calls Andean-Amazonian capitalism, García Linera argues that a transition to socialism in Bolivia is impossible for at least fifty to one hundred years due precisely to the immaturity of productive forces in the country (García Linera, 2006a, 2006b, 2006c. 2007). Instead, García Linera posits that Bolivia must first build an industrial capitalist base. The capitalist model he envisions—Andean-Amazonian capitalism—projects a greater role for state intervention in the market. The formula essentially means capitalist development with a stronger state to support a petty bourgeoisie that will eventually become a powerful national bourgeoisie to drive Bolivia into successful capitalist development. This national bourgeoisie will be indigenous, or "Andean-Amazonian." Only after this long intermediary phase of industrial capitalism has matured will the fulfillment of socialism be materially plausible (García Linera, 2006d).

García Linera expounds further on notions of stagism in his characterization of the Morales government, and specifically his attempt to define the ideology of "Evismo." The indigenous, democratic, and cultural "revolution," he reminds us, does not imply "radical" economic change, or even transformative restructuring of political institutions. Rather, "modifications" in the existing political structures of power and elite rule are all that is promised in the current context. A democratic cultural revolution is possible today in Bolivia, he argues, but any attempt to move toward socialism would be foolhardy given the lack of a fully developed industrial base.

The alternative to stagism is not, as some would have it, the full and immediate installation of socialism. To construct such a society, rooted in social justice and equality, will require a prolonged historical process, whereby norms and institutions of competition and exploitation are overcome with time. It is also the case that in peripheral countries such as those in Latin America, this process presupposes the maturation of certain economic foundations that will allow for the qualitative improvement in the lives of the majority of the population.[2] However, if it is obvious that none of this can be accomplished overnight, the transition nonetheless requires a rupture with the capitalist system today and the substitution of the preeminence of an economy regulated by exchange values toward one regulated by the satisfaction of social necessities, or use values. This is the necessary precondition for whatever type of subsequent advances might take place. A postcapitalist society, it should be stressed, will never emerge automatically in some future "stage" of development if a push toward socialism, a break with capitalism, is not pursued through struggle in the present (Katz, 2008: 104). Such a rupture is necessarily counterposed to neostructuralist plans for market regulation and "systemic competitiveness," just as it runs against the premises of stagist theories of socialist transition, some fifty to one hundred years after a painful, capitalist interregnum. Only by beginning the eradication of capitalism in the present will a road be opened toward social emancipation in the future.

It is true that Latin America occupies a peripheral position in the capitalist world system, but it is a region nonetheless endowed with fertile earth, mineral wealth, hydropower, energy resources, and industrial bases, all of which have been underutilized in terms of redirecting their utility toward satisfying real human needs rather than the needs of capital. The way in which Latin America has been integrated into the world market historically, and the retrograde form of capitalist accumulation that accompanied this dependent insertion, accounts for the unevenness and distorted quality of regional development patterns. Rather than a shortage of local savings, the situation is better understood as an excess of surplus transfers to the core of the world economy. Problems such as inadequate agricultural production, low productivity in industry, and scandalous levels of inequality are the results of a destructive capitalist imperialism and will be reproduced systematically without an overthrow of that system. There is in fact space in the present to begin immediately popular socioeconomic programs of transformation that are not predicated on a prolonged capitalist phase of further development of productive forces.

Part of this initiative must be an audacious broadening of socialist vision. The ruling classes of the region are quite adept at envisioning their interests on a regional scale, through the promotion of neoliberal trade agreements and accords, such as Mercosur and NAFTA. It is necessary for the Latin American Left to think strategically about building socialism regionally, through initiatives such as the Alianza Bolivariana para los Pueblos de Nuestra América (Bolivarian Alliance for the Peoples of Our America, ALBA). Such cross-national socialist orientation and commitment might counter the capitalist foundations of existing trade agreements rooted in exchange values and profit seeking, with values of regionwide cooperation and economic complementarities. The stakes are high, as Katz suggests in this volume: "the socialist option is not a Keynesian program to turn around recessive market trends. It is a platform to overcome the exploitation and inequality inherent in capitalism. It seeks to abolish poverty and unemployment, eradicate environmental disasters, and put an end to the nightmares of war and the financial cataclysms that enrich a minuscule percentage of millionaires at the expense of millions of individuals."

Apart from neostructuralist economics and stagist theories of transition, one of the prominent schools of thought coming out of the last decade of Latin American tumult can be categorized loosely as anarchism, although certainly not all of the movements and thinkers that broadly adhere to this current think of themselves in this way. Perhaps the most widely celebrated thinker to have expressed the ideas of the new Latin American anarchism is John Holloway, particularly in his book *Change the World without Taking Power* (2005). His thesis, distilled to its barest elements, is as follows: it may or may not be possible to change the world without taking power (we cannot know for sure); within this context of uncertainty, the best way to imagine revolutionary change is to seek the dissolution of power rather than the conquest of power; and it is particularly important to avoid a strategy focused on the conquest of *state* power, which was ruinous for the revolutionary Left in the twentieth century.

Many have pointed out important flaws in Holloway's perspective: oversimplification of a very complex history of competing theoretical and strategic debates in the international history of the workers' movement (Bensaïd, 2005); too little account taken of a vast critical literature within the Marxist tradition on the state; lack of serious theoretical and analytical treatment of history and the role of the revolutionary Left therein (Bensaïd, 2005); mystification of the Zapatista experience in Mexico through an analysis rooted in discourse rather than the real contradictions of the political situation on the ground; and abandonment of the terrain of politics and strategic orientation, a vacuum that will inevitably be filled by capitalist or procapitalist forces if left empty.

The ideas that Holloway has sought to clarify need to be taken seriously, and they continue to resonate in particular settings within the Latin American Left, especially among "autonomists" and "horizontalists" in Argentina and some adherents of Zapatismo in Mexico and elsewhere (Katz, 2005; Sitrin, 2006; Zibechi, 2003). Various authors in this volume address the theory and praxis of contemporary Latin American anarchism as they relate to the specific countries and case studies under investigation.

Diversity of Social and Political Subjects

If socialist strategy must engage theoretically and practically with the *izquierda permitida*, stagist theorists, and anarchists, it is increasingly evident that it must also grasp the diversity of social subjects driving the resurgence in radicalism across the region. The theoretical and empirical content of each of the chapters of this book grapples with different social actors at the heart of social change in the region, whether it be the new working classes, the peasantry, women, or indigenous movements.

Women

In this volume, Sujatha Fernandes discusses the complexities of gendered community politics inside the Latin American Left today. She points specifically to the contradictory dynamics in the barrios, or shantytowns, of Caracas, Venezuela, since Chávez assumed office in 1999. On the one hand, Fernandes finds that most of the community leaders continue to be men and that social programs in the barrios continue to be administered by male-dominated bureaucracies. On the other hand, women's participation in local activism has significantly increased over the last decade, and this collective protagonism from below has begun to challenge traditional gender roles, in spite of enduring patriarchal legacies. Women's popular participation in grassroots politics, Fernandes suggests, has collectivized private tasks and created alternatives to male-centric politics in contemporary Venezuela. This tension in the country, of increased participation of women in popular politics at the base running alongside residual, institutionalized sexism, is reproduced—with national particularities of course—in other countries in the region transitioning in various ways toward the New Left.

The Working Classes

While women are arguably assuming new levels of participation in the social movements of the new lefts, old social subjects have taken on new forms as well. While it is fashionable to suggest that the decline in numbers of a formally employed industrial working class in some parts of the region since the onset of neoliberalism has meant the end of the working class itself, Susan Spronk's chapter powerfully refutes this claim. It is true that the uneven spread of neoliberal economic transformation throughout the world economy since the 1970s has engendered a proliferation of part-time, unprotected, fragmented, and informal work in Latin America. However, this has not led to the dissolution of the working class into some kind of amorphous "multitude" or "civil society," nor spelled the end of class struggle as such. Rather, drawing on the theoretical and historical tradition of the British Marxist E. P. Thompson, Spronk argues that while traditional forms of trade unionism have stepped back from center stage in Latin American popular struggles, a multiplicity of "class struggles without class" have taken their place. The Latin American working class is actually bigger than ever and workers are slowly building repertoires of resistance appropriate to the new contexts they face.

Peasants

In the post–World War II period in Latin America, the role of the peasantry in economic transformation began to emerge as the central focus in the development question as policy makers in advanced capitalist countries sought capitalist development in the Third World (especially in agriculture) to stave off communism. In the context of the Cold War, and particularly with regard to Latin America, the 1959 Cuban revolution provided new impetus in this direction. The development question, and the agrarian question in particular, came to occupy center stage in American foreign policy and consequently in academia as well. Moderate land reform as a defensive response to thwart socialist advance became the predominant policy concern of Latin American states.

For those on the Left, the emergence of rural *guerrillero* movements following the Cuban revolution were a source of inspiration, and the countryside was seen as the necessary and obvious site of revolution. The question for the Left revolved around strategy, leadership, alliances, organization, or, in short, *how* revolutions were to happen. As William Roseberry points out, "That a revolution was possible, that it would include the peasantry, and that much of it would be fought in the countryside was . . . not a subject for serious doubt" (1993: 322). For those on the right, the Sierra Maestra and the burgeoning guerrilla groups in various countries were also a symbol: a challenge to develop rural and urban areas in order to diffuse revolutionary protagonism.

With the advent of neoliberal reforms throughout Latin America in the 1980s and 1990s, the issue of redistributive land reform was no longer on the agenda of governments in the region. Despite the ubiquitous rhetoric of "free trade" and "globalization," the United States and the European Union continued to heavily subsidize their food and grain exporters, while the International Monetary Fund (IMF) and the World Bank demanded budget cuts and open borders from Latin American countries.

Despite a relative dearth of literature on the topic, peasant movements have been at the heart of popular left challenges to neoliberalism over the last two decades, from the Movement of Landless Rural Workers (MST) in Brazil to land-seizing peasants in Paraguay to indigenous-peasant resistance in Ecuador, Guatemala, Chile, and Bolivia, among many other mobilizations in different settings. However, the ethnic character of these movements tends to be privileged while the often interrelated component of social class is downplayed if not totally disregarded.

Leandro Vergara-Camus's contribution to this volume is an exemplary deviation from this trend in the broader literature. He points out that classical Marxist theory tended to downplay the centrality of the peasantry in revolutionary transformation. Whereas peasants have never accomplished a revolutionary overthrow on their own, they have been crucial actors in alliance with other social classes. Examining closely the Movimento dos Trabalhadores Rurais Sem Terra (Movement of Landless Rural Workers, MST) from Brazil and the Ejército Zapatista de Liberación Nacional (Zapatista Army of National Liberation, EZLN) from Chiapas, Mexico, Vergara-Camus suggests that the peasant character of these movements actually provides them with an advantage over other radical movements in the region because they are able to control territory. Once they have established their encampments—for Vergara-Camus liberated zones within a sea of capitalism—both movements have sought to build alternative structures of power that facilitate the self-government of the exploited and oppressed, through wide-scale political participation from below and the establishment of noncapitalist forms of production. Through these activities they challenge the limits of representative liberal democracy and the capitalist institution of private property. The EZLN and the MST, therefore, clearly fall in the camp of the radical Left in contemporary Latin America. The difficulties they have encountered in building alliances with other popular movements and parties of the Left in Brazil and Mexico, according to Vergara-Camus, are a consequence of the greater susceptibility of other movements and parties to incorporation into existing corporatist institutions—that is, becoming a part of the *izquierda permitida*.

Indigenous Movements

Rural and urban indigenous resistance has been at the center of the left turn in many countries in the region. Unfortunately, the study of indigenous politics has been dominated by perspectives that analytically separate indigenous struggle from its organic, if often tense, relationship with wider left formations. The idea that indigenous movements are essentially nonleft, nonclass, rural, and ethnic phenomena that arose principally in response to changes in political party systems and citizenship regimes is deeply flawed. Recent popular struggles in Bolivia, for example, have been characterized by the deep interpenetration of race and class. Their strongest manifestations, moreover, have been urban and working class rather than rural and peasant, although both rural and urban movements have been important. The most powerful insurrections were rooted in El Alto, an informal proletarian and indigenous city. Movements there responded to the social costs of neoliberal economic restructuring and tied together the aims of indigenous liberation from racial oppression and socialist emancipation from class exploitation and imperialism. Such movements are best understood as the foundation of a reconstituted indigenous Left that takes the politics of indigenous liberation seriously while not abandoning questions of class. It is a misleading simplification at best to suggest that the politics of the Left in Bolivia has been replaced by a politics of ethnic conflict and strife. Comparable left-indigenous dynamics played themselves out over the course of twentieth-century Ecuadorian politics and continue into the present century (see Marc Becker chapter in this volume).

Separating indigenous political struggle from the sphere of capitalist social relations within which, and often against which, these struggles occur has caused liberal-institutionalists to reach political conclusions very distant from the movements they purport to study. As William I. Robinson argues, "Transnational capital seeks to integrate indigenous into the global market as dependent workers and consumers, to convert their lands into private property, and to make the natural resources in their territories available for transnational corporate exploitation" (2008: 303–4). Threatened in this fashion by the implications of global capitalism, indigenous populations have often responded in kind: "Indigenous struggles spearhead popular class demands; these are *struggles against (transnational) capital* and for a transformation of property relations. Ethnicity and class have fused in the new round of indigenous resistance, which has become a—perhaps *the*—leading edge of popular class mobilisation" (Robinson, 2008: 303, emphasis in original).

Imperialism

The U.S. invasions and occupations of Iraq and Afghanistan helped to spur a major renewal in Marxist theory around the "new" imperialism of George W. Bush. The diverse collection of writings under this broad rubric has tended to focus almost exclusively on the Middle East and Central Asia (the wars in Iraq and Afghanistan) and debates around interimperial rivalry (especially the rise of China), as well as the relative fragility or strength of the American empire in the current period. With few exceptions, Latin America has been marginalized from the key debates. In his contribution to this volume, Henry Veltmeyer traces six foundational pillars of the U.S. imperialist system since the end of the Second World War and situates Latin America centrally in this panoramic analysis. He charts the role of the United States in consolidating a liberal-capitalist world order through the Bretton Woods institutions and, later, beginning in the 1980s, in transforming this into a neoliberal order. He explains the strategy of building a network of military bases around the world as a means of projecting military power and force where and when necessary. Veltmeyer also points to the centrality of development "aid" and "cooperation" for consolidating compliant regimes by way of financial and technical assistance. U.S.-led "free trade" initiatives under the banner of "regional integration" in Latin America are also seen as instruments through which the power and interests of U.S. capital and empire are consolidated and promoted throughout the region. Finally, U.S. imperialism promotes a multifaceted "globalization" policy, designed essentially to provide "maximum freedom to the operating units of the global empire." All of these interrelated elements of the U.S. state's informal empire are inherently unstable, vulnerable as they are to countervailing forces of resistance generated in the countries at the receiving end of the imperialist exploitation and oppression.

In the 1990s and early 2000s, it was evident that due to the U.S. state's overextension in Eurasia and the Persian Gulf region Latin America had indeed fallen outside its principal geopolitical lens. But the emergence over the last decade of radical social-movement struggles and a center-left counter-axis across a number of states south of its border has stoked the empire's interests in regaining control and reversing the tide. The move to tighten relations with far-right administrations in Peru, Colombia, and Mexico was reignited under Bush and has accelerated under Obama. Strong relations have been established with the new Sebastián Piñera administration in Chile, for example, and there are now seven new U.S. military bases set up in Colombia. Haiti, meanwhile, has been flooded with U.S. military troops, apparently destined to stay put for an extended period under the pretext of aid delivery following the devastating earthquake of 2010. At the same time, Obama has reached out to the regimes of the *izquierda permitida* in Brazil, Argentina, Uruguay, and elsewhere in an attempt to counterbalance the influence of Hugo Chávez and his Bolivarian Revolution throughout the region. This has been complicated, as Veltmeyer notes, by the increasing willingness of the governments of Lula and Rouseff in Brazil to flex its economic and political muscles throughout the region.

The most important recent development in imperial relations was the Honduran coup of June 2009, which ousted the democratically elected President Manuel Zelaya, who had been moving further to the left, making Honduras a member of ALBA, for example. It is vital to note the subsequent consolidation of that coup under a democratic guise with the fraudulent elections of November 2009, which brought Porfirio "Pepe" Lobo to office in January 2010. The U.S. and Canadian governments were quick to legitimize these elections and to seek to normalize relations with the new Honduran regime (see the chapter by Todd Gordon and Jeffery R. Webber in this volume). As the U.S. state finds its control over the region increasingly called into question by anti-imperialist rural and urban popular movements, center-left governments, and incipient counter-hegemonic blocs such as ALBA, future research will need to stay open to the possibilities of a renewal of interimperial rivalry for influence in the region. China, the European Union (EU), Canada, Russia, and other imperialist forces have already begun to express the interests of their states and capital in the region.

The Global Economic Meltdown and Latin America's Left Turn

By April 2008, the International Monetary Fund suggested that we were witnessing the largest financial crisis in the United States since the Great Depression. However, as David McNally has observed, this underestimated the scale of the crisis. First, while originating in the United States, the crisis reverberated around the globe. Second, the crisis quickly escaped a narrowly financial profile, deeply impacting the core of the "real economy." Bankruptcies, factory closures, and layoffs were a response to overaccumulation—over 250,000 jobs have been lost in the North American automobile industry alone. Waves of downsizing in nonfinancial corporations feed the underconsumption dynamic of this crisis. "As world demand and world-sales d[ove]," McNally points out, "the effects of overcapacity (factories, machines, buildings that cannot be profitably utilized), which have been masked by credit-creation over the past decade, [kicked] in with a vengeance" (McNally, 2009: 37).

The early suggestion of Luiz Inácio Lula da Silva, president of Brazil at the time, that the crisis would not seriously affect Latin America now appears exaggerated. The slowdown of the 2003–2007 commodity-driven boom deepened in Latin America over the first two quarters of 2008, sharpening severely, if perhaps temporarily, thereafter. The significant accumulation of foreign exchange reserves and reduction of dollar-denominated public debt during the boom years provided a temporary cushioning of the global crisis in Latin America, but this situation is unlikely to matter if the world recession turns into a prolonged slump. The effects of collapsing remittance flows have been uneven across different Latin American countries based on fragmentary evidence but are likely to inflict increasing pain on the popular classes over time as xenophobia, "draconian restrictions on the movement of migrant-labor," and "tighter control and regulation of the movement of labour" in the countries of the Global North deepen and expand (McNally, 2011: 78).

Latin America's biggest expansionary period in four decades, driven by the commodities boom, was interrupted by the onset of the crisis. The financial crisis in the core of the world system was channeled to Latin America through slumping external trade and export prices and declines in remittances (ECLAC, 2009). The fallout from the crisis has been uneven in Latin America and the Caribbean, with Mexico and Central America being hardest hit due to the unique depth of their integration into the U.S. economy. However, if the world slump extends into protracted crisis as some expect, South American economies will increasingly feel its effects. Venezuela, for example, is already weathering the contradictions thrown up by ongoing rentier capitalism in a context of fluxuating international oil prices. Center-left regimes will come under increasing pressure to shift back toward orthodox neoliberal austerity in an effort to displace the costs of the crisis onto the popular and working classes. Whether this leads to the delegitimation of these regimes and a shift to the right across the region, or a similar delegitimation of center-left politics followed by a sharper turn to the left, will depend less on economics than on the politics of struggle between left resistance from below and right-wing restoration from above, and the shifting balance of class forces underlying these developments.

Case Studies

Part II of this volume includes a range of country case studies. These examine regimes, parties, and social movements spanning the *izquierda permitida* to radical Left continuum. Brazil, as one of the emergent BRIC countries (together with Russia, India, and China), is a major economic and geopolitical player inside Latin America, and increasingly outside the region as well. Ricardo Antunes situates the Lula regime squarely in the camp of the *izquierda permitida* in his chapter. Lula's Brazil, for Antunes, belongs together with Chilean president Michelle Bachelet (until the recent electoral shift to the right) and Vázquez and Mojica, the last two Uruguayan presidents. More broadly, Brazil is sandwiched between regimes further to the left, such as those of Chávez, Morales, and Correa, and those on the hard right, like Álvaro Uribe (and now Manuel Santos) in Colombia, Alan García (until the recent election of center-left Ollanta Humala) in Peru, and Felipe Calderón (and now Enrique Peña Nieto) in Mexico. We can now include recent additions to that group on the right: Porfirio "Pepe" Lobo in Honduras and Sebastián Piñera in Chile. As Antunes suggests, the United States and the EU, and international financial institutions such as the IMF, have been happy with Lula and Roussef's conciliatory politics of the *izquierda permitida*, despite the fact that Brazil's projection of its state and capital power in the region sometimes conflicts with the immediate interests of other capitals and imperial states. Antunes goes much further than an analysis of the regime, however, discussing in detail the dynamics of the labor movement and wider popular left struggles in contemporary Brazil.

Argentina's recent governments, first of Néstor Kirchner and since then of his wife, Cristina Fernández de Kirchner, are also examples of the *izquierda permitida* at the regime level. Indeed, Emilia Castorina suggests in this volume that Argentina's Kirchners represent a paradigmatic case study of the *permitida* wing of the region's left turn. In the early part of the twenty-first century, the country looked as though it might break fundamentally with the neoliberal model. In the midst of a massive financial crisis in 2001 and 2002, popular rebellions exploded on the scene, demanding that the entire political class be tossed out—"Que se vayan todos!" was the call: "Out with them all!" However, Castorina suggests that, despite many premature announcements of the death of neoliberalism in the country from observers across the political spectrum, the basic ways in which politics and the economy are run have not been altered. She develops an analytical framework that explores how the ruling class engaged in a process of political recomposition under the Kirchners, allowing ultimately for the reinvigoration of capital accumulation in the country. Castorina's chapter combines a systematic explanation and critique of the *izquierda permitida* in Argentina with a guide to the limits of social movements from below committed ideologically to autonomist politics. The Peronist electoral machine and the ghost of normal capitalism have been given new life under the Kirchners, and the political alternatives on offer from below have not been able to resist co-optation from above.

The Chilean case arrives at a similar destination, albeit from a different starting point. Post-Pinochet Chile, Fernando Leiva argues in his chapter, was unique in that it witnessed a center-left coalition initiate, consolidate, and then institutionalize a new capitalist order based in the political economic model of the *izquierda permitida* described above. The coalition, Concertación de Partidos por la Democracia, or Concertación, governed the country for twenty years, between 1990 and 2010. The Chilean Left, broadly conceived, is constituted, according to Leiva, by the following parts: an *izquierda permitida* characteristic of the successive Concertación coalitions that, while in office, served transnational capital faithfully while employing anti-neoliberal discourse; a historic Left with a weak social base, ossified in the practices of the past and therefore unable to intervene effectively in the current socioeconomic, political, and cultural terrain characterized by increasingly female, young, and unstably employed workers; a new radical Left, influenced by autonomist and horizontalist ideas of building popular power from the grassroots up, which has made inroads in the student movement and a variety of other sectors, but which represents no measurable political alternative at the national level; and, finally, a highly fractured social Left, which has attempted to fill the abyss left by market, state, and party solutions to the myriad problems facing Chile's popular classes with a set of small-scale, local forms of collective action. Until the recent ouster of the Concertación from office, then, Chilean politics had been characterized by a governing *izquierda permitida* above and a highly segmented array of popular left alternatives below, attempting unsuccessfully to cohere into an authentic radical-left alternative for the country's exploited and oppressed.

The trajectory of the Central American Left over the last two decades is perhaps more open to debate. How best to characterize the path traced by many of the region's left forces from mass-based guerrilla movements to electoral political parties? The editors of this volume would tend to argue that the FSLN in Nicaragua, the Frente Farabundo Martí para la Liberación Nacional (Farabundo Martí National Liberation Front, FMLN) in El Salvador, and the Unidad Revolucionara Nacional Gautemalteca (Guatemalan National Revolutionary Union, URNG) have navigated a complex road from the radical Left to the *izquierda permitida* since the 1980s. This transition was obviously not without contradiction and division within their own ranks, but it is difficult to maintain that since coming to office Daniel Ortega (2006) of the FSLN in Nicaragua, Mauricio Funes (2009) of the FMLN in El Salvador, and Álvaro Colom (2007)—supported by the URNG—in Guatemala have started their countries on a transition toward the goals of the radical Left. Rather, the vast majority of their domestic and foreign social, political, and economic decisions places them in the camp of the *izquierda permitida*, together with Brazil, Argentina, Uruguay, and Chile (until recently).

However, this assessment is challenged by Héctor Perla Jr., Marco Mojica, and Jared Bibler in their chapter on the Left in Nicaragua, El Salvador, and Guatemala. First, at the level of theory, they take issue with what they see as our "dichotomization of the Left" between an *izquierda permitida* and a radical wing. They argue that this cannot adequately take into account the fact that middle-class reformers, socialists, and communists are all operating simultaneously within the administrations of these three countries. The same parties in power are therefore a simultaneous configuration of the radical and moderate. They also contend that our ideal-type continuum is politically dangerous. It falls into the hands, they suggest, of those on the right who see in Latin America a "good" and "bad" Left and in so doing "does nothing to formulate a counter-hegemonic narrative around which center-left and left forces can coalesce for progressive social change." Perla, Mojica, and Bibler are uncritical of what they see as these three government's commitment to building a progressive capitalist stage of capitalism to build productive forces before any transition to socialism. For them, this necessarily involves "national coalitions with patriotic elements of the bourgeoisie and middle classes."

The case of Ecuador also reveals the complexities of the contemporary Latin American Left. In this volume, Marc Becker challenges any easy characterization of Rafael Correa's government as part of the radical Left in the region. While Correa has condemned capitalism and embraced the banner of twenty-first-century socialism in many international forums, his domestic policies have often fallen far short of the rhetoric. That is not to say the radical Left does not exist in Ecuador. For Becker, this radical Left is embodied in the country's militant indigenous movements, which have clashed with Correa on several fronts, mainly around the president's ongoing commitments to pursuing capitalist resource extraction in their rural communities. In many ways, Correa seems to be a part of an emergent *izquierda permitida* in his domestic development policies, Becker suggests, even as he condemns imperialism and capitalism abroad. Meanwhile, indigenous movements in the country have much more aggressively supported the liberation of the oppressed and exploited classes and groups in Ecuadorian society, especially through their orientation toward building their collective social power from below. An increasingly conflictual dynamic seems to be establishing itself in Ecuador, then, with Correa representing the *izquierda permitida* from above and the indigenous movements representing the radical Left from below.

For many, Venezuela represents the closest example of the ideal-typical radical Left available in the region today (Lebowitz, 2006, 2007; Raby, 2006). However, it is important not to leap to conclusions on this front either. A number of authors have pointed out how far away Venezuela continues to be from a socialist society and economy (Ellner, 2008, 2010a, 2010b; Webber, 2010). "Venezuela is still a capitalist country in which the law of value, of capital accumulation, is operative," William I. Robinson (2010) has pointed out. Similarly, Sujatha Fernandes describes Venezuela's social order under Chávez as "a hybrid state formation that has mounted certain challenges to the neoliberal paradigm but which remains subject to the internal and external constraints of global capital" (Fernandes, 2010: 23). "The national government claims to be attempting to take this country to an open, democratic and participatory socialism," Venezuelan activist Roland Denis points out. "But the situation in this regard is very complex. Socialist propaganda and discourse are constantly in the media, and on the lips of Chávez and the most intelligent state representatives. However, the practical behaviour of the state, its concrete policies and its relations with the transnationals and private sector leave a lot to be desired" (Stobart, 2010). While acknowledging some of these contradictions—bureaucratization, corruption, and government alliances with fractions of the domestic capitalist class—Gregory Wilpert's contribution to this volume stresses that the government is gradually transforming Venezuela into a socialist economy and participatory democratic polity. For Wilpert, one of the central dangers of this transition is its dependence on Chávez's leadership.

In some ways, the case of Bolivia is most similar to that of Ecuador. Between 2000 and 2005, Jeffery R. Webber argues in his chapter, Bolivia witnessed a left-indigenous insurrectionary cycle incomparable in collective strength and organization from below to any other popular movement in the region. Inaugurated by the Water War against privatization in the city of Cochabamba in 2000, the cycle of revolt led eventually to the overthrow of two neoliberal presidents through two mass, extra-parliamentary mobilizations. They were known as the Gas Wars because of the centrality of the demand to renationalize the natural gas industry, and they deposed Presidents Gonzalo Sánchez de Lozada in October 2003 and Carlos Mesa in June 2005. The left-indigenous movements in Bolivia in the early part of this century, Webber argues, were imbued with a collective consciousness that embraced both anticapitalism and indigenous liberation and saw it as necessary to achieve liberation from both forms of oppression in a combined way. The political visions articulated by movement activists during this period closely adhere to the ideal-typical radical Left, according to Webber.

The tide of social movement activity paved the way for the electoral victory of Evo Morales in the elections of December of 2005. As leader of the Movimiento al Socialismo (Movement Toward Socialism, MAS) party, he became the republic's first indigenous president. More controversially, Webber argues that while there have certainly been reforms to the inherited neoliberal development model under the Morales government between 2006 and 2010—such as the significant shift in the tax and royalty regime of the hydrocarbon (natural gas and oil) sector introduced in 2006—in terms of fiscal austerity, central bank independence, low inflation caps, labor flexibility, low rates of social spending, and other factors, the continuities of neoliberalism seem to outweigh the modest reforms introduced thus far. This can be explained by two principal domestic factors. First, since roughly 2002 the MAS had become progressively more moderate in its political economic-strategic orientation than most observers tended to believe. Second, the new government initially overestimated the political strength of its right-wing opposition in the eastern lowlands. In seeking to appease that opposition through moderate economic initiatives, it paradoxically provided the necessary breathing space for the opposition to eventually transform itself into the political threat the government had only imagined it to be when Morales first assumed office. Webber ultimately contends that the regime of Bolivia's Evo Morales is best situated precariously in the middle of the two ideal types, with societal and state forces pulling the government in both directions. In terms of policy outcomes thus far, the government is closer to the *izquierda permitida*, but unlike Brazil, Argentina, Uruguay, Chile, and the Central American countries, Morales faces a real possibility of the rearticulation of radical autonomous social movements from below resolutely aligned with the radical Left. His ability to fully embrace the model of the *izquierda permitida* is therefore constantly under threat from below.

Mexico is also included in this volume as an example where the Far Right maintains control over the state apparatus, but where there are incipient signs of radical left activity from below. In Richard Roman and Edur Velasco Arregui's chapter, we find that Mexico has been on a significantly different political trajectory than many states in South America. Whereas in many of the latter countries, according to Roman and Velasco Arregui, there have been national reformist solutions to organic crises of neoliberal capitalism, in Mexico a similar set of crises has instead led to the consolidation at the regime level of a new conservative-neoliberal power bloc. The new bloc has triumphed in the last four presidential elections and has been able to transform economy and society in such a way than many of the previously won social rights of citizenship have been abolished. In a parallel transformation, the state has become ever more repressive, militarized, and exclusionary. The general context that the radical social Left has had to confront, then, has been one of an increasingly repressive state, democratic only insofar as it holds highly constrained elections. Neoliberalism has ravaged the lives of millions of working-class and peasant Mexicans, but emigration to the United States has provided a precarious and partial safety valve against potentially explosive urban and rural discontent. With the heart of the global economic crisis centered in the United States, and especially in sectors of the economy that had employed many Mexicans, this safety valve may now be in question.

While the political context facing the radical social Left has thrown up severe obstacles, there have nonetheless been a string of popular insurgencies in recent years. The ongoing struggles of the Zapatistas, the experience of the Oaxaca Commune in 2006, and the mass antifraud movement of the same year are all part of this trend. But specific explosions of extra-parliamentary resistance have not translated into sustained victories for the popular classes, nor the formation of durable national organizations representing left forces. At the same time, while the party Left made small inroads into the electoral process, they have still consistently lost to the Far Right in presidential contests.

While much of the weakness of the Mexican Left can be explained by the repressive character of the neoliberal state, there are also a set of internal weaknesses that cannot be sidestepped, suggest Roman and Velasco Arregui. The Mexican political culture of patrimonial administration of government subsidies and the distinct lack of rank-and-file control over formally democratic institutions throughout society are part of this scenario. The electoral Left is prone to cooptation and the moderation of its extra-parliamentary activity and alliances through the state subsidies siphoned to officially registered parties that play by the rules. The extra-parliamentary Left, meanwhile, has often been subject to the same state-society pressures of clientelism, as broad popular movements attempt to make tangible gains for their members that require state action in return for moderation of movement activities and compliance with wider state objectives. In constant tension with these hierarchical and clientelistic components of Mexico's political culture are the democratic and participatory components of long-standing revolutionary traditions in the country. While this reservoir of revolutionary tradition is a source of hope, the present situation presents formidable obstacles standing in the way of left advance. The electoral and social Left are politically and regionally divided. In fact, there are no left parties with a national scope or any degree of political cohesion. On the social Left, the Zapatista movement and the Oaxaca Commune experience have been primarily regional. It appears that for the moment the Left remains in a very weak position from which to mount offensives against the conservative-neoliberal bloc presently in power.

Notes

1. The case of Cuba is not explored in this volume. For useful debates with a range of perspectives from the radical Left on the character of the Cuban revolution and its trajectory since 1959, see the special issues of *Latin American Perspectives*, vol. 36, nos. 1–3 (2009), and *Against the Current*, nos. 141 and 142 (2009). Also see Farber, 2010; Gott, 2004; Habel, 1991; Raby, 2006.

2. For discussion relevant to critiques of stagism, see Chilcote's (2009) exploration of Leon Trotsky's concepts of backwardnesss, combined and uneven development, permanent revolution, and socialist transition and revolution, as they have been theorized in the Latin American context.

References

Aguiar de Medeiros, Carlos. 2009. "Asset-Stripping the State: Political Economy of Privatization in Latin America." *New Left Review* 2 (55): 109–32.

Bensaïd, Daniel. 2005. "On a Recent Book by John Holloway." In *Change the World without Taking Power? . . . or . . . Take Power to Change the World?*, 4–18. Amsterdam: International Institute for Research and Education.

Carr, Barry, and Steve Ellner, eds. 1993. *The Latin American Left since Allende*. Boulder, CO, and London: Westview Press and the Latin American Bureau.

Castañeda, Jorge. 2006. "Latin America's Left Turn." *Foreign Affairs*, May–June, 28–43.

Charnock, Greig. 2009. "Why Do Institutions Matter? Global Competitiveness and the Politics of Policies in Latin America." *Capital and Class* 33 (2): 67–99.

Chilcote, Ronald. 2009. "Trotsky and Development Theory in Latin America." *Critical Sociology* 35 (6): 719–41.

Coatsworth, John H. 2005. "Structures, Endowments and Institutions in the Economic History of Latin America." *Latin American Research Review* 40 (3): 126–44.

Damián, Araceli, and Julio Boltvinik. 2006. "A Table to Eat On: The Meaning and Measurement of Poverty in Latin America." In *Latin America after Neoliberalism: Turning the Tide in the 21st Century?*, ed. Eric Hershberg and Fred Rosen. New York: New Press.

ECLAC. 2009. *Economic Survey of Latin America and the Caribbean 2008–2009*. Santiago: Economic Commission for Latin America and the Caribbean.

Ellner, Steve. 2008. *Rethinking Venezuelan Politics: Class, Conflict, and the Chávez Phenomenon*. Boulder, CO: Lynne Rienner.

———. 2010a. "The Perennial Debate over Socialist Goals Played Out in Venezuela." *Science and Society* 74 (1): 63–84.

———. 2010b. "Hugo Chávez's First Decade in Office: Breakthroughs and Shortcomings." *Latin American Perspectives* 37 (1): 77–86.

Farber, Samuel. 2011. *Cuba Since the Revolution of 1959: A Critical Assessment*. Chicago: Haymarket.

Fernandes, Sujatha. 2010. *Who Can Stop the Drums? Urban Social Movements in Chávez's Venezuela*. Durham, NC: Duke University Press.

García Linera, Álvaro. 2006a. "La gente quire autonomía pero conducida por el MAS." *Página/12*, July 5.

———. 2006b. "No estamos pensando en socialismo sino en revolución democratizadora." *Página/12*, April 10.

———. 2006c. "Tres temas de reflexión." *Rebelión*, November 4.

———. 2006d. "El capitalismo andino-amazónico." *Le Monde Diplomatique*, edición Boliviana, January.

———. 2006e. "El Evismo: Lo nacional-popular en acción." *El Juguete Rabioso*, April 2.

———. 2007. "Hay múltiples modelos para la izquierda." *Página/12*, June 11.

Gott, Richard. 2004. *Cuba: A New History*. New Haven: Yale University Press.

Grandin, Greg. 2004. *Last Colonial Massacre: Latin America in the Cold War*. Chicago: University of Chicago Press.

———. 2006. *Empire's Workshop: Latin America, the United States, and the Rise of the New Imperialism.* New York: Metropolitan Books.

Habel, Jeanette. 1991. *Cuba: The Revolution in Peril.* London: Verso.

Hale, Charles R. 1996. *Resistance and Contradiction: Miskitu Indians and the Nicaraguan State, 1894–1987.* Stanford, CA: Stanford University Press.

———. 2002. "Does Multiculturalism Menace? Governance, Cultural Rights and the Politics of Identity in Guatemala." *Journal of Latin American Studies* 34:485–524.

———. 2004. "Rethinking Indigenous Politics in the Era of the 'Indio Permitido.'" *NACLA Report on the Americas* 38 (2): 16–21.

———. 2006. *Más Que un Indio (More Than an Indian): Racial Ambivalence and Neoliberal Multiculturlism in Guatemala.* Santa Fe, NM: SAR Press.

Holloway, John. 2005. *Change the World without Taking Power: The Meaning of Revolution Today.* 2nd ed. London: Pluto.

Holloway, John, and Alex Callinicos. 2005. "A Debate Between John Holloway and Alex Callinicos: 'Can We Change the World without Taking Power?'" In *Change the World without Taking Power? . . . or . . . Take Power to Change the World?,* 60–72. Amsterdam: International Institute for Research and Education.

Katz, Claudio. 2008. *Las disyuntivas de la izquierda en América Latina.* Buenos Aires: Ediciones Luxemburg.

Lebowitz, Michael. 2006. *Build It Now! Socialism for the Twenty-first Century.* New York: Monthly Review Press.

———. 2007. "Venezuela: A Good Example of the Bad Left." *Monthly Review* 59 (3): 38–54.

Leiva, Fernando. 2008. *Latin American Neostructuralism: The Contradictions of Post-Neoliberal Development.* Minneapolis: University of Minnesota Press.

Love, Joseph L. 2005. "The Rise and Decline of Economic Structuralism in Latin America: New Dimensions." *Latin American Research Review* 40 (3): 100–125.

McNally, David. 2011. *Global Slump: The Economics and Politics of Crisis and Resistance.* Oakland, CA: PM Press.

Petras, James, and Henry Veltmeyer. 2005. *Social Movements and State Power: Argentina, Brazil, Bolivia, Ecuador.* London: Pluto Press.

———. 2009. *What's Left in Latin America: Regime Change in New Times.* Burlington, VT: Ashgate.

———. 2010. "A Class Perspective on Social Ecology and the Indigenous Movement." *Critical Sociology* 36:437–52.

Raby, D. L. 2006. *Democracy and Revolution: Latin America and Socialism Today.* London: Pluto.

Ramírez Gallegos, Franklin. 2006. "Más que dos izquierdas." *Nueva Sociedad* 205:30–44.

Reygadas, Luis. 2006. "Latin America: Persistent Inequality and Recent Transformations." In *Latin America After Neoliberalism: Turnign the Tide in the 21st Century?,* ed. Eric Hershberg and Fred Rosen, 120–43. New York: New Press.

Roberts, Kenneth M. 2008. "Is Social Democracy Possible in Latin America?" *Nueva Sociedad* 217 (September-October): 96–98.

Robinson, William I. 2007. "Transformative Possibilities in Latin America." *Socialist Register* 44:1–19.

——. 2008. *Latin America and Global Capitalism: A Critical Globalization Perspective.* Baltimore: Johns Hopkins University Press.

——. 2010. "The Challenges of Twenty-First Century Socialism in Venezuela," *Znet,* January 31. http://www.zcommunications.org/the-challenges-of-21st-century-socialism-in-venezuela-by-william-i-robinson.

Roseberry, William. 1993. "Beyond the Agrarian Question in Latin America." In *Confronting Historical Paradigms: Peasants, Labor, and the Capitalist World System in Africa and Latin America,* ed. Frederick Cooper, Florencia E. Mallon, Steve J. Stern, Allen F. Isaacman, and William Roseberry, 318–70. Madison: University of Wisconsin Press.

Sandbrook, Richard, Marc Edelman, Patrick Heller, and Judith Teichman. 2006. "Can Social Democracies Survive in the Global South?" *Dissent,* Spring. http://www.dissentmagazine.org/article/?article=427.

Sitrin, Marina. 2006. *Horizontalism: Voices of Popular Power in Argentina.* Oakland, CA: AK Press.

Stobart, Luke. 2010. "Venezuela at the Crossroads: Voices from Inside the Revolution." *International Socialism* 126:19–28. http://www.isj.org.uk/index.php4?id=635&issue=126#126stobart5.

Veltmeyer, Henry. 1997. "New Social Movements in Latin America: The Dynamics of Class and Identity." *Journal of Peasant Studies* 25 (1): 139–69.

Webber, Jeffery R. 2010. "Venezuela under Chávez: The Prospects and Limitations of Twenty-first-Century Socialism, 1998–2009." *Socialist Studies/Études Socialistes* 6 (1): 11–44.

Wilpert, Gregory. 2007. *Changing Venezuela by Taking Power: The History and Policies of the Chávez Government.* London: Verso.

Zibechi, Raúl. 2003. *Gegealogía de la revuelta: Argentina, la sociedad en movimiento.* Montevideo: Nordan Comunidad.

I
THEORETICAL ISSUES

2

Socialist Strategies in Latin America

Claudio Katz
Translated by Leonard Morin

T HE LATIN AMERICAN LEFT IS ONCE AGAIN DISCUSSING the paths to socialism. The correlation of forces has changed through popular action, the
crisis of neoliberalism, and U.S. imperialism's loss of offensive capability. It
is no longer relevant to juxtapose a revolutionary political period of the past
with a conservative present. The social weakness of the industrial working
class does not impede anticapitalist progress, which depends on the exploited
and the oppressed uniting in common struggle.

What is crucial is the level of popular consciousness. The latter has forged new
antiliberal and anti-imperialist convictions, but an anticapitalist link, which an
open debate about twenty-first-century socialism could foster, is still missing.

The constitutional framework that replaced the dictatorships does not impede the Left's development. But the Left must avoid institutional co-optation
without turning its back on the electoral process. Electoral participation can
be made compatible with the promotion of people's power.

Movements and parties fulfill a complementary function since social struggle is not self-sufficient and partisan organization is necessary. Yet it is essential to avoid sectarian posturing and to include immediate improvements as
part of the revolutionary agenda. This principle governs all socialist strategy.

Socialist Strategies in Latin America

After several years of silence, strategic discussion is reemerging on the Latin
American Left, which once again is analyzing assessments and courses of

action in order to advance toward the socialist goal. This reflection includes six major themes: material conditions, relationships of force, social subjects, popular consciousness, institutional frameworks, and organizing the oppressed.

Maturity of the Productive Forces

The first debate revisits a classic controversy. Have the productive forces in Latin America matured enough to permit undertaking an anticapitalist transformation? Are the existing resources, technologies, and skills sufficient to initiate a socialist process?

The countries of the region are less prepared than the developed nations—but more pressed—to confront this change. They suffer more intense nutritional, educational, and sanitary disasters than the advanced economies but have fewer material resources at their disposal to solve these problems. This paradox is the consequence of Latin America's peripheral situation and its resulting agricultural backwardness, fragmentary industrialization, and financial dependence.

On the left there have been two traditional responses to this dilemma: promote a progressive capitalist stage, or initiate a socialist transition adapted to the region's shortcomings. In a recent article, I advocated the second option (Katz, 2006).

But another equally important debate concerns the timeliness of this course. Recovering from a traumatic period of industrial slump and bank meltdown, Latin America is experiencing a phase of growth, boom in exports, and recovery of entrepreneurial profits. One could object that, under these conditions, there is no likelihood of a collapse that would justify anticapitalist transformation.

But the socialist option is not a Keynesian program to turn around recessive market trends. It is a platform to overcome the exploitation and inequality inherent in capitalism. It seeks to abolish poverty and unemployment, eradicate environmental disasters, and put an end to the nightmares of war and the financial cataclysms that enrich a minuscule percentage of millionaires at the expense of millions of individuals.[1]

This polarization is evident in current Latin American market trends. The rise in profits and consumption of the well-to-do contrasts with terrifying indices of extreme poverty. These misfortunes that justify the battle for socialism become more visible in the pit of a recession. But situations of collapse do not furnish the only apt moment to uproot the system. The anticapitalist turn is an option open for an entire epoch and can begin at different moments in the economic cycle. The experience of the twentieth century confirms this possibility.

No socialist revolution ever coincided with the depths of a financial crisis. In the majority of cases, it erupted as a consequence of war, colonial occupation, or dictatorial oppression. It was under such conditions that the Bolsheviks took power in Russia, Mao succeeded in China, Tito prevailed in Yugoslavia, the Vietnamese drove out the United States, and the Cuban revolution triumphed. Many of these victories were consummated at the height of a postwar boom, that is, during a stage of intense capitalist growth. No mechanism, therefore, shackles the debut of socialism to an economic collapse. The misery that capitalism generates is sufficient to inspire the overthrow of this system in any phase of its periodic fluctuations.

Only catastrophist theorists see an unwavering link between socialism and financial meltdown. This supposed connection forms part of their habitual portrayal of capitalism as a system that always operates on the verge of final collapse. Waiting for this fall, they identify any banking slump as a global depression, and they confuse a simple stock market downturn with a general crash. These exaggerations ignore the basic workings of the system that they intend to uproot and make it impossible to tackle any of the problems of socialist transition.[2]

Globalization and Small Countries

One objection to the initiation of socialist processes emphasizes the impediments that globalization creates. It argues that the current internationalization of capital makes an anticapitalist challenge impracticable in Latin America.[3]

But where exactly is the obstacle rooted? Globalization does not constitute a barrier to the socialist project, which has universal reach. Expansion across borders amplifies capitalism's imbalances and creates greater objective bases for overcoming it.

Only those who conceive of the construction of socialism as a "competition between two systems" can view globalization as a great obstacle. This approach is a remnant of the theory of the "socialist camp" proclaimed by supporters of the old Soviet model. They gambled on defeating the enemy by means of a series of economic successes and geopolitical achievements, forgetting that one cannot defeat capitalism at its own game.

Peripheral—or less industrialized—economies in particular can never triumph in a competition with imperialist powers that have controlled the world market for centuries. The success of socialism requires a continuous sequence of processes that undermine global capitalism. Achieving socialism in a single country (or single bloc) is an illusion that repeatedly has led to subordinating the possibilities of revolutionary transformation to a diplomatic rivalry between two blocs of nations.

The portrayal of globalization as blocking the development of other models is an offshoot of the neoliberal vision, which proclaims the nonexistence of alternatives to the right-wing path. But if one accepts this premise, one must also discard any scheme of regulated or Keynesian capitalism. It is incongruent to affirm that the totalitarianism of globalization has buried the anticapitalist project, but that it tolerates interventionist regimes of accumulation. If one closes the first option, one also rules out chances for neo-developmentalist endeavors (since these depend on the power of the national state to resist externally imposed measures).

But since globalization is not in reality the end of history, every alternative remains open. What we are witnessing is merely a new period of accumulation, sustained by recovery of the rate of yield that the oppressed of every country pay. This regressive flow makes socialism an immediate necessity as the sole popular response to the new stage. Only socialism can correct the disorders created by the global expansion of capital in the current framework of financial speculation and imperialist polarization.

Many theorists recognize the global viability of the socialist option but question its feasibility in small Latin American countries. They believe that this beginning ought to be postponed—for example in Bolivia—some thirty or fifty years to allow the prior formation of an "Andean-Amazonian capitalism" (García Linera, 2005, 2006a). But why thirty years and not ten or one hundred and fifty? In the past, these time frames were associated with calculations of the emergence of national bourgeoisies in charge of carrying out the presocialist stage. But currently it is evident that the impediments to developing a competitive capitalist system in countries such as Bolivia are at least as great as the obstacles to initiating socialist transformations. One need merely imagine the concessions that the large foreign corporations would demand for participation in their project and the conflicts that these commitments would generate with the popular majorities.

The difficulty is even greater if one conceives of "Andean-Amazonian capitalism" as a model compatible with the reconstruction of indigenous communities (García Linera, 2006b, 2006c). In any scheme that is driven by commercial competition, the abuses against these communities would persist. The step to socialism in countries as peripheral as Bolivia is complex, yet possible and desirable. It requires promoting a transition together with similar programs and alliances in other countries of Latin America.

What Is the Correlation of Forces?

Socialist change depends on a balance of forces favorable to the oppressed. The popular majority cannot prevail over its antagonists if this balance is negative. But how does one evaluate this parameter?

The correlation of forces in Latin America is determined by the positions that are won, threatened, or lost by three sectors: the local capitalist classes, the mass of the oppressed, and U.S. imperialism. During the 1990s, capital carried out a global offensive against labor. This offensive weakened in the last few years, but it left a climate adverse to wage earners on an international scale. Nonetheless, in Latin America one can note several peculiarities.

The capitalists actively participated in the neoliberal assault but ended up suffering various side effects of this process. They lost competitive positions with the opening of markets and relinquished defenses against their external competitors with the denationalization of the productive apparatus. The financial crises also battered the establishment and reduced its direct political presence. The Right thus ended up in the minority, and center-left governments have replaced many conservative governments in national administrations (especially in the Southern Cone). The capitalist elites no longer set the entire region's agenda with impunity. A crisis of neoliberalism, which could lead to the structural decline of this project, has affected them.

Great popular upheavals, which precipitated the fall of several heads of state in South America, have also modified the regional relationship of forces. Uprisings in Bolivia, Ecuador, Argentina, and Venezuela have affected the totality of the dominant classes. They have challenged ruling-class aggressiveness and have imposed in many countries a certain degree of accommodation with the masses.

The combative impulse differs widely. In certain countries (Bolivia, Venezuela, Argentina, and Ecuador), one finds popular initiative (*protagonismo*), but in others (Brazil and Uruguay) there has been an ebb brought about by disappointments. What is new is the awakening of union and student struggles in countries that led the neoliberal ranking (Chile) and in countries asphyxiated by social abuses and the hemorrhage of emigrants (Mexico). The correlation of forces in Latin America varies greatly, but one can affirm a general surge of popular initiatives in the entire region.

At the start of the 1990s, U.S. imperialism embarked on the political recolonization of its backyard through free trade and the installation of military bases. This panorama also changed. The original version of the Free Trade Area of the Americas (FTAA) failed because of three factors: (1) conflicts between globalized corporations and those dependent on internal markets,

(2) clashes between exporters and industrialists, and (3) widespread popular rejection. The counteroffensive through bilateral treaties launched by the U.S. State Department does not compensate for this setback.

Bush's international isolation (the Republican electoral debacle, failure in Iraq, and the loss of allies in Europe) has left him less room for unilateralism and has incited the resurgence of geopolitical blocs adverse to the United States (such as the Non-Aligned Movement). The absence of a military response to the Venezuelan challenge is clearly symptomatic of this U.S. retreat.

The correlation of forces in Latin America has therefore undergone several significant changes. The dominant classes can no longer rely on their strategic neoliberal compass, the popular movement has recovered its street presence, and U.S. imperialism has forfeited its capacity to intervene.

The New Period

Changes in the domination from above, in the combativeness from below, and in the behavior of the external gendarme compel one to revise a common traditional diagnosis by various theorists of the Left. This assessment tended to highlight the obstacles to socialism on the basis of a contrast between two stages: the favorable period that began with the Cuban Revolution (1959) and the unfavorable phase that opened with the fall of the Soviet Union (1989–1991). The first cycle—revolutionary and anti-imperialist—gave way to the second phase of conservative regression (Harnecker, 2002). Is this scheme still valid?

The current political climate in many countries seems to contradict this vision at all three levels of the correlation of forces. First of all, the local capitalists have lost the aggressive confidence they had during the past decade. Unlike in the 1970s, they can no longer resort to dictatorial savagery. They have lost the instrument of the coup d'état as a means to avoid crisis and to crush popular rebellion with mass killings. In various countries, state terrorism persists (not only in Colombia but also in a selective form currently in Mexico), but in general, the establishment must accept a framework of institutional restrictions that they did not know in the past. This limitation constitutes a popular victory that works in favor of the exploited in the balance of forces.

Second, the intensity of the social struggles—measured by their magnitude and immediate political impact—has much in common with the resistances of the 1960s and 1970s. The uprisings that have occurred in Ecuador, Bolivia, and Argentina, and the actions of students and the community rebellions in the entire region, are comparable to the great upheavals of the past generation.

Third, the obstacles to intervention that imperialism confronts are very visible. While in the 1980s Reagan waged an open counterrevolutionary war in Central America, Bush has had to limit his operations in the region.

An analysis of the correlation of forces must take into account these three processes and avoid an outlook that pays attention only to the context at the top (relations between powers), omitting what happens below (social antagonisms). Such an outlook characterizes the traditional focus on the two stages, which sees a sharp break in regional history marked by the collapse of the Soviet Union. Based on this division, the socialist possibilities of the first period are idealized, and the anticapitalist prospects of the second are minimized.

The existence or disappearance of the Soviet Union constitutes an element of the analysis that does not define the correlation of forces. It is worth remembering that a bureaucracy hostile to socialism commanded this regime long before its reconversion into a capitalist class. It confronted the United States in the international chess game, but it supported anti-imperialist movements only as a function of its geopolitical interests. It was therefore not an engine of the anticapitalist project. The differences with the '70s exist and are significant, but they are not differences in the correlation of forces.

The Diversity of Subjects

The agents of a socialist transformation are the victims of capitalist domination, but the specific subjects of this process in Latin America are very diverse. In some regions, the indigenous communities have played a leading role in the rebellions (Ecuador, Bolivia, and Mexico), and in others, *campesinos* have led the resistance (Brazil, Peru, and Paraguay). In certain countries, the protagonists have been urban wage laborers (Argentina and Uruguay) or the precariously employed (in the Caribbean and Central America). Also striking are the new roles of the indigenous communities and the less influential roles of industrial unions. This multiplicity of sectors reflects the differentiated social structure and the political peculiarities of each country.

Yet this diversity also demonstrates the variety of participants in a socialist transformation. Since the development of capitalism expands the exploitation of wage labor and collateral forms of oppression, the potential agents of a socialist process are all of the exploited and oppressed. This role falls not only on the wage earners who directly generate business profits, but on all of the victims of capitalist inequality. What is essential is the convergence of these sectors in a common battle around constantly changing focal points of rebellion. Victory depends on such convergence against an enemy that dominates by dividing the popular camp.

In this struggle, certain segments of wage laborers tend to play a more influential role because of the place they occupy in vital branches of the economy (mining, factories, and banks). The capitalists benefit from the privations of all the dispossessed, but their earnings depend specifically on the direct labor efforts of the exploited.

This centrality is shown in the present phase of economic recovery, which tends to restore the significance of wage earners. In Argentina, the unions are regaining their influence on the street, in comparison to the role played by the unemployed and the middle class during the crisis of 2001. In Chile, the miners' strikes are having an impact, in Mexico certain unions are growing in strength, and in Venezuela the influence exerted by the oil workers during their battle against *golpismo* (the attempted shutdown of the oil industry in 2002) persists.

Absent Subject?

Some theorists believe that currently "no subject exists to undertake socialism" in Latin America (Dieterich, 2005). Yet they do not clearly define what the missing conglomeration is. The implicit response is the weakness of the regional working class, which represents a reduced fraction of the population as a consequence of capitalist underdevelopment. This position argues for postponing the realization of socialism until a bigger and more extensive working class emerges.

But the development of contemporary capitalism is synonymous with high productivity, technological change, and the consequent spread of contingent work or unemployment. This evolution calls into question the traditional link between growing accumulation and the massive increase of the industrial working class. If unemployment and informal labor make the battle for socialism impossible for now, they will also impede it in the future. It is evident that both scourges will continue to reinforce the army of the unemployed and the fragmentation of wage earners.

One must also bear in mind that an entirely uniform and homogenous proletariat has never existed and that the current expansion of the informal sector is an additional reason to favor socialism. The necessary actors for initiating this transformation are amply present in Latin America.

It is true that the working class does not possess the ideal profile for this change, yet neither does the bourgeoisie have perfect traits for capitalist development. For this reason, the neo-developmentalists intensely debate the degree to which this national business class exists, and yet, whatever their conclusion, they never discard capitalism. For some theorists of the Left, however, the quantitative limitations of the working class constitute grounds to argue for the postponement of socialism.

This difference of approach is instructive. While the dominant classes exhibit enormous flexibility in confronting adversities with different remedies (for example, increased state intervention), the response of some socialists is timid. They only see obstacles to the popular project, while their opponents attempt one model after another of capitalism.

With idealized conceptions of the industrial working class—as the sole architects of socialism—there will always be obstacles to conceptualizing an anticapitalist agenda in the periphery. But if one abandons that narrow notion, there is no reason to question the viability of this project on the basis of class deficiencies.

The assimilation of traditions of struggle is more important for an anticapitalist process than is the hierarchy of the participating subjects. If the experiences of resistance are shared, the potential for a revolutionary change increases. An example of such sharing was the conversion of Argentine ex-workers into militants of a great movement of the unemployed. Another case was the transformation of the ex-miners in Bolivia into organizers of informal workers.

The change of status (from the exploited to the oppressed and vice versa) does not make a major difference if the level of combativeness persists and if the channels of popular activism are constantly renewed. This second aspect is more relevant to the socialist project than any changes in social configurations. And so sociological analysis must not replace the political characterization of a revolutionary process.

The supposed absence of subjects has informed a great variety of arguments challenging socialism. In some small nations, this objection highlights the demographic scarcity of the proletariat, as in Bolivia where the latter suffered severe defeats since the privatization of the mining industry and its importance waned in relation to family agriculture (García Linera, 2006d, 2006e).

Yet all the anticapitalist revolutions of the twentieth century were consummated in backward countries where wage workers were in the minority. The defeats suffered by the miners of the Bolivian Altiplano have been amply offset by a succession of popular rebellions. And agrarian communities are potential allies and not adversaries of socialist change.

The problem of the absent subject tends to generate sterile debates. Finding ways to guarantee unity between the oppressed and the exploited is much more important than settling which of them would be the greater protagonist in a leap toward socialism.

Problems of Popular Consciousness

The eradication of capitalism is a project entirely dependent on the level of consciousness of the oppressed. Only their convictions can guide a process of struggle toward socialism.

The primitive view of this transformation as a historically inevitable process has lost intellectual consensus and political appeal. No pattern of historical evolution of this type exists. Either socialism will be a voluntary creation of the great majorities, or it will never emerge. The experience of "actually existing socialism" illustrates how damaging it is to substitute the paternalism of functionaries for the initiative of the people.

But the consciousness of the oppressed is subject to strong mutations. Two opposing forces influence its development: the lessons learned by the exploited in their resistance to capital, and the discouragement they suffer as a result of burdensome labor, survival anxieties, and everyday alienation.

The inclination of wage earners to question or accept the established order arises from the changing outcomes of this conflict. Under certain circumstances, the critical view predominates, and at other moments resignation prevails. These attitudes depend on many factors and are reflected in very different generational perceptions of capitalism. The bulk of contemporary youth, for example, grew up without the expectation of improvement in labor conditions and education that prevailed in the postwar period and view exclusion, unemployment, or inequality as normal operating patterns of the system. This outlook on the established order has not prevented the new generation of Latin Americans from resuming the combativeness of its predecessors.

The predominant image of capitalism influences socialist consciousness but does not determine its continuity. In this regard, what is essential are the conclusions drawn from the class struggle and the impact generated by great revolutions in other countries. These benchmarks determine the existence of certain "average degrees of socialist consciousness" that translate into levels of greater enthusiasm or disappointment about the anticapitalist project. The victories achieved in Russia, China, Yugoslavia, Vietnam, and Cuba, for example, promoted a positive socialist perception, which the numerous defeats that also occurred in those periods did not dissipate.

The present generation of Latin Americans did not grow up like their parents in a context marked by revolutionary triumphs. This absence of a successful anticapitalist reference—close to their immediate personal experiences—explains their spontaneously distancing themselves further away from the socialist project.

The great differences between the current period and that of 1960–1980 lie more on this plane of political consciousness than in the realm of relationships of force or in the change of the popular subjects. It is not the intensity of the social conflicts, the willingness of the oppressed to struggle, or the capacity of the oppressors to control that has substantially changed, but the visibility of—and confidence in—a socialist model.

Ruptures and Continuities

The fall of the Soviet Union provoked an international crisis of credibility for the socialist project that has conditioned action on the left. Latin America was no exception to this effect, but some theorists exaggerate its repercussions and tend to suppose that it would rule out prospects for socialism for a long period. This view has given rise to the categorical distinction between a revolutionary period (until 1989) and a conservative one (from that date on).

This separation overlooks the fact that the Latin American Left had distanced itself from the Soviet model before the collapse of the "socialist camp." The disenchantment of the 1990s corresponded more to the inheritance left by the dictatorships, to the failure of the Sandinistas, and to the blocking of the Central American insurgency. In this dimension, the survival of the Cuban Revolution constituted a significant counterbalance.

In any case, it is evident that an impulse to reconstruct the emancipatory program has replaced the climate of disappointment. The prosocialist stance of various popular movements confirms this impetus. The big question to be answered at present is this: To what extent has this project been assimilated by the new generations who led the rebellions of the last decade?

These groups' overwhelming rejection of privatization and deregulation (much stronger than that observed in other regions, such as Eastern Europe) demonstrates the advance of antiliberal consciousness in their ranks. One can also observe the rebirth of an anti-imperialist consciousness without the regressive components in terms of ethics or religion that prevail in the Arab world. In Latin America, a framework conducive to a revival of leftist thought has developed because the break with this tradition that one observes in various countries of Eastern Europe has not occurred.[4]

Yet the anticapitalist nexus is the great missing link in the region, and this deficiency has up to now inhibited the radicalization of popular consciousness. In this regard, open debate about socialism in the twenty-first century can play a decisive role.

The Constitutional Framework

The Latin American Left faces a relatively novel strategic problem: the general presence of constitutional regimes. For the first time in the history of the region, the dominant classes govern through nondictatorial institutions in almost every country and have done so for a significant period. Not even economic collapses, political meltdown, or popular insurrections have modified this pattern of administration.

The return of the military is an option that the majority of the hemisphere's elites have abandoned. In the most critical situations, old presidents are replaced by new chief executives with some kind of civilian-military interregnum government, but this substitution does not lead to the reinstallation of dictatorships to resolve the disintegration from above or the rebellion from below.

Most of the current regimes are plutocracies at the service of capitalists and are thus completely removed from real democracy. The institutions of these systems have committed social abuses that many dictatorships never even dared to insinuate. These aggressions have robbed the system of its legitimacy, but they have not led people to reject the constitutional regime in the way they rejected the old tyrannies.

This change in the mode of capitalist domination has contradictory effects on the action of the Latin American Left. On the one hand, it broadens the possibilities of action in a context of civil liberties. On the other, it imposes a framework marked by the confidence that capitalists have in the institutions of their system.

A regime that limits and at the same time consolidates the power of the oppressors entails a great challenge for the Left, especially when this structure is seen by the majority as the natural *modus operandi* of any modern society.

This latter belief has been fostered by the Right—which has seized the opportunity to pursue its course within the constitutional context—and also by the center-left, which upholds the status quo with progressive pretences. Both sides incite false electoral polarizations to mask the simple alternation of the figures who hold power.

The current example of this complementary arrangement is the "modern and civilized left" that has acceded to government with Lula da Silva, Tabaré Vázquez, or Michelle Bachelet to perpetuate the supremacy of the capitalists. But other situations are more problematic because institutional continuity was broken up by fraud (Mexico) or by presidential resignation (Bolivia, Ecuador, and Argentina).

In certain cases, these convulsions ended up reestablishing the bourgeois order (Néstor Kirchner). But in other countries, the crises led to unforeseen access to government by left nationalist or radical reformist presidents who are rejected by the establishment. This is the case with Hugo Chávez and Evo Morales, and probably with Rafael Correa—because the crises and uprisings in these nations occurred initially outside the established institutions.

In these processes, the electoral terrain has proven to be a site of struggle against reaction and a setting for proposing radical transformations. This conclusion is vital for the Left. One must not forget that in Venezuela, for example, from 1998 to the present, every election ratified the legitimacy of the Bolivarian process and transferred to the ballot box the defeats it had delivered to the Right on the streets. The electoral sphere served to complement the victories of mass mobilization.

Answers from the Left

The constitutional framework significantly alters the context of leftist activity, which for decades had been directed against military tyrannies. The battle within the current system is not simple because the current institutionalism renews bourgeois domination in multiple disguises.

This plasticity initially disconcerted a generation of militants prepared to fight against a very brutal but not very devious dictatorial enemy. Some activists were demoralized by these difficulties and ended up accepting the accusations from the right. They began to flay themselves for their former "underestimation of democracy," forgetting that civil liberties were an achievement of popular resistance (and not of a bourgeois party regime complicit with authoritarianism).

The constitutional framework induced other militants to proclaim the end of "revolutionary utopia" and the beginning of a new era of gradual advances toward a postcapitalist future. They returned to the gradualist scheme and proposed to embark on the road to socialism through an initial consensus with the oppressors. They advocated taking this path to gaining hegemony for the workers.

But the vast trajectory of social democracy has proved the unreality of this option. The dominant classes do not give up power. They only co-opt partners to recreate the pillars of an oppression based on private ownership of the big banks and corporations. They will never permit this control to be corroded by the political or cultural weight of their antagonists.

For this reason, any policy that indefinitely postpones the anticapitalist goal ends up reinforcing oppression. Socialism requires preparing and consummating anticapitalist ruptures. If one forgets this principle, the strategy of the Left lacks a compass.

But the confrontation with constitutionalism has also generated positive effects in recent years. It has allowed, for example, debate on the left about the form that a genuine democracy under socialism would adopt. This reflection introduced a significant change in the way of conceptualizing the anticapitalist perspective. In the 1970s, democracy was a topic that the critics of the Soviet bureaucracy omitted or barely put forth. Now almost no one skirts this problem. Socialism has ceased to be imagined as a prolongation of the tyranny that reigned in the Soviet Union and has currently begun to be perceived as a regime of growing participation, representation, and popular control.

But this future also depends on the immediate responses to constitutionalism. Two positions prevail on the left: one focus proposes winning space within the institutional structure, and the other promotes parallel organs of people's power (Harnecker, 2000; Petras and Veltmeyer, 2005).

The first path argues for advancing by climbing from the local to the provincial levels to subsequently reach the national governments. It follows from the experiences of community administrations that the Brazilian Workers' Party (Partido dos Trabalhadores) and the Broad Front (Frente Amplio) of Uruguay pursued in the early 1990s. It recognizes the bitter concessions granted to the establishment during these administrations (business commitments and postponement of social improvements), but it construes the final outcome as positive.

Undeniably, this "municipal socialism" led to old activists turning into confidence men of capital. They debated at city halls, exhibited hostility toward the social movement, and ended up governing on behalf of the dominant classes. First they moderated programs, then they called for responsibility, and finally they changed sides.

The participatory budget did not counteract this regression. Discussing how to distribute a local expenditure limited by the constraints of neoliberal policy leads to imposing a self-adjustment upon the citizenry. Participatory democracy only awakens radical consciousness of the people when it resists and denounces the tyranny of capital. If it renounces this goal, it turns into an instrument for preserving the established order.

An opposite strategy to the institutional path exists that encourages social mobilization and rejects electoral participation. It denounces the corruption of the Workers' Party or the passivity of the Broad Front and advocates the emergence of direct options for people's power. It also questions the electoral traps that, in the Andean countries, have led to channeling resistance through the system.

This vision ignores the influence of the electoral arena and minimizes the negative consequences of abandoning it. Citizenship, voting, and electoral rights are not just instruments of bourgeois manipulation. They are also popular conquests achieved against dictatorships, which under certain conditions allow one to take a stand against the Right. If elections were pure trickery, they would not have been able to fulfill the progressive role that they have played, for example, in Venezuela.

It is vital to denounce the circumscribed character that civil rights have under a social system governed by profit. But democratic advances must be broadened and not disdained. They constitute the basis of a future regime of social equality that will grant substantial content to the formal mechanisms of democracy.

Participation in the constitutional framework fosters the political practices necessary for the future socialist democracy. Rejecting electoral participation is as pernicious on a tactical level (isolation) as it is in terms of strategy (preparing this socialist future).

In the face of the false dilemma of accepting or ignoring the rules of constitutionalism, there is a third viable path: to combine direct action with electoral participation. With this approach, the expressions of people's power—which any revolutionary process requires—would be made compatible with the maturation of socialist consciousness, which to a certain extent takes place in the constitutional arena.

Only Movements?

Popular consciousness translates into organization. The grouping of the oppressed is essential to creating the instruments of an anticapitalist transformation, since without their own organizations, the exploited cannot gestate another society.

Movements and parties constitute two modes of contemporary popular organization. Both are essential to the development of socialist convictions. They reinforce confidence in self-organization, and they develop the norms for the future exercise of people's power.

Movements sustain the immediate social struggle, and parties fuel a more fully developed political activity. Both are necessary for facilitating direct action and electoral participation. But this complementarity is frequently questioned by exclusivist advocates of movement or party. Some movement-oriented theorists—who subscribe to autonomist points of view—believe that party organization is obsolete, useless, and pernicious (Katz, 2005).

But their objections apply only to the actions of certain parties and not to the general operation of these structures. No emancipatory project can evolve exclusively in the social realm, nor can it do without the specific platforms—the links between demands and power strategies—that party groupings provide. These groupings help overcome the limitations of a spontaneous rebellion. The party facilitates the maturation of an anticapitalist conscious-ness that does not emerge abruptly from protest actions but requires a certain processing in order to transform the battle for immediate improvements into a struggle for socialist objectives.

The critics of parties have drawn support from the favorable climate toward movements that has predominated at the World Social Forums in recent years. Nonetheless, from Seattle (1999) to Caracas-Bamako (2006), much has changed. Confidence in the self-sufficiency of movements has declined, especially in the current Latin American scenario marked by electoral defeats of the Right. The foundational "utopian moment" of the forums has shrunk, clearing the way for debating strategies that include parties. This change also reflects the turn of various movement-oriented theorists, who continue to aggressively question leftist organizations while now defending Lula or Kirchner (Cocco, 2006; Negri, 2005; Negri and Cocco, 2006).

The rejection of parties also persists among authors who propose "chang-ing the world without taking power." They dissent from political organiza-tions that defend the need to conquer state power, but without ever clarifying how a postcapitalist society lacking governmental forms would emerge. The state is the target of all social demands, and its transformation is the condition for any anticapitalist transition. Not even the most basic democratic changes that we currently see in Latin America are conceivable without the state. This instrument is necessary to implement social reforms, create constituent as-semblies, and nationalize basic resources. Those who deny this necessity have become disconcerted in the face of the new scenario that exists in Venezuela and Bolivia.

Notes

1. This article originally appeared in *Monthly Review* 59, no. 4 (2007): 25–41.
One percent of the planet's population currently controls 40 percent of the wealth (Aizpeolea, 2006).

2. An extreme example of this conception—which assumes catastrophe as a quality—is set forth by Pablo Rieznik (2006).

3. Marta Harnecker (2000) describes how this debate arose on the left in the early 1990s.

4. The breaks in wage laborers' historic identification with the Left, which one can note in the Old World, do not exist. See Francois Vercammen (2002).

References

Aizpeolea, Horacio. 2006. "Como se reparte la torta." *La Nación*, September 15.

Cocco, Giuseppe. 2006. "Los nuevos gobiernos no se entienden sin los movimientos sociales." *Página/12*, March 20.

Dieterich, Heinz. 2005. *Hugo Chávez y el socialismo del siglo XXI. Caracas: Por los caminos de América.*

García Linera, Álvaro. 2005. "Somos partidarios de un modelo socialista con un capitalismo boliviano." *Clarín, December 23.*

———. 2006a. "El capitalismo andino-amazónico." *Enfoques Críticos* 2 (April–May).

———. 2006b. "El evismo." *OSAL* 19 (January–April).

———. 2006c. "Tres temas de reflexión." *Argenpress, November 14.*

———. 2006d. "No estamos pensando en socialismo sino en revolución democratizadora." *Página/12, April 10.*

———. 2006e. "La gente quiere autonomía pero conducida por el MAS." *Página/12,* July 5.

Harnecker, Marta. 2000. *La izquierda en el umbral del siglo XXI. Madrid: Siglo Veintiuno.*

———. *2002. La izquierda después de Seattle.* Madrid: Siglo Veintiuno.

Katz, Claudio. 2005. "Crítica del autonomismo." *Memoria* 197 (July).

———. 2006. "Socialismo o neodesarrollismo." *LaHaine.org*, December. http://www.lahaine.org/index.php?p=18867.

Negri, Toni. 2005. "La derrota de EEUU es una derrota política." *Página/12*, November 1.

Negri, Toni, and Giuseppe Cocco. 2006. "América Latina está viviendo un momento de ruptura." *Página/12*, August 14.

Petras, James, and Henry Veltmeyer. 2005. *Movimientos sociales y poder estatal.* Mexico: Lumen.

Rieznik, Pablo. 2006. "En defensa del catastrofismo." *En defensa del marxismo* 34 (October).

Vercammen, Francois. 2002. "Europe: la gauche radicale est de retour." *Critique Communiste* 167 (Autumn).

3

The Latin American Left in the Face of the New Imperialism

Henry Veltmeyer

FINDING ITSELF IN MILITARY OCCUPATION of much of the world in the immediate wake of a second world war, and possessing an estimated 38 percent of world industrial capacity and half of the financial resources available for investment, the U.S. government strove to consolidate this power into dominion of the "free world." The motivation behind the subsequent empire-building project is clear enough: the perception of U.S. state officials of its military and economic power, its geopolitical strategic interests in an emerging bipolar world, as well as considerations of profit and national security (to make the world safe for U.S. investments as well as activating a systemwide capital-accumulation process). It was to be an empire of free trade and capitalist development, plus democracy if and where possible—a system of capitalist democracies backed by the authority and power of a system of international institutions dominated by the United States, and a global network of military bases concentrated in Europe and East Asia (Hearden, 2002).

Fast-forwarding from the post–World War II era of the welfare-developmentalist state to the 1980s and the installation of a "new" (neoliberal) world order, and with it a renewed assault on the working classes and the rural poor in the name of "structural reform" (adjustment to the requirements of this order), the twentieth century ended with a resurgence of the political Left in the form of antisystemic social movements led by rural landless workers, peasants, and indigenous communities. As the "actually existing" socialist system collapsed, with the transition from one form of imperialism (economic) to another (military)—and the advance of imperial wars in other areas of the capitalist world—Latin America served as a beacon of popular hope, a major site of resistance against neoliberalism and U.S. imperialism.

The organized resistance to the new world order revived the spark of social revolution, even as the fires of revolutionary ferment were being dampened by the forces of state reaction and the forces of resistance were put on the defensive in other parts of the empire. To counter this perceived threat to "order," the architects and guardians of imperial rule adjusted and revised the "new economic model" of neoliberal globalization with a new post-Washington consensus (PWC) on the need to "bring the state back in," effect a better balance between state and market, and establish a more socially inclusive and pragmatic form of neoliberalism (Craig and Porter, 2006; Ocampo, 2006; Sunkel and Infante, 2009). Under conditions of this new policy agenda and widespread disenchantment with neoliberalism, together with a shift in the structure of international trade (a primary commodities boom) and a consequent windfall in private profit and fiscal resources, a number of center-left governments were formed and assumed power across Latin America—in Argentina, Brazil, Chile, Bolivia, Ecuador, Uruguay, Paraguay, and Nicaragua, as well as Venezuela (Barrett, Chavez, and Rodríguez Garavito, 2008; Castañeda and Morales, 2009; Levitsky and Roberts, 2011; Petras and Veltmeyer, 2009).

But this leftist tilt in national politics did not necessarily mean progress in the form of a more equitable distribution of the social product and freedom from oppression and exploitation. On the one hand, Hugo Chávez actively promoted and sought to bring about the "socialism of the twenty-first century," bringing Bolivia and Ecuador with him in alliance with Cuba, and several countries in the immediate backyard of the U.S. empire. Bolivia, Ecuador, Cuba, Nicaragua, Honduras, the Dominican Republic, El Salvador, and several Caribbean island states joined Venezuela's lead in establishing a new anti-imperialist front of regional integration, Alianza Bolivariana para los Pueblos de Nuestra América (Bolivarian Alliance for the Peoples of Our America, ALBA). On the other hand, the installation of a number of left-leaning regimes only served to perpetuate the neoliberal capitalist projects that preceded them, and paradoxically at the level of class struggle (i.e., in the streets), in some places (Argentina, Bolivia) it actually strengthened the Right and weakened the Left, provoking the retreat of the social movements that had dominated the political landscape in the 1990s (Petras and Veltmeyer, 2009).

Latin America in this new context—after five years of a primary commodity boom and the onset of the so-called global financial crisis—remains at a crossroads, caught in the vortex of forces that cut toward both the left and the right, raising questions about the plausibility of advancing a twenty-first-century form of socialism in conditions of a system in crisis. This chapter will explore several dimensions of this issue with an emphasis on the response of American imperialism to the resurgence of the Left and the prospects for substantive or transformative change in the face of this response.

The Imperial Project: Pillars of the U.S. Empire

The United States has always been imperialist in its approach to national development, but the situation in which it found itself (as an occupying power of major proportions)[1] awakened in U.S. policy-making circles and the foreign-policy establishment a renewed sense of the country's historic mission regarding the Americas, provoking a quest to bring about its dominion in the preferred form of an "informal empire." A key element of this project was to set up the rules for what would later be termed "global governance," securing its economic and geopolitical strategic interests in a world freed from colonial rule and competing empires. The resulting world order, dubbed "Bretton Woods I" by some,[2] also provided a framework for advancing the geopolitical strategic interests of the United States in the context of a "cold war" waged against the emerging power of the USSR and for advancing an agenda for cooperation for international development, a policy designed to ensure that the economically backward countries seeking to liberate themselves from the yoke of colonialism would not fall to the siren song of communism, but rather undertake a nation-building and development process along a capitalist path.

This nation-building and development project required the United States to assume the lead but also share power with its major allies—strategic partners in a common enterprise organized as the Organization for Economic Cooperation and Development (OECD) and a united Europe, with a United Nations system to provide a multilateral response to security threats (to prevent any one country from seeking world domination via unilateral action). This was the price that the United States had to pay for national security under conditions of an emerging external threat presented by the USSR—Soviet Communism backed up by a growing industrial might and state power.

In this context, the United States undertook building an empire on the foundation of six pillars: (1) consolidation of the liberal capitalist world order, renovating it on neoliberal lines in the early 1980s when conditions allowed; (2) a system of military bases to provide the staging point and logistics for the projection of military power and rule by military force, when circumstances would dictate; (3) a project of cooperation for international development, providing financial and technical assistance to countries and regimes willing or forced to sign on, while also securing safe havens for U.S. economic interests; (4) implementation of a neoliberal agenda for policy reform, to adjust national policies and institutions to the requirements of a new world order in which the forces of freedom would be released from the constraints of welfare development; (5) regional integration in the form of economic integration in the diverse macro-regions of the empire; and (6) globalization—the integration of economies across the world into the global economy in a system designed to give maximum freedom to the operating units of the global empire.

Each strategy not only served as a pillar of the empire, but it also provided the focal point for the projection of state power as circumstances required or permitted. Together they constituted what might be termed the imperialist system. Each element of the system was dynamic in its operations but ultimately unstable and difficult to govern because of the countervailing forces of resistance they would generate in the popular sector of society.

Imperialism as Armed Force: War in the Informal Empire

Within U.S. ruling-class circles there has been an open acceptance that theirs is an imperial state and that the United States should act so as to maintain or restore its dominant position in the twenty-first century by any means, and certainly by force if need be.

The whole tenor of the debate in the past two decades over U.S. foreign policy was framed in these terms. In this connection, Richard Hass, the current director of policy planning in the State Department, wrote an essay in November 2000 advocating that the United States adopt an "imperial" foreign policy. He defined this as "a foreign policy that attempts to organize the world along certain principles affecting relations between states and conditions within them" (quoted in Halevi and Varoufakis, 2004: 85). This would not be achieved through colonization or colonies but thorough what he termed "informal control" based on "a good neighbor policy" backed up by military force if and when necessary—harking back to the "informal empire" of a previous era (McLean, 1995; Roorda, 1998).

Institutional arrangements such as international financial markets and structural reforms in macroeconomic policy, and agencies such as the World Bank, the World Trade Organization (WTO), and the International Monetary Fund (IMF), would work to ensure the dominance of U.S. interests, with the military iron fist backing up the invisible hand of the market and any failure in multilateral security arrangements. This system of "economic imperialism," maintained by U.S. hegemony as leader of the "free world" (representing the virtues of capitalist democracy), was in place and fully functioning from the 1950s throughout the 1980s and the reign of Ronald Reagan. In the 1990s, with the disappearance of the threat of the Soviet Union and international Communism, this system of economic imperialism, based as it was on the hegemony of "democracy and freedom" as well as multilateralism in international security arrangements, did not so much break down as become eclipsed by the emergence of the "new imperialism" based on the unilateral projection of military force as a means of securing world domination in "the American century."[3]

This concept of a new imperialism, a "raw imperialism" that would not "hesitate to use [coercive] force if, when and where necessary" (Cooper, 2000), based on "aggressive multilateralism" or the unilateral projection and strategic use of state power, including emphatic military force, was advanced in neoconservative circles over years of largely internal debate and put into practice by a succession of regimes, both Democratic (Clinton in the 1990s) and Republican. It achieved its consummate form in George W. Bush's White House, with the Gang of Four (Donald Rumsfeld, Paul Wolfowitz, Condoleeza Rice, and Dick Cheney), and its maximum expression in a policy of imperial war in the Middle East and the Persian Gulf region. Although the United States also projected its military power in other theaters of imperial war, such as in Yugoslavia and Colombia, the policy of imperial war and the strategy of military force were primarily directed toward the Persian Gulf region.

The issue of the specific or dominant form taken by imperialism has not been framed as a matter of when and under what circumstances military force might be needed or legitimately used (generally seen not as a "last resort" but rather as the necessary part of the arsenal of force available to the state, conceived of as the only legitimate repository of the use of violence in the "national interest"). Rather, the issue of armed force in the imperialist projection of military power has been framed in terms of an understanding that imperial order cannot be maintained by force and coercion. It requires hegemony, which is to say acquiescence by the subalterns to imperial power achieved by a widespread belief in the legitimacy of that power generated by an overarching myth or dominant ideology—the idea of freedom in the post–World War II context of the cold war against communism and the idea of globalization in the new imperial order established in the 1980s. Power relations of domination and subordination, even when backed up by coercive or armed force, invariably give rise to resistance, and they are only sustainable if and when they are legitimated by an effective ideology—ideas of democracy and freedom in the case of the American empire or globalization in the case of the new form of imperialism that came into play in the 1990s.

It is hardly coincidental that the 1990s saw the advent of a new form of imperialism based on the projection of armed force. The idea of globalization, used to legitimate and justify neoliberal policies of stabilization and structural reform, had lost its commanding force—its hold over the minds of people, particularly among classes within the popular sector. As a result, the 1990s in

Latin America saw the advent and workings of powerful forces of resistance to the neoliberal policy agenda and the machinations of U.S. imperialism. To combat these forces of resistance, state officials resorted to different strategies and tactics as dictated by circumstances, generally by combining development assistance and outright repression (Petras and Veltmeyer, 2003).

How this worked in practice can be illustrated in the case of Paraguay. In 1996 the then government presided over by Nicanor Duarte decreed the presence of military and paramilitary forces in the countryside as legal because the police were unable to contain the peasant struggle. At the same time, the regime authorized the presence of American troops, giving them immunity for any violation of the country's laws that might occur in the process of their "humanitarian assistance" (counterinsurgency training) provided to the Paraguayan troops. It has been alleged by the peasant organizations in the country that some of the nongovernmental organizations operating in the area and financed by U.S. Agency for International Development (USAID) were also enlisted to provide assistance in controlling the population—to divert the rural poor away from the social movements and have them opt for local micro-development projects instead. In this sense, what happened in Paraguay is part of the time-honored U.S. tradition of combining the iron fist of armed force with the velvet glove of local development on the front lines of rural poverty.

Elsewhere in the empire, neither neoliberalism in policy or resistance in the form of social movements were as virulent as they were in Latin America. As a result, the idea of globalization had more force in other macro-regions of the empire than it ever had in Latin America (Bowles et al., 2007a, 2007b). Consequently, it would require the events of 9/11 and the resurrection and reconstruction of the United States' global mission (to defend the free world) for the administrators of the empire under George W. Bush to escape the confines of globalization and dispense with its constraints, allowing the administration to institute the new imperialism unilaterally and with overt military force.

Imperialism as Development, International Cooperation as Imperialism

Overseas development assistance (ODA)—foreign aid, in more common parlance—is widely viewed as a catalyst of economic development, a boost to developing societies' economies to assist them in following the path toward progress and prosperity traced out by the club of rich or advanced capitalist countries. But it is possible to look at foreign aid differently—as a means of advancing the geopolitical and strategic interests of the governments and international organizations that provide this "aid." In 1971, at the height (but impending crisis) of the Bretton Woods world economic order, this view was expressed in the notion of "imperialism as aid." The purpose of aid was essentially geopolitical: to ensure that the former colonies of British-led European imperialism, upon achieving national independence, would not fall prey to the lure of communism and that they would follow a capitalist path toward their national development.

After the Cuban Revolution in 1959, the United States redirected its development efforts away from nation building toward the countryside in various developing societies where there was a buildup of revolutionary ferment. In Latin America, where this new strategy was concentrated, this entailed the construction of the Alliance for Progress, a new policy and institutional framework of international cooperation for rural development, aimed at the rural poor—to turn them away from revolutionary movements and opt instead for local development mediated by the nongovernmental organizations brought into play (Veltmeyer, 2005).

In the 1960s and 1970s, a combination of this approach with a strategy of co-optation of the leadership of the social movements, and strategic use of its repressive apparatus, resulted in the defeat of the revolutionary impulse among the rural poor and destruction of the armies for national liberation that had sprouted throughout the Latin American countryside under conditions of imperialist and class exploitation. The Revolutionary Armed Forces of Colombia—People's Army (FARC-EP) was one of the few such revolutionary organizations in the region that survived. The occasional and fragile unity of the forces of resistance mounted by organized labor in the cities and the proletarianized peasants in the countryside was everywhere broken, and the remaining resistance was demobilized and went underground, awaiting more favorable conditions. As it turned out, such conditions only materialized in Chiapas, allowing the grounded forces of resistance to reappear under changed conditions—erupting, in this case, on January 1, 1994, the day on which NAFTA, a major new offensive in the imperialist war, was launched.

This particular offensive would also be ultimately defeated—not by armed force but by a policy of strategic isolation and encirclement. In other contexts—particularly in Brazil, Ecuador, and Bolivia—the forces of resistance against neoliberalism and U.S. imperialism were more successful. Indeed, the social movements in these countries succeeded in either halting, slowing down, and even in some cases reversing the neoliberal agenda, placing state officials in these countries, as well as the agencies of U.S. imperialism, on the defensive. It would take another decade of concerted actions against these movements to hold them at bay. Again, it was not armed force but international cooperation for "development," implemented within the new policy framework of the post-Washington consensus, that was responsible for taming the forces of revolutionary change. This consensus is at the heart of the economic vision of the new Latin American Left embodied in the new developmentalist policies of the so-called post-neoliberal state (Bresser-Pereira, 2009; Burdick, Oxhorn, and Roberts, 2009; Levitsky and Roberts, 2011; Lievesley and Ludlam, 2009; MacDonald and Ruckert, 2009; Silva, 2009)—what Jeffery Webber and Barry Carr, in the introduction to this volume, term *la izquierda permitida.*

The Left, it turned out, having abandoned the revolutionary struggle, was complicit in this defeat of the social movements. Certain elements of the Left (see in particular the "situationists" in Argentina)[4] took up positions on the basis of what John Holloway (2002), among others, views as the "no power" approach to social change (change without taking power). Others on the Left, such as Antonio Negri (2001) and others associated with MAS (the Movement Toward Socialism) in Bolivia, joined or formed the "political class" opting for democratic elections or what used to be termed the parliamentary road to state power. By 2004, with the notable exception of Bolivia, where the revolutionary forces were actively mobilized in the struggle to prevent the privatization of the country's strategic natural resources, the wave of social movements that had washed over the neoliberal state in the 1990s had ebbed, leading to retreat by the very center-left that had assumed state power.

Imperialism as Neoliberal Economic Reform

The neoliberal agenda, a prominent feature of the economic imperialism of recent years, was decades in the making, but it was not till the early 1980s, in the vortex of two crises, that the conditions needed for its implementation became available. The fiscal crisis provided the political conditions of a conservative counterrevolution in development thinking and practice—for the advent of neoliberalism. On the other hand, the debt crisis provided a lever for adjusting government policies to the requirements of this new world order.

While the World Bank and the IMF might well be considered agents of the empire, and the multinationals its operational units, the brain trust of the system was made up of an array of neoconservative institutions, including the Pelerin Society, a neoliberal thought collective constituted to advance free-market capitalism at the level of national policy. It also includes the Council on Foreign Relations, a complex of policy forums and Washington-based foundations. The institutional structure of this new world order encompasses the World Bank, the IMF, and the WTO, the latter stillborn until 1994.

The impetus behind the call for a new world order was to advance capitalism on a global scale and to create a policy agenda in support of the economic interests at play, interests associated with a system of multinational corporations, the largest cluster of which were headquartered in the United States (Petras and Veltmeyer, 2003, 2005a, 2009). The economic and political dynamics of this "development" are well documented and have been analyzed at the level of the multinational corporations that dominate the world economy (see, for example, Harvey, 2003).

The neoliberal agenda was advanced in the form of globalization, an ideology constructed to mobilize support for this agenda, presenting it as a policy consensus and even as a development program, the only way forward to general prosperity—and to establish hegemony over the whole system. By the end of the decade, however, the idea of globalization had lost its luster and mobilizing power, and it gave rise to diverse and at times powerful forces of resistance. No longer was it able to effectively serve as an ideology to justify and mask the neoliberal policy agenda, leading to a major revision in the framework, an effort to provide it with a human face and present it as a more inclusive form of national and local development, designed to empower and capacitate the poor. By the new millennium, this PWC was achieved in the form of the *izquierda permitida*—the pragmatic (new developmentalist) form of neoliberalism pursued by the center-left regimes in the region.

The Dynamics of Empire Building in Latin America

The U.S. empire, built in the postwar years (see the discussion above on the pillars of empire), extended into and held sway in different regions of the world economy. The dynamics of these forces and the workings of imperialism in each region are substantively different. But we are particularly concerned with Latin America, where the U.S. empire was extended from its original base in Central America and Mexico further south to encompass virtually the entire region, and where neoliberalism as an institutional and policy framework for imperialism had its major expression and the forces of resistance have been most virulent.

The workings of empire in the region can be traced out in four major phases that more or less correspond to empire-building efforts elsewhere.

Phase 1: 1945–1973—U.S. Imperialism in the Golden Age of Capitalism

After World War II, the informal U.S. empire remained largely unchanged in the American hemisphere, although it began to creep further south. The region was seen as having a relatively low strategic and economic value and received relatively less economic or military attention from the United States than other regions. The bigger states in the hemisphere pursued their own development path, while the United States was content to influence the smaller states in its backyard through comprador regimes that shared the preference of the United States for authoritarian forms of capitalism.

However, these regimes more often than not were confronted by forces of resistance—workers in the cities and peasants in the countryside who demanded and actively mobilized for revolutionary change. If and when these forces achieved power, as they did in Cuba in 1959, they drove a hard bargain with American corporations and financial interests as well as the ruling classes—threatening U.S. "interests," leading U.S. officials to brand them as communists and enemies of the forces of freedom and democracy. Alternatively, where local class conflict intensified, the United States perceived a danger of escalation to "chaos" and then perhaps to communism. Both outcomes were perceived to threaten U.S. interests. In response, or in some conjunctures in anticipation of this threat, the United States mobilized its military assets in attempting to overthrow regimes deemed antithetical to its interests—Arbenz in Guatemala (1954), Castro in Cuba (1961), Bosch in the Dominican Republic (1963), Goulart in Brazil (1964), the Dominican Republic again (1965), Jagan in Guyana (1953), and then Allende in Chile (1973).[5]

Arbenz was deposed by military force in a direct military invasion, but the dismal failure of this tactic in Cuba (the Bay of Pigs debacle) led the United States to pursue an alternative strategy of sponsoring military coups and "dirty war" by proxy against subversives, using the armed forces of the countries in question, arming them and training them within the framework of the National Security Doctrine (NSD) constructed for the purpose. In 1964 this strategy was successful in removing Goulart from power in Brazil because of the nationalist threat to U.S. interests posed by his moderate nationalism—the proposal to nationalize (with compensation) some U.S. assets and property. Within hours of his removal from state power by the U.S.-trained Brazilian Armed Forces, the junta was congratulated by President Johnson for "having restored democracy" to Brazil. A decade later, Salvador Allende, also democratically elected but unlike the moderate reformer Goulart a proclaimed "socialist," was removed from power by means of a violent coup engineered from and financed by the United States, allowing the head of the military junta, Augusto Pinochet, to assume power and implement a neoliberal agenda at the level of national policy—and also "teach the world a lesson in democracy" (Morley, 2010). Other NSD-based military coups, all of them supported by the U.S., took place in Uruguay (1972) and Argentina (1976).

During this forty-year period, the United States launched several open military interventions but a far greater number of covert or proxy ones. It was an informal empire, mixing armed force with clientelism, but by proxy and without colonies. It was generally justified or legitimated as the spread of freedom and democracy, with communism presented as the antithesis of democracy and the enemy of freedom. But this presented image was undercut by the clear U.S. preference for authoritarian allies and the sponsoring as well as active support and propping up of military dictatorships in the region.

In reviewing the dynamics of U.S. imperialism over this period, we can identify permutations of two basic strategies pursued with diverse tactics. The two-pronged strategy included use of the iron fist of military force within the velvet glove of development assistance or foreign aid (Petras and Veltmeyer, 2005a). The resort to military force has already been alluded to in the sponsoring or support of military coups across the region from 1964 to 1976. However, an equally important use of imperial power took the form of rural development—NGO-mediated assistance to the rural poor to prevent them from joining or forming social movements pressing for revolutionary change.

Phase 2: The 1980s—Economic Imperialism, Reagan, and the Washington Consensus

By 1980 the countryside was pacified and labor was on the defensive in a protracted class war waged against it by capital and the state. Its leadership was co-opted, its forces in disarray, and its ties to the peasant movement disarticulated. At the macro-level, virtually every capitalist state in the global north had to contend with a decade-long unresolved production crisis (despite diverse efforts to restructure the system out of the crisis) and an emerging fiscal crisis, as well as imperial and popular pressures to restore democracy, not in the authoritarian form preferred by the United States but as regimes committed to the rule of law and elected civilian administrations that were responsive to demands from the people. As for the fiscal crisis, and the detritus of the systemwide production crisis (stagnant output and runaway inflation), it combined in the early 1980s with conditions created by the Reagan administration's turn toward a high-interest-rate policy and an unfavorable turn in the export markets to precipitate a decade-long debt crisis—and create conditions for the new world order.

Unfortunately for the Sandinista revolutionaries in Nicaragua, these conditions coincided with their capture of state power in 1979, provoking the Iran-Contra Affair, as the U.S. state used its proxies to launch covert military operations against the revolutionary regime. As it turned out, this would be the last military adventure of U.S. imperialism, its agents resorting instead to structural reform of macroeconomic policy (to create conditions for a renewal of foreign investment and reactivation of an accumulation process), international cooperation for local development (to demobilize or turn the rural poor away from the social movements), and co-opting "civil society" organizations in the responsibility of restoring order—"good (participatory) governance" in the lingo of the new imperialism and the new development paradigm.

The emergence of neoconservative regimes in the United States, the United Kingdom, and elsewhere in the Global North, formed under conditions of a fiscal crisis, facilitated the implementation of the neoliberal agenda under the Washington Consensus on correct policy. Under these conditions, U.S. imperialism turned away from their protégé generals, allowing them to retreat to the military barracks, and turned from armed force toward the IMF and the World Bank, essential adjuncts of the imperialist state system, in making Latin America safe for U.S. capital. This would take close to a decade. But the turn of every major country in the region to the "new economic model" amid the retreat of the state under the auspices of Washington tells the tale.

The contras affair closed one chapter in U.S. imperialism, and the installation of a new world order of neoliberal globalization opened another—a chapter characterized not by armed force and the projection of military power, but rather what we might term "economic imperialism"—the engineering of free market structural reforms in national policy, the penetration of foreign capital in the form of multinational corporations (the shock troops of the old imperialism), and a free-trade regime. Agents of this form of imperialism included the IMF, the World Bank, and the WTO—the "unholy trinity" (Peet, 2003)—as well as a host of neoconservatives, neoliberal economists, and policy makers who serve the "global ruling class," as described by John Pilger (2002).

The new imperial order of neoliberal globalization was made possible and facilitated not only by a political turn toward neoconservatism but by a new reserve of ideological power: the idea of globalization, presented as the only road to general prosperity, the necessary condition for reactivating growth and the capital-accumulation process. The project of globalization, which served to justify the "structural adjustment program," was launched mid-decade. The World Bank's 1995 World Development Report (*Workers in an Integrating World*) can be seen as one of its most important programmatic statements—a capitalist manifesto on the need to adjust to the requirements of a new world order in which the forces of freedom would hold sway over the global economy.

As for the political adjustment to this world order, the United States was constrained in part by its own declared mission to spread democracy and make the world safe for freedom, to support the widespread movement in diverse regions toward political democracy. As for Latin America, the United States adapted to the spread of democracy across the hemisphere, conducting a policy of "democracy by applause" from the sidelines, as Latin

Americans made their own democratic gains (Carrothers, 1991), in a process of redemocratization that saw the negotiated retreat of the generals to their barracks.

The neoliberal policies implemented in the 1980s were unpopular to say the least, with the core opposition coming from organized labor. Democratic governments in most cases, as in Jamaica and Mexico, were reluctant to sign up for the reform agenda, and most structural adjustment programs were introduced by presidential decree or administrative fiat rather than legislation, which made the IMF appear to favor dictatorship over democracy (Biersteker, 1992: 114–16; Vreeland, 2003; 90–102). However, in Latin America, the reforms mandated by the World Bank and the IMF were generally implemented by the civilian democratically elected regimes that came to power after the first experiments in neoliberalism crashed and burned in the early 1980s.

Phase 3: The 1990s—The Golden Age of U.S. Imperialism, Clinton, and the Post-Washington Consensus

The 1990s was a decade of major gains for U.S. imperialism in Latin America, at a time in which it experienced serious setbacks and an erosion of economic and political power in other regions of the world. At the same time, the 1990s can be viewed as a decade of major gains for the social movements in their resistance to the neoliberal agenda and the operations and machinations of U.S. imperialism. Already in the 1980s the push toward neoliberalism had generated widespread opposition and protest, which, in the case of Venezuela, resulted in a major social and political crisis—the Caracazo of 1989, in which hundreds if not thousands of protesters against the high price of food and IMF policies were massacred (see Ellner, 2008: 95). More generally, conditions of structural adjustment across the region generated widespread opposition and resistance in the form of protest actions and social movements. They also led to a reorganization and mobilization of the forces of resistance in the popular sector. By the 1990s these organizations took form as antisystemic social movements formed on the social base of indigenous communities, landless workers, and peasants.

The most dynamic of these movements were the Movement of Landless Rural Workers in Brazil (MST) and the Confederation of Indigenous Nationalities in Ecuador (CONAIE). In a number of cases, such as Ecuador, these movements managed to halt and even reverse the policies implemented under the neoliberal agenda. In this context it is possible to see the decade as the leaders of the indigenous movement see it—as one of major gains.

However, the neoliberalism in these conditions and at this time was not the neoliberalism of the Washington Consensus. Already by the end of the 1980s, it was widely recognized by the guardians of the new world order and U.S. imperialism that neoliberalism was economically dysfunctional and politically unsustainable, generating as it does forces of resistance that could be mobilized against not just the policy framework but the entire system. The solution, from the perspective of class power and imperial rule, was a more socially inclusive form of neoliberalism—to give the structural-adjustment process a human face via a new development paradigm and social policy targeted at the poor, empowering and capacitating them to act on their own behalf in taking advantage of their "opportunities" for self-advancement (Sandbrook, Edelman, Heller, and Teichman 2007; World Bank, 2007).

Under these political conditions, the 1990s gave way to a major shift in the correlation of class forces. On the left, the political class was largely on the defensive, unable to make gains under conditions of a divided and demobilized working class—and with few ties to the new, principally rural forces of resistance mounted by organizations such as CONAIE. The Left at the time materialized basically in the form of social movements and, to some extent, social organizations for local development and the nongovernmental organizations that mushroomed in the dirty soil of neoliberal policies.

Most political regimes at the time were still aligned with the United States. But the United States, seeking to reverse major setbacks in Asia and other parts of the world, was rapidly losing influence as well as the capacity to dictate policy, or to counter the growing power of the social movements in the region. Major exceptions here were Colombia, where the United States continued to have a major military presence, and Argentina under Carlos Menem, who, together with Alberto Fujimori in Peru, presided over one of the most radical neoliberal reform programs in the region and aligned the country with the United States.

Phase 4: 2000–2008—U.S. Imperialism in an Era of Neoliberal Decline

The first decade of the new millennium opened with a regionwide production crisis and is closing with a crisis of global proportions and multiple dimensions. On the diverse dynamics of the latter crisis, see in particular Walden Bello (2009) and John Bellamy Foster and Fred Magdoff (2009). During this phase, some six years under the presidency of George W. Bush and a decided tilt to the left in Latin American politics, the region participated in a primary commodities boom on the world market, a development that changed and to some extent reversed a historic pattern in the terms of north-south trade, bringing windfall profits to the Latin American private sector in agro-export production and unanticipated gains in fiscal revenues for the center-left and leftist regimes that had formed in the wake of a spreading disenchantment with neoliberalism. Unfortunately for the Left and the popular sector organizations that had pinned their hopes on these regimes, the opportunity to change the course of national development in a popular or populist direction was missed (Petras and Veltmeyer, 2009).

It would take a global crisis, precipitated in the third quarter of 2008, to bring about a change in the pattern of deployment of fiscal expenditures, and then not in the interest of social justice (a more equitable distribution of the social product) but as part of a countercyclical strategy to prime demand and boost employment. Throughout the decade, what has prevailed is a policy program once again engineered in Washington as part of a new consensus constructed as a way of saving capitalism from itself—from its propensity toward crisis and from widespread forces of resistance mobilized and to some extent held in abeyance by the political class on both the left and the center of Latin American regime politics.

By the turn into this new millennium, the distraction of U.S. power elsewhere in the world had borne fruit in the weakening of neoliberalism as a policy agenda and the formation of center-left regimes that rode the wave of anti-neoliberal sentiment to state power. Under these conditions, U.S.–Latin American relations and the projection of U.S. imperial power must be understood in terms of three different types of political regimes that have emerged in the region. First, there are regimes such as those in Colombia and Mexico that continue to stay the course of neoliberal structural reform and that remain on the side of U.S. imperialism, accepting its dominion and well disposed to bilateral trade relations with the United States even with the collapse of the United States' project for a regional free-trade agreement (under pressures exerted by the Workers' Party (PT) government in Brazil in its efforts to advance the interests of the agro-mineral exporters and, arguably, to reassert it role and status as a subimperialist power). Then there are regimes such as those in Chile, Argentina, and Brazil that have chosen to pursue a center-left path of pragmatic neoliberalism under the PWC and that—particularly in regard to Brazil under Lula's Workers' Party regime—are concerned to diversify trade relations and escape the clutches of the United States' free-trade imperialism by pushing for greater independence vis-à-vis in both national policy and international relations. A third bloc of countries, led by Venezuela and encompassing Bolivia and Ecuador (and perhaps the Dominican Republic, Paraguay, Nicaragua, and Honduras under Manuel "Mel" Zelaya were he to be reinstated), have struck out in a Bolivarian nationalist (and socialist) direction against U.S. imperialism, countering the United States' proposed hemispheric free-trade agreement with the Bolivarian Alliance for the

Peoples of Our America (ALBA), an alternative mechanism of regional integration allied to Cuba and opposed to both neoliberalism and U.S. imperialism. With the support of a growing popular movement of resistance against neoliberal globalization, ALBA[6] has become major focal point of resistance to U.S. imperialism in the region.

In these conditions, the United States has lost a significant degree of influence in the region, certainly relative to the capacity it had in the 1980s and 1990s to dictate policy or even, as in the case of Ecuador and Bolivia, to maintain its network of military bases. In this context, the United States in recent years (and continuing under Obama) has redoubled its efforts on the fronts of policy reform (pragmatic or social neoliberalism), regional and bilateral free-trade agreements (the Free Trade Area of the Americas [FTAA]), cooperation for international development (local development based on self-help, empowerment of the poor, and social capital), and military intervention via its remaining client states in the region. Key to the latter is strengthening relations with Colombia, massively increasing funding and support to the Uribe regime as the nodal point and staging ground of its regionwide war against drugs and drug trafficking, the hub of its military operations.[7]

In 2009 the United States stepped up the military phase of Plan Colombia instituted a decade ago to tighten the noose around the neck of the one remaining "army of national liberation" in the region, FARC, redefined for this purpose after 9/11 as a terrorist organization and thus fair game in the global war on international terrorism. The most dramatic development on this front has been recent plans, and an agreement with the Colombian government, to give the United States access to seven military bases in the country. Despite the vehement opposition to this plan from most Organization of American States (OAS) member countries, the Colombian government has signed the agreement, demonstrating both its subservience to the United States and the pivotal importance of Colombia to its strategy vis-à-vis Latin America—protecting its economic interests and containing the forces of resistance and subversion.

U.S. Imperialism in Latin America Today: Dispatches from Peru and Honduras

One of the ironies of the recent pattern of regime change—the tilt to left—effected over the course of the past decade has been a weakening of the forces of resistance against neoliberalism, a retreat of the social movements, and in some contexts (Argentina, Bolivia, Peru, Mexico), a weakening of the Left and a strengthening of the Right. This is evident, for example, in both Argentina and Bolivia, where at the turn into the new millennium the forces on the Right were disarticulated but have since been allowed to regroup (on this point, see Petras and Veltmeyer, 2009). In part this is the result of somewhat misplaced views on the Left that these regimes are progressive and on their side—anti-neoliberal in economic policy and anti-imperialist in their relations with the United States. But this is not necessarily the case—certainly not in Argentina, Brazil, and Chile, where the social movements have been held in abeyance by the governing regime. Except for Venezuela and of course Cuba, and to some extent Bolivia and Ecuador, these regimes are only formally populist and can best be characterized as pragmatic neoliberal, or *izquierda permitida*. In some cases, particularly Peru, Colombia, and Mexico, the current and recent regimes can even be described as dogmatically neoliberal. Unlike in Chile, Argentina, and Brazil, the governments of Peru, Colombia, and Mexico are not even concerned with adapting the neoliberal agenda to the post-Washington consensus on the need for a more inclusive form of neoliberalism.

Perhaps the clearest example of this can be found in Peru, where the efforts of the government to protect the economic operations of the U.S. empire in June 2009 resulted in a major confrontation with the indigenous communities adversely affected by these interests, leading the government to resort to its own repressive apparatus and resulting in the deaths of twenty-four police officers and ten indigenous people. The day after Alan Garcia announced a new cabinet in response to the growing wave of social and class conflict, and a month into the wave of conflict arising from the confrontation with the indigenous communities, the People's Defense Command (Defensoría del Pueblo) identified up to 226 "active" social conflicts in the country. Transportation and public-sector workers were on strike, joining the march organized by the General Confederation of Workers (CGTP), the major workers' central in the country. At the same time, on the periphery of Lima, numerous street blockades were reported, harking back to the quasi-revolutionary situation or insurrection that emerged in Ecuador in 2000 and in Bolivia at various points between 2000 and 2005 (Webber, 2011).

At the center of this class struggle was the government's neoliberal policy, even without a free-trade agreement, designed to grant free access of the multinational forms of capital to the country's mineral resources and the guaranteed right to expatriate its profits. The ongoing struggle of the indigenous communities in Peru's Amazon against the incursions of multinational (especially Canadian) capital is one manifestation of this fight (Bebbington and Burneo, 2008; De Echave et al., 2009). Another, one of many others, has affected in a major way the country's cotton producers and textile workers. Peru, like several other countries in the region, has been subject to dumping by U.S. cotton producers able to "export" their product with government subsidies that allow their product to enter the local market with super-low prices, undercutting and destroying local producers. This is similar to the situation confronted by corn producers in Mexico. In both cases, the government, under the pressure of likely U.S. trade sanctions, refused to provide a matching subsidy to protect local producers. In both cases, workers and producers ("no aguantamos más") have responded by taking their struggle into the streets.

Similar situations are brewing in other countries in the region. But none of these are as meaningful for U.S. imperialism as the current situation in Honduras brought about by the actions of the ruling class, in control of the Congress and the Supreme Court—and, it would seem, the army—against a sitting and democratically elected president. For U.S. imperialism, Honduras represents not so much a political crisis or a crisis in U.S.–Latin American relations as a crossroads in imperial power and policy, influencing if the U.S. administration under President Obama might be able to recover its position and influence in the region.

U.S. imperialism in the region today is at a crossroads. In the 1990s the U.S. administration was too distracted by the greater game in Eurasia and the Persian Gulf region, and too overextended in its operations there, to attend to its Latin American affairs. Various political developments in the new millennium (especially the emergence of a left-of-center axis of political power) forced the administration to engage in efforts to halt and reverse the trend toward declining influence and power; to renew and repair relations with its former allies, especially Chile, Peru, Colombia, and Mexico; and to develop a counterpoint and weight to the growing influence of Hugo Chávez and his Bolivarian Revolution. Under the Obama administration, these efforts have been redoubled, but with mixed results thus far.

The significance of Honduras in this context is that it represents an opportunity for the United States to counter the growing influence of Chávez in the region, particularly in its Central American domain where Nicaragua and even El Salvador, not to mention Honduras, have fallen into the orbit of Chávez's Bolivarian Revolution and an alliance with Cuba, the major irritant and obstacle to U.S. hegemony in the region for five decades. When Chávez was deposed briefly from power in 2002, the U.S. administration was forced to backtrack from its initial and immediate recognition of the de facto regime. In the case of Honduras, however, the immediate and definitive response of the OAS, and its demand that Zelaya in the case of Honduras be restored to office, presented the United States with little room to maneuver, forcing the administration into a lukewarm "demand" that Zelaya be allowed to negotiate his return to power.[8]

The problem from the standpoint of Honduras's ruling class is that Zelaya's proposal for a nonbinding referendum for a constituent assembly had for them all the marks of a Chávez-type move to extend his term in office to push the country into and along a socialist path. And they have absolutely no intention to allow Zelaya to track this path. Nor does the United States have any intention to allow it—if it can be helped. And it is safe to assume that the State Department will stick at little or nothing short of outright support for a military coup in Honduras and elsewhere to prevent another Chávez. The lines of an emerging imperial war in the region are being drawn in the sands of class struggle in Honduras.

Conclusion

A number of observers of current developments in Honduras have speculated on whether the political crisis in Honduras might create conditions for the resort to military force by the ruling classes elsewhere in the region and working hand in glove with the U.S. imperial state to help restore U.S. dominion if not hegemony in the region. Quite apart from the anticipated, albeit covert, support from the United States for the "lesson in democracy" (that democracy is good as long as the people do not mistakenly elect a potential despot) provided by the tilt to the left in Latin American politics, particularly in regard to Chávez and Zelaya, it is conceivable that conditions for a military solution to political crises, namely a class-divided country, might materialize not only in Honduras but possibly in Ecuador and Bolivia, Nicaragua, or even in Venezuela—and perhaps in El Salvador. This scenario is undoubtedly on the drawing board used by the intelligence and security services of the imperial state to design a covert response and an appropriate public-policy stance by the United States.

Apart from Honduras, which provides the United States both a challenge and an opportunity to recover lost political space, other issues that the Obama administration will have to deal with immediately include Cuba and how to counter the leftward drift in Latin American electoral and regime politics and the widespread rejection of U.S. policies. Since 2001 a growing number of countries in the region have taken or are taking positions on policy and trade issues (the search to diversify trade relations, joining ALBA) that are not in the U.S. national interest, and Obama is undoubtedly being briefed as to how to respond to this challenge to U.S. power and influence.

Of particular concern for U.S. imperialism is the movement of more and more countries in its immediate backyard and former sphere of influence, the Caribbean and Central America, into the orbit of nationalism and socialism. In this panorama, both Colombia and Honduras provide favorable conditions for a Washington-made solution—a U.S. military base, intimate day-to-day relations with armed forces personnel, a malleable and supportive Congress and Supreme Court, a ruling class that shares its concerns about the actual and possible forces of subversion in the country and region.

In some ways, the situation confronted by Obama in Central America is similar to that faced by President Reagan in the early 1980s vis-à-vis Nicaragua. But Reagan had on his side a number of cronies and dictators—Álvarez in Uruguay, Videla in Argentina, Pinochet in Chile, Stroessner in Paraguay. In this regard, at least the political landscape in Latin America has changed. Today the vast majority of countries in the region might be described as centrist and pragmatic in terms of macroeconomic policy, rather than leftist or rightist, but they are also concerned to keep the United States at bay on matters of foreign relations and policies. Thus it is that a number of countries, and Argentina and Brazil in particular, are concerned to diversify their relations of international trade, and even in some cases to align themselves with alternative mechanisms of regional integration such as ALBA and enter into relations with Cuba. This is, in fact, the case for the countries in Central America and the Caribbean basin that have entered ALBA.

What this means for the current Obama administration might be gauged by its reaction to the nomination for secretary general of the OAS of José Miguel Insulza, a social democrat close to, and a candidate of, Chile's former president Michelle Bachelet. It seems that the United States, as announced by Secretary of State Hilary Clinton, was implacably against this nomination, apparently (according to several Washington insiders) because of Insulza's support for Cuba's entry into the OAS (a consensus view today, except for the United States), his campaign against the *golpistas* (coupists) in Honduras, and his earlier denunciation of U.S. intervention in Venezuela. If this is the attitude and position of the United States vis-à-vis a noted progressive and liberal social democrat, a representative of a centrist and pragmatic position in Latin American politics, and the nominee of a country supportive of the United States and allied with it at the level of bilateral trade, what might be the position of the Obama administration regarding relations with regimes seeking to strike a more independent line and steer a leftward course? Needless to say, a supportive or even tolerant position on this political development would be totally offline—unless the U.S. administration thought that it could thus gain some leverage with this support, and only then if this worked to contain this development within acceptable limits.

Obama's administration at the outset made various overtures to governments in the region, such as Lula's in Brazil, with which previous U.S. administrations had strained relations, but how the Obama administration copes with an emergent push in the region for greater independence, and how it relates to Chávez and to the right-wing opposition in countries such as Bolivia and Venezuela, and how it deals with the "Honduras question"—after the coup of June 2009 was consolidated through fraudulent elections that saw Porfirio "Pepe" Lobo come to office in January 2010—will provide a clear sign of the direction that U.S. imperialism is likely to take in the region. It is not impossible that if the Obama regime's current diplomatic stance fails to bear fruit, and politics in the region tilt or turn further to the left, that the United States might return to its earlier policy of support for military coups—this time as a "last resort."

Notes

1. U.S. occupation of Germany and Japan was seen as temporary only and not as part of a colonization policy. In this context, Germans and Japanese and people elsewhere welcomed U.S. military bases, seeing them as part of their own defences. And in the same spirit, they accepted the rule of the dollar and welcomed U.S. investment and multinational corporations. Lundestad (1998) calls the resulting system "empire by invitation."

2. In the Bretton Woods negotiations, the British were overruled, while the others were allowed almost no contribution. However, everyone was all too aware of the coercive element in the new international regime. But they accepted American hegemony as the price for economic growth and military protection from Soviet communism—leadership of the "free world" based on the virtuous marriage of democracy and capitalism.

3. The 1992 Wolfowitz Report asserted explicitly that the United States had to maintain a military machine so powerful as to discourage local or global rivalries. Under George W. Bush, this doctrine was converted into policy.

4. See, among others, Colectivo Situaciones (2001) and Negri (2001).

5. The U.S. interventionist success in Guatemala (1954) led the United States to repeat its policy with Cuba in 1961—a policy that led to defeat. The successful U.S. orchestrated military coups in Brazil (1964) and Indonesia (1965) and the invasion of the Dominican Republic (1965) encouraged the United States to deepen and extend its military invasion of Indo-China, which led to a historic but temporary defeat of imperial policy makers and the profound weakening of domestic political support.

6. Based on the principles of Bolivarian Revolution, ALBA is much more than a simple trade agreement. It has diverse social and economic dimensions, including cooperative programs of health and education, as well as projects related to development finance (the Bank of the South) and energy (Petrocaribe).

7. The U.S. ambassador to Colombia, William Brownfield, refused to make any declarations regarding stepped-up support and expansion of Plan Colombia, which entails the biggest outlay of funds for maintaining the empire in the region. However, he did insist that the United States would not construct any new military bases in Colombia. The policy was to "modernize" existing bases. Brownfield was ambassador to Venezuela in 2002 when the U.S.-supported conspiracy to oust Chávez failed. In the context of this failure, Colombia has become increasingly central to the U.S. strategy of "containing" the forces of revolutionary change in the region. In this connection, Colombia's immediate neighbors, Venezuela and Ecuador, have been the objects of diverse provocations from both Colombia and Washington.

8. On the actual and apparent dynamics of U.S. policy on this issue, and the opportunity and dilemma presented by the coup, there is a large and growing literature, much of it from the coordinated voice of the popular movement in the country and region. See in particular works by James Petras (2009) and Atilio Borón (2009).

References

Bacevich, Andrew. 2002. *American Empire. The Realities and Consequences of U.S. Diplomacy.* Cambridge, MA: Harvard University Press.

Barrett, Patrick, Daniel Chavez, and César A. Rodríguez Garavito. 2008. *The New Latin American Left: Utopia Reborn.* London: Pluto Press.

Bebbington, Anthony, and María Luisa Burneo. 2008. "Conflictos mineros: ¿Freno al desarrollo o expresión ciudadana?" In *Pobreza, desigualdad y desarrollo en el Perú. Informe Anual 2007–2008*, 44–51. Lima: Oxfam.

Bello, Walden. 2009. *The Food Wars.* London: Verso.

Biersteker, Thomas J. 1992. "The 'Triumph' of Neoclassical Economics in the Developing World: Policy Convergence and the Bases of Government in the International Economic Order." In *Governance without Government: Order and Change in World Politics*, ed. James Rosenau and Ernst-Otto Czempiel, 102–31. Cambridge: Cambridge University Press.

Blustein, Paul. 2001. *The Chastening: Inside the Crisis That Rocked the Global Financial System and Humbled the IMF.* New York: Public Affairs.

Boot, Max. 2002. *The Savage Wars of Peace: Small Wars and the Rise of American Power.* New York: Basic Books.

Borón, Atilio. 2009. "Honduras y la SIP." *Alai Amlatina*, July 25.

Bowles, Paul, et al., eds. 2007a. *National Perspectives on Globalization: A Critical Reader.* International Political Economy Series. Basingstoke, UK: Palgrave Macmillan.

———. 2007b. *Regional Perspectives on Globalization: A Critical Reader.* International Political Economy Series. Basingstoke, UK: Palgrave Macmillan.

Brands, H. W. 1999. "The Idea of the National Interest." In *The Ambiguous Legacy: U.S. Foreign Relations in the American Century*, ed. Michael Hogan, 120–51. New York: Cambridge University Press.

Bresser-Pereira, Luiz Carlos. 2009. *Developing Brazil: Overcoming the Failure of the Washington Consensus.* Boulder, CO: Lynne Rienner.

Burdick, John, Philip Oxhorn, and Kenneth M. Roberts, eds. 2009. *Beyond Neoliberalism in Latin America? Societies and Politics at the Crossroads*. New York: Palgrave Macmillan.

Bush, George, and Brent Scowcroft. 1998. *A World Transformed*. New York: Alfred A. Knopf.

Carrothers, Thomas. 1991. "The Reagan Years: The 1980s." In *Exporting Democracy: The United States and Latin America*, ed. Abraham Lowenthal, 90–122. Baltimore: Johns Hopkins University Press.

Castañeda, Jorge G., and Marco A. Morales. 2009. "The Emergence of a New Left." In *Which Way Latin America? Hemispheric Politics Meets Globalization*, ed. Andrew F. Cooper and Jorge Heine, 64–78. Tokyo: United Nations University Press.

Colectivo Situaciones. 2001. *Contrapoder: una introducción*. Buenos Aires: Ediciones de Mano en Mano.

Cooper, Robert. 2000. "The New Liberal Imperialism." *Guardian*, April 7.

Craig, David, and Doug Porter. 2006. *Development Beyond Neoliberalism? Governance, Poverty Reduction and Political Economy*. Abingdon, UK: Routledge.

Cypher, J., and R. Delgado Wise. 2007. "Subordinate Economic Integration through the Labor-Export Model: A Perspective from Mexico." In *National Perspectives on Globalization: A Critical Reader*, ed. Paul Bowles et al., 27–43. New York: Palgrave Macmillan.

Daalder, Ivo, and James Lindsay. 2003. *America Unbound: The Bush Revolution in Foreign Policy*. Washington, DC: Brookings Institution Press.

De Echave, José, et al. 2009. *Minería y territorio en el Perú: Conflictos, resistencias y propuestas en tiempos de globalización*. Lima: CooperAccion / Programa democracia y Transformación Global / CNCPAM—Confederación Nacional de Comunidades del Perú Afectadas por la Minería, Universidad Nacional Mayor de San Marcos.

Eichengreen, Barry. 1996. *Globalizing Capital: A History of the International Monetary System*. Princeton, NJ: Princeton University Press.

Ellner, Steve. 2008. *Rethinking Venezuelan Politics: Class, Conflict, and the Chávez Phenomenon*. Boulder, CO: Lynne Rienner.

Ferguson, Niall. 2004. *Colossus: The Price of America's Empire*. London: Penguin.

Foster, John Bellamy, and Fred Magdoff. 2009. *The Great Financial Crisis: Causes and Consequences*. New York: Monthly Review Press.

Gallagher, John A., and Ronald E. Robinson. 1953. "The Imperialism of Free Trade." *Economic History Review* 6 (l): 1–15.

Gowan, Peter. 1999. *The Global Gamble: Washington's Faustian Bid for World Domination*. London: Verso.

Grugel, Jean, and Pia Riggirozzi. 2012. "Post Neoliberalism: Rebuilding and Reclaiming the State in Latin America." *Development and Change* 43 (1): 1–21.

Halevi, Joseph, and Yanis Varoufakis. 2004. "The Global Minotaur." In *Pox Americana: Exposing the American Empire*, ed. J. Bellamy Foster and R. W. McChesney, 77–94. New York: Monthly Review Press.

Harvey, David. 2003. *The New Imperialism*. Oxford: Oxford University Press.

Hearden, Patrick. 2002. *Architects of Globalism: Building a New World Order during World War II*. Fayetteville: University of Arkansas Press.

Holloway, John. 2002. *Change the World without Taking Power: The Meaning of Revolution Today*. London: Pluto Press.

Hudson, Michael. 2003. *Super Imperialism: The Origins and Fundamentals of U.S. World Dominance*. 2nd ed. London: Pluto Press.

Kagan, Robert, and William Kristol, eds. 2000. *Present Dangers: Crisis and Opportunity in American Foreign and Defense Policy*. New York: Encounter.

Kurtz, Marcus. 2004. *Free Market Democracy and the Chilean and Mexican Countryside*. Cambridge: Cambridge University Press.

LaFeber, Waiter. 1984. *Inevitable Revolutions: The United States in Central America*. 2nd ed. New York: Norton.

Levitsky, Steven, and Kenneth Roberts, eds. 2011. *The Resurgence of the Latin American Left*. Baltimore: Johns Hopkins University Press.

Lievesley, Geraldine, and Steve Ludlam, eds. 2009. *Reclaiming Latin America: Experiments in Radical Social Democracy*. London: Zed Books.

Lundestad, Geir. 1998. *Empire by Invitation: The United States and European Integration, 1945–1997*. New York: Oxford University Press.

MacDonald, Laura, and Arne Ruckert. 2009. *Post-Neoliberalism in the Americas*. Basingstoke, UK: Palgrave Macmillan.

Maier, Charles. 1987. "The Politics of Productivity: Foundations of American Economic Policy after World War II." In *In Search of Stability: Explorations in Historical Political Economy*, ed. Charles Maier, 121–52. Cambridge: Cambridge University Press.

Mann, James. 2004. *The Rise of the Vulcans: The History of Bush's War Cabinet*. New York: Viking.

Mann, Michael. 2003. *Incoherent Empire*. London: Verso.

McLean, David. 1995. *War, Diplomacy and Informal Empire: Britain, France and Latin America, 1836–1852*. London: Tauris.

Mirowski, Philip, and Dieter Plehwe, eds. 2009. *The Road from Mont Pelerin; The Making of the Neoliberal Thought Collective*. Cambridge University Press.

Morley, Morris. 2010. "'Not about to Lose Chile': Democratic Socialism Confronts the Imperial State." In *Imperialism, Crisis and Class Struggle*, ed. Henry Veltmeyer, 193–224. Leiden: Brill.

Negri, Antonio. 2001. "Contrapoder." In *Contrapoder: una intrcducción*, ed. Colectivo Situaciones, 83–92. Buenos Aires: Ediciones de Mano en Mano.

Ocampo, José Antonio. 1998. "Beyond the Washington Consensus: An ECLAC Perspective." *CEPAL Review* 66 (December): 7–28.

———. 2007. "Markets, Social Cohesion and Democracy." In *Policy Matters: Economic and Social Policies to Sustain Equitable Development*, ed. J. A. Ocampo, K. S. Jomo and S. Kahn, 1–31. London: Zed Books.

Peet Richard. 2003. *Unholy Trinity: The IMF, World Bank and WTO*. London: Zed Books.

Petras, James. 2005. "Latin American Strategies: Class-Based Direct Action versus Populist Electoral Politics." *Science and Society* 69 (2): 152–59.

———. 2009. Interview. *CX36 Radio Centenario*, July 20.

Petras, James, and Henry Veltmeyer. 2001. *Unmasking Globalization: The New Face of Imperialism*. London: Zed Books / Halifax, NS: Fernwood.

———. 2003. *System in Crisis: The Dynamics of Free Market Capitalism*. London: Zed Books / Halifax, NS: Fernwood.

———. 2005a. *Empire with Imperialism*. London: Zed Books / Halifax, NS: Fernwood.

———. 2005b. *Social Movements and the State: Argentina, Bolivia, Brazil, Ecuador*. London: Pluto Press.

———. 2009. *What's Left in Latin America*. London: Ashgate.

Petras, James, and Henry Veltmeyer, eds. 2002 *Las privatizaciónes y la desnacionalización en América Latina*. Buenos Aires: Libros Prometeo.

Pilger, John. 2002. *The New Rulers of the World*. London: Verso.

Roorda, Eric. 1998. *The Dictator Next Door: The Good Neighbor Policy and the Trujillo Regime in the Dominican Republic, 1930–1945*. Durham, NC: Duke University Press.

Sandbrook, Richard, Marc Edelman, Patrick Heller, and Judith Teichman. 2007. *Social Democracy on the Periphery*. Cambridge: Cambridge University Press.

Saxe-Fernández, John, and Omar Núñez. 2001. "Globalización e Imperialismo: La transferencia de Excedentes de América Latina." In *Globalización, Imperialismo y Clase Social*, ed. John Saxe-Fernández, James Petras, Henry Veltmeyer, and Oman Núñez. Buenos Aires: Editorial Lúmen.

Schumpeter, Joseph. 1955. "The Sociology of Imperialism." In *Imperialism and Social Classes*. Cleveland: World Publishing.

Sell, Susan. 2002. "Intellectual Property Rights." In *Governing Globalization: Power, Authority and Global Governance*, ed. David Held and Anthony McGrew, 171–88. Cambridge: Polity.

Silva, Eduardo. 2009. *Challenging Neoliberalism in Latin America*. New York: Cambridge University Press.

Smith, Peter. 2000. *Talons of the Eagle: Dynamics of U.S.–Latin American Relations*. New York: Oxford University Press.

Soederbert, Susanne. 2004. *The Politics of the New International Financial Architecture: Reimposing Neoliberal Domination in the Global South*. New York: Zed Books.

Sunkel, Osvaldo, and Ricardo Infante, eds. 2009. *Hacia un desarrollo inclusivo: El caso de Chile*. Santiago: CEPAL.

Vaitney, Robert. 2001. *State and Revolution in Cuba: Mass Mobilization and Political Change, 1920–1940*. Chapel Hill: University of North Carolina Press.

Veltmeyer, Henry. 2005. "The Dynamics of Land Occupation in Latin America." In *Reclaiming the Land: The Resurgence of Rural Movements in Africa, Asia, and Latin America*, ed. Sam Moyo and Paris Yeros, 285–316. London: Zed Books.

Veltmeyer, Henry, ed. 2010. *Imperialism, Crisis and Class Struggle*. Leiden: Brill

Veltmeyer, Henry, and James Petras. 2005. "Foreign Aid, Neoliberalism and US Imperialism." In *Neoliberalism: A Critical Reader*, ed. Alfredo Saad-Filho and Deborah Johnston, 120–26. London: Pluto Press.

Vreeland, James. 2003. *The IMF and Economic Development*. Cambridge: Cambridge University Press.

Wallerstein, Immanuel. 2003. *The Decline of American Power: The U.S. in a Chaotic World*. New York: New Press.

Weaver, Frederick. 2000. *Latin America in the World Economy: Mercantile Colonialism to Global Capitalism*. Boulder, CO: Westview.

Webber, Jeffery. 2011. *Red October: Left Indigenous Struggle in Modern Bolivia*. Leiden: Brill.

World Bank. 2007. *Meeting the Challenges of Global Development*. Washington, DC: World Bank.

4

Neoliberal Class Formation(s)

The Informal Proletariat and "New" Workers' Organizations in Latin America

Susan Spronk

D RAMATIC CHANGES IN THE WORLD ECONOMY in the past quarter century have posed major challenges to trade unions in Latin America.[1] Labor markets throughout the region have been made more flexible, and patterns of production and employment in Latin America have also been transformed by economic integration, a process known as neoliberal globalization (Garza Toledo and Salas Páez, 2000; Hershberg, 2007; Patroni and Poitras, 2002; Stillerman and Winn, 2006). Most notably, there has been a shift away from standard full-time regular employment (the traditional trade union base) to atypical forms, such as part-time, contract, and unprotected, informal types of work. The labor force has become increasingly scattered and fragmented, rendering collective organization at the workplace more and more difficult (Abramo, et al., 1997; Olivera and Lewis, 2004).

Due to these socioeconomic changes, traditional forms of trade unionism no longer dominate the landscape of popular struggle in Latin America. As César Rodríguez-Garavito, Patrick Barrett, Daniel Chávez (2008) argue, the "New Left" differs from the "historic left" in several respects, including the prevalence of coalition building among different social sectors and the predominance of "civil society" over the "working class." While trade unions and socialist political parties still participate in these broad coalitions, they argue, they are no longer the leaders of these initiatives as was often the case during the middle decades of the twentieth century.

This chapter argues that the political decline of trade unions does not mean, as some scholars are wont to argue, that the "working class" has dissolved into a more inchoate "multitude" or "civil society."[2] While class struggle today takes many forms that do not fit the description of proletarian revolution described by Marx and Engels in the *Communist Manifesto* over 150 years ago, it is equally amiss to describe all forms of struggle as "new." Rather, I argue that many of the class struggles waged by working peoples in the neoliberal period can be understood in terms of what British Marxist historian E. P. Thompson (1978a) called "class struggle without class," which is pertinent to understand some of the challenges and limitations of the contemporary Latin American Left. The first part of the chapter outlines a class-struggle analysis of working-class formations in Latin America. The second section provides a historical context for understanding contemporary developments in the region. The third section provides examples of innovative forms of working-class resistance in Argentina, Venezuela, and Bolivia.

Class-Struggle Analysis of Working-Class Formations

The labor movement was the most visible social movement in Latin America for most of the twentieth century. This observation has not only to do with the fact that the dominant paradigm in Latin American left social analysis for most of the century was a form of Marxism that tended to privilege industrial workers as the revolutionary subject, but also because as the formal proletariat grew in size and strength with industrialization over the period more and more workers organized and joined trade unions. Today, by contrast, the development of capitalism has continued apace, but the labor movement in Latin America is a shadow of its former self.

Theoretically, Marxism has also entered a crisis due to the decline of "really existing socialism" that inspired the communist parties and trade unions of the past. The combined effect of the "crisis of the Leninist subject" (Rodríguez-Garavito, Barrett, and Chávez, 2008: 8) and the ascendancy to political prominence of "new" social-movement actors in Latin America has led many academic observers to eschew the traditional emphasis on "class," "socialism," and "class struggle" in favor of "identity," "radical democracy," and "social movements" (Escobar and Álvarez, 1992; Laclau and Mouffe, 1985). By the mid-1990s, as Paul Haber put it in a review of books on Latin American social movements, "Marxist variations, so popular during the 1970s, were out, and democratic theories starring actors from civil society were in" (1996: 171–72). Some critical observers have traced this shift to changing political and intellectual fashions in Europe (Borón, 2000; Chilcote, 1990) or to the "retreat of intellectuals" from active engagement with radical left politics (Petras, 1990). While critics are correct to point out that many "post-Marxist" scholars such as Ernesto Laclau and Chantal Mouffe have erroneously replaced "class reductionism" with "class rejectionism" (Vilas, 1993), I contend that the latter were correct to point out some serious theoretical blinders in the form of Marxism that dominated radical thought in Latin America in the 1960s and 1970s.[3] Nonetheless, I further contend that it is not necessary to reject Marxism on these grounds, for alternative interpretations exist *within* Marxism that allow for a more nuanced understanding of the relationship between class, class consciousness, and other forms of identity such as race, gender, and sexuality.

Ever present in structuralist forms of Marxism are two problematic assumptions that lie behind the vanguardist and teleological model of historical development. First is the assumption that the socialist proletariat is the only revolutionary subject, an ideological position that is predetermined by its economic class location. Second, there is an assumption that the "normal" course of history would lead to the abolition of capitalism. According to some variations of this essentialist construction, such as that elaborated by Louis Althusser (1971), the continued existence of capitalism proved that the capitalists dominated the working class ideologically.

One of the most influential and persuasive critiques of structuralist versions of Marxism was put forward by British historian E. P. Thompson in *The Poverty of Theory* (1978b). Thompson was particularly concerned about Althusser's tendency to "put the cart before the horse" in social analysis by theorizing in abstraction from "real history" (read: without reference to the concrete lived experiences of workers). Contrary to the abstract, ahistorical, theoretical gymnastics favored by Althusser, Thompson stressed the *historical* dimension of class, the need to study class consciousness as a cultural experience, and the multi-arena nature of class struggle and class formation. For Thompson, class is not a static category—so many people standing in this or that relation to the means of production—and cannot be measured in positivistic or quantitative terms, but rather a historical category, describing people in relationship over time and the ways in which they become conscious of their relationships, separate, unite, enter into struggle, form institutions, and transmit values in class ways (Thompson, 1977: 264). Class is at once a process rooted in relationships of economic exploitation and an identity. As Thompson argued,

> Classes arise because men and women, in determinative productive relations, identify their antagonistic interests, and come to struggle, to think and to value in class ways: thus the process of class formation is a process of self-making, although under conditions which are "given." (Thompson, 1978b: 297–98)

Some scholars, such as Gareth Stedman Jones (1983), have interpreted Thompson's work to indicate that there is no such thing as class beyond its construction in theory or language. Cultural-historical materialists caution against such a reading, since Thompson clearly retained materialist notions such as "mode of production," which understands socioeconomic systems to be conditioned by class relationships of exploitation (e.g., feudal lord–peasant under feudalism, worker–capitalist under capitalism) (Camfield, 2004; Wood, 1995). As Thompson explains, class is a relationship that must exist before it can be experienced. In this way, class can also be an identity similar to race or gender; actors are said to be "class conscious" when they act upon their politicized notions of their class differences.

To say that class is a relationship that must exist *before* it can be experienced is not to say that it *will always be* experienced. In the early stages of capitalist industrialization in England, for example, class struggle was expressed in a form that Thompson labels "class struggle without class." In observing the dynamics of the bread riots that rocked England on the eve of the industrial revolution, Thompson wrote that the English working class was still in a process of formation, as they began to rebel against perceived social injustice rooted in the economic system:

> People find themselves in a society structured in determined ways (crucially, but not exclusively, in productive relations), they experience exploitation (or the need to maintain power over those whom they exploit), they identify points of antagonistic interest, they commence to struggle around these issues and in the process of struggling they discover themselves as classes, they come to know this discovery as class consciousness. Class and class consciousness are always the last, not the first, stage in the real historical process. (Thompson, 1978a, cited by Camfield, 2004: 436)

In other words, class struggle does not always occur in a conscious way; much depends on the capacity of political agents and the forms of collective action taken by workers' movements. Furthermore, the construction of class identities is always an uneven process, replete with internal contradictions. In any given national context, the working class is divided into factions that display a host of views and attitudes. In short, while the division of society into social classes is a constant feature of capitalist society, class consciousness is something that emerges from time to time and unevenly when workers decide to act collectively to resist exploitation and domination by employers or the state.

Class Struggle in Twentieth-Century Latin America: From Populism to Neoliberalism

In Latin America, as with other places in the world, class struggle has given rise to various forms of workers' organizations of diverse ideological currents.

In the early stages of capitalist development in the first decades of the twentieth century, Latin American trade unions tended to be more radical than today's unions, owing to the influence of socialist, communist, and anarchist ideologies. Over the course of the century, however, radical unions eventually gave way to more conservative forms under the influence of the national-populist political parties and the corporatist state, which was consolidated during a period of state-led industrialization. In the past thirty years, however, corporatist unions have confronted a crisis of legitimacy, opening up opportunities for the emergence of new, independent workers' organizations.

At the turn of the century, early trade unions in Latin America were influenced by the ideas of anarcho-syndicalism imported by immigrants from Europe (Greenfield and Maram, 1987; Stillerman and Winn, 2007). Anarcho-syndicalist organizers aimed to build expansive general unions—*one big union*—organized on the basis of territorial affiliation rather workplace or occupation and controlled by the rank and file. Since this radical form of unionism was so threatening to the status quo, anarcho-syndicalist trade unionists faced severe state repression. Following many explosive episodes of labor unrest in the early 1900s, many labor leaders were jailed or killed, and those who were foreign-born were sent back to their countries of origin.

As labor radicalism gave way to reformism, the idea that the state should legalize unions in order to contain their explosive potential took hold. From 1930 to 1970, Latin America underwent a profound transformation from a mostly rural to a mostly urban region. The old elite—the iron triangle of landowners, military leaders, and the church—gave way to new social forces: industrialists, the urban middle classes, and the working class. Over the course of this period, states took control over the main sectors of economic activity in an economic development project known as import-substitution industrialization (ISI). In order to contain working-class radicalism and guarantee popular support for this state-led industrialization project, populist leaders such as Getúlio Vargas in Brazil, Lázaro Cárdenas in Mexico, and Juan Perón in Argentina pounded home the message of the importance of the working class in building the new society.

Under these powerful national-populist governments, class conflict was institutionalized over the ISI period through the consolidation of state corporatism (Collier and Collier, 1991). This system of labor control implied that unions were conceived as public and political organisms that had co-responsibility for the continuity of the socioeconomic system. This function was put into practice through informal and formal mechanisms, the most significant of which was the inclusion of unions as organizations within the structure of the governing party and their consequent organic participation in the party system. Official labor federations were dominated by the powerful national-populist parties: the CGT by the Peronists (Justicalistas) in Argentina; the CTV by Democratic Action (AD) in Venezuela; and the CTM by the Institutional Revolutionary Party (PRI) in Mexico. The consolidation of state corporatism severely thwarted the emergence of democratic, leftist, and militant unions, which were punished for their oppositional stance by being marginalized in this system. Meanwhile, official labor leaders were handed government posts and rank-and-file workers benefited from higher salaries, paid vacations, health care, pensions, and even housing. Within the corporatist system of labor control, only the *izquierda permitida* (see Jeffery Webber and Barry Carr in this volume), which was willing to sacrifice democratic forms of unionism in exchange for exclusive benefits, was given a place at the bargaining table with the state and employers. To this day, official trade unions in countries with strong corporatist systems like Mexico—known as "yellow" or "white" unions—do not represent workers but serve employers' interests (Bensusán and Cook, 2003).

The neoliberal structural adjustment policies that were imposed throughout the region in the 1980s and 1990s reversed the fortune of labor. In order to facilitate market-based growth and economic integration into the world economy, these policies liberalized trade, deregulated capital markets, privatized state-owned enterprises, and dismantled labor regulations. As Fernando Leiva (2006) argues, the neoliberal project was sold on the promises that labor reforms and increased labor flexibility would bring about substantial reductions in unemployment, poverty, inequality, and social conflict in Latin America. These promises have not been borne out. To the contrary, real wages have declined, in some cases dramatically, and unemployment has increased throughout Latin America (Weeks, 1999: 156). Between 1970 and 1998, labor's relative position in income distribution fell in almost every country. In Bolivia, for example, real wages fell more than 50 percent between 1983 and 1996. In Peru, real wages in 1998 were 40 percent of their early 1980 levels. In Central American countries, such as Nicaragua and El Salvador, real wages fell by over 80 percent and 40 percent respectively over roughly the same period. As economist John Weeks argues, "Such real wage declines are probably unprecedented in Latin America in the twentieth century" (1999: 157).[4]

Unionization rates in the region have always been low compared to the majority of the advanced industrialized countries, but the dual processes of privatization and economic restructuring deprived official trade unionism of its principal areas of strength. As Ken Roberts (2008: 6) notes, the regional average for trade union density in the 1990s was approximately 13 percent, where it remains to this day, down from about 22 percent at the peak level of labor mobilization during the ISI era. The sectors where labor was once the strongest—oil, automobile, steel, copper, meatpacking, and public services—were hit hard by the downsizing that accompanied privatization, swelling the ranks of the unemployed. The introduction of new technologies has also led to a restructuring of the economy along the lines of "flexible accumulation" to allow for just-in-time production. Instead of hiring full-time staff with salaries and benefits, local and international businesses increasingly prefer to hire on temporary or short-term contract, depending on the needs of production at the moment (Garza Toledo and Almaraz, 1998; Iranzo and Patrayo, 2002).

In the neoliberal era, many of the newly unemployed have sought refuge by making due with informal forms of work, striking another blow to trade unionism. While the informal sector has been a fairly constant feature of Latin American economies in the latter half of the twentieth century, during the neoliberal period high rates of informality have increasingly come to be considered a "normal" part of capitalist development in the South. Indeed, several studies have suggested that the informal sector has become the most dynamic part of the economy in Latin America. Based on International Labour Organization data, Peruvian economist Norberto Garcia (2007: 66) estimates, for example, that between 1990 and 2005 more that 55 percent of the new jobs that were created in Latin America were created in the informal sector, most of which is precarious employment. According to the estimates of sociologists Alejandro Portes and Kelly Hoffman (2003: 49), almost half of the workforce in Latin America receives unregulated wages, irregular profits, or nonmonetary compensation for their work. In short, the working class in Latin America can be described as an "informal proletariat."

In the face of these dramatic changes and declining membership, between 1985 and 2000, most official labor unions in Latin America negotiated their organizational survival instead of engaging in militant action against state policies (Clifton, 2000; Murillo, 2001). It bears emphasizing that throughout Latin America radical programs of neoliberal structural adjustment were often implemented by the traditional national-populist parties, which made a hard turn to the right after being elected to office, often in defiance of their electoral mandates (Stokes, 2001). Due to strong corporatist ties forged between unions and political parties in Argentina, Mexico, and Venezuela, union leaders often remained loyal to the parties in power with the hopes that their collaboration with government would encourage the latter to mitigate the worst effects of neoliberal restructuring on union members (Murillo, 2001). In Argentina, for example, when President Carlos Menem privatized the very same companies nationalized by Perón fifty years before, the Peronist unions affiliated with the CGT not only accepted privatization but also became private entrepreneurs as owners of public utilities, trains, cargo ships, and pension funds.

While the crisis engendered by neoliberalism meant the destruction of trade unions and the informalization of work, it also opened new windows for insurgents within the labor movement who were dissatisfied with the corporatist pacts struck by their leaders. As the old national-populist parties embraced neoliberalism, their vice grip on the labor movement loosened (La Botz, 2007). The corporatist relations that were once the greatest basis of trade union strength became their main source of weakness. As working and living conditions deteriorated for the majority of the population, workers—both organized and unorganized—began to question the collaborationist policies of the official union leadership and traditional political parties. As Mexican sociologist Graciela Bensusán argues, corporatist ties "prevented [the labor movement's] renewal, reduced its representativeness, and increased its fragility through growing dependence on the power resources" (cited in Iranzo and Patrayo, 2002: 60–61), thus leaving official trade unions vulnerable to ideological attack by members of the rank and file who yearned for democracy within their unions. Over the neoliberal period, new oppositional labor confederations emerged, such as the CUT in Brazil, the FAT and, more recently, the UNT in Mexico, and the CTA in Argentina. Although these new confederations have not changed the balance of power in industrial relations systems to the extent hoped (Antunes and Hallewell, 2000; Bensusán and Cook, 2003; Patroni, 2004), they are a welcome sign that neoliberal restructuring has broken some of the corporatist ties that have traditionally wedded the labor movement to populist political parties in the region.

The most notable trend in social-movement organizing over the neoliberal period has been the shift in the locus of class struggle from the factory floor to neighborhoods and communities, which is reflected in the characteristics of the New Left in Latin America. As anthropologist June Nash observes, in times of economic retrenchment, "marginalized subsistence and survival activities both in developed economies and in the new frontiers of capitalist penetration have become a central arena for the development of consciousness and action" (1994: 10). Similar to the commoners on the eve of the Industrial Revolution in England, the primary concern of the majority of the working population on the margins of capitalist development during the neoliberal era has become "the right to live in a world with a diminishing subsistence base" rather than "class struggle against exploitation defined in the workplace" (Nash, 1994: 10). In short, with the devastation caused by neoliberal restructuring on the livelihoods of many people in Latin America, the focus of class struggle has shifted from demands for better wages and working conditions to demands for basic subsistence.

Workers' Organizations and the New Left in Latin America

Since the "informal proletariat" is now arguably the largest electoral constituency, the main protagonists of the New Left have a distinctly "plebeian" character, reflecting the fracturing and displacing effect that neoliberalism has exerted all over Latin America—unemployed workers in Argentina, informal workers in Bolivia, and indigenous communities left on the margins of development. In general, since trade unions have been unable to break out of the collective bargaining framework, the working class has created and adhered to other vehicles of struggle, such as the *piquetero* (unemployed) movement in Argentina, coalitions of residents in Bolivia, and workers' cooperatives in Argentina and Venezuela. As aforementioned, for optimistic observers of the New Left, these particular experiences are to be welcomed precisely because they erode the primacy of trade unions and political parties, representing examples of new emancipatory self-organization. Yet leaders of these "new" forms of organization face the same intractable dilemma of left politics: how to transform the local struggles that Thompson described as "class struggle without class" into broader social movements that address the causes rather than the symptoms of inequality.

Territorially Based Organizations in Argentina and Bolivia: *Piqueteros* and Neighborhood Committees

Two of the most celebrated expressions of the New Left—coalitions of residents in Bolivia and the *piquetero* movement in Argentina—demonstrate that innovative strategies for organizing the working class have tended to emerge from the ranks of the unemployed and urban poor excluded from traditional forms of workplace-based trade unions. These associations of unemployed workers, neighborhood committees, and citizens' coalitions can be defined as "territorially based" organizations rather than functional organizations such as trade unions in that they bring together people from different walks of life on an issue of regional concern (Spronk, 2007). In Bolivia, organizations of residents, such as the Federación de Juntas Vecinales de El Alto (Federation of Neighborhood Committees of El Alto, FEJUVE) and the Coordinadora de Defensa del Agua y de la Vida (Coalition for Defense of Water and Life, the Coordinadora), played fundamental roles in coordinating the protests known as the Water Wars and Gas Wars between 2000 and 2005 in the cities of Cochabamba and El Alto, which successfully pressured the government to reverse its privatization policies. The FEJUVE and the Coordinadora have been heralded as new forms of inclusive, horizontal, and popular organizations that have replaced trade unions as a vehicle of popular struggle (García Linera, 2004; Tapia, 2008). Much has also been written on the novel aspects of the *piquetero* movement in Argentina, which first emerged in the mid-1990s when workers laid off from the state-owned oil company in the province of Nequen took to the streets demanding the removal of all politicians from office (Dinerstein, 2003; Zibechi, 2003).

Unlike trade unions, they were thought to "do politics differently" because they lack formal leaders and the rigid hierarchies associated with the closed membership structures of trade unions and include a much broader range of participants (Crespo Flores, 2000; Dinerstein, 2003; García Linera, 2004; Zibechi, 2003). In the words of Rodríguez-Garavito, Barrett, and Chávez, these new organizations broaden the social bases and political agendas of the Left, thereby breaking "the monopoly of the struggle against class inequality within the heart of the left" (2008: 14). In her study of the *piquetero* movements in Argentina, Ana Dinerstein (2003) makes the claim that politics itself has been "reinvented," noting that new identities that have resulted from collective action on the picket lines have taken on a distinctly territorial rather than class dimension as the participants chose to self-identify as "neighbors" rather than member of the "working class" in a broader struggle against class inequality.

While the *piquetero* protests were heralded by enthusiasts of the New Left because of their initial attempts to distance themselves from the corrupt Peronist trade unions and political parties, it did not take long for the old political system to reestablish itself. In 2002 the Peronist government enacted Work Plans ("*Planes Trabajar*"), a welfare scheme that distributed benefits through the leaders of the *piquetero* organizations. By recreating the old patronage networks, the government managed to fragment and dismember the movement as various factions of the *piquetero* movement became increasingly dependent on state programs. Only the more radical elements of the movement with independent sources of funding, such as the Movimiento Territorial de Liberación (Movement for Territorial Liberation, MTL), continued to pursue a militant anticapitalist politics (Alcañiz and Scheier, 2007), while the sections of the movement that allied with the Peronist government were almost completely demobilized a few months into Kirchner's first term in office (see Emilia Castorina's chapter in this volume).

The demobilization of the *piqueteros* demonstrates that the line between "old" and "new" forms of politics of trade unions and social movements is not as clear as some analysts suggest. Rather, social-movement leaders face an interminable challenge to transform local struggles that focus on the issues of "everyday life" into broader movements that politicize the conflict between labor and capital. One of the main spokespersons of the struggle against water privatization in Bolivia and labor leader, Oscar Olivera, confirms the Thompsonian view that struggles to meet basic needs such as welfare payments and drinking water are examples of "class struggle without class." In recounting

his experience of social organizing during the 2000 Water War in Cochabamba, Olivera argues that it is important for social leaders to speak about
issues that affect peoples' "everyday lives" before talking about socialism. He
believes that the task of building socialism from below in contemporary Bolivia entails the following:

> Social fighters across the continent . . . need to develop the ability to listen to
> people. Left-wing leaders often prefer to hear themselves talk rather than listen to
> others. . . . I have met people in various countries with an extraordinary capacity
> for analysis, and for knowing what people want. But I have also encountered or-
> ganizations in these same countries that talk big but are terribly bureaucratized.
> Their leaders keep talking about socialism as the only alternative, as if socialism
> were just around the corner. But if you say this in a neighbourhood today, people
> will call you a "traditional politician"—not just because they do not believe in
> socialism, but rather because they would say, "What I want right now is that the
> city politicians stop robbing me in order to pay for the sewers." People want this
> kind of thing first, and then we can discuss socialism. (Olivera, 2004: 149)

Olivera goes on to argue that the struggle for basic services in Bolivia is not
simply a struggle for services but for social justice, which cannot be achieved
under the current socioeconomic system of neoliberal capitalism. The task at
hand, according to Olivera, is to build popular consciousness on a step-by-
step basis, gradually working toward socialism.

As with the outcome of the *piquetero* movement in Argentina, however,
concrete gains from the mobilizations against the privatization of water and
gas in Bolivia have been minimal. Despite the return of the municipal water
company to government control, many taps in Cochabamba still run dry.
The "nationalization" of gas by the MAS government in 2006 has delivered
some benefits in the forms of a public pension program and improvements
to health and education, but most Bolivians continue to live in poverty. In the
realm of politics, the election of the MAS in 2005 has created divisions within
the popular sectors. The FEJUVE has returned to the clientelist politics of the
past and the ad hoc coalition once known as the Coordinadora has more or
less dissolved (Spronk, 2007, 2008). Social-movement leaders who participated in these struggles have been unable to build on the momentum of the
"revolutionary moment" opened by the Water War (Hylton and Thomson,
2007; Webber, 2011).

Workers' Cooperatives in the Occupied Enterprises of Venezuela and Argentina

The occupied-factory movements in Argentina and Venezuela are among
the most dynamic class-conscious movements in Latin America, drawing

on former experiences with workers' control and the horizontal forms of decision making characteristic of the New Left. Due to the radical threat that these workers movements' pose to the status quo, however, they have often come into conflict with the left governments in office. The Kirchner administration has been outright hostile to worker movements that it cannot co-opt. While Chávez—arguably one of the most radical leaders of the pink tide—speaks passionately about alternatives to capitalism, his actions in the first ten years of the Bolivarian Revolution have indicated that the primary goal of his "twenty-first-century socialism" has been the construction of a capitalist welfare state with pockets of cooperativism on the margins of the economy.

In the wake of the 2001 economic crisis in Argentina, about two hundred Argentine companies threatened with bankruptcy were "recovered" by their workers and turned into cooperatives. By 2005 it has been estimated that about seven thousand workers were employed in recuperated enterprises in Argentina (Atzeni and Ghigliani, 2007: 654). The recuperated enterprise movement did not emerge in a vacuum. A law passed by Menem in the 1990s allowed for the formation of cooperatives within enterprises facing bankruptcy as a cost-saving and "crisis prevention" measure. When owners and bosses abandoned various factories, plants, hotels, and shops following the economic meltdown, former employees decided to take matters into their own hands, following the battle cry, "To Occupy, to Resist, to Produce!" Often there was evidence that the economic crisis was used as an excuse by the owners "to decapitalize their firms, attain millions of dollars in governmental credits for non-production related financial speculation and, ultimately to deprive the workers of their earned wages as they broke the labor contracts and often simply walked away from the factory or enterprise" (Ranis, 2006b: 61).

Once having occupied the enterprises, the workers found themselves fighting intense battles against capital and the state. After devaluation, many recuperated businesses, such as the BAUEN hotel, the Zanon ceramics factory, the La Foresta meatpacking plant, and the Chilavert print shop became profitable again, and the old bosses returned wanting their companies back (Trigona, 2006). In a show of solidarity, entire communities—members of the *piquetero* movement, human rights groups such as the Madres of the Plaza de Mayo, salaried workers allied with the CTA—held solidarity picket lines to fend off the police who were sent to evict the workers. Siding with capital rather than labor, the Kirchner government refused protestors' demands to pass a national expropriation law, instead preferring to decide the legality of each recuperated enterprise on a case-by-case basis. As a result, the workers of many of the enterprises face lengthy, complicated legal battles and the constant threat of eviction.

While the occupied factories have struggled to survive in the absence of state support as Kirchner returns Argentina to "normal capitalism" (see Castorina's chapter in this volume), the movement for workers' control in Venezuela was born in slightly more favorable economic and political circumstances. Prior to his election in 1998, Venezuelan president Hugo Chávez did not challenge the right to own capitalist property or the right to profit from the exploitation of working people. Article 115 of the Bolivarian Constitution establishes the "right to private property" but allows for expropriation by the state only for reasons of public benefit or social interest and only with timely payment of just compensation. Chávez's political coalition has also attracted the support of revolutionary workers' organizations, who have tried to push for a socialist economy based on worker control in key industries.

The movement for worker control was born in the heat of the management-sponsored lockout of workers at the PDVSA state oil company. Between December 2002 and January 2003, the management of the PDVSA, which had become a "state within the state" that served elite interests, launched a production strike in an attempt to cut off the main source of government revenue. The economy ground to a halt due to shortages of gasoline and fuel oil, shutting down production in various sectors. Determined not to let the opposition management commit this act of economic sabotage, blue-collar workers supportive of Chavez restarted production under their own control. They brought in technicians from abroad where necessary and brought in the army to transport gasoline and deliver foodstuffs. As Mike Lebowitz (2006) observes, the economic coup galvanized support for Chávez within many sections of the middle class and organized labor. Workers who refused to go along with the lockout from across the country formed a new labor federation, the National Union of Workers (Unión Nacional de Trabajadores, UNT) in August 2003. In its founding document, the UNT calls for the transformation of "capitalist society into a self-managing society" and for a "new model of anti-capitalist and autonomous development that emancipates human beings from class exploitation, oppression, discrimination, and exclusion" (cited in Lebowitz, 2006: 103).

Since then, it has been estimated that 1,200 business and factories have been occupied by their workers after bosses and owners abandoned them, although very few have been recognized by the government (Trigona, 2007). One of the highest profile cases of "comanagement" is a large paper mill located in Morón, about two hundred kilometers from Caracas. While Venepal had been in financial trouble since the late 1990s, it lost so much money during the two-month strike that it was unable to continue production. When the owners declared bankruptcy toward the end of 2003, the workers, who had not been paid for several months, seized the plant and continued operations under a successful but short-lived experience of workers' control. After a two-year battle to keep their jobs, the workers finally turned to Chávez, who announced the nationalization of Venepal (renamed Invepal) in January 2005. In a joint management arrangement between workers and the state, the workers' cooperative was given majority representation on the company's board and 49 percent of the shares, with majority ownership by the state (Gindin, 2005).

Despite having some support from the government, workers at the co-managed factories such as Invepal have been faced with the same dilemmas as the recovered factories in Argentina: how to survive in a sea of capitalist economic relations, how to ensure a steady supply of raw materials, and how to secure a buyer for the finished product (Janicke, 2007). The relationship between these workers and the Venezuelan government has also been con-flictive. State managers have been reluctant to recognize workers' control, insisting that the state is the majority owner and should have final say over management decisions. The experiment in comanagement turned sour when the government-appointed management decided to contract out work in the company's Maracay operation, hiring workers at lower wages. Protests by cooperative workers at the home plant in Morón resulted in the firing of 120 workers (Ramírez and Prada, 2006). In general, experiments in comanage-ment such as that at Invepal are exceptions to the rule, for there is a strong belief within significant segments of the Chávez administration that coman-agement has no place in "strategic industries" such as telecommunications and oil. Due to the reluctance of the Chávez administration to embrace new forms of democratic self-management, Mike Lebowitz concludes that the "threat to [the Bolivarian Revolution] is from within the Bolivarian Revolu-tion itself" (2006: 105).

Even once the legal challenges have been settled, the recuperated enter-prises face a further difficulty concerning their relation to the capitalist sys-tem as a whole. As Maurizio Atzeni and Pablo Ghigliani note, this aspect of the struggle is "neglected in the current literature on workers' occupations in Argentina as scholars, while often acknowledging the existence of market limitations, have preferred to explain the changes that occurred in the facto-ries by focusing on agency rather than structural factors" (2007: 657). In con-trast to studies of cooperative enterprises by Peter Ranis (2005, 2006a) and Karen Faulk (2008), Atzeni and Ghigliani do not find that the "logic of coop-erativism" breaks with the "logic of [neoliberal] capitalism." In their study of four recuperated enterprises in Argentina, workers noted improvements in the quality of their working lives in the absence of bosses, but old hierarchies within the workplace have been reestablished as workers found themselves under constant pressure to respond quickly to market demands, forcing a division of labor between manual and intellectual work. Furthermore, due to a lack of initial capital and obsolete technology, the cooperatives under study had little chance of survival without increasing the rate of self-exploitation by lengthening the working day or intensifying production.

Conclusion: Capitalist Crisis and the Future of the Left

This chapter has argued that class analysis is necessary to understand some of the most celebrated expressions of the New Left in Latin America, particularly the organizations of the "informal proletariat." The fact that social subjects of the New Left do not express their demands in explicit class terms does not suggest that the working class has disappeared but that it has been transformed by neoliberalism. Indeed, if poverty in a capitalist society is connected to the growth of precarious forms of work and a lack of employment, "the informal proletariat" is engaged in a form of class struggle even if it is not expressed explicitly as such. Furthermore, by surveying the changes to working-class formation over the past few decades, it was demonstrated that workers' organizations of the contemporary Left—from unemployed workers' movements to coalitions of informal workers fighting against the privatization of natural resources to the cooperatives established in recuperated enterprises—are not really as "new" as some theorists claim but rather confront many of the same classic dilemmas of left politics.

This chapter has also argued that the crisis of neoliberalism opened up opportunities for the emergence of "new" forms of working-class organizations in Latin America, which are new not in the sense that they have never been seen before but because they resurrect forms of struggle that were eclipsed in the middle decades of the twentieth century when salaried workers dominated the landscape of popular struggle. Workers moved from defensive struggles focusing on basic subsistence to more offensive struggles focusing on taking control of production, as indicated by the combative movements for workers' control within enterprises abandoned by their owners.

With the specter of the global financial crisis looming, these experiments with local democracy at the point of production will be particularly important because they point the way to an alternative form of society in which production could be based on human need rather than profit based upon coordinated societal self-management. To date, it has been possible for left governments in office to delay more radical reforms; the social programs demanded by the unemployed and the working poor that aimed to repair the damage to living standards suffered under neoliberal austerity programs of the 1980s and 1990s could be met by the lucrative rents retrieved from the exploitation of nonrenewable natural resources. As commodity prices plummet with the advance of the global recession, however, there may be little choice for radical leaders like Chávez to change words into action. Indeed, Chávez's enthusiastic call for worker control at a conference in the industrial city of Guayana in May 2009 indicates that the administration may be taking a new course.

Unfortunately, the economic situation is likely to get much worse before the political situation gets better. Similar to neoliberal structural adjustment, the immediate effects of the shrinking of the economies sponsored by the global financial crisis are likely to be felt most by those on the bottom rungs of the labor market, struggling to make ends meet in the informal economy. With the International Labour Organization predicting that global job losses could reach as high as fifty-one million for 2009, the already bloated informal sector will likely multiply even further as millions of unemployed crowd the streets, competing fiercely in a shrinking labor market. Where the impact hits will not be determined by economics but politics—by the level of organization of the poorest rather than by the action of governments or states.

Notes

1. For the purposes of this discussion, "Latin America" does not include the Caribbean.

2. See, for example, Michael Hardt and Antonio Negri (2004) and César Rodríguez-Garavito, Patrick Barrett, and Daniel Chávez (2008).

3. See the article by Richard L. Harris (1979) for a description of structuralist Marxism's influence on the intellectual Left in Latin America.

4. Weeks adds that there is no reliable data for comparison for the early part of the century; hence, his use of the term "probably."

References

Abramo, Luís, et al. 1997. "The Institutionalization of the Sociology of Work in Latin America." *Work and Occupations* 24 (3): 348–63.

Alcañiz, Isabella, and Melissa Scheier. 2007. "New Social Movements with Old Party Politics: The MTL Piqueteros and the Communist Party in Argentina." *Latin American Perspectives* 34 (2): 157–71.

Althusser, Louis. 1971. *Lenin and Philosophy, and Other Essays.* New York: Monthly Review Press.

Antunes, Ricardo, and Laurence Hallewell. 2000. "The World of Work, the Restructuring of Production, and Challenges to Trade Unionism and Social Struggles in Brazil." *Latin American Perspectives* 27 (6): 9–26.

Atzeni, Maurizio, and Pablo Ghigliani. 2007. "Labor Process and Decision-Making in Factories under Workers' Self-Management: Empirical Evidence from Argentina." *Work Employment and Society* 21 (4): 653–71.

Bensusán, Graciela, and Maria Lorena Cook. 2003. "Political Transition and Labor Revitalization in Mexico." *Research in the Sociology of Work* 11:229–67.

Borón, Atilio A. 2000. "Embattled Legacy: 'Post-Marxism' and the Social and Political Theory of Karl Marx." *Latin American Perspectives* 27 (4): 49–79.

Camfield, David. 2004. "Re-orienting Class Analysis: Working Classes as Historical Formations." *Science and Society* 68 (4): 421–46.

Chilcote, Ronald H. 1990. "Post-Marxism: The Retreat from Class in Latin-America—Introduction." *Latin American Perspectives* 17 (2): 3–24.

Clifton, Judith. 2000. "On the Political Consequences of Privatisation: The Case of Teléfonos de México." *Bulletin of Latin American Research* 19 (1): 63–79.

Collier, Ruth Berins, and David Collier. 1991. *Shaping the Political Arena: Critical Junctures, the Labor Movement, and Regime Dynamics in Latin America*. Princeton, NJ: Princeton University Press.

Crespo Flores, Carlos. 2000. "La guerra del agua en Cochabamba: movimientos sociales y crisis de dispositivos de poder." *Ecología Política* 20:59–70.

Dinerstein, Ana C. 2003. "¡Que se Vayan Todos! Popular Insurrection and the *Asambleas Barriales* in Argentina." *Bulletin of Latin American Research* 22 (2): 187–200.

Escobar, Arturo, and Sonia E. Álvarez. 1992. *The Making of Social Movements in Latin America: Identity, Strategy and Democracy*. Boulder, CO: Westview.

Faulk, Karen Ann. 2008. "*If They Touch One of Us, They Touch All of Us*: Cooperativism as a Counterlogic to Neoliberal Capitalism." *Anthropological Quarterly* 81 (3): 579–614.

Garcia, Norberto E. 2007. "Employment and Globalization in Latin America." *Revista De Economia Mundial* 17:51–75.

García Linera, Álvaro. 2004. "The 'Multitude.'" In *¡Cochabamba! Water War in Bolivia*, ed. Oscar Olivera and Tom Lewis, 65–86. Cambridge, MA: South End Press.

Garza Toledo, Enrique de la, and Araceli Almaraz. 1998. *Estrategias de modernización empresarial en México: Flexibilidad y control sobre el proceso de trabajo*. México: Rayuela Editores.

Garza Toledo, Enrique de la, and Carlos Salas Páez. 2000. *Reestructuración productiva, mercado de trabajo y sindicatos en América Latina*. Buenos Aires: Consejo Latinoamericano de Ciencias Sociales.

Gindin, Jonah. 2005. "Venezuela's Venepal under Workers Control after Bankruptcy and Expropriation." *VenezuelAnalysis.com*, January 20.

Greenfield, Gerald Michael, and Sheldon L. Maram, eds. 1987. *Latin American Labor Organizations*. New York: Greenwood.

Haber, Paul Lawrence. 1996. "Identity and Political Process: Recent Trends in the Study of Latin American Social Movements." *Latin American Research Review* 31 (1): 171–89.

Hardt, Michael, and Antonio Negri. 2004. *Multitude: War and Democracy in the Age of Empire*. New York: Penguin.

Harris, Richard L. 1979. "The Influence of Marxist Structuralism on the Intellectual Left in Latin America." *Insurgent Sociologist* 9 (1): 62–73.

Hershberg, Eric. 2007. "Globalization and Labor: Reflections on Contemporary Latin America." *International Labor and Working-Class History* 72:164–72.

Hylton, Forrest, and Sinclair Thomson. 2007. *Revolutionary Horizons: Past and Present in Bolivian Politics*. London: Verso.

Iranzo, Consuela, and Thanali Patrayo. 2002. "Trade Unionism and Globalization: Thoughts from Latin America." *Current Sociology* 50 (1): 57–74.

Janicke, Kiraz. 2007. "Venezuela's Co-managed Inveval: Surviving in a Sea of Capitalism." *VenezuelAnalysis.com*, July 27.

Jones, Gareth Stedman. 1983. *Languages of Class: Studies in English Working Class History, 1832–1982*. Cambridge: Cambridge University Press.

La Botz, Dan. 2007. "Latin America Leans Left: Labor and the Politics of Anti-Imperialism." *New Labor Forum* 16 (2): 61–70.

Laclau, Ernesto, and Chantal Mouffe. 1985. *Hegemony and Socialist Strategy: Towards a Radical Democratic Politics*. London: Verso.

Lebowitz, Michael A. 2006. *Build It Now! Socialism for the Twenty-first Century*. New York: Monthly Review Press.

Leiva, Fernando Ignacio. 2006. "Neoliberal and Neostructuralist Perspectives on Labor Flexibility, Poverty and Inequality: A Critical Appraisal." *New Political Economy* 11 (3): 337–59.

Murillo, Maria Victoria. 2001. *Labor Unions, Partisan Coalitions, and Market Reforms in Latin America*. Cambridge: Cambridge University Press.

Nash, June C. 1994. "Global Integration and Subsistence Insecurity." *American Anthropologist* 96 (1): 7–30.

Olivera, Oscar. 2004. "Toward a National Continental Rebellion." *¡Cochabamba! Water War in Bolivia*, ed. Oscar Olivera and Tom Lewis, 141–52 Cambridge, MA: South End Press.

Olivera, Oscar, and Tom Lewis. 2004. *¡Cochabamba! Water War in Bolivia*. Cambridge, MA: South End Press.

Patroni, Viviana. 2004. "Disciplining Labor, Creating Poverty: Neoliberal Structural Reform and the Political Conflict in Argentina." *Research in Political Economy* 21:91–119.

Patroni, Viviana, and Manuel Poitras. 2002. "Labor in Neoliberal Latin America: An Introduction." *Labor, Capital, Society* 35 (2): 207–20.

Petras, James. 1990. "The Metamorphosis of Latin America's Intellectuals." *Latin American Perspectives* 17 (2): 102–12.

Portes, Alejandro, and Kelly Hoffman. 2003. "Latin American Class Structures: Their Composition and Change during the Neoliberal Era." *Latin American Research Review* 38 (1): 41–82.

Ramírez, Luisana, and Ramón Prada. 2006. "Los trabajadores despedidos de INVEPAL Maracay tras 8 meses de lucha seguimos sin ser reintegrados a nuestros puestos de trabajo." *Aporrea.org*, June 26. http://www.aporrea.org/trabajadores/a23050.html.

Ranis, Peter. 2005. "Argentina's Worker-Occupied Factories and Enterprises." *Socialism and Democracy* 19 (3): 1–23.

———. 2006a. "Factories without Bosses: Argentina's Experience with Worker-Run Enterprises." *Labor: Studies in Working-Class History of the Americas* 3 (1): 11–23.

———. 2006b. "Learning from the Argentine Worker: To Occupy, to Resist, to Produce." *Situations: Project of the Radical Imagination* 1 (2): 57–72.

Roberts, Kenneth M. 2008. "Is Social Democracy Possible in Latin America?" *Nueva Sociedad* 217:70–86.

Rodríguez-Garavito, César, Patrick Barrett, and Daniel Chávez. 2008. "Utopia Reborn? Introduction to the Study of the New Latin American Left." In *The New Latin American Left: Utopia Reborn*, ed. Paul S. Barrett, Daniel Chavez, and Cesar Rodriguez-Garavito, 1–41. London: Pluto Press.

Spronk, Susan. 2007. "Roots of Resistance to Urban Water Privatization in Bolivia: The 'New Working Class,' the Crisis of Neoliberalism, and Public Services." *International Labor and Working-Class History* 71:8–28.

———. 2008. "After the Water Wars in Bolivia: The Struggle for a 'Social-Public' Alternative." UpsidedownWorld.or, April 29.

Stillerman, Joseph, and Peter Winn. 2006. "Introduction: Globalization and the Latin-American Workplace." *International Labor and Working-Class History* 70:1–10.

———. 2007. "Introduction: New Studies/New Organizations; Labor Organization in Latin America and Beyond." *International Labor and Working-Class History* 72:2–17.

Stokes, Susan Carol. 2001. *Mandates and Democracy: Neoliberalism by Surprise in Latin America*. Cambridge: Cambridge University Press.

Tapia, Luis. 2008. "Bolivia: The Left and the Social Movements." In *The New Latin American Left: Utopia Reborn*, ed. Paul S. Barrett, Daniel Chavez, and Cesar Rodriguez-Garavito, 21531 London: Pluto Press.

Thompson, E. P. 1977. "Folklore, Anthropology and Social History." *Indian Historical Review* 3:247–66.

———. 1978a. "Eighteenth-Century English Society: Class Struggle Without Class?" *Social History* 3 (2): 133–65.

———. 1978b. *The Poverty of Theory & Other Essays*. New York: Monthly Review Press.

Trigona, Marie. 2006. "Recuperated Enterprises in Argentina: Reversing the Logic of Capitalism." Centre for International Policy Americas Program, March 16. http://www.cipamericas.org/archives/1005.

———. 2007. "Workers in Control: Venezuela's Occupied Factories." *Synthesis/Regeneration* 43 (Spring). http://www.greens.org/s-r/43/43-15.html.

Vilas, Carlos M. 1993. "Back to the Dangerous Classes? Capitalist Restructuring, State Reform and the Working Class in Latin America." Studies Series Paper 43, Institute of Latin American and Iberian Studies, Columbia University.

Webber, Jeffery R. 2011. *From Rebellion to Reform in Bolivia: Class Struggle, Indigenous Liberation and the Politics of Evo Morales*. Chicago: Haymarket.

Weeks, John. 1999. "Wages, Employment and Workers' Rights in Latin America, 1970–98." *International Labor Review* 138 (2): 151–69.

Wood, Ellen Meiksins. 1995. *Democracy Against Capitalism: Renewing Historical Materialism*. Cambridge: Cambridge University Press.

Zibechi, Raúl. 2003. *Genealogía de la revuelta: Argentina, la sociedad en movimiento*. Montevideo: Nordan Comunidad and Letra Libre.

5

Revolution in Times of Neoliberal Hegemony

The Political Strategy of the MST in Brazil and the EZLN in Mexico

Leandro Vergara-Camus

MARXIST THEORY HAS TRADITIONALLY UNDERESTIMATED the role and importance of the peasantry in revolutionary processes even though peasants and agricultural workers have been crucial actors in many revolutions. Nevertheless, peasants have never carried out a revolution all by themselves. The outcome of revolutionary processes has depended on the nature of their alliance with other classes.

In Latin America today, two of the most important and openly revolutionary social movements, the Movimento dos Trabalhadores Rurais Sem Terra (Movement of Landless Rural Workers, MST) from Brazil and the Ejército Zapatista de Liberación Nacional (Zapatista Army of National Liberation, EZLN) from Chiapas, are peasant movements. This peasant nature gives them an advantage over other popular movements because it allows them to control a territory—encampments and settlements in the case of the MST and indigenous communities and municipalities in the case of the EZLN. Within these "liberated territories," both movements have created alternative structures of power that promote people's self-government through the active participation and politicization of their membership. Simultaneously, access to land provides the basis for the reproduction of noncapitalist forms of production, allowing peasant families to partially de-link from the market (Vergara-Camus, 2009a).

Because they challenge the limits of liberal democracy and attack the most sacred institution of the capitalist society—private property of the means of production—these movements have been subjected to harassment, repression, and state terror. Hence, they fall within the ranks of the "*izquierda no permitida.*" Regardless, the MST and the EZLN have been very successful in their struggles for land. The MST began in 1984 in a few regions of southern Brazil and is now present in twenty-three out of the twenty-seven Brazilian states, while the EZLN grew from a clandestine guerrilla organization embedded in a remote area of the Lacandona jungle in 1994 into a movement that has now established autonomous rebel municipalities in half the territory of Chiapas.

Like previous peasant movements, in order to resist and protect their achievements, these two groups have sought to build alliances with organizations representing popular classes. The outcome of their strategies has depended to a great extent on the political and ideological evolution of these other forces. This chapter will argue that the MST and the EZLN have had difficulty in bringing about a coalition of forces to fight neoliberalism because most left-wing popular movements and political parties in Brazil and Mexico have remained within the corporatist tradition and have *willingly* accepted their role as *izquierdas permitidas*. The chapter will also show that both the MST and the EZLN reached out to left-wing parties, notably the Partido dos Trabalhadores (Workers' Party, PT) and the Partido de la Revolución Democrática (Democratic Revolution Party, PRD), respectively. In spite of the fact that the MST developed a much closer cooperation with the PT than the EZLN did with the PRD, as both parties became further inserted within their political regime, the political and ideological distance grew between the movements and the parties.

State Power, Radical Social Change, and the Corporatist Legacy

Traditionally, the strength of the Latin American Left has lain in its capacity to simultaneously mobilize and politicize the working classes while fighting to take state power through elections or armed revolution. In addition, most revolutionary movements in Cuba, Chile, Peru, and Nicaragua also promoted forms of class power through the creation of neighborhood councils, factory committees, cooperatives, and other forms of collective self-management or self-government.

Zapatismo has brought back an old debate within the Left. Should a revolutionary movement ultimately seek state power in order to change society, or should its objective be to change society from within in order to abolish the state and replace it with new political institutions controlled by the laboring classes? Should and can it combine both objectives? Can a revolutionary movement use the contradictions within the capitalist state to occupy institutional spaces and pressure for policies that can reinforce popular struggles without being co-opted?

The MST and the EZLN have very different understanding of the role of state power within the process of social change. However, for these social movements, the question of state power is a very practical one. It is a question to be approached by taking into consideration the actual history of national state formation and the concrete experience of each movement with the state. After forty years of broken promises and betrayals from state officials, indigenous subsistence peasants have come to see the state as the main class enemy (Vergara-Camus, 2009a: 371). The Zapatista rejection of state power and their decision to build forms of self-government derives as much from this experience as from an ideological reflection on how best to radically transform society. In contrast, throughout its history the MST has had a dual strategy toward the state and has always believed that it was important to struggle for political space within the state, be it at the local, regional, or national level, the legislative or executive branch, or even within specific ministries or state agencies. The success of its struggle for land depends on the state's decision to expropriate land and allocate resources to agrarian reform settlements. Hence, the MST has, at times, confronted state policies while negotiating and collaborating with it in other occasions. Thus it is important for the MST to influence or count on allies within the state. However, like the Zapatistas, the MST has always privileged the politicization of its membership by promoting broad political participation in the organizational structure of the movement (Vergara-Camus, 2009b: 181–82).

The State in Brazil and Mexico and the Corporatist Legacy

During the twentieth century, the relationship between the state and civil society in Brazil and Mexico followed corporatist lines. The state created political organizations in order to control the popular classes and impede the development of autonomous organizations.[1] In Brazil this was carried out first during President Getúlio Vargas's dictatorship by linking unions to the state and later by creating the Partido Trabalhista Brasileiro (Brazilian Labor Party, PTB) in 1945, while in Mexico the Partido Revolucionario Institucional (Revolutionary Institutional Party, PRI), which remained in power under different names for more than seventy years, was so omnipresent in society that people have referred to it as the party-state. The clientelist legacy of corporatism is thus much denser in Mexico because popular classes were organically linked to the regime as early as the 1930s. In Brazil no party has stayed in power that long, and peasants only began to be the subject of attention from the state in the late 1950s.

Until the mid-1980s, Brazil and Mexico were ruled by authoritarian regimes, Brazil under a military dictatorship since 1964 and Mexico under a one-party state since the 1920s. In both countries, the process of transition to liberal democracy was very slow and controlled by the ruling elite. In Brazil the transition had two distinctive dynamics. On the one hand, the transition was being negotiated from above, as several sectors of the bourgeoisie and the upper middle class wanted to move to a civilian regime in which they would have more power. On the other hand, it was pushed through by the rise of social movements, particularly the new unionism in the city and the countryside, which led to the creation of the Central Única de Trabalhadores (Worker's Unitary Union, CUT) and later the PT. In Mexico, although the 1968 student movement and the subsequent rise of underground guerilla movements in the 1970s signaled rising discontent, the transition was much slower than in Brazil. Although the right-wing Partido Acción Nacional (National Action Party, PAN) was making some headway in municipal elections before, the transition really began to unfold in the runoff to the presidential elections of 1988 with a split inside the PRI between neoliberals aligned with Carlos Salinas de Gortari, the official presidential candidate, and the nationalists led by Cuauhtémoc Cárdenas. Banking on his prestige and popularity, Cárdenas broke with the PRI and built a coalition to support his candidacy, which later became the PRD. By the end of the 1980s, most left-wing parties ended up dismantling and merging into the PRD and the leaders of the old Left subordinated themselves to the PRI runaways. The great majority of the social movements stayed with the PRI, except for a few independent movements, such as the Asamblea de Barrios of Mexico City or the Coalición Obrera, Campesina e Estudiantil del Istmo (COCEI) of Oaxaca.

Throughout their history, the PT and the PRD have opposed neoliberal policies. However, beyond a return to a modified developmental-populist state, neither elaborated an alternative political project. The PT emerged from a process of radicalization of unions and the rise of popular movements who wanted to create a political party that would truly represent their interests. It inherited a militant culture that emphasized politicization and participation of the grassroots membership and combined street mobilizations with inventive experiences of direct democracy, such as participatory budgeting. Internally, made up of several highly organized tendencies, the PT was extremely dynamic. Nothing in the history of the PRD resembles the trajectory of the PT. Despite the fact that left-wing parties that had merged into the PRD had a long history of involvement in working-class struggles, once the ex-*priistas* took control of the PRD, they brought with them the old PRI practices. Although mobilizations were important in the earlier years of the party, the more the PRD integrated within the political regime, the more electoral politics came to dominate the party. Like the PRI, the PRD's relationship with social movements has been characterized by the co-optation of leaders and clientelist links with the grassroots. As they became part of the political regime, both Brazil's PT and Mexico's PRD began to accommodate their discourse to neoliberalism and adopted a narrower understanding of politics, increasingly restricted to elite negotiations in the corridors of parliament.

The MST: Occupying All Possible Spaces

The most important struggle of the MST is the struggle for agrarian reform. Hence, most of its actions are geared to pressuring the state in accelerating land distribution, improving credit schemes, and supporting programs for small agricultural producers. Hence, since its creation in 1984, the MST has always recognized the need to participate in all fronts to generate support for its struggle.

The political strategy of the MST toward civil society is mainly preoccupied with building alliances with concrete organizations, in particular other rural movements and unions. In the countryside, the closest allies of the MST are the Movimento de Atengidos dos Barragems (Movement of Those Displaced by Hydro-electric Dams, MAB), the Movimento dos Pequenos Agricultores (Movement of Small Agricultural Producers, MPA), the rubber tappers movement, and the indigenous movement. They participate in numerous campaigns together and very often organize combined mobilizations. However, the MST has not been able to forge a strongly unified alliance with the most important rural organizations, the Confederação Nacional de Trabalhadores na Agricultura (National Confederation of Workers in Agriculture, CONTAG) and the rural branch of the CUT, because they consider each other rivals and hence do not have a common strategy.

The MST's strategy toward political parties and institutional politics is pragmatic and complementary to the mobilization and politicization of landless people. The MST does not consider institutional politics as the fundamental arena of its struggle but recognizes the importance of counting on allies within that sphere. Individually, members of the MST participate in several left-wing political parties but have overwhelmingly favored the PT. They participate in party politics and electoral campaigns, and in certain regions MST members have been elected as representatives at different levels of the state (Vergara-Camus, 2009b: 185–87). When the PT had a more radical profile, MST militants saw the PT as another instrument to modify the correlation of forces in Brazil.

Today, they simply believe that left-wing politicians can contribute to defend and promote agrarian reform and push for slightly more progressive policies.

If the emergence of the MST coincided with the rise of the Left in Brazil, the MST acquired national status at the moment of the decline of radicalism, particularly within unions and the PT. This context explains why the MST gradually became the most visible opposition movement to President Fernando Cardoso's (1995–2002) neoliberal policies, but also why the MST's radicalism was at odds with the strategies adopted by other leftist organizations.

The Struggle for Democracy, New Unionism, and the MST

The foundation of the MST in 1984 is part of the same process that gave birth to the new unionism movement, which culminated in the creation of the CUT and the PT. In many regions, members of the MST have participated in the process of electing more combative and democratic leadership to their local rural unions. In several regions in the early 1990s, the MST carried out land occupations and mobilizations in cooperation with rural unions that were affiliated to the CUT. At the time, both the CUT and the MST did not limit themselves to representing their constituency but understood their respective struggles as a battle for citizenship rights that could only be acquired through the eradication of socioeconomic inequalities within society at large. Thus they tackled issues such as education, health, and housing (Riethof, 2004: 34, 36).

These links with the CUT also incited MST members to participate in the foundation of the PT, but without organically tying the movement to the party. Landless people participated in numerous mobilizations and campaigns promoted by the PT such as the Diretas Ja campaign in 1984 to demand the organization of direct elections for president. Ever since, members of the MST have always supported Lula in his bid for the presidency and campaigned for the PT during local, state, and national elections. This support has been constant even when in the mid-1990s the PT top leaders and Lula made the strategic choice of abandoning grassroots mobilization and adopting a watered-down version of neoliberalism in order to attract middle-class voters and gain "respectability" within the political establishment.

The Cardoso Administration, the Rise of the MST, and the Decline of the CUT

In July 1995 the MST held its third national congress, in which delegates established two priorities: to continue the struggle for agrarian reform, and to oppose the neoliberal policies of the Cardoso government. The MST hence decided to deepen its contact with other civil-society organizations. It was during the first administration of President Cardoso (1995–1998) that the MST really came to have the stature of a national movement. A series of factors can explain the increased visibility of the MST during this period, but the public reaction to two massacres of MST members—in the municipality of Corumbiará in the state of Ceará in 1995 and in Eldorado dos Carajás in the state of Pará on April 17, 1996—stands out. These events broke the MST's isolation from the rest of Brazilian society, as the MST decided to counterattack in 1997 by organizing the National March for Land Reform, Jobs, and Justice. The two-months-long march proceeded to Brasília in three columns of MST families from different regions. The participants arrived to the capital on April 17, 1997, exactly a year after the Eldorado dos Carajás massacre. This was the first major protest against Cardoso's government, and it drew media coverage almost every day (Almeida and Sanchez, 2000). The effects of the march on the progressive sectors of Brazilian society were surprising. In the context of the retreat of the Brazilian Left in general, the MST represented for many the emergence of new possibilities. The MST benefited greatly from this visibility, as the number of land occupations and families involved in them increased dramatically (Ondetti, 2008: 157–60).

By the mid-1990s, even if at the local level CUT unions were collaborating with the MST, at the leadership level both organizations were taking separate paths. After a failed attempt to carry out a general strike against the Cardoso government in 1996 in response to the increased threat of unemployment, the CUT moved away from a strategy where strikes were a key element to one that emphasized negotiations (Riethof, 2004: 38–41; see also Ricardo Antunes's chapter in this book). Most rural unions now also favored participation within the Conselhos de Desenvolvimento Rural (Rural Development Councils), neo-corporatist regional consultative councils inscribed in the constitution of 1988.

In response to this divergence with unions, the MST has reached out to urban movements by helping to organize a coalition of popular organizations called the Central dos Movimentos Populares (Union of Popular Movements, CMP) and by promoting the construction of an alternative "popular project." This popular project has taken form gradually through public meetings forming a *consulta popular* (a sort of popular referendum) where groups representing marginalized sectors of society come together to coordinate opposition campaigns and propose alternative policies.

The MST has partly succeeded in its attempt to link up with urban movements. The CMP has not turned into a movement with significant political capacity, but it is a valuable forum where popular organizations can maintain a certain degree of communication among themselves. Recently, the urban movement with which the MST has been able to develop a better working relationship has been the Movimento dos Trabalhadores Sem Teto (Movement of the Homeless Workers, MTST). The MST helps to train leaders and members of the MTST. Although this collaboration is fairly recent, it is one of the most promising for the MST because the Sem Teto movement has the potential for developing some of the characteristics that explain the strength of the MST (i.e., the ability to control a neighborhood and establish forms of self-government).

The difficulty that the MST has had in building a coalition of movements can be explained by the tendency toward institutionalization that predominates within civil-society organizations, as it does within unions. In the 1980s popular movements and NGOs within Brazilian civil society were known for being extremely active and involved in challenging the dominant political culture. However, in more recent years, many of these movements and organizations have institutionalized, as they participate in the various consultative channels created to increase public participation in policies. Since participation within these channels is dominated by NGOs, the representation of interests is no longer accompanied by mobilization of the poor as it once was (Baierle, 2005).

During Cardoso's second term (1999–2002), halting the growth of the MST became an important priority for the government. Cardoso adopted a much more militaristic approach toward the movement by creating the Department of Agrarian Conflicts within the federal police force, and undercover police and informants infiltrated the movement. On December 27, 2000, in order to discourage land occupations, the Cardoso administration passed a decree prohibiting the institution in charge of agrarian reform from auditing land that had been occupied by landless families. In spite of this political harassment, the MST continued to carry out land occupations, marches, and sit-ins during Cardoso's second term. In January 2001, as part of the Brazilian campaign against genetically modified (GM) crops, members of the MST in coordination with Via Campesina[2] invaded a property of the Monsanto Company in order to destroy the GM maize that was being grown there.

The Lula Administration: The Rise of Neo-corporatism

Even though it was evident that Lula would not implement substantial reforms, many on the left thought he would at least distinguish himself from Cardoso. However, Lula (2003–2010) governed almost in direct line with his immediate predecessor, partly because in order to maintain a majority in Congress he had to rely on a broad coalition with parties from the Right.

His monetary policy and the reforms of the public-sector pension plan represented the completion of Fernando Henrique Cardoso's agenda. Lula also decided to follow the trend toward the promotion of conditional cash transfer programs in social policy by creating Fome Zero (Zero Hunger) and Bolsa Familia (Family Basket). Under these programs, a family living under poverty or extreme poverty can receive up to a monthly maximum of R$95, the equivalent of $43 U.S. Since these programs are administered by municipal governments and are open to all kinds of political manipulation, they are contributing to reinforcing the long tradition of corporatist and clientelist politics. In the case of the founders of the CUT and PT in particular, Francisco de Oliveira saw Lula's policies within a larger context of the emergence of a new patronage system in which a new class of former labor leaders use their links with the PT in order to occupy positions within large state firms and pension funds and favor their subordinates with public-sector jobs (Oliveira, 2006: 17).

Lula also followed in Cardoso's footsteps by promoting the interests of agribusiness and large agricultural producers due to the large export revenues they generate. Early in his mandate, he lifted the ban on GM crops and made the production of ethanol from sugar cane, controlled by large corporations, one of the new economic "engines of growth" of Brazil. With respect to the distribution of land, which is the most important measure for landless people, Lula did not quite live up to his promises. In his first mandate, the government stated that it had distributed land to 448,000 families between 2003 and 2007, but several experts contest these numbers and argue that most of the actions were legalization of old settlements. Lula would have settled only 192,257 new families in his first mandate (Fernandes, 2008: 79), which is far from the 550,000 he had promised.

Although it held back during the first year of the Lula government, the MST resumed its actions in June 2004 by launching a series of land occupations throughout Brazil and undertook another march to Brasília in May 2005. To compensate for the lack of swift agrarian reform, Lula's government took some steps to help small agricultural producers. Debts were renegotiated and partially cancelled, and credits were increased and made available before harvest. The Lula administration also decided to buy up to 30 percent of food crops from small producers for its poverty-relief programs. However, since it depends on the president's will and the collaboration of municipal governments, this measure is another way of reinforcing the clientelist pattern between small farmers, the PT, and the state.

For Lula's reelection bid in 2006, the MST remained silent throughout the campaign, giving its support to Lula only a few days before the second-round vote. The MST has since pursued its direct-action tactics, but under conditions of decreasing unemployment and increasing public welfare, they no longer seem to attract as many people. The MST has thus been playing a pivotal role in reinvigorating popular mobilization by participating in national campaigns to recover national sovereignty, such as A Vale é Nossa and O Petróleo é Nosso. The first campaign began in 2007, as an effort of social movements and civil-society organizations to revert the highly irregular privatization by President Cardoso of the world's largest state mining company, Vale do Rio Doce, in 1997. Its highpoint was a week of popular referendums in September 2007 in which 94 percent of the 3.7 million participants voted against the privatization. In 2008 the second campaign, now to avoid the privatization of the oil sector, was launch in collaboration with the oil workers union and other organizations. Grassroots assemblies were held to discuss and elaborate a project of law that would ensure state control over the sector and the reinvestment of oil revenues in social policies. The campaign culminated in August 2009 with the submission of a law signed by 1.3 million people to the Brazilian Congress. Beyond all the contradictions involved in the revival of the developmental state, tactically for the MST, campaigns represent an opportunity of recomposing a broad coalition of forces against neoliberalism, through which it can win support to put agrarian reform back on the political agenda.

Even though Lula's policies have been disappointing for its militants, the MST is not ready to turn its back on the PT. The MST still believes that social movements have to concentrate on pressuring the state into adopting measures more favorable to popular sectors. Lula's balancing act between capital and popular sectors seems to only partly confirm this analysis. In 2008 in comparison to 2003, the budget for infrastructure and sustainable development on agrarian reform settlements increased by a factor of ten, and the credits that help the families that have been awarded land set up their farm increased by five (INCRA, 2011: 49, 83). In September 2009, Lula's administration sent to the Congress a project of law that revises—although only for a small proportion of the territory—the productivity indexes that determine which properties are subject to expropriation. This had been a longstanding demand of rural movements because the current indexes are based on the productivity and technological level of 1975. The same month, Lula also sent his own plan regarding oil exploration and exploitation to the Congress. The project includes elements proposed by the O Petróleo é Nosso campaign, such as a social fund, but also provides ample opportunities for the private sector. However, these two mild measures seemed to respond much more to the electoral calendar of the presidential elections of 2010 than to a real commitment to social movements and organized sectors of the working class.

An unambiguous governmental decision came at the end of Lula's administration. On June 26, 2009, by ratifying Decree 458, which legalizes 67.4 million hectares of Amazonian land (equivalent to the size of Germany and France combined), against the critiques of his former minister of the environment, Marina Silva, Lula definitively sided with the landed class. This decision was very controversial because, even though thousands of squatters will be able to legalize their access to land, several clauses of Decree 458 could open the door to a new round of illegal land grabbing and consolidation of large *latifundios* in the Amazon region, which will directly benefit the large capitalist farmers and agribusiness. Agrarian reform numbers at the end of his second mandate cast further doubts on how much the PT is committed to agrarian reform. According to official sources, his government would have distributed land to 614,000 families during his two terms, making him the president to have distributed more land in the history of Brazil, in front of Cardoso, who benefited 541,000 families. However, scholars of agrarian reform, such as Ariovaldo Umbelino de Oliveira from the University of São Paulo, have once again questioned these numbers and contend that most of the distributions, like in the time of Cardoso, were actually legalization of land that was already being farmed, and that Lula distributed land to a mere 211,000 new families (Arruda, 2011).

Lula's presidency remains a puzzling experience for the MST. The movement is divided on how to rebuild a popular political alternative for poor Brazilians, but there are no signs that the MST will invest its activist time in the construction of the Partido Socialismo e Liberdad (Socialism and Liberty Party, PSOL), created in 2004 by PT parliamentarians expelled for criticizing Lula's policies. The MST's pragmatic position toward institutional politics and the local nature of the militancy of MST members within the PT seem to weigh more than the need to create a new political instrument for the laboring classes. At least for the moment, many MST members still prefer to use the PT machinery to wage their local battles in their municipalities and states, even if it means sacrificing the possibility of more far-reaching change. The MST's critical support of Dilma Rousseff, the presidential candidate of the PT, at the end of the second round in 2010 signals that the movement is not ready to change its strategy.

The EZLN: Another Way of Doing Politics

When, following the uprising of January 1994, the EZLN declared that it did not seek state power but rather to change the relationship between the rulers and the ruled, it generated enormous confusion within the Left. Although the development of self-governed indigenous communities and municipalities in Chiapas showed that the objective was to build political institutions controlled by the popular classes, most organizations of the Left have had difficulty in envisioning a similar process within Mexican society at large. Ever since, the Zapatistas have had difficulties articulating their proposal, given that most organizations in the country believe that relevant change would come through the election of a progressive government.

Throughout the years, the EZLN's main aim has been to build up the local autonomous power of its member communities, which has replaced the Mexican state by providing education, health, microdevelopment, and justice to indigenous communities. In order to achieve this, its national strategy has had many objectives. First and foremost, it has been preoccupied with maintaining a network that can support the movement and shield the autonomous municipalities from the attacks of the Mexican state. The second objective has been the formation of a broad opposition front of popular organizations of the Left—including political parties—to defeat the PRI and its neoliberal policies and rewrite a constitution that would allow for indigenous and non-indigenous forms of self-government. The third objective has been the construction of a national political organization geared toward the organization of civil society rather than electoral politics.

Even if in 1994 the PRD was finally allowing the Left to reach unprecedented levels of electoral support, the EZLN burst into the public scene during a low point in the history of the Mexican Left: it had not manage to mount a real opposition to President Salinas's electoral fraud of 1988; popular movements were either disorganized, repressed or co-opted through Salinas' Solidaridad program (Hellman, 1994); and large sectors of the intelligentsia had given into neoliberal hegemony.

Refounding the Nation-State

The Convención Nacional Democrática (National Democratic Convention, CND), organized from August 6 to 8, 1994, in the Lacandona jungle, was the first attempt by the EZLN to establish formal links with the different sectors of the Mexican Left and elaborate a common platform for action. The EZLN saw the CND as the first step toward the organization of a constituent assembly responsible for writing a new constitution that would reverse the modifications of the social clauses of the constitution of 1917 and respond to the new demands for greater political participation (EZLN, 1994: 275; Womack, 1999: 284).

The victory of the PRI's Ernesto Zedillo (1994–2000) cut short these ambitions and forced the EZLN to reconsider its strategy and alliances. Through the "Third Declaration of the Lacandona Jungle," the EZLN called for the creation of the Movimiento de Liberación Nacional (National Liberation Movement, MLN) to organize the resistance against the Zedillo government and coordinate efforts with the PRD. The EZLN proposed to refuse to recognize Zedillo's victory, form a transition government, and call for a constituent assembly (EZLN, 1995a: 192–93; Womack, 1999: 293). However, the MLN did not progress, and by the end of 1995 it was already evident that the organization would not survive.

The initiative did not prosper because the adoption of an insurrectional stand was far from the PRD's analysis of the conjuncture. First, the PRD did not think it had the capacity to contest the results of the elections. Second, the party had been struggling for years to win elections and have its electoral victories recognized, so it was not ready to challenge the Mexican state. Even though it opposed neoliberal policies, the PRD was not seeking to fundamentally transform the political system but simply to be integrated into it. The failure of the Zapatista strategy can be explained by their inability to read the PRD's intention correctly and by the decision of President Zedillo to negotiate an electoral reform with the PRD that gave parties access to enormous amount of public funds for electoral campaigns. In a contradictory twist of history, the Zapatista rebellion and the possibility of seeing the radicalization of the electoral Left forced the Zedillo government to negotiate an electoral reform that he would not have accepted under other circumstances. As a result, the PRD became further inserted into the political regime, and the possibility of a real alliance between the EZLN and the PRD disappeared (Anguiano, 1997: 159, 162–63, García de León, 2002: 252).

At the same time that it was attempting to radicalize the PRD, the EZLN used the negotiations with the Mexican state (October 1995 to February 1996) to put into practice its idea of pushing for a constituent assembly. After the federal congress voted on a law that called for a negotiated solution to the conflict in Chiapas and gave some guarantees to the EZLN, the Zapatistas pressured the government into accepting a series of talks (the San Andrés Accords) that would touch upon all the major national issues. The idea was to transform the different dialogues in something equivalent to a constituent assembly. The talks were supposed to be comprised of six separate dialogues: (1) indigenous rights and culture, (2) democracy and justice, (3) well-being and development, (4) conciliation in Chiapas, (5) women's rights in Chiapas, (6) and an end of hostilities (EZLN, 1995b: 445–46).

During the negotiations on indigenous rights and culture, the EZLN invited leaders of other indigenous movements and well-known scholars to sit on its side of the negotiating table or to attend as guests. The debate that the negotiations generated within society, as well as the fact that the agreement would apply to *all* indigenous peoples and not only to the EZLN, gave to the event the character of a de facto constituent assembly on indigenous rights. At the end of this dialogue in 1996, the government signed the San Andrés Accords with the EZLN, promising to transform it into legislation and have it ratified by the federal congress. In November 1996, the Comisión para la Concordia y la Pacificación (Commission for Agreement and Pacification, COCOPA)[3] worked on a legislative text based on the San Andrés Accords. A legislation based on the accords was extremely important for the Zapatistas because through it their local experiences of indigenous autonomy would be legitimized and protected. Both parties agreed to the text in late November, but Zedillo finally rejected it a month later. In addition, the federal government broke up talks right at the beginning of the second dialogue on democracy and justice and blocked the strategy of the EZLN of using the negotiations to build direct links with other social movements. As a consequence, the strongest political ally of the EZLN has been the indigenous movement through the Congreso Nacional Indígena (CNI), the only organization created by the Zapatistas that acquired a national status and persisted (Bartra and Otero, 2005: 400).

The refusal by the Mexican state to uphold what it had signed in San Andrés was a major turning point. Since then, the EZLN has dedicated the greatest part of its efforts to getting the state to uphold its engagement, and the movement's political agenda has been limited, to a large extent, to indigenous autonomy. The Mexican state thus managed to limit the EZLN and downplay its national character. As a consequence, the Zapatista proposal of "refounding the nation" has not been given serious consideration by any other political forces.[4]

Nevertheless, from 1994 to the end of Zedillo's term, the PRD denounced the government's military strategy in the conflict and pushed for the recognition of the San Andrés Accords. In turn, in the midterm elections of 1997, the EZLN congratulated Cuauhtémoc Cárdenas on his victory in the elections for Mayor of Mexico City but reminded Mexicans that the high level of military presence and political repression in Chiapas and other southern states were no conditions for democratic and free elections. Since 1998, as the years and electoral campaigns passed and the new electoral politics became more and more characterized by overpragmatism, the EZLN definitively rejected electoral and institutional politics as a path for social change.

Counterinsurgency and Political Isolation

The Zapatista uprising unleashed a significant wave of land occupations throughout Chiapas by independent peasant organizations as well as organizations linked to the PRI. The independent organizations created a coalition in support of the Zapatistas, the Consejo Estatal de Organizaciones Indíge- nas y Campesina (State Council of Indigenous and Peasant Organizations, CEOIC). The EZLN welcomed the support and asked the organizations not to negotiate separately with the federal state. However, in 1996, while the federal government was negotiating with the EZLN in San Andrés, most indepen- dent organizations agreed to sign individual agreements with the state that legalized their land occupations and the CEIOC crumbled (García de León, 2002: 263). As it did during the final phase of the San Andrés negotiations, the federal government, now using very traditional clientelist tactics, managed to isolate the EZLN from Chiapan peasant organizations.

In 1997 the table was set for President Zedillo to unleash a counterinsur- gency campaign against Zapatista autonomous municipalities. The Mexican Army intensified its actions within Zapatista territory, destroyed the infra- structure that the Zapatista autonomous municipalities had built, imprisoned dozens of Zapatista supporters, and encouraged the creation of indigenous paramilitary groups. One of the worst atrocities of this campaign was the massacre of eighteen children, twenty-two women, and six men in the village of Acteal on December 22, 1997. The state tried to further weaken the EZLN by attempting to co-opt its social base through microdevelopment programs, infrastructure work, and poverty-relief programs.

In response to this campaign, the EZLN adopted its policy of resistance[5] and intensified its efforts to mobilize Zapatista supporters. In September 1997, the EZLN organized the March of the 1,111, where one thousand one hundred and eleven Zapatista community members from Chiapas were sent to Mexico City for the creation of the Frente Zapatista de Liberación Nacio- nal (Zapatista Front of National Liberation, FZLN). The FZLN was intended to be a new political force that would not seek state power but rather would organize civil society with the objective of generating a counterpower to the state and forms of self-government. The EZLN would eventually participate directly within the FZLN, but only once the military and political conflict could be solved. However, lacking concrete struggles of its own, the FZLN fell into sectarian battles and gradually turned simply into a solidarity network for the Zapatista rebels.

Very little is known about the exchanges and dialogues that the EZLN has had with leaders of popular movements. What is clear though is that the Zapatistas have refused to enter into any kind of collaboration or alliance with organiza- tions that have links to political parties. They have avoided dissident sectors of the corporatist structure of the PRI and have been critical of leaders of inde- pendent organizations that have chosen to negotiate with the state. Hence, the Zapatistas have consciously chosen not to add their voice to certain struggles and have only sought alliances with movements that remain autonomous of political parties and the state, which in Mexico are still a minority.

The decision to not collaborate with movements that seek to extract concessions from the state has had a high political cost for the Zapatistas. It has isolated them and has impeded their ability to influence these movements. In contrast to the MST in Brazil, the inability of the EZLN to find ways to reach out to these movements and incorporate them into common tactical objectives, expressed through specific campaigns, has led the Zapatistas to rely more and more on a "politics of events" (i.e., the organization of encounters, marches, referendums), which has been essential for resisting the counterinsurgency campaign but has not provided the foundation for a broad coalition of forces.

With the failure of all its attempts to create a national organization, the EZLN reverted to its sporadic and spontaneous relationship with groups from civil society (students, popular movements, collectives, NGOs, etc.) through the call to organize a popular referendum on indigenous rights, which lasted from November 1998 to May 1999. The process mobilized tens of thousands of supporters, and 2.8 million people are said to have participated in the referendum.

The Zapatista attempts to have the San Andrés Accords recognized ended in February and March 2001 with another march, La Marcha del Color de la Tierra—the largest ever organized by the EZLN. After having waited for President Vicente Fox (2000–2006) to define his government's position on the issue of indigenous rights, the EZLN sent Subcomandante Marcos and all members of the top leadership of the organization from Chiapas to Mexico City to convince the Mexican Congress to ratify the COCOPA law. The enthusiastic response of hundreds of thousands of people all along the caravan route confirmed the support that the Zapatistas had garnered within Mexican society, especially among indigenous people, peasants, workers, and sectors of the middle class and youth. The arrival of the *comandancia* of the EZLN to Mexico City's Zócalo in March 2001 is one of the biggest mass events in recent Mexican history.

However, even if this enthusiastic response obliged political parties to allow a Zapatista delegation to speak at the tribune of the Mexican Congress, the Congress did not approve the COCOPA law but rather a very watered down version of it, far from the spirit of what had been negotiated. This was the coup de grâce to institutional politics because all political parties represented in Congress, including the PRD, adopted that law.

The Otra Campaña: From Below and to the Left

With the passing of the indigenous law in 2001, a new phase of the Zapatista struggle was opened. In 2003 the Zapatistas further consolidated their presence over the indigenous regions of Chiapas by creating the Juntas de Buen Gobierno, councils that coordinate several autonomous municipalities. Even though various peasant movements staged an important protest movement in 2003 and 2004, the EZLN remained silent as peasant organizations negotiated an agreement with the Fox administration that led nowhere. In June 2005 the EZLN decided to take the offensive once again and issued the "Sixth Declaration of the Lacandona Jungle." The "Sexta" puts the issue of class exploitation at the core of the Zapatista analysis of Mexico, reiterates the need for a constituent assembly, and calls for a new national movement. The Otra Campaña (the Other Campaign) was the result of these meetings and began in January 2006 as a sort of "reconnaissance" tour across Mexico. Subcomandante Marcos and fifteen Zapatista commanders toured the country to meet face-to-face with groups interested in joining a national Zapatista movement that would be clearly anticapitalist and nonelectoral. The Otra Campaña broke with previous attempts because it sought to transcend the politics of events by creating direct links between the EZLN and other organizations. However, the Otra Campaña repeated the limitations of the past by refusing any collaboration with organizations that did not follow the Zapatista path of resistance.

When Subcomandante Marcos harshly criticized elections as a path for social change and associated Andrés Manuel López Obrador, the candidate of the PRD in the presidential race of 2006, with neoliberalism and the heritage of Carlos Salinas, many leftist intellectuals were infuriated. But Subcomandante Marcos was echoing the criticism that many on the left shared, which included the preoccupation with López Obrador's highly personalist and populist style, his opportunistic use of popular mobilization without real politicization and participation, his ties to Carlos Slim, who benefited from the privatization of the state-owned telephone company under Salinas, and the presence of several close collaborators of Salinas in his team. The attack was not a turnaround in the Zapatista position toward institutional politics but rather a reminder that for the EZLN social change would not come by changing politicians at the top but rather by changing the way of doing politics from below. The objective was to clearly establish itself within the radical Left and build alliances from there. However, tactically it cost the movement the support of more moderate sectors of the Left.

On May 4, 2006, just a few days after the Zapatistas reached Mexico City, the federal police attacked the village of Atenco, killing two, sexually assaulting more than thirty women, and imprisoning over two hundred people. The event halted the EZLN caravan in Mexico City as the EZLN tried to coordinate efforts to liberate the prisoners. A few months later in December 2006, the PRI governor of the state of Oaxaca called on the federal police to violently repress the Asamblea Popular de los Pueblos de Oaxaca (Popular Assembly of the Peoples of Oaxaca, APPO), which had been carrying out an intense experience of self-government that took control of numerous neighborhoods of the state's capital city.

Although several groups within APPO were strongly influenced by Zapatismo and the political practices of the movement mirrored their own, the EZLN remained distant from the process and only expressed its solidarity with it. In a certain sense, this speaks to the limitations of the Zapatista strategy because, in the absence of direct organizational links that could have been created throughout the years through coalition building, the ideological influence of Zapatismo within APPO did not lead to a national protest movement. The Oaxaca case suggests also that popular organizations that negotiate with the state, like a teachers union, can escape corporatism and be the basis for radical politicization and self-government and eventually be the seed of radical social change.

The EZLN seems to be reflecting on the issue because it has established links with some groups from the APPO, as with groups from Atenco and Mexico City, notably the Movimiento Popular Francisco Villa Independiente, an important squatter movement. However, Zapatistas have not changed their attitude toward traditional organizations, and the Festival de la Digna Rabia in January 2009 looked more like a return to their "politics of events" than the beginning of the construction of a broad coalition of mass organizations. The repression that many popular movements have been facing under President Felipe Calderon (2006–2012) could lead certain movements into aligning themselves with the EZLN, but most of them are probably still awaiting the results of the next presidential election, which might very well see the comeback of the PRI, to decide on their strategy. As for the Zapatista decision not to collaborate with the PRD, it is not likely to change since the PRD is moving ever further from its initial oppositional roots and has even been flirting recently with the idea of building local alliances with the party ideologically more to the right, the PAN, in order to block the PRI. Considering López Obrador's failure to rally the whole party around him when he adopted an insurrectional stand in 2006–2007 and the rise of several contenders within the party since then, the battle for the PRD's presidential nomination in 2011–2012 could bring to the fore all the dirty politics inherited from the PRI. This is bound to further degrade the image of the PRD within Mexican society, not to mention in the eyes of the Zapatistas.

Conclusion

As with previous peasant movements, the strength of the MST and the EZLN lies not in their ability to build national alliances but in their ability to control a territory, provide and protect the access to land, and organize their member-ship around their own self-governed structures of power. This provides them with the ability to mobilize entire communities behind their strategy and con-duct massive direct action that attracts media attention and generates solidar-ity for their cause. Both movements have been very successful on this front.

Building a national coalition of organizations to oppose neoliberalism and struggle for radical social change has turned out to be a task that far exceeded their organizational capacities. In Brazil and Mexico, unlike in Venezuela or Bolivia, fundamental social change did not become the objective of a historic bloc of popular social forces. As most organizations were choosing insertion into the political regime, the MST and the EZLN found themselves going against the current, without real allies for their national strategy.

For the MST, the task of building a coalition has become more difficult in recent years due to the institutionalization of the CUT and many movements and civil-society organizations. Regardless, even though the MST adopts a more radical perspective then most organizations, it has decided to continue to collaborate with them in specific campaigns with the objective of influenc-ing them and gaining support for its cause. The EZLN faced an even worst situation because it was trying to build a political front while facing a coun-terinsurgency campaign, which succeeded in isolating it. The Mexican state outplayed the Zapatistas by pretending to negotiate with them in San Andrés while co-opting independent peasant movements and signing an electoral reform that provided funds for the PRD. The Zapatistas' subsequent refusal to collaborate with organizations that do not adopt their policy of resistance further diminished the number of potential allies and impeded them from influencing social movements and coordinating actions. The limit of this strategy became evident during the experience of the Oaxaca commune.

The two movements have also adopted different strategies in regard to political parties and the state. The MST recognizes that social forces seek-ing radical social transformation cannot progress without counting on allies within the state. They thus give their support to the PT with the hope of af-fecting change in public policy. The disappointing achievements under Lula's administration have generated a discussion within the movement, but there has been no real break with their traditional pragmatic attitude toward insti-tutional politics yet. It is still uncertain though how the militants and the lead-ership of the MST are going to rethink their traditional alliance with the PT. In contrast, the Zapatistas believe that the capitalist state cannot be reformed and that new working-class institutions and ways of doing politics should re-place it. They nevertheless still attempted to build bridges with the PRD until 1998, at which point they came to the conclusion that the PRD was simply another version of the PRI. The endless episodes of internal frauds, corrup-tions, and intrigues to control the party or choose candidates for elected office have confirmed the Zapatista analysis. However, their complete rejection of elections has cut them off from large sectors of the population that could have otherwise been allies.

The MST's more pragmatic politics of alliance has probably yielded more short-term results than the Zapatistas' maximalist one. The results, however, if we consider the way Lula's policies combine a strong support for capital with small concessions to popular sectors, have been very modest. The MST has accepted that in the current context it is the most that can be expected. The EZLN refuses to limit itself to this perspective.

The MST and the EZLN have transformed the everyday lives of the rural communities that they control by reaching significant levels of autonomy. In that respect, they are examples for other peasant movements. However, without allies from other classes, they cannot translate their achievements into a proposal for other sectors of society. But they remain more than "cracks in the Empire" because, in the context of the current global economic crisis, the experience they have acquired within an unfavorable conjuncture could contribute to the arduous task of rebuilding an alternative to the *izquierda permitida* in Brazil and Mexico.

Notes

1. One of the most important aspects of a corporatist state is that class conflict is channeled through formal or informal negotiations between the leadership of sectoral organizations (labor, business, etc.) and state officials. Through this process, sectoral representatives tend to count less on the mobilization of their membership than on their ability to have access to politicians, to whom they are tied through a patronage system that turns grassroots members into clients of their representatives and politicians.

2. Via Campesina is the most important peasant coalition in the world. It was created in 1993 and brings together organizations representing small and medium farmers, landless peasants, and rural workers from Asia, Africa, the Americas, and Europe.

3. The COCPA was a parliamentary commission, made up of deputies and senators from the different parties represented in Congress, created to assist in the negotiations.

4. During his campaign against the alleged fraud that robed him of his victory in the presidential election of 2006, Andrés Manuel López Obrador revived the idea of refounding the nation by rewriting the Constitution, but he did not give the process a genuinely participatory character. It was simply a way of putting pressure on its political rivals (see Richard Roman and Edur Velasco Arregui's chapter in this book).

5. The policy of resistance implied the end of any sort of cooperation between the EZLN and the state and called upon all Zapatista families to refuse any state program or subsidy until the state ratified the San Andrés Accords.

References

Almeida, Lúcio Flávio de, and Félix Ruiz Sánchez. 2000. "The Landless Workers' Movement and Social Struggle against Neoliberalism." *Latin American Perspectives* 27 (5): 11–32.

Anguiano, Arturo. 1997. *Entre el pasado y el futuro: La izquierda en México, 1969–1995.* México: Universidad Autónoma Metropolitana-Unidad Xochimilco.

Arruda, Roldão. 2011. "INCRA infla números de reforma agrária." *Estadão.com.br,* February 27. http://www.estadao.com.br/noticias/nacional,incra-infla-numeros-de-reforma-agraria,685346,0.htm.

Baierle, Sergio. 2005. "Lula's Swamp." *Journal of Iberian and Latin American Studies* 11 (2): 109–16.

Bartra, Armando, and Gerardo Otero. 2005. "Indian Peasant Movement in Mexico: The Struggle for Land, Autonomy and Democracy." In *Reclaiming the Land: The Resurgence of Rural Movements in Africa, Asia and Latin America,* ed. Sam Moyo and Paris Yeros, 383–410. London: Zed Books.

EZLN. 1994. "Segunda Declaración de la Selva Lacandona." In *Documentos y Comunicados. Tomo 1,* 269–78. Mexico: Editorial Era.

———. 1995a. "Tercera Declaración de la Selva Lacandona." In *Documentos y Comunicados. Tomo 2,* 187–93. Mexico: Editorial Era.

———. 1995b. "Propuesta sobre mesas y reglas para el diálogo, 12 de septiembre." In *Documentos y Comunicados. Tomo 2,* 445–47. Mexico: Editorial Era.

Fernandes, Bernardo Mançano. 2008. "O MST e as reformas agrarias no Brasil." *OSAL: Observatorio Social de América Latina* 24:73–85.

García de León, Antonio. 2002. *Fronteras interiores: Chiapas, una modernidad particular.* Mexico: Editorial Oceano.

Hellman, Judith. 1994. "Mexican Popular Movements, Clientelism, and the Process of Democratization." *Latin American Perspectives* 21 (2): 124–42.

INCRA (Instituto de Colonização e Reforma Agrária). 2011. *Prestação de contas ordinárias anual. Relatorio de gestão de exercício de 2010.* Brasília: Ministerio de Desenvolvimento Agrário.

Oliveira, Francisco de. 2006. "Lula in the Labyrinth." *New Left Review* 42:5–22.

Ondetti, Gabriel. 2008. *Land, Protest, and Politics: The Landless Movement and the Struggle for Agrarian Reform in Brazil.* University Park: Pennsylvania State University Press.

Riethof, Marieke. 2004. "Changing Strategies of the Brazilian Labor Movement: From Opposition to Participation." *Latin American Perspectives* 31 (6): 31–47.

Vergara-Camus, Leandro. 2009a. "The MST and the EZLN's Struggle for Land: New Forms of Peasant Rebellions." *Journal of Agrarian Change* 9 (3): 365–91.

———. 2009b. "The Politics of the MST: Autonomous Rural Communities, the State and Electoral Politics." *Latin American Perspectives* 36 (4): 178–91.

Womack, John, Jr. 1999. *Rebellion in Chiapas: An Historical Reader.* New York: New Press.

6

Barrio Women and Popular Politics in Chávez's Venezuela

Sujatha Fernandes

SINCE LEFTIST PRESIDENT HUGO CHÁVEZ came to power in Venezuela in 1998, ordinary women from the barrios, or shantytowns, of Caracas have become more engaged in politics at the grassroots level. Given the use of images of black and poor women in Chávez's television campaigns; his creation of programs such as Barrio Adentro and Misión Ribas, related to concerns that affect women such as health and education; and the general politicization of the population in this movement, it is not surprising that women from the barrios have become major protagonists in the current urban social movements in Venezuela. But the majority of community leaders in the barrios continue to be men. Chávez's programs are controlled by male-dominated bureaucracies. Indeed, many women activists still look toward the president himself as the main source of direction and inspiration. What is the outcome of women's increasing political participation that was and continues to be generated under male-directed and -initiated campaigns from above? What possibilities exist for poor women mobilized in the framework of state-managed programs in a revolutionary-populist state?

In this chapter I argue that the ability of barrio women in Caracas to build local spaces of participation partly outside of state control has increased their power of negotiation within state-sponsored programs such as soup kitchens. Despite male leadership and authority, the growing presence of women in local committees, assemblies, and communal kitchens has created forms of popular participation that challenge gender roles, collectivize private tasks, and create alternatives to male-centric politics. Women's experiences of shared struggle from previous decades, along with their use of democratic methods of popular control such as local assemblies, help to prevent the state's appropriation of women's labor for its own ends. But these spaces of popular participation exist in dynamic tension with more vertical, populist notions of politics that are characteristic of official sectors of Chavismo.

Understanding the gendered dimensions of popular participation is crucial to an analysis of the nature of urban social movements, especially how these movements differ from traditional forms of political participation, such as political parties and trade unions. Such an analysis is particularly important given the recent upsurge of popular participation in the barrios since Chávez assumed the presidency. Although women play a key role in these social movements, most scholars have failed to incorporate gender into their analysis or to look at the specific gains made by women through their participation.

Drawing on theoretical frameworks developed by scholars of popular women's activism and those looking at gender politics in revolutionary and populist states, this chapter seeks to develop a specific analysis of barrio women's activism in Chávez's Venezuela that can also shed light on debates about popular women's organizing in general. It begins with an overview of these various literatures, provides background to the Chávez government, and traces the rise in barrio women's participation since Chávez came to power in 1998. It then looks at experiences of local organizing in a popular sector of Caracas known as the Carretera Negra of La Vega.

The analysis is based on eight months of field research conducted in three parishes of Caracas: San Agustín, 23 de Enero, and La Vega, between January 2004 and February 2006. The study comprises individual and collective interviews with women activists, observations of local committee meetings and assemblies, and documents produced by the various community organizations. Residence in a popular barrio for the eight months, moreover, allowed time to get to know the women and to accompany them to various official events and meetings.

Urban Social Movements, Women's Activism, and Populism

Urban social movements in Latin America have generated a large literature, some of which has addressed the predominant role of poor women in these movements. Surprisingly little literature, however, focuses on the gendered aspects of popular participation in Venezuela. The literature on urban popular movements in Venezuela tends to represent popular subjects as androgynous (Ellner, 2005; Grohmann, 1996; López-Maya, Smilde, and Stephany, 1999; Ramos Rollon, 1995).

The scholarship on Venezuelan women's movement politics has provided crucial insights about women's challenge to unequal gender relations, and a few of these accounts look historically at the intersections between class and gender in popular women's organizing. For instance, Elisabeth Friedman (2000: 173) describes the emergence of Popular Women's Circles (Círculos Femeninos Populares, CPF) in the barrios of Caracas in the 1970s, which sought to "address the effects of discriminatory gender relations within the context of popular women's daily lives." But most accounts of gender politics in contemporary Venezuela have not addressed the daily struggles of women in popular classes. Some, such as Cathy Rakowski (2003: 400), see popular women organized in Chavista groupings as "new to feminism and women's rights," most of whom "have no understanding of the history of women's struggle in Venezuela" and "reject feminism as antifamily." Certainly there are differences between those women who have become newly politicized under Chávez and those with a longer-term political involvement. But this literature does not give us a sense of what kinds of gender-based struggles popular women have engaged in under Chávez or their relationship to the history of the women's movement and feminism. In this chapter I suggest that popular women's organizing contains its own unique history, struggles, and trajectories that cannot be reduced to the history of feminism in Venezuela.

One dominant approach to studying the activism of women in popular sectors in Latin America emphasizes the practical versus strategic needs of these women. Based on her work on the Nicaraguan revolution during the 1980s, Maxine Molyneux (1985: 284) suggests that we look at the participation of poorer women in terms of "practical gender interests," which include daily struggles over food, shelter, and health, and are counterposed to "strategic gender interests," which "entail a strategic goal such as women's emancipation or gender equality." Various scholars have drawn on this distinction to show how the struggles of women in popular classes may differ from those of middle- and upper-class women, and that struggles for practical needs can lead to a growing consciousness and questioning of gender hierarchy (Barrig, 1989; Caldeira, 1990; Díaz-Barriga, 1998; Massolo, 1999; Rodriguez, 1994; Safa, 1990). Likewise, the experiences of popular women's organizing in Caracas demonstrate how involvement in everyday political organizing has brought about changes in how barrio women view themselves and their place in the world. But while barrio women may come to challenge certain aspects of gender subordination, they generally do not adopt feminist outlooks as these have been traditionally defined. Moreover, they do not always express their reasons for becoming active in terms of economic or practical interests.

Scholars have argued that the distinction between "practical" and "strategic" gender interests incorrectly assumes that women's daily struggles for basic goods and services in themselves are prepolitical and do not represent a challenge to patriarchy or established gender relations (Lind, 1992; Westwood and Radcliffe, 1993), that the distinction indirectly reinforces women's structural position by assuming a public/private dichotomy (Stephen, 1997: 12), and as Molyneux (2001: 155) herself has clarified in later work, that popular women's organizations may combine "practical" and "strategic" interests in their daily organizing experiences. In this chapter I seek to build on the contributions of these scholars. I follow Amy Lind's (1992: 137) suggestion that rather than creating false barriers between "practical" and "strategic" gender interests, we need to focus on "how poor women negotiate power, construct collective identities, and develop critical perspectives on the world in which they live—all factors that challenge dominant gender representations." As Lind (2005: 96) argues in her book on Ecuadorian women's popular organizing, poor women organized not to explicitly confront gender relations but "to improve the gendered conditions of their daily lives," something quite distinct.

This study seeks to locate popular women's organizing in Caracas within the complexities of a revolutionary-populist system, where women's local participation is both nationally valorized and initiated from above. Following Kenneth Roberts (2003: 35), this study defines populism as "a form of personalistic leadership that mobilize[s] diverse popular constituencies behind statist, nationalistic and redistributive development models." It qualifies this definition, however, by noting that the concept of populism cannot describe all aspects of Venezuelan politics under Chávez; it is one privileged element of political discourse and culture that interacts among other elements (Burbano de Lara, 1998: 24).

Gender politics in Chávez's Venezuela is distinct from the postrevolutionary contexts of Cuba, China, and Nicaragua, where political leaders created state women's agencies in order to promote women's interests and rights within a broader project of state building (Chun, 2001; Craske, 1999; Howell, 1998; Molyneux, 2000). Popular women participated en masse in organizations such as the Federation of Cuban Women, the All-China Women's Federation, and the Luisa Amanda Espinoza Association of Nicaraguan Women. These organizations provided some scope for addressing gender inequalities, but women's interests were often secondary to greater political goals of national unity and development. Looking at Cuba and Nicaragua, Nikki Craske (1999: 140) suggests that rather than becoming subsumed into the state, women need to maintain an independent women's movement in order to "provide alternative agendas and strategies, which in turn maintain pressure on the regime." The experiences of barrio women in Chávez's Venezuela, however, do not fit neatly into the categories of either mass women's organizations or independent women's movements as defined in this literature.

Barrio women in Venezuela are not organized within mass women's organizations. Women in the Chávez administration created a new National Institute for Women, known as INAMujer, which was established by presidential decree in 2000. INAMujer's predecessors were the National Women's Council (CONAMU), created in 1992, and the Presidential Women's Advisory Commission (COFEAPRE), established in 1974 (Friedman, 2000). INAMujer works together with barrio women, but this organization does not have a mass membership like its counterparts in Cuba and Nicaragua. INAMujer presides over such women's groupings as the Bolivarian Forces (Fuerzas Bolivarianas) and the Meeting Points (Puntos de Encuentro), but to date neither of these organizations has succeeded in incorporating barrio women to a significant degree. Nor have barrio women formed autonomous women's movements like Women for Dignity and Life (Mujeres por la Dignidad y la Vida) in the revolutionary context of El Salvador or the Mothers of the Plaza de Mayo in Argentina. The Círculos Femeninos of the 1970s were not an autonomous social movement; they were linked to a Christian nongovernmental organization known as the Popular Action Service Center (Centro al Servicio de Acción Popular, CESAP).

Instead of forming either mass organizations or independent movements, barrio women in Venezuela work in the context of local community organizations, some of which have long histories. Yet while these women tend to work in local spaces and engage in struggles outside of the state, they still strongly identify with government-directed programs and leaders such as Chávez. How can we conceptualize this kind of political activism? As argued elsewhere, we need alternatives to dichotomous classifications of state feminism and independent movements (Fernandes, 2006). That earlier article draws on the distinctions made by various scholars between "independent movements," which set their own goals; "associational linkages," where autonomous groups choose to work with other political organizations; and "directed mobilization," where authority and initiative come from outside (Molyneux, 1998; Randall, 1998). Like the activists of the Cuban feminist organization Magín (Fernandes, 2006), barrio women in Venezuela also work in association with official institutions and programs, while maintaining a degree of autonomy through their local organizing work in domestic and community spaces. But at the same time, barrio women are always vulnerable to directed mobilization from above and the institutionalization of their struggles, which Amy Lind (2005: 90) argues may lead to increased work responsibilities without changes in women's conditions of life.

In addition to the practical consequences of women's involvement in state-managed programs, this chapter seeks to explore the role of discourse, self-esteem, and nurturance in women's mobilization under a populist system. Lola Luna has described the impact of populist discourse on women's movements in Latin America. On the one hand, she suggests that the populist regimes of Perón in Argentina, Cárdenas in Mexico, and Vargas in Brazil developed a maternalist ideology that sought to maintain reproductive control over women, to utilize their capacities as social agents of development, and to exploit their economic productivity (Luna, 1995: 252). On the other hand, the contradictions of this maternalist ideology, and the new social order that it represented, opened possibilities for women to construct new subjectivities in response to their political exclusion (Luna, 1995: 254). This schema needs to be retooled for an analysis of contemporary populism, where maternalist ideology is no longer rooted in developmentalist concerns of labor discipline, particularly given changing regimes of labor and capital. But women's emerging activism does need to be understood in relation to what Magdalena Valdivieso (2004) has called "the foundational imaginary of heroism," latent in much of Chávez's political rhetoric, as well as ideological constructions of women as nurturers and carers. Like the Sandinista maternal ideal of Madres Sufridas that Lorraine Bayard de Volo (2001: 121) discusses in Nicaragua, notions of revolutionary motherhood are also used in Venezuela to appeal to barrio women, a construction that both reinforces older roles and creates the groundwork for new possible roles and identities to emerge.

Histories of Gender and Politics

Barrio women's activism under Chávez must be located within the history of women's organizing in Venezuela and also the history of grassroots community movements in the barrios. In the early phase of the women's movement in Venezuela during the 1940s, it was mainly middle-class women who mobilized in support of civil and economic demands (Friedman, 2000: 6). But during the struggle against the Marcos Pérez Jiménez dictatorship in the 1950s, women from a range of social strata became engaged in politics. Veteran feminist activist Argelia Laya recalls defending her rights as a woman in the base committees (*comités de base*) of the Communist Youth in the barrios: "I never accepted that they assigned me secondary roles or they discriminated against me. I always protested it" (cited in Petzoldt and Bevilacqua, 1979: 226).

Cross-party and cross-class organizing were facilitated by the creation of a Women's Committee (Comité Femenino). But following the transition to democracy in 1958, women were demobilized. Terry Karl (1987) refers to

Venezuela democracy after 1958 as a "pacted democracy" because fundamental issues, including a development model based on foreign capital and state intervention in processes of union bargaining, were decided before they could be open to public debate through the holding of elections. According to Friedman (1998), the united activism of women was seen as a threat to this pacted democracy, which sought to exclude the Community Party and independent social actors. The Women's Committee was converted into the National Women's Union and was then disbanded in 1961 (Friedman, 2000: 128). Women of different classes were excluded from participation in the posttransition period as they faced gender bias within dominant parties and their own organizations were closed down.

Women were involved in the guerrilla struggles of the 1960s that arose to contest the conditions of pacted democracy. But given the male-dominated structures of guerrilla organizations, women did not often play a primary role alongside men. It was not until the 1970s that women would again engage in grassroots activism. During this period, women began to organize autonomously in response to their exclusion from political life. As Friedman (2000: 163) shows, this new phase in women's organizing was often divided by issues of class as middle-class women organized in the feminist movement and lower-class women in local community organizations. Like elsewhere in Latin America, feminist groups sought to establish independence from party politics and were often informed by a socialist perspective. These efforts continued into the 1980s, with a campaign to reform the civil code led by a professional women's organization, the Venezuelan Federation of Female Lawyers (FEVA). The campaign sought equal rights for wives and husbands regarding property and divorce, and equal rights for children born out of wedlock (Friedman, 2000: 176). The success of the reform, passed by the Congress in July 1982, was due to the coalition building and broad tactics applied by the women. Some of the reform provisions did affect poor women, many of whom did have children out of wedlock, and women from the Círculos Femeninos helped create links with popular women (Friedman, 2000: 186). But as Friedman (2000: 186) notes, "Most of the reform provisions reflected a middle- or upper-class perspective—for example, because poor women rarely got married, they would not benefit from a changed divorce law, and their partners usually did not have property to share or inheritance to leave." These class biases were also reflected in later campaigns, such as the campaign to reform the labor law. Since most of the reform leaders were elite women who relied on domestic labor, the rights of domestic workers were not included in the campaign (Friedman, 2000: 194). While efforts in women's organizing did impact poor women somewhat, they were more focused on the demands of educated, professional women.

Popular women's organizing in the early 1970s emerged with the formation of the Círculos Femeninos. The Círculos Femeninos sought to address
the specific problems of poor women, they rejected interference by political
parties, and they sought to build a decentralized and nonhierarchical movement (Friedman, 2000: 169–71). The aims of the Círculos Femeninos were
closely linked to problems in the barrio, such as health, education, jobs, and
facilities (García Guadilla, 1993: 76). But at the same time, the Círculos were
a part of CESAP, a large male-dominated NGO. Being part of this institution
prevented the poor women from taking up more radical feminist demands,
but as the women started to participate in coalitions with feminist groups
during the 1980s, they began to question the male leadership of CESAP and
the gendered division of labor in the organization (García Guadilla, 1993: 77).
The Círculos Femeninos were an important initiative in support of popular
women, but the organization relied on outside facilitators to "train" women,
and their dependence on outside funding reduced their autonomy and spon-
taneity as a women's organization.

At the same time, barrio women had begun to engage in organic forms
of community activism jointly with the men in the barrio. One of the most
important campaigns in which women engaged in the early 1970s was the
struggle against urban remodeling. In San Agustín, Christian Democratic
president Rafael Caldera (1969–1974) promoted a housing program known
as "The New San Agustín" that proposed to eliminate the *ranchos* (small
dwellings) and to build houses in the lower and middle ranges of the hills,
while the higher hills would become public gardens, uniting the Botanical
Gardens and the Parque los Caobos. The residents of San Agustín del Sur
formed a Committee Against Displacement (Comité Contra los Desalojos),
which proved that the price being paid for each square of land was not that indicated by the Municipal Office of Urban Planning (OMPU). Carlos Andrés
Pérez from Democratic Action (AD) came to power in 1974, and in his "V
Plan of the Nation" he continued his predecessor's plans for urban remodeling and displacement of barrio residents (Baptista and Marchionda, 1992). In
response, the movement of community resistance grew stronger and spread
to other parishes such as La Vega, El Valle, and La Pastora, where residents
also formed Committees Against Displacement to challenge the government
policy.

In San Agustín, the campaign against displacement was linked to broader
community issues through the movement El Afinque de Marín, started by
the Grupo Madera in 1977. The original Grupo Madera was a radical cultural
movement that was concerned with building solidarity and unity among the
members of the barrio. Most members of the group perished in a tragic ac-
cident in the Orinoco river while touring the country in 1980. According to

one of the surviving members of the group, Nelly Ramos (2004: 176), Grupo Madera wanted to "forge an ideological consciousness . . . above all, to give incentive to all the participants to define their corresponding role as the protagonists of a cultural response that was emerging in the heart of the community." Like the black women in the Black Power movement in the United States, the women of Grupo Madera sought to revive a sense of black pride and dignity.

One of the members, Alejandrina Ramos, reinterpreted the poem "El Negro Lorenzo" by Venezuelan poet Miguel Otero Silva in a composition known as "Ritual" or "La Negra Lorenza." The subject of Ramos's song composition is the black woman: while Otero Silva's "negro" is the slave of all, Ramos's "negra" is slave to men as well. The reworking of the song with the black woman as the subject points to the intersectionality of race, gender, and class oppression, and attempts to overcome this oppression: "Black woman, slave of all, I am no one's slave." With their natural afro hairstyles and African clothing, the black women of Grupo Madera launched a struggle of cultural resistance, what the song refers to as "rebelde el pelo," or "rebellion of hair." Grupo Madera reclaimed black subjectivity and revindicated black culture as the basis of an autochthonous culture.

The 1970s was a moment of community-based activism in many parishes and barrios across Caracas. Large numbers of barrio women mobilized during the protests and hunger strikes led by Jesuit worker priests (*curas obreros*) such as Francisco Wuytack and José Antonio Angós. Wuytack was based in the barrio Carmen, in the parish of La Vega. When Wuytack arrived in the barrio in 1966, he noticed the poor schooling conditions of the local children, who did not have adequate facilities above the third grade. When he asked if the children could attend the private Colegio San José de Tarbes in the neighboring middle-class enclave of Paraiso, he was told that he was a dreamer.[1] Wuytack went several times to the school with the children and their mothers, who were accused of being a disturbance. Wuytack and the women stayed outside the school, singing hymns and chanting, but several were taken to prison and beaten.[2]

The activities helped the women of the community to organize and realize the injustices they faced as compared with the neighboring urbanization of Paraiso. In 1976 there was a major landslide in the sector Los Canjilones, and several barrio residents were trapped and died. Hermelinda Machado, a barrio resident from Callejon 19 de Abril, recalls that the women of the barrio launched large protests against the government for its failure to carry out rescue efforts.[3] Together with Angós, they organized a hunger strike against the proposed relocation of the surviving barrio residents (Herrera de Weishaar, Ferreira, and Cabrera, 1977: 168). The worker priests played an important role in facilitating women's protest and community activism in La Vega during this time.

In the parish of 23 de Enero, women had also begun to participate in sport, cultural, and community-based organizations with close links to the community during the 1970s. The residents of public housing engaged in similar protest actions as residents of other barrios. On December 23, 1981, to protest the buildings' severe states of disrepair, residents engaged in hijackings of public and private vehicles, demanding that the government address the problems. Four weeks later, the government agreed to fix the elevators and the open sewers, to provide electricity cables and telephone service, and to provide permanent services of garbage collection (Contreras, 2000: 54–56). As barrio residents united around shared goals of community work, they created new spaces of activism outside of the organized left groups who had predominated in the previous decade of urban guerrilla struggle, as well as the political parties and their organisms in the barrios. Popular women played an important role in community organizations and struggles, but unlike the middle-class feminists, they had less access to the political arena (García Guadilla, 1993: 84). As Machado says, "We had a voice, but we were not heard."[4]

During the period of the 1980s and 1990s, Venezuelan women faced a new series of challenges given the economic and political crisis that hit the country. On February 18, 1983, otherwise known as "Black Friday," the currency collapsed, leading to a period of hyperinflation and economic stagnation (Levine, 1998; Silva Michelena, 1999). As a response to rising interest rates, the government of Luis Herrera Campíns devalued the currency and initiated a set of controls over the economy to prevent the massive flight of private capital (Silva Michelena, 1999: 92). When Pérez returned to office in 1989, he announced the adoption of a "neoliberal packet," consisting of austerity measures such as dismantling government subsidies to local industries, deregulating prices, and reducing social spending.

The initial price increases associated with these measures led to massive popular riots on February 27, 1989, which induced the government to implement some social policies for an interim period. The neoliberal packet was revived in April 1996 in consultation with the IMF as a program of macroeconomic stabilization known as Agenda Venezuela (Silva Michelena, 1999: 103). While Agenda Venezuela did succeed in stabilizing the economy to some degree, it also contributed to the increase in marginality, poverty, and unemployment. Between 1984 and 1995, those living below the poverty line went from 36 to 66 percent, and those in extreme poverty tripled from 11 to 36 percent (Roberts, 2004: 59). In December 1997 there were 3 million homes in poverty and more than 1.6 million homes in situations of extreme poverty (Silva Michelena, 1999: 95). The growth in poverty was related to a number of factors, including the large-scale loss of employment, higher prices and reduced purchasing power due to inflation, and reduced government spending on social programs. There were major cuts in social spending, including cuts of over 40 percent in education, 70 percent in housing, and 37 percent in health (Roberts, 2004: 59). Unemployment, inflation, and cuts in social spending impacted the poorest 40 percent of the population most strongly, leading to growing urban segregation.

In the context of growing urban poverty and declining services, women created their own alternative organizations and survival networks to confront the crisis. In 1992 the Círculos Femeninos split from their parent organization, CESAP, and began to organize more autonomously. At the same time, there was increasing funding available from international donors and agencies for women's organizations constituted as NGOs. The Coordinating Committee of Women's NGOs (Coordinadora de Organizaciones No-Gubernamentales de Mujeres, CONG), founded in the 1980s, received international support and finance during the preparations for the UN World Conferences on Women in Nairobi and Beijing in 1985 and 1995 (Friedman, 1999).

Many theorists have noted the paradoxes of international donor funding for women's organizations (Alvarez, 1999; Lind, 1997, 2005; Schild, 1998). In a context of privatization and cutbacks to social welfare, women in NGOs often find themselves providing the services that used to be the responsibility of the state. In Venezuela, international foundations such as UNICEF and the National Fund for Infant Attention (El Fondo Nacional de Atención a la Infancia, FONAIN) provided funding for Day Care Centers (Hogares de Cuidado Diario) in 1987, with the aim of establishing forty-two thousand centers by 1993. This program, which involved large numbers of women as "carer mothers," was a continuation of programs established during the first administration of Pérez (Delgado Arria, 1995: 62). The Círculos Femeninos were also incorporated into the World Bank–funded Social Fund (El Fondo Social), in charge of over fourteen compensatory programs.[5] While providing some relief for women in a context of economic crisis, these programs also served to institutionalize women's struggles for survival (Lind, 2005: 89). This often meant an increased workload for poorer women and a lower likelihood that the conditions of structural adjustment policies would be challenged.

Chávez and the Resurgence of Women's Participation

While the events of the Caracazo came in the context of a growing crisis, they also helped to spark the reemergence of urban social movements in the barrios of Venezuela. In the early 1990s, the community movement Macarao and Its People (Macarao y su Gente) emerged in the parish of Macarao (Grohmann, 1996). After a series of protests and organizing efforts in the parish 23 de Enero, barrio residents formed the Coordinadora Simón Bolívar in 1993. As compared to the petitioning, lobbying, and negotiation favored by the middle-class neighborhood movements, urban social movements in the barrios pursued more radical tactics of protests, hijackings of public vehicles, and community takeovers of public spaces (Ramos Rollon, 1995). Coinciding with growing activism in the barrios was the emergence of a clandestine radical grouping within the military known as the Movimiento Bolivariano Revolucionario 200 (MBR-200), which was led by Chávez (López Maya, 2004). The coup attempt by this group in February 1992 was crushed, but Chávez asked to be allowed to speak on television to advise insurgents in other cities to surrender peacefully (Gott, 2000: 70). In his appearance, Chávez said that, "For now, the objectives that we had set ourselves have not been achieved in the capital." The phrase, "For now," or "Por Ahora," became the rallying cry of diverse sectors who were frustrated with the orientation of the mainstream parties and were looking for alternatives. According to Margarita López Maya, David Smilde, and Keta Stephany (1999: 205), Chávez was a powerful counterimage projected as capable of unifying social movements and opposing neoliberalism. Following the unsuccessful February coup, Chávez was imprisoned in military jail, and in November of the same year his fellow officers launched a second coup attempt, which was also unsuccessful.

But the coup attempts and the final attainment of office by Chávez in 1998 were important catalysts in the politicization and growing participation of broader sectors of society, including women, in new spheres of popular action. Women organized to elect women-friendly candidates to the new constituent assembly that Chávez convened in 1999, and they lobbied to include articles pertaining to sexual and reproductive rights in the drafting of the new constitution, approved by referendum in 1999 (Castillo and Salvatierra, 2000; Muñoz, 2000; Rakowski, 2003). In July 2000, Chávez again stood for election under the new constitution and was reelected for a six-year term of office. On April 11, 2002, there was a brief opposition-led coup against Chávez, who was brought back to power two days later as a result of massive popular protests, mainly involving women from the popular classes. Popular women mobilized again during the recall referendum in May 2004, called by the opposition to determine whether Chávez should be recalled from office. They played a major role in campaigns to register and mobilize people to vote, and they staffed voter registration centers in the barrios, ultimately leading to the success of Chávez in the referendum.

Longtime feminists have occupied important positions in the Chávez government and in the state women's agency, INAMujer. Some women have been involved in the movement of Chavismo, which includes Chávez's party, the Fifth Republic Movement (Movimiento Quinta República, MVR), mass organizations such as the Francisco Miranda Front (Frente Francisco Miranda), and the National Union of Workers (Unión Nacional de Trabajadores, UNT). But Chavista organizations tend to be hierarchically organized and male dominated, along the lines of traditional political parties and unions. For this reason, rather than entering Chavista organizations, many barrio women have become involved in a parallel social revolution known as the *proceso*. José Roberto Duque (2004) defines the proceso as a parallel and underground movement that defends the Chávez government but which has its own trajectory independent of directives from the central government. Many women participating in the *proceso* do not identify as Chavista. They may participate in Chávez's programs, such as soup kitchens, land committees, and the "missions," and they may even look toward Chávez for leadership and direction. But they have sources of identity that come from their barrio or parish and which form the basis of alternative social and community networks.

New sectors of women have entered into community work through the social programs introduced by the Chávez government. One of the programs introduced by Chávez is a college-level work-study program known as Misión Ribas. Billboards for the program placed strategically in subways and at the intersections of central roads and highways in the barrios appeal specifically to women. One of these shows a young mestiza woman, Ana Guerrero, standing in front of her small house, or *rancho*. The caption says that while today she is a housewife, tomorrow she will be a business administrator. Others show black and indigenous women who are moving out of their traditional roles of domestic workers and craftspersons to become social workers and doctors. The presence of black and mestiza women on billboards is a radical departure from standard commercial advertisements, such as the ads for Polar beer dotting the city landscape, which present highly sexualized portraits of women in skimpy bikinis, with European features and long flowing blond hair. The representation of barrio women as business administrators, social workers, and doctors is also a dramatic change from conventional representations and class expectations.

In additional to the educational programs, which range from literacy programs (Misión Robinson) to work-study programs (Misión Ribas) and university courses (Misión Sucre), Chávez has encouraged barrio residents to create a range of committees and cooperative organizations. By an executive decree in 2002, Chávez provided the basis for Urban Land Committees (Comités de Tierra), in order to rationalize land tenancy through surveys, distribution of land deeds, and development of property belonging to the community (Ellner, 2005: 24). Since most dwellings in the barrios were constructed through a process of mass occupation as people moved to Caracas from the countryside, few homeowners possess the deeds or title to their land. In March 2005 there were more than four thousand Urban Land Committees in the urban capitals of Venezuela that had distributed about 170,000 property titles (Botía, 2005). Through the program Barrio Adentro, Chávez has created a series of popular clinics in the barrios, staffed by some twelve thousand Cuban doctors (Ellner, 2005: 23). In March 2005 there were over five thousand Health Committees (Comités de Salud), which were created to supervise and help out with the Barrio Adentro program (Botía, 2005). Another initiative introduced by the Chávez government are soup kitchens (*casas alimentarias*), where needy children and single mothers from the barrios receive one free meal a day. During 2004 there were 4,052 soup kitchens established in Venezuela.[6] In 2001 the government also created a women's lending agency, known as the Woman's Bank (Banco de la Mujer), to make financial services available to poorer women (Castañeda, 2004: 27).

Not surprisingly, the participants in these programs and committees have overwhelmingly been women.[7] As many scholars have noted, the centrality of women to the life of the barrio (Martín-Barbero, 1993: 198), gender roles that assign domestic and reproductive tasks to women (Rodriguez, 1994: 34), and women's exclusion from traditional male spheres of politics such as parties and trade unions (Caldeira, 1990) have bolstered their participation in such domestic, community-related concerns as health, education, and rights to land title. Women themselves reaffirmed these reasons when asked about their participation. In June 2004, a group of women from San Agustín were going door-to-door to carry out a census of the residents of the *ranchos* in the upper reaches of the barrio Hornos de Cal and other barrios of the parish, for the purposes of new social programs. One of the women, Clara Brinson, related that women were mobilizing in the social programs because "we women are the ones who almost always have to carry the burden of housework; we are the ones who most feel the weight of this work. Men, by nature, are used to coming home on Fridays, having their beer." It is this awareness of domestic responsibility that encourages some women to become central actors in community and social work.

However, other women pointed to the importance of Chávez as a catalyst for the mass involvement of women in popular politics. Carmen Teresa Barrios, an activist from the Carretera Negra of La Vega, pointed to the April 2002 coup against Chávez and the role of women in bringing him back to power:

> For me this comes since Chávez. I am forty-something years old, and never in my life have I cared about what was happening in my country, and I'm saying my country, but also my Carretera where I live. . . . It's like I am fulfilled. This work fulfills me. I want to be involved in everything, I want to participate in

everything, I really feel that someone needs me and I can do it. . . . That's why I say it was Chávez who awoke the woman. He gave us importance, value. . . . I studied, but I never felt interested to participate or do other things, to care about people other than myself. . . . It was this voice that told us we could do it, that if we are united we can achieve something. I was one of those people who never thought about taking to the streets, like I did on April 11th, when they overthrew our president. I said, "My God, is this what you feel when you fight for what is yours?" I went all the way to Maracay in a car. I took a flag and I said to the others, "My God, what am I doing?" I didn't recognize myself. . . . This was all asleep within me and because of this man, his calling, his way of being, or I don't know what, I got involved in this thing. . . . And then I wanted to face the president himself, and tell him how things should be; you may want to do it this way, but I don't agree, that we should do it in this other way in order to achieve what we aim to do. That's why I tell you it was an awakening, a calling, and he made us women go out into the streets, he made us realize that as women we can also struggle, we can do it and be involved.

Carmen Teresa's narrative contains several layers. On the one hand, there is a story of an awakening of almost biblical proportions: there is a "calling" and women have responded to this calling of the president. As Richard Gott (2000: 146) argues, Chávez often appeals to a highly religious population with his rhetoric of an evangelical preacher, invoking love and redemption; his millenarian notion of a new start after the evils of the past; and his campaign posters that contain portraits not dissimilar to evangelical pictures of Christ. Carmen Teresa's narrative reflects this kind of popular religious discourse appropriated by Chavismo. On the other hand, there is an awareness that Carmen Teresa knows best her "Carretera," as she refers to her barrio, and if she does not agree with the president, she can tell him the right way to do things. This latter aspect disrupts our ability to read the narrative as a populist manipulation of women's agency, as Carmen Teresa is expressing an initiative to decide what is best for her community, rather than waiting for orders from above. This aspect is important and will be further demonstrated through examples below. Carmen Teresa's narrative further expresses the importance that poor women activists feel as a result of Chávez's emphasis on the protagonism of the poorer classes as a motor force for change in society.

The other notable aspect of Carmen Teresa's narrative, and one found in other narratives as well, is the quality of nurturance: "I really feel that someone needs me and I can do it." Many women's narratives strongly brought out these emotive aspects of community participation, which also go beyond the more economy-focused explanations of "practical needs" prevalent in the literature. This aspect of nurturance and maternal caring is not only common to the new activists who have been spurred into action through Chávez. Susana Rodríguez, a leftist militant for over twenty years in the parish 23 de Enero, noted that,

"Women are always at the forefront, and I think this has to do with maternity, with this necessity to look after and protect. To look after the fatherland, to look after the barrio, to look after friends, to look after the husband, to look after the president. It is a feeling that is generated among us women." Veteran women activists, as well as newer ones, used tropes of motherhood as a way of describing their involvement in politics. Various scholars have also found that women use discourses of nurturance and their maternal role to frame their participation and construct a sense of collective identity (Bayard de Volo, 2001; James, 2000; Lind, 2005; Morgen, 1988). But as Lynn Stephen (1997) argues, rather than understanding women's participation in terms of essentialized or uniform identities of motherhood, we need to look at the internal contradictions and differences being negotiated among women. While for some barrio women their history of local community organizing is at the center of their approach to politics, to others it is their maternal feelings toward the president, and for others still some combination of these, that has spurred their involvement in politics.

Daily Life and Popular Organizing

By looking at the intersection of everyday life and popular organizing, what Elizabeth Jelin (1987: 11) refers to as *lo cotidiano*, or "the everyday," this section attempts to give greater depth to the daily experience of popular organizing. I focus on the experiences of activists in the Carretera Negra, where I have carried out ongoing research with the women of the barrio. The barrio consists of a line of houses located along a stretch of highway road, as indicated by its name, "Black Highway," and along three smaller lanes, Oriente, 24 de Julio, and Justicia, situated in the broader parish of La Vega, in the west of Caracas. The barrio is composed of about 140 families and is a close-knit community with a long history of organizing tied to the parish of La Vega. One of the main community leaders in the Carretera Negra, Freddy Mendoza, came to Caracas as a child. From a young age, he was involved in community activism with other young people such as Edgar "El Gordo" Pérez from the sector Las Casitas. These leaders came of age during the struggles of the 1970s, when residents from the Carretera Negra participated in the protests and hunger strikes for education, employment, and basic services. In the 1980s they banded together with residents from sectors to demand the removal of a local cement factory that was contaminating the area, to protest the building of a prison in the barrio, and to protect large green areas of the neighborhood from being taken over for other government projects. Through this process, the activists developed a community newspaper, organized cultural and sporting events for members of the community, and built a sense of collectivity.

Many women of the Carretera Negra such as Carmen Pérez, Freddy's wife, were also involved in these struggles. Through these struggles and the history of democratic participation in the sector, involving decision making by popular assembly, the activists have been able to retain a sense of their individual identity as they participate in the *proceso*. Stephen (1997: 138) has argued that it is in "cohesive neighborhoods with a history of shared struggle" that collective strategies such as communal kitchens may find fertile ground. Moreover, she argues that women who have participated alongside men through these struggles are also more likely to be valued for their independent contributions (1997: 138). Stephen's observations are borne out in the context of the Carretera Negra, where women activists took the lead in implementing programs such as Barrio Adentro and the communal kitchens. The women of the Carretera Negra first formed their Health Committee in July 2003, when a Cuban doctor was sent to the barrio. The women found a house that was to be used as the popular clinic; they looked for equipment, chairs, and beds; and they found him a residence within the barrio. They organized meetings between the Cuban doctor and the community, they took health censuses, and they visited families to explain the idea of the popular clinics. In September 2003 the women started up an Urban Land Committee, which consisted of twenty-one people who took censuses of families, and began to distribute land titles, giving titles to ninety-eight families by June 2004. A year later, in September 2004, the community activists set up a soup kitchen, and this was functioning by October.

The premises of the soup kitchen are rooms in the house of barrio resident Osvaldo Mendoza, a police officer who had never before participated in community work. Osvaldo noted, "I was never a *vecino* [neighbor] who was very involved with the community because of my work . . . but seeing the necessities of our communities, what I've seen as a police officer, the necessities you see in the streets, I offered my house when this opportunity came." Osvaldo and his family worked together with the women of the community to set up the kitchen, and he is actively involved in its activities, unloading materials from the trucks, serving the children, and carrying out surveys in the barrio. He is often the only man present in community assemblies, which tend to be dominated by women. According to Osvaldo, people even joke about his presence as a man: "In the meetings we have a joke, a game that when they speak of '*ellas*' [the women] or '*nosotras*' [us women], I'm included. The women make fun of me: 'Well, the señora Osvalda. . . .'" The jokes reveal the gendered nature of community work: like domestic chores, it is still assumed to be women's work. But the participation of men in community work is also changing perspectives about domestic responsibility. As Osvaldo said, "I don't feel bad because this is women's work; no, this is also men's work." The participation of men in the soup kitchen is a signal to other men that cooking and domestic work are not only women's work.

This section draws on material from two popular assemblies held in the homes and meeting spaces of the Carretera Negra. The first was a general assembly held on January 27, 2005, and it brought together activists from various barrios in La Vega. The second popular assembly was on June 22, 2005, and it convened the activists of the barrio to discuss the progress of the soup kitchen. These assemblies and the discussions in which people engaged illustrate the possibilities and the limitations of popular organizing for creating new forms of gender relations and popular politics. Following other work that has been done on experiences of soup kitchens in Lima, Peru, I find that participation in collective experiences such as popular assemblies and soup kitchens, while not explicitly feminist enterprises, are important in challenging a gendered division of labor and perceptions of women's role in politics (Lind, 1997; Mujica, 1992).

The first assembly was particularly notable because it was an example of the kinds of discussions that have begun to lead to the challenging of gender hierarchies and male dominance in popular organizing. In January 2005 we were gathered in Zaida's living room, a large room with windows overlooking the hills of the parish. More than thirty people filled the room and spilled out into the adjoining rooms of her *rancho*. Those present were mainly women, and as the night went on, people came and left the room. Various topics were discussed, including the relationship between the community and institutions, the local council elections scheduled for August, and activities being organized by the community. Freddy Mendoza had told me earlier that during the assembly he also wanted to have a serious discussion about the participation of women and issues of gender. When Freddy opened the discussion, his wife Carmen responded, "We women participate more because the majority of us are unemployed. We are in the home, and our husbands, whoever they are, are out there working, so we collaborate with each other, we are aware of the problems that exist in the community." Carmen Teresa disagreed with her, saying that it's only because of Chávez that women have begun to participate: "For me all of this comes from Chávez." Lina agreed with her: "Chávez has opened my eyes and won me over. I began to get involved in the cooperative, in the community." "El Gordo" Edgar put forward his point of view:

We have always had a strong presence of women in all the revolutionary movements of this parish, but they have been discriminated [against] by history that is based in the macro and not in *cotidianeidad* [daily life]. . . . Carmen Teresa had her political awakening with the discourse of Chávez, the fall of the government, the coup. By contrast, I have strong memories of women participating; in fact, I think that the women are fighters and the men are a hindrance. My mother arrived here in the year 1964, because these barrios up in Las Casitas were built by people from the communities and they put down the pipes for water to reach there. It was the women, together with the children, who carried up the pipes. The men arrived at five in the evening from work, and they worked on the pipes till ten at night. This is what I remember of here in Caracas, where women had a very important role. We also have to have another discussion when we talk about gender, without falling into economism. I am black and I define myself as black. . . . I think we have to fight these battles together.

As a long-term community activist, El Gordo thus dates his political awakening to before Chávez, with roots in a longer historical struggle over race and class. Freddy summarized the discussion:

There are some key points. First, that it's not just now that women are participating to address the problems of the community. We are talking about experiences of thirty-something years that we have lived through. . . . Recently we protested INOS [National Institute of Sanitary Works, Instituto Nacional de Obras Sanitarias] so that they would resolve our water issues, and 90 percent of the people protesting were women with their children. . . . I think that this is a natural attitude women have because they are permanently in the community and this produces a sensibility toward problems faced by the community. Meanwhile the husband is occupied with his work, exploitation, he leaves at six in the morning and returns at eight at night to ask for food and watch television. He doesn't have this same kind of sensibility, and on weekends he just restricts the time of women, because of jealousy, because of machismo, for a range of factors.

The discussion seemed to center on the historical and contemporary role of women in the barrios, with Carmen, Freddy and El Gordo suggesting that women play an important role in community activism because the barrio is the location of their daily lives and work. Carmen Teresa and Lina, who have become politicized much more recently, point out that large numbers of women have only become involved in politics since Chávez has come into power. While for Carmen Teresa and Lina, their involvement in politics is more dependent on Chávez's charismatic leadership, El Gordo seeks to build local and independent leadership. He said,

The government has many problems, we are trying to construct something here, from ourselves, together. It's our only possibility. It might happen that the United States wants to come here and intervene, but they're not going to stop our *proceso*, because our *proceso* didn't begin with Chávez and it won't end with Chávez.

In their discussions, the long-term and newer activists articulate and negotiate these questions of autonomy versus dependency and the relationship of their movements to the government.

Freddy then reoriented the discussion to address questions of machismo and how it affects women's participation:

> And in this revolutionary process today, I find it strange that we have not addressed issues of machismo. I think that in this moment we are living, we have to think about how we as males can help, for example, in the work of the home so that women can have time to participate and become leaders.... For example, José Luis cooks and I'm sure his food has more flavor than his wife's cooking. He doesn't lose his manhood because she drinks a cold beer.... That is, share the work of the home and work together with your *compañera*.... Manhood is not about never cooking, washing the dishes, or washing your own clothes; it is a conception of power. And if we are in this revolution, we have to break with the structures of power that are being generated in the home. These are structures of domination of men over women.

José Luis, another man present at the meeting, responded that "yes, to be a real man is to assume responsibility.... To assume the kind of responsibilities that Venezuelan women do is difficult. There in the hills [points out the window] we have a number of *ranchos*, and the majority of women living there are single women who work, attend to their children, and carry the responsibility of the home.... Really, here the woman is relegated to a second-class status; women are very mistreated by their families." The fact that this discussion was being initiated by men and not women is partly related to the structures of male privilege themselves that have enabled men to contemplate these questions and promote new lines of thinking. Yet the involvement of these men alongside their *compañeras* in community work has opened their eyes to these gender differences and made them more sensitive to questions of male privilege.

Carlos, a representative of the mayor's office, had been invited to the assembly to listen to the community's perspective. Since Juan Barreto, a Chavista mayor, was elected in November 2004, community leaders had been trying to make connections with the mayor's office in order for the community to have access to funding and projects being channeled through there. But Carlos's perspective provided a strong contrast to José Luis, Freddy, and El Gordo. Carlos dominated the discussion where José Luis, Freddy, and El Gordo held back so that others could speak. When women were invited to respond to particular points, Carlos interjected with his opinion. Following José Luis's incisive comment about the problems faced by single women in the barrios, Carlos responded by saying, "I don't want to change the subject, but I can add the anecdote that they say in the home, when there are no men, women urinate standing up." This kind of crude joke, combined with Carlos's domineering presence, provided an alternative pole to the kind of awareness and self-criticism that the male community activists present were trying to encourage.

At the second assembly, five months later, the women of the Carretera had begun to take a much more proactive role. This assembly was convened to discuss the progress of the soup kitchen. The process of organizing the soup kitchen had been a positive organizational experience for the women. Like with the popular clinic, they had taken the initiative in repainting the rooms, stocking it with the necessary cookware, and carrying out a census in the barrio to determine the needy families who were eligible for meals. Every day a government truck arrives with supplies, and Osvaldo is usually on hand to help the women unload these, but all the work of preparing the food is done by the women. While the participation of the women activists in the soup kitchen is not overtly challenging traditional gender roles, it is bringing about other changes, as Helen Safa (1990: 361) has argued in another context: "the collectivization of private tasks, such as food preparation and child care, is transforming women's roles, even though they are not undertaken as conscious challenges to gender subordination." Food preparation is increasingly being seen as a job, performed for the most part by women, that should be assumed by the community and not by individual women. The basis of the soup kitchen is women's voluntary participation and the networks of mutual support that have existed for many years in the barrio.

The assembly was convened for three in the afternoon, but since the *vecinas* all live close by one another, they just called to each other and knocked on each others' doors as they made their way up to the premises of the soup kitchen. In the soup kitchen, we sat around on wooden chairs, mostly borrowed from neighbors. There was a total of twenty-five people, consisting of twenty-two women and three men. The soup kitchen is run by five women, who work full-time, five days a week, to provide lunch to over 140 to 150 people daily. The women began the assembly by raising concerns about the amount of work involved in maintaining the soup kitchen. One of the cooks, Gladys, recounted that the women must begin the work the evening before, washing and soaking the beans, cleaning the rice, cutting the chicken, and generally preparing the food. At 1:30 p.m. the children come for lunch, and they must be served and attended to. Afterward, the women spend several hours cleaning up. Gladys said that since the women are not being paid, they must simultaneously attend to the needs of their own families. The problem raised by Gladys is akin to what Caroline Moser (1986) has referred to as a "triple burden," which includes productive work, reproductive work, and community-managing work.

Some scholars have noted the ways in which women's labor has been appropriated under populist governments, such as Alberto Fujimori in Peru or Sixto Durán-Ballén in Ecuador, as a means of providing essential services to households as the neoliberal state retreats from this role (Barrig, 1996; Lind, 2005; Paley, 2001). This devolving of responsibility for welfare services was characteristic of the day-care centers and World Bank–funded women's projects under previous administrations of Herrera Campíns and Pérez in Venezuela. Social policy under Chávez is guided by contradictory principles that retain some aspects of this neoliberal approach toward decentralization of service provision, shifting responsibility toward poorer sectors. But at the same time, state-sponsored programs under Chávez constitute part of a range of other social-welfare strategies that aim to channel funds toward social development and away from a neoliberal market model. Moreover, in contrast to the "privatization of the struggle for daily survival" (Lind, 1997: 1208), the women's use of popular assemblies is a means for exercising democratic control over the soup kitchens and thinking through collective solutions to the dilemma of a double or triple workload. The assembly had been called for precisely this reason. Various people proposed that they roster extra people to help with the work so that it does not fall on the five women only, and others suggested gathering donations in the community to pay the women a small wage.

Another woman, Judy, then raised another problem, related to the ingredients delivered by the government. While they received fixed menus from the government, often the ingredients do not match the menus. Like women as mothers are accustomed to employing creative strategies to stretch the family income and resolve problems (Safa, 1990: 357), so too in the soup kitchen they must invent new recipes in order to spread the scarce food that comes from the government in order to feed more mouths. If the spaghetti does not arrive, they may need to make tuna croquettes for lunch instead.

Gladys posed as a solution to this problem that they reject the government-dictated menus and come up with their own weekly menus, as this would give more leverage to the women and make them feel more creative with their work. Since there are five cooks, each could have a particular day of the week when they determined the menu, she suggested. For instance, they had been receiving an oversupply of black beans for several weeks and would need to start finding creative ways of preparing the beans. The women discussed various options, including letting the diners decide the menu. But they concluded that this would promote the idea of the soup kitchen as a consumer service, when it reality it was intended as a survival strategy to lessen the burden of those women in the barrio who were not able to provide their children with nutritious meals. In the daily work of organizing a soup kitchen, the women were engaging in a range of debates that included their leverage and agency in a state-directed program and the meaning of what they were doing in the context of the community.

At one point, Orlando sought to raise an issue. He said that on the previous day militants from the Chavista vanguard youth organization Frente Francisco de Miranda had stopped by the soup kitchen and demanded that the community activists put a banner outside the kitchen with the insignia of the Chavista mayor and a name taken from one of the founding heroes, such as Bolívar or Sucre. Orlando was bitter that these Chavista militants should be dictating to the community what they should do when the community has put all the work into constructing and maintaining the kitchen. Freddy responded to Orlando's story with disgust, saying,

> Why should we name our soup kitchen after Simón Bolívar or Sucre? It's always the same old heroes of the republic. We have to think with our heads. Until when will be stuck in the same old schema? Why can't we name the soup kitchen after Benita Mendoza, a working woman here in the barrio who has raised three kids, been left by three husbands, studied in spite of all the difficulties, and retired to work here as a volunteer?

Gladys agreed with Freddy, saying that "if the militants from the Frente come by here again, tell them to come to the next assembly and put it to the community, because that is who makes decisions in this barrio." Like Carlos from the mayor's office, the Frente Francisco de Miranda represents a machistic conception of politics that marks the official sphere, or "*oficialismo*." As Valdivieso (2004: 141) argues, a heroic conception of politics in Chavismo, marked by grand stories of liberation, is taken directly from republican discourse. By contrast, in their discussions and praxis, community activists challenge the current political rhetoric and seek to place barrio women at the center of new liberatory imaginaries. Moreover, Orlando's account evoked similarities to "family kitchens" under the populist government of Fernando Belaúnde in Peru, where, Maruja Barrig (1996: 60) notes, the provision of infrastructure and food was given in exchange for support for the governing political party. Through their discussions, the Carretera Negra activists rejected this kind of clientelism as it ran counter to a politics of collective accountability and participation that they were trying to build.

At this point in the assembly, three of the women cooks, Ana, Mercedes, and Judy, left the room and entered the adjoining kitchen to begin preparations for the next days' meal. Gladys stayed in the room. The three men present began discussing questions of financing for the soup kitchen. Gladys noticed that the women were being left out of the conversation, and she called out to them, "Leave your *caraotas* [beans] and come and join in the discussion." Through her involvement in politics, Gladys was more alert to the gender differences that emerge in the process of popular organizing, and she was more ready than the men to call this out. The women came back in the room and the activists finished up with the meeting quickly, and then I was surprised to see all three men enter the kitchen and help with cleaning the rice, washing the beans, and cutting meat. The point seemed to be understood by those present that rather than replicating gender divisions in community organizing, with women doing the cooking and men discussing the finances, men and women should have equal participation in all aspects of community organizing. Treating the soup kitchen as a collective responsibility, and not as the sole work of the women volunteers, had the effect of challenging the notion that cooking is the sole domain of women. Community activism is a space where men and women are attempting to jointly define new perspectives based in the realities of daily life. Even though men continue to dominate as leaders, through the process of community activism, both men and women are learning to call out instances of gender domination, as women take on positions of leadership and responsibility.

Conclusion

In this chapter, I have argued that we must conceptualize the mobilization of poor women in the barrios of Caracas as part of a historical trajectory of community struggle and in terms of their engagement with male community activists and a revolutionary populist state. Barrio women drew on their associational links with a revolutionary-populist president, state officials, and state-managed programs in order to build new spaces of community participation. They utilized a maternal-centered notion of responsibility and nurturance as the basis of their political identity. Like the Mothers of Heroes and Martyrs in wartime revolutionary Nicaragua, who, according to Bayard de Volo (2001: 214), asserted themselves as active participants in the revolution rather than passive recipients, barrio women in Chávez's Venezuela also sought to take the initiative at the local level to make decisions regarding their community and the implementation of local programs. In contrast to other accounts of barrio women, which see them as merely reactive or manipulated by a populist state, I have argued that these women are agents who are building new spaces of democratic community participation.

Chávez's state-sponsored programs such as soup kitchens may perpetuate the appropriation of women's labor and the institutionalization of their struggles for survival, like the day-care centers implemented under previous Venezuelan governments and the communal kitchens operating in contexts of neoliberal restructuring in other Latin American countries. But there is also a difference in that Chávez has sought to reverse some neoliberal austerity measures of previous governments. He has reintroduced the idea of social welfare as the responsibility of the state and has alleviated women's burden through a range of social services, including Mercal, Barrio Adentro, and the missions. Moreover, in those parishes such as La Vega that have a long history of community activism, women have sought to retain community control over the programs through the practices of local assemblies. They view food preparation in soup kitchens as a collective task rather than the responsibility of individual cooks, and hence they seek collective rather than private solutions to the problems presented. When women's increasing participation occurs in the framework of cohesive community networks, there is much more opportunity to build democratic and sustainable projects.

The space of the barrio, as the location of community organizing, is generally more conducive to the participation of women and their developing political awareness than Chavista organizations, which tend to operate in a machistic manner. As the example of the visiting Chavista official and the militants from the Frente Francisco de Miranda showed, these bodies tend to operate with a much more vertical and clientelist notion of politics than the community activists. But even in the community spaces, it is still men who tend to occupy leadership roles, and they were the ones who initiated the discussions about gender and machismo in the assemblies. Women from La Vega had always been at the forefront of campaigns in the community, and their experiences in earlier struggles guide their current work. But the gendered division of labor that underlies women's participation in community work also restricts them from having time for the kinds of education and reflection that the men of the community have had available to them. Where men can gather to discuss, read, or attend lectures, women are often at home with the children or taking care of other domestic responsibilities such as cooking and cleaning. In this context, it is men from the community who have thought more about gender inequality and machismo and who raise these questions in the assembly. This finding points to the ongoing challenges that barrio women face in becoming leaders in their communities, but also the possibilities for community work as a space for generating change within the context of a revolutionary-populist system.

Notes

I would like to thank the community activists of the Carretera Negra and Las Casitas in La Vega for sharing their experiences and ideas. Thank you to my research assistant Paola Cortes-Rocca for her work in transcribing interviews. This research was made possible by faculty research grants from the University Committee on Research in the Humanities and Social Sciences and the Program in Latin American Studies at Princeton University. I would also like to thank Elisabeth Friedman, Cathy Rakowski, and two anonymous reviewers of *Latin American Politics and Society* for their helpful comments on earlier drafts of this essay. An earlier version of this article was presented at the American Political Science Association conference in Washington, DC, September 2005. This chapter originally appeared in *Latin American Politics and Society*, vol. 49, no. 3.

1. Interview with Francisco Wuytack, August 2005.
2. Ibid.
3. Cited in *La Vega Resiste*, a documentary produced by Consejo Nacional de la Cultura, 2004.
4. Ibid.
5. Thanks to Cathy Rakowski for providing this information.
6. http://www.infocentro.gov.ve/viewusuario/detalleNoticia.php?id=2288&cc=93, retrieved March 2006.
7. Although there has been no data available on the percentages of women participating in these programs, from my own observations and conversations with others it is clear that most committees, especially Health Committees, generally consist of over 90 percent women.

References

Alvarez, Sonia. 1999. "Advocating Feminism: The Latin American Feminist NGO 'Boom.'" *International Feminist Journal of Politics* 1 (2): 181–209.

Baptista, Felix, and Oswaldo Marchionda. 1992. "¿Para Que Afinques?" BA thesis, Escuela de Antropología, Universidad Central de Venezuela.

Barrig, Maruja. 1989. "The Difficult Equilibrium between Bread and Roses: Women's Organizations and the Transition from Dictatorship to Democracy in Peru." In *The Women's Movement in Latin America: Feminism and the Transition to Democracy*, ed. Jane Jaquette, 114–48. Boston: Unwin Hyman.

———. 1996. "Women, Collective Kitchens, and the Crisis of the State in Peru." In *Emergences: Women's Struggles for Livelihood in Latin America*, ed. John Friedman, Rebecca Abers, and Lilian Autler, 59–77. Los Angeles: UCLA Latin American Center Publications, University of California.

Bayard de Volo, Lorraine. 2001. *Mothers of Heroes and Martyrs: Gender Identity Politics in Nicaragua, 1979–1999*. Baltimore: Johns Hopkins University Press.

Botía, Alejandro. 2005. "Círculos Bolivarianos parecen burbujas en el limbo." *Últimas Noticias*, March, 20.

Burbano de Lara, Felipe. 1998. "A modo de introducción: el impertinente populismo." In *El Fantsma del Populismo: Aproximación a un tema [siempre] actual*, ed. Felipe Burbano de Lara, 9–24. Caracas: Nueva Sociedad.

Caldeira, Teresa. 1990. "Women, Daily Life, and Politics." In *Women and Social Change in Latin America*, ed. Elizabeth Jelin, 47–78. London: Zed Books.

Castañeda, Nora. 2004. "Por una Sociedad Justa y Amante de la Paz." In *Bolivarianas: El Protagonismo de las Mujeres en la Revolución Venezolana*, ed. Mónica Saiz, 25–36. Caracas: Ediciones Emancipacion.

Castillo, Adicea, and Isolda H. de Salvatierra. 2000. "Las Mujeres y el Proceso Constituyente Venezolano." *Revista Venezolana de Estudios de la Mujer* 5 (14): 37–88.

Chun, Lin. 2001. "Whither Feminism: A Note on China." *Signs: Journal of Women in Culture and Society* 26 (4): 1281–86.

Contreras Juan. 2000. "La Coordinadora Cultural Simón Bolívar: Una Experiencia de Construcción del Poder Local en la Parroquia '23 de Enero.'" BA thesis, Escuela del Trabajo Social, Universidad Central de Venezuela.

Craske, Nikki. 1999. *Women and Politics in Latin America*. Cambridge: Polity Press.

Delgado Arria, Carol. 1995. *Mujeres: Una Fuerza Social en Movimiento*. Caracas: Comite Juntas por Venezuela Camino a Beijing.

Díaz-Barriga, Miguel. 1998. "Beyond the Domestic and the Public: *Colonas* Participation in Urban Movements in Mexico City." In *Cultures of Politics/Politics of Cultures: Re-visioning Latin American Social Movements*, ed. Sonia Alvarez, Evelina Dagnino, and Arturo Escobar, 252–77. Boulder, CO: Westview.

Duque, José Roberto. 2004. "Un Gobierno, Un Proceso." *Patriadentro*, May 21–27.

Ellner, Steve. 2005. "The Revolutionary and Non-Revolutionary Paths of Radical Populism: Directions of the Chavista Movement in Venezuela." *Science and Society* 69 (2): 160–90.

Fernandes, Sujatha. 2006. "Transnationalism and Feminist Activism in Cuba: The Case of Magín." *Politics and Gender* 1 (3): 1–22.

Friedman, Elisabeth. 1998. "Paradoxes of Gendered Political Opportunity in the Venezuelan Transition to Democracy." *Latin American Research Review* 33 (3): 87–135.

———. 1999. "The Effects of 'Transnationalism Reversed' in Venezuela: Assessing the Impact of UN Global Conferences on the Women's Movement." *International Feminist Journal of Politics* 1 (3): 357–81.

———. 2000. *Unfinished Transitions: Women and the Gendered Development of Democracy in Venezuela, 1936–1996*. University Park: Pennsylvania State University Press.

García Guadilla, María-Pilar. 1993. "*Ecologia*: Women, Environment and Politics in Venezuela." In *"Viva": Women and Popular Protest in Latin America*, ed. Sarah Radcliffe and Sallie Westwood, 65–87. London: Routledge.

Gott, Richard. 2000. *In the Shadow of the Liberator: Hugo Chávez and the Transformation of Venezuela*. London: Verso.

Grohmann, Peter. 1996. *Macarao y Su Gente: Movimiento Popular y Autogestion en los Barrios de Caracas*. Caracas: Nueva Sociedad.

Herrera de Weishaar, Maria Luisa, Maria Ferreira, and Carlos Cabrera. 1977. *Parroquia la Vega: Estudio Micro-Historico*. Caracas: Consejo Minucipal del Distrito Federal.

Howell, Jude. 1998. "Gender, Civil Society and the State in China." In *Gender, Politics, and the State*, ed. Vicky Randall and Georgina Waylen, 166–84. London: Routledge.

James, Daniel. 2000. *Doña María's Story: Life History, Memory, and Political Identity.* Durham, NC: Duke University Press.

Jelin, Elizabeth. 1987. *Movimientos Sociales y Democracia Emergente.* Buenos Aires: Centro Editor de América Latina.

Karl, Terry. 1987. "Petroleum and Political Pacts: The Transition to Democracy in Venezuela." *Latin American Research Review* 22 (1): 63–94.

Levine, Daniel. 1998. "Beyond the Exhaustion of the Model: Survival and Transformation of Democracy in Venezuela." In *Reinventing Legitimacy: Democracy and Political Change in Venezuela,* ed. Damarys Canache and Michael R. Kulisheck, 187–214. Westport CT: Greenwood Press.

Lind, Amy Conger. 1992. "Power, Gender, and Development: Popular Women's Organizations and the Politics of Needs in Ecuador." In *The Making of Social Movements in Latin America: Identity, Strategy, and Democracy,* ed. Arturo Escobar and Sonia Alvarez, 134–49. Boulder, CO: Westview.

———. 1997. "Gender, Development and Urban Social Change: Women's Community Action in Global Cities." *World Development* 25 (8): 1205–23.

———. 2005. *Gendered Paradoxes: Women's Movements, State Restructuring, and Global Development in Ecuador.* University Park: Pennsylvania State University Press.

López Maya, Margarita. 2004. "Hugo Chávez Frías: His Movement and His Presidency." In *Venezuelan Politics in the Chávez Era: Class, Polarization, and Conflict,* ed. Steve Ellner and Daniel Hellinger, 73–92. Boulder, CO: Lynne Rienner.

López Maya, Margarita, David Smilde, and Keta Stephany. 1999. *Protesta y Cultura en Venezuela: Los Marcos de Acción Colectiva en 1999.* Caracas: CENDES.

Luna, Lola. 1995. "Los Movimientos de Mujeres an América Latina o Hacia una Nueva Interpretación de la Participatión Política." *Boletín Americanista* 35:249–56.

Martín-Barbero, Jesús. 1993. Communication, Culture and Hegemony: From the Media to Mediations. London: Sage.

Massolo, Alejandra. 1999. "Defender y cambiar la vida. Mujeres en movimientos populares urbanos." *Cuicuilco* 6 (17): 13–23.

Molyneux, Maxine. 1985. "Mobilization without Emancipation? Women's Interest, the State, and Revolution in Nicaragua." In *Transition and Development: Problems of Third World Socialism,* ed. Richard R. Fagen, Carmen Diana Deere, and Jose Luis Goraggio, 280–302. New York: Monthly Review Press and Center for the Study of the Americas.

———. 1998. "Analysing Women's Movements." *Development and Change* 29:219–45.

———. 2000. "State, Gender, and Institutional Change: The Federación de Mujeres Cubanas." In *Hidden Histories of Gender and the State in Latin America,* ed. Elizabeth Dore and Maxine Molyneux, 291–321. Durham, NC: Duke University Press.

———. 2001. *Women's Movements in International Perspective: Latin America and Beyond.* New York: Palgrave.

Morgen, Sandra. 1988. "'It Is the Whole Power of the City against Us': The Development of Political Consciousness in a Women's Health Care Coalition." In *Women and the Politics of Empowerment*, ed. Sandra Morgen and Ann Bookman, 97–115. Philadelphia: Temple University Press.

Moser, Caroline. 1986. "Women's Needs in the Urban System: Training Strategies in Gender Aware Planning." In *Learning about Women and Urban Services in Latin America and the Caribbean*, ed. Judith Bruce, Marilyn Kohn, and Marianne Schmink, 39–61. New York: Population Council.

Mujica, Maria-Elena. 1992. "Nourishing Life and Justice: Communal Kitchens in Lima, Peru." *Latin American Anthropology Review* 4 (2): 99–101.

Muñoz, Mercedes. 2000. "Derechos Sexuales y Reproductivos y Proceso Constituyente." *Revista Venezolana de Estudios de la Mujer* 5 (14): 123–46.

Paley, Julia. 2001. *Marketing Democracy: Power and Social Movements in Post-Dictatorship Chile*. Berkeley: University of California Press.

Petzoldt, Fania, and Jacinta Bevilacqua. 1979. *Nosotras también nos jugamos la vida: Testimonios de la Mujer Venezolana en la Lucha Clandestina: 1948–1958*. Caracas: Editorial Ateneo de Caracas.

Rakowski, Cathy. 2003. "Women's Coalitions as a Strategy at the Intersection of Economic and Political Change in Venezuela." *International Journal of Politics, Culture, and Society* 16 (3): 387–405.

Ramos, Nelly. 2004. Trabajadora cultural a tiempo completo." In *San Agustin: Un Santo Pecador o un Pueblo Creador*, ed. Antonio Marrero, 173–82. Caracas: Fundarte.

Ramos Rollon, Maria Luisa. 1995. *De las Protestas a Las Propuestas: Identidad, Accion y Relevancia Politica del Movimiento Vecinal en Venezuela*. Caracas: Instituto de Estudios de Iberoamerica y Portugal.

Randall, Vicky. 1998. "Gender and Power: Women Engage the State." In *Gender, Politics, and the State*, ed. Vicky Randall and Georgina Waylen, 185–205. London: Routledge.

Roberts, Kenneth. 2003. "Social Correlates of Party System Demise and Populist Resurgence in Venezuela." *Latin American Politics and Society* 45 (3): 35–57.

———. 2004. "Social Polarization and the Populist Resurgence in Venezuela." In *Venezuelan Politics in the Chavez Era: Class, Polarization and Conflict*, ed. Steve Ellner and Daniel Hellinger, 55–72. Boulder, CO: Lynne Rienner.

Rodriguez, Lilia. 1994. "Barrio Women: Between the Urban and the Feminist Movement," *Latin American Perspectives* 21 (3): 32–48.

Safa, Helen. 1990. "Women's Social Movements in Latin America." *Gender and Society* 4 (3): 354–69.

Schild, Veronica. 1998. "New Subjects of Rights? Women's Movements and the Construction of Citizenship in the 'New Democracies.'" In *Cultures of Politics/Politics of Cultures: Re-visioning Latin American Social Movements*, ed. Sonia Alvarez, Evelina Dagnino, and Arturo Escobar, 93–117. Boulder, CO: Westview.

Silva Michelena, Héctor. 1999. "La política social en Venezuela durante los años ochenta y noventa." In *Política Social: Exclusión y Equidad en Venezuela Durante los Años Noventa*, ed. Lourdes Alvares, Helia Isabel del Rosario, and Jesús Robles, 85–114. Caracas: Nueva Sociedad.

Stephen, Lynn. 1997. *Women and Social Movements in Latin America: Power from Below*. Austin: University of Texas Press.

Valdivieso, Magdalena. 2004. "Confrontación, Machismo y Democracia: Representaciones del 'Heroismo' en la Polarización Política en Venezuela." *Revista Venezolana de Economía y Ciencias Sociales* 10 (2): 137–54.

Westwood, Sallie, and Sarah Radcliffe. 1993. "Gender, Racism and the Politics of Identities in Latin America." In *"Viva": Women and Popular Protest in Latin America*, ed. Sarah Radcliffe and Sallie Westwood, 1–29. London: Routledge.

II

CASE STUDIES OF THE
NEW LATIN AMERICAN LEFT

7

From Left-Indigenous Insurrection to Reconstituted Neoliberalism in Bolivia

Political Economy, Indigenous Liberation, and Class Struggle, 2000–2011

Jeffery R. Webber

A N EXTRAORDINARY WAVE of left-indigenous extra-parliamentary mobilizations shook Bolivian politics to its foundations between 2000 and
2005. Two neoliberal presidents were overthrown in under two years, and
the basis was laid for the successful bid by Evo Morales, as leader of the Movimiento al Socialismo (Movement Toward Socialism, MAS) party, to become
the country's first indigenous president. Morales won the December 2005
elections decisively and then consolidated this electoral strength by winning a
second term in office in the December 2009 elections with an unprecedented
64 percent of the popular vote.

Against this backdrop, a critique is required of the two broadest prevailing
caricatures of contemporary Bolivian politics. On the one hand, mainstream
liberal and conservative analyses of the Bolivian government, and much of
the English-language press coverage internationally, tends to depict the Morales regime as radically populist, even socialist, in its economic policies and
indigenous-nationalist in its sociopolitical orientation. These analyses from
the right describe such qualities in pejorative terms and sometimes raise the
specter of Morales's supposed tendencies toward authoritarianism and the
threats he may therefore pose to liberal democratic stability and the sanctity
of private property. The Right, in other words, engages in a sort of ritualized
demonization of the Morales government and the social movements associated with his political base.

On the other hand, much of the scholarly and popular interpretations of
the regime coming from the left internationally tend to celebrate uncritically
alleged advances in the social, economic, political, and especially cultural

rights of the impoverished indigenous majority, enacted, it is contended, under the Morales administrations between 2006 and the present moment. The international Left often accepts quite literally the regime's rhetorical embrace of slogans such as "communitarian socialism" and "democratic cultural revolution." Thus, if the Right, taking its cues from Washington, engages in ritual demonization, the Left has too often descended into casual celebration of communiqués issued from the Presidential Palace in La Paz.

In contrast to these two misleading caricatures, the central argument of this chapter is that between 2000 and 2005 Bolivia witnessed a left-indigenous insurrection whose scope and aims closely mirrored what this volume refers to as the radical Left; however, the revolutionary anticapitalist and indigenous-liberationist possibilities of this epoch were considerably dampened through the diversion of mass energies from the domain of extra-parliamentary organization and mobilization toward electoral participation in December 2005. After assuming office, the Morales government introduced what I call a political economy of reconstituted neoliberalism, the Bolivian expression of the *izquierda permitida*, or the authorized Left (see Jeffery Webber and Barry Carr in the introduction to this volume).

The chapter proceeds in three parts. First, the trajectory and character of the left-indigenous cycle of revolt between 2000 and 2005 is explained in considerable detail. The Cochabamba Water War of 2000, Aymara peasant insurrections of 2000 and 2001, antitax revolts of February 2003, and the Gas Wars of 2003 and 2005 are analyzed as the key moments of the cycle. Second, the political economy of reconstituted neoliberalism under Morales, between 2006 and 2011, is introduced and interrogated. Third, the sociopolitical contradictions of reconstituted neoliberalism in Bolivia are analyzed, with particular emphasis being placed on growing conflict between different organized sections of the popular classes and the Morales administration.

Neoliberal Crisis, Revolutionary Epoch, 2000–2005

Between 1989 and 1996, average annual growth in Bolivia was just over 4 percent, reaching a high of 5.27 percent in 1991, a low of 1.65 percent in 1992, and a new peak of 5.03 percent in 1998. Agriculture was the fastest-growing sector between 1992 and 1997, but hydrocarbons and minerals still accounted for more than half of legal exports.[1] Soybean and vegetable oil exports from the eastern lowlands had grown to ten times their size since 1990, attracting significant amounts of Brazilian investment into commercial agricultural enterprises (Kohl and Farthing, 2006: 121). As a result of overall growth in the economy, between 1993 and 1999 the World Bank claims urban poverty declined from 52 percent to 46 percent (World Bank, 2005: 1).[2] However, contradictions in neoliberal capitalism at the global, regional, and national levels struck Bolivia hard in 1999. GDP growth plummeted to 0.43 percent that year, rose only to 2.28 percent in 2000, and declined again to 1.51 percent in 2001. Between 1999 and 2003 the average growth rate was 1.9 percent, which measured out to roughly 0 percent in per capita terms. As a consequence, World Bank figures suggest that between 1999 and 2002 overall poverty rates in the country increased from 62 percent to 65 percent, and extreme poverty also experienced a slight increase. Income inequality also increased during this period (World Bank, 2005: 1–3).[3]

The national economic crisis was deepened further by the loss of state revenue as a result of the massive sell-off of valuable state-owned enterprises, particularly YPFB, the national petroleum company. State revenue from hydrocarbons and mining that used to trickle down to poor rural municipalities dried up almost completely, sewing widespread discontent (Kohl and Farthing, 2006: 151–52). The effect of privatizing hydrocarbons was indeed a catastrophic contribution to the budget crisis suffered by the state (Kohl, 2003: 346). From 1997 to 2002 Bolivia's budget borrowing increased from 3.3 to 8.6 percent of its gross national income (GNI) (Schultz, 2005: 16–17). This gave international financial institutions and the United States even more leverage over the Bolivian government's policy response to the crisis (Fernández Terán, 2003: 112–39). As others have pointed out, privatization of the hydrocarbons sector was a key component in the World Bank's and International Monetary Fund's overall plan for Bolivia. In a cruelly ironic twist, when that privatization helped to worsen the economic crisis by sapping a key source of revenue, the IMF demanded that the budget shortfall be made up through cuts in social spending and increases in regressive taxes that hit poor Bolivians the hardest (Schultz, 2005).

Popular discontent with the social consequences of neoliberalism began to grow quite dramatically in the late 1990s and early 2000s. This can be seen through a number of different indicators. By 2001, according to polls conducted by Latinobarómetro, over 90 percent of the Bolivian population reported that they thought the income distribution in the country was "unfair" or "very unfair" (World Bank, 2005: 3). Data compiled by the Bolivian Ministry of Labor between 1982 and 2000 attempts to track episodes of strikes or slowdowns as reported in national newspapers (Gray Molina and Chávez, 2005: 86).[4] Under Paz Zamora (1989–1993) there were 968 strikes and slowdowns, under Sánchez de Lozada (1993–1997) 631, and under Bánzer (1997–2001) 1,364. Clearly, there was a discernible expression of discontent from the population as a response to the social consequences of neoliberalism. The reproduction of the neoliberal form of state power in Bolivia was increasingly undermined by changes in the balance of racialized class forces, economic recession, and the declining legitimacy of neoliberalism.

The Cochabamba Water War of 2000, Aymara peasant insurrections of the western *altiplano* (high plateau) in 2000 and 2001, and proletarian antitax revolt in La Paz and El Alto in February 2003 constituted the opening acts of what developed into a five-year cycle of left-indigenous insurrection in Bolivia. This gradual extension of popular class power from below helped shift the balance of class forces in society and opened up a crisis within the ruling class by 2003, as well as an extended crisis of the Bolivian neoliberal state. The reactive sequences of popular mobilization and state repression over these five years provided the basis for an escalating scale of radicalism. The anticapitalist and indigenous-liberationist demands of protesters broadened in scope, and the repertoires of struggle became more confrontational with time. The cycle culminated in the Gas Wars of September–October 2003 and May–June 2005, which witnessed the ousting—through mass demonstrations in the capital, street confrontations with police and military forces, and strikes, road blockades, and marches in the western part of the country—of Presidents Gonzalo Sánchez de Lozada and Carlos Mesa, respectively.

The Cochabamba Water War

The privatization of water in the city of Cochabamba grew naturally out of the earlier stages of economic restructuring. Through pressure from the IMF and the World Bank and violation of Bolivian legal procedures and regulations, water that had been under the control of a public water utility or, in some areas, communal water system was transferred to private ownership (Albro, 2005; Finnegan, 2002; Spronk, 2007). Beginning in 1994, the World Bank repeatedly demanded that SEMAPA, Cochabamba's municipal water system, be auctioned off as a condition for new or renegotiated credits (Arze Vargas, 2000). Two critical acts by the Hugo Bánzer government (1997–2001) during this process set the stage for future conflict over the commodification of water. First, in September 1999 a forty-year concession to control the Cochabamba water system was granted to Aguas del Tunari, an international consortium legally registered as International Water in the Cayman Islands. The Italian multinational Edison SpA and the American giant Bechtel owned 50 percent of International Water, while 25 percent was owned by Abengoa of Spain. The remaining 25 percent was divided between four different Bolivian investment groups, all with ties to parties in the government (Arze Vargas, 2000). The auction for SEMAPA drew one bidder, and the terms of the contract reflected the lack of competition. Aguas del Tunari was guaranteed an annual return of 15 percent on its investment, to be adjusted to the consumer price index in the United States, for forty years (Finnegan, 2002). The concession, in this respect, failed to comply with existing Bolivian legislation, according to which three proposals were required for a valid auction (Crespo, 2000). The characteristics of fraud and legal manipulation common in other privatized sectors were also visible, then, in the case of water.

Second, in October 1999 the government passed the Ley de Servicios de Agua Potable y Alcantarillado Sanitario (Law 2029 on Potable Water and Sanitary Drainage), which legalized the concession granted in September. This law facilitating the privatization of water passed through Congress at breathtaking speed with little to no consultation with those who would endure its consequences (Crabrtree, 2005). Theoretically, Law 2029 could grant concessions and licenses for water management to any legally recognized institution. In practice, however, the conditions for obtaining concessions and licenses were heavily biased toward large enterprises that operated according to market criteria. Further, the law stipulated that once concessions were granted concessionaires had exclusive rights over the concession area, meaning preexisting communal forms of water governance—in both rural and urban areas—would be forced to enter into contracts with the concessionaires, likely large enterprises operating within market logic (Assies, 2003). In other words, this indicated an unmitigated transition from communal property to exclusive private property through a secretive state process with the backing of powerful international financial institutions and interested multinational water corporations. Because the contract granted to Aguas del Tunari awarded the company a guaranteed rate of return, and because the World Bank had stipulated to the Bolivian government that state revenue could not be used to generate this money, the obvious source was the water-consuming residents of Cochabamba. Aguas del Tunari skyrocketed water tariffs accordingly (Spronk and Webber, 2007: 39). The working-class and lower-middle-class residents of the city and peasants in the surrounding countryside did not take this lightly. Tariff increases were the catalyst to the Cochabamba Water War of 2000, the opening act of a five-year left-indigenous insurrectionary cycle throughout Bolivia's countryside and major cities.

The Water War consisted of an anti-neoliberal popular movement struggling against the commodification of perhaps the most important of public goods. Social-movement actors articulated a powerful understanding of the rebellion, wedding it to *usos y costumbres*, or the customary use of commonly governed water supplies of the Quechua indigenous communities dating back centuries in rural areas surrounding Cochabamba and decades in some poor neighborhoods in the city. The privatization of water was a fundamental violation of these *usos y costumbres*. Activists also emphasized the notion that water is a resource that is biologically and socially critical for life itself. To privatize water would be to privatize life itself. Water scarcity and the threat posed by privatization in the Cochabamba context fundamentally impacted a multiclass, rural, and urban layer of the population simultaneously.

The role of the international financial institutions and a consortium of multinational corporations fueled the revitalization of a rich Bolivian tradition of anti-imperialism. The formation—through collective action and confrontation with the state—of a deepened oppositional consciousness, a stronger sense of solidarity, and a heightened awareness of the power of collective mass action contributed to the radicalization of measures and demands as the protest developed (Tapia, 2000). The Cochabamba Water War was of fundamental importance in part because it represented the first left-indigenous popular victory following fifteen years of relatively weak and impotent popular resistance on the part of the popular sectors of Bolivian society. The indigenous peasant and proletarian classes of Bolivia were perceived to have won, if perhaps only temporarily, in a battle against the Bolivian ruling class, the neoliberal state, the World Bank, and a transnational water consortium led by American transnational Bechtel.

With the concession to Aguas del Tunari and the passing of Law 2029 in 1999, the Water War began in earnest. The height of the conflict, however, was distilled in three intense episodes in January, February, and April 2000, remembered by participants as the three "battles" of the Water War. Popular urban and rural movements, working together under the Coordinadora, an umbrella organization, occupied the city of Cochabamba, confronted the coercive forces of the state, and practiced direct democracy in the streets through mass popular assemblies. On April 10, 2000, the Coordinadora and the government signed an agreement that annulled the contract with Aguas del Tunari and ensured the reassertion of SEMAPA as the public water system, although now with representatives from the Coordinadora on its board. Detainees were released and the wounded cared for at the expense of the government (Assies, 2003). Oscar Olivera, the most visible leader of the Water War, declared victory, and the Water War wound its way to a close with social movements soon declaring it a major conquest over neoliberalism. In the words of Olivera:

> They tossed a foreign corporation out of the country. Even better, they briefly replaced the government, the political parties, the prefects, and the state itself with a new type of popular government based on assemblies and town meetings held at the regional and state levels. For one week, the state had been demolished. In its place stood the *self-government* of the poor based on their local and regional organizational structures. (Olivera, 2004: 125)

It is important to repeat that the Water War initiated a cycle of left-indigenous protest that spread throughout the country. It proved to be the spark of

Bolivia's most recent left-indigenous cycle of revolt. Olivera expressed this dynamic to me in a powerful fashion:

> The people realized that it's possible to defeat the system, that it's possible to defeat the transnationals, and that it's possible to dispense with the political parties of the institutional state system that up until that moment had been privatized by the political parties. They had privatized the right to speak and to make decisions. Therefore, I think that we broke not only the monopoly of the transnationals and their plundering of our natural resources, but the monopoly on the right to speak and make decisions held by the political parties. The people, since 2000, since the Water War, began a process of self-organization, a process of mobilization, a process of proposals and demands that culminated . . . in the great popular uprising of October 2003, which threw out . . . the most symbolic, the most emblematic figure of neoliberalism, Gonzalo Sánchez de Lozada. (personal interview, July 2005)

The Insurrectionary Aymara Peasantry

If the Water War in Cochabamba was one regional axis of the emergent insurrectionary cycle in 2000, another critical zone was the western *altiplano* of the departments of Oruro and La Paz, as well as the northern valleys of the latter (García Linera, 2002a; Gutiérrez and García Linera, 2002; Kohl and Farthing, 2006). In April and September–October 2000, as well as in June–July 2001, the Aymara peasantry in these regions, organized through the Central Sindical de Trabajadores Campesinos de Bolivia (Bolivian Peasant Trade Union Confederation, CSUTCB) and led by Aymara radical Felipe Quispe, orchestrated wide-scale mobilizations with massive road blockades. The protests marked the historic reemergence of the Aymara peasantry, who had not made a political intervention of this magnitude since the rural component of the 1979 struggles for democracy led by Genaro Flores.

The immediate causes of the Aymara regional uprising were similar to those that ignited protest in Cochabamba. Fundamental as a spark to the insurrection in the *altiplano* was a bill before Congress that would have privatized access to water in the region. Just as the Quechua indigenous peasants of Cochabamba had appealed to *usos y costumbres* to contest water privatization, Aymara peasants in Oruro and La Paz demanded that the new water bill not be passed because it violated communal indigenous understandings of water: "in the logic of the *ayllus* [independent indigenous communities], water cannot be bought or sold, or subjected to market logic because water is a vital part of life: it is the blood of the pachamama. . . . Mother earth, pachamama, would die if it [water] became a commodity with market value" (Mamani Ramírez, 2004: 81).

The Aymara insurgents also demanded the annulment of the law of the Instituto Nacional de Reforma Agraria (National Agrarian Reform Institute,

INRA), promulgated by the Sánchez de Lozada government in 1996 as part of its Plan de Todos (Plan for Everyone). The Aymara peasants saw the law as a threat to their traditional *ayllu* systems of land governance in the *altiplano*, especially as the INRA process increasingly emphasized land titling and individual property rights, a response to pressures from the World Bank and large landholding lobbyists (Crabtree, 2005: 79). Protesters were also motivated to act on a host of other short-term demands, including the need for agricultural subsidies and access to new agricultural technologies, the creation of rural indigenous universities, and an end to the eradication of coca crops in the Yungas region of the department of La Paz.

The CSUTCB initiated its road blockade on April 3, 2000. Roadblocks were concentrated in La Paz and Oruro, but also extended to the departments of Cochabamba, Chuquisaca, and Tarija. Over the next few days, blockades were extended throughout the departments of Beni and Potosí (García Linera, Chávez León, and Costas Monje, 2005: 122). Between April 5 and 9, roads were blocked at a national level. Aymara peasants from the communities of Huatajata, Juarina, and Achacachi in the province of Omasuyos, in the department of La Paz, were the pivotal social force behind the rebellions. The Bánzer government, having already declared a state of siege to deal with the mounting problems in Cochabamba, militarized the city of Achacachi as well as many surrounding towns and villages. Felipe Quispe and other leaders were arrested and shipped off to remote prisons within the country (Mamani Ramírez, 2004: 46). In the following confrontations between the military and mobilized peasants, two Aymaras were killed (Mamani Ramírez, 2004: 26–42). Throughout Omasuyos, protesters destroyed state offices and institutions, such as the Palace of Justice and the offices of the sub-prefect. The insurgent peasants managed also to liberate prisoners from the jail in Achacachi. State repression intensified further, with over a thousand new troops deployed to the area by land and air, raiding houses in the early-morning hours and torturing some of their occupants. Battles between Aymara peasants and the coercive apparatuses of the state extended into other provinces of La Paz (Patzi, 2005: 207–8). Negotiations were initiated with the government, and by April 14, 2000, this round of Aymara protest wound down.

The lull in activity was short lived. April's mobilizations in the *altiplano* were followed by a massive wave of blockades and protests over many of the same issues, starting on September 11 and lasting until October 7, 2000. Tens of thousands of peasants blocked the central highways connecting Cochabamba and Santa Cruz and Oruro and Potosí. They also occupied all the roads and highways connecting the city of La Paz with the rest of the provinces and the main thoroughfares to the other departments in the country. The blockades were so effective at shutting down the flow of goods that basic supplies for the city of La Paz had to be flown in under the order of President Bánzer and the prefect of La Paz.[5] Peasants from the valleys of Inquisivi and Loayza occupied the La Paz–Oruro highway. Over fifty thousand assembled in Achacachi from provinces throughout the department of La Paz to decide on further actions. Talk of an Aymara nation, civil war, and a march on La Paz were in the air (Patzi, 2005: 212).

Forrest Hylton and Sinclair Thomson (2005: 50) note, "By September–October 2000, the road blockades organised by the CSUTCB and their calls for a march on the capital raised the revolutionary spectre of 1781 [when indigenous forces rose up in an insurrection led by Túpaj Katari against the Spanish colonizers]. Food shortages started to affect La Paz." During the September–October actions, discussion circulated throughout many of the rural provinces of La Paz of more fully realizing indigenous self-governance in the region. This sentiment found its expression in the establishment of the *cuarta general indígena* (general headquarters) of Qalachaka, located near Achacachi. All the while, the Aymara peasantry of the *altiplano* engaged in what Quispe termed Plan Pulga, or Operation Flea, whereby peasants would sweep into one area of a highway, piling up rocks and debris. While the military cleared that area, the peasants moved elsewhere, perpetually tying up troops in one section of the highway and maintaining the blockades in others. Like fleas, they caused the state to scratch in one place, leading only to itches all over (Mamani Ramírez, 2004: 47).

By June–July 2001, a third wave of Aymara peasant uprisings emerged. At this stage, the principal domains of struggle and mobilization were contained in the La Paz provinces of Los Andes, Omasuyos, Manco Cápac, Camacho, and Franz Tamayo. On June 21 roadblocks were initiated in the highways at Huarina and Achacachi, followed shortly thereafter by state repression. State ammunition destroyed the lungs of indigenous peasant protester Severo Madani and fatally wound Isabel Quispe with a gunshot to her stomach (García Linera, Chávez León, and Costas Monje, 2005: 126–27). Undoubtedly, the most important component of the days of June through July was the official consolidation of the general headquarters of Qalachaka, conceived of as a militarized confederation of *ayllus* (independent indigenous communities) and other indigenous communities of the *altiplano* (García Linera, 2002b: 22–26). Over twenty thousand indigenous activists gathered at Qalachaka, apparently armed with clubs, rocks, and old Mauser rifles from the Chaco War of the 1930s (García Linera, Chávez León, and Costas Monje, 2005: 127). A photo, likely taken on one of the hills of Achacahi, circulated through the mainstream daily newspapers, showing a group of teenagers apparently "armed" and sporting balaclavas in the style of the Zapatistas of the Lacandon jungle of southern Mexico.[6]

This series of revolts centered in the *altiplano* was a racialized peasant class struggle. The protesters sought to defend indigenous *usos y costumbres* in the communal management of water and land—under threat from privatization laws. They sought to assert Aymara indigenous pride in the face of racist state repression that led to several civilian deaths. These were struggles for indigenous liberation. They were also anticapitalist, as peasants sought to defend communal customs against the blood-and-fire processes of capitalist expansion.

The more radical sectors of the rebellions of 2000 and 2001 were ideologically oriented toward a fundamental, revolutionary challenge to the neoliberal capitalist model in place since 1985. Large sections of the Aymara *altiplano*, aligned with Quispe in these contentious moments of confrontation with the state, were building the incipient ideological and organizational foundations for an alternative revolutionary and democratic state (Patzi, 2005: 66). This alternative democracy envisioned by the indigenous activists on the road blockades has been expressed intellectually by scholars working in the Bolivian context as *ayllu*, or communal, democracy versus liberal-capitalist, representative democracy (Rivera Cusicanqui, 1991: 20). Quispe conceived of the rebellions as a communitarian socialist challenge to the neocolonial capitalist Bolivian state. He spoke of the reassertion of the communal system of the *ayllu*, adapted to the twenty-first-century context, as a way of replacing the colonial institutions and practices inherited by the republicans at Bolivian independence in 1825 (Quispe, 2005: 71–75). In many respects, this notion of communitarian socialism in the countryside was the rural counterpart to the revolutionary, assemblyist forms of urban democracy experienced during the Water War in Cochabamba through the creation of the Coordinadora and mass meetings in the streets and plazas.

The February 12–13, 2003, *Impuestazo*

The epoch of left-indigenous insurrection begun in Cochabamba in 2000 surged forward dramatically in February 2003 with a historic insurrection by low-ranking police officers in the city of La Paz, armed confrontation between the police and the military, and largely spontaneous revolts by the informal and formal sectors of the urban working classes and public university and high school students of La Paz and El Alto (APDHB et al., 2004: 1–22.). The police insurrection and popular rebellion spread, albeit on a smaller scale, to the cities of Cochabamba, Santa Cruz, Trinidad, Oruro, and Sucre (García Mérida, 2003; Hylton, 2003; Peredo, 2003). The armed assault on the protesting police forces by the military protecting the presidential palace in the Plaza Murillo set off popular indignation throughout the urban working classes of La Paz and

El Alto and led to two days of revolt. The crisis of neoliberalism had reached a crescendo as the two wings of the state's coercive apparatus—the military and the police—disintegrated into internecine conflict. The workers in the streets were primarily indigenous, particularly so in the city of El Alto. Claudia Espinoza and Gozalo Gosálvez describe the masses in the streets as "in the majority unemployed young men and women between 13 and 18 years of age, families congregated in protest, students, unemployed adults, self-employed informal workers, and to a lesser extent workers from the organised sectors" (Espinoza and Gozálvez, 2003). The protests in February reignited the urban dimension of left-indigenous insurrection that had been eclipsed somewhat by the rural Aymara indigenous insurrections and various *cocalero* battles following the more urbanized Cochabamba Water War. The antitax protests in El Alto and La Paz had a more spontaneous character than the Cochabamba Water War and the Aymara peasant insurrections. The importance of the existing urban infrastructure of class struggle in building and leading the rebellion was less obvious. Various unions and social-movement organizations did play a part, but they tailed rather than led the February events.

The September–October 2003 Gas War

The Cochabamba Water War, the Aymara uprisings, and the proletarian antitax revolt together laid the basis for the first Gas War and the overthrow of the most hated Bolivian president in recent memory, Gonzalo Sánchez de Lozada. At the outset of September 2003, the popularity of Sánchez de Lozada's administration was in steep decline. In an urban poll of residents of Cochabamba, El Alto, La Paz, and Santa Cruz, 70 percent of respondents disapproved of the government's record during its first year in office. A remarkable 84 percent of residents of El Alto held this view. The future of natural gas development in Bolivia had already deeply penetrated popular political discussions in the streets and countryside, and continued to be a contentious subject in the halls of Congress as well. The state-owned natural gas and oil company, YPFB, was privatized in 1996. Under the administration of ex-dictator Hugo Bánzer (1997–2001), a deal was then initiated between the Bolivian state and the Spanish-British-U.S. energy consortium Pacific LNG and San Diego-based Sempra Energy. Under the proposed arrangement, natural gas would be exported through a Chilean port to markets in Mexico and the Californian coast of the United States. A year after the start of his second mandate as president in 2002, Sánchez de Lozada sought to close the gas export deal, contributing a focal point and unifying issue to the left-indigenous social forces in insurrection during September and October 2003 (Hylton and Thomson, 2004: 18).

The idea of using a Chilean port to export gas was provocative to Bolivian nationalist sentiments across the political spectrum, which have long sustained an antipathy toward Chile, rooted in the latter's annexation of Bolivia's coastline during the Pacific War of the late 1870s and early 1880s. However, much more important than basic resentment of Chile's nineteenth-century foreign relations was a profound sense that, since natural gas had been privatized in 1996, the resource had been pillaged by transnational corporations with little to no benefit accruing to the Bolivian population. Reestablishing Bolivian social control over natural gas—and other natural resources—soon was understood by left-indigenous movements as the only way to avoid the cruel repetition of hundreds of years of exploitation of domestic natural resources—silver and tin historically—and of the laborers used by capital to extract them.

The Aymara peasantry of the western *altiplano* were the first to act (Álvaro García Linera, personal interview, April 10, 2005). The initial "insurrectionary energy" of the 2003 rebellions emerged from the overwhelmingly Aymara indigenous province of Omasuyos, next to Lake Titicaca and close to the country's capital city (Hylton and Thomson, 2004: 16). They mobilized initially around a list of demands, including broad anti-neoliberal themes as well as more specific conjunctural issues relating both to their sector's economic interests and to defending their collective right to indigenous self-government. Under the leadership of Felipe Quispe, the CSUTCB was central to articulating this peasant mobilization, as was the Federación Única Departamental de Trabajadores Campesinos de La Paz—Tupaj Katari (Departmental Federation of Peasant Workers of La Paz, FUDTCLP-TK), led by Rufo Calle.[7] A peasant march on September 8, 2003, from the community of Batalla to El Alto was the first mobilization of the Gas War.

Coinciding with the Aymara peasant convergence on El Alto was a civic strike in the city organized by the Federación de Juntas Vecinales de El Alto (Federation of Neighborhood Committees of El Alto, FEJUVE) and Central Obrera Regional de El Alto (Regional Workers' Central of El Alto, COR) against new municipal legislation, *maya y paya*, that would have increased taxes on building and home construction (Hylton and Thomson, 2007: 111). Two days later, on September 10, with no government response to their demands forthcoming, CSUTCB and FUDTCLP-TK militants, with the help of *jilaqatas* and *mama t'allas* (traditional authorities) from the Aymara peasant communities of the rural provinces of La Paz, initiated a hunger strike in the auditorium of the Aymara-language radio station in El Alto, Radio San Gabriel. The hunger strike quickly garnered the support and solidarity of several other urban and rural popular organizations, including the Central Obrera Boliviana (Bolivian Workers' Central, COB), and plans to erect roadblocks in the *altiplano* were finalized. *Cocaleros*, or coca growers, of the Yungas and the Chapare regions expressed their solidarity with peasant actions developing in the *altiplano*.

Urban protests toward the end of September demonstrated that while the Aymara peasantry had started the cycle of insurrection known as the Gas War of 2003, El Alto had become the new fulcrum of popular mobilization in the country (Espinoza, 2003). The FEJUVE and the COR coordinated roadblocks of the principal routes connecting La Paz to El Alto. Schools were shut down, the streets of the city were completely barricaded, and stores and street vendors ceased operations. Thousands of *alteño* marchers snaked their way down the La Paz hillsides to join the large concentrations of people in the Plaza San Francisco. The columns of protesters from El Alto were met in La Paz by teachers, factory workers, peasants, truckers, street vendors, health-care workers, and pensioners. The COB let it be known that it would be holding an emergency national assembly on October 1 in Huanuni, in the department of Oruro, where strategic discussion over a possible general strike and coordinated nationwide campaign of roadblocks would occur. The basis of an insurrectionary alliance led by the largely informal working classes of El Alto, and supported by the peasantry, the formal working class, and sections of the middle class, was beginning to emerge. New levels of state coercion soon acted as the spark that consolidated these forces.

The first shock of state repression since the *impuestazo* of February 2003 radicalized social movements. On September 20, military troops invaded Warisata and began killing indigenous community members (García Linera, 2004: 62). Immediately after the Warisata killings, President Sánchez de Lozada's approval rating fell to 9 percent. Rather than suppress the movements of September, this moment of state repression extended, deepened, and radicalized left-indigenous struggle both within the rural Aymara zone where the killing took place and, crucially, in El Alto over the next couple of weeks. By mid-October, protests, road blockades, hunger strikes, and militant clashes with the military and police forces shook huge swathes of the country. In the context of September and October 2003, the deaths caused by state repression "evoked a feeling of unity, of solidarity, of identification with those abused by power" (Suárez, 2003: 17).

The state had lost all control over El Alto. Beneath the waves of repression between October 10 and 17, a collective sentiment of resistance radiated throughout the neighborhoods of the city. Bonds of solidarity and coordination between adjacent neighborhood councils, districts, and zones of El Alto were created. Virtually every space in the city was occupied and controlled by neighborhood councils, in near-constant confrontation with the state (Mamani Ramírez, 2005: 69). As the strength of left-indigenous social forces grew and consolidated, the *alteño* working classes began to mirror a process Marx identified as "revolutionary practice" (Lebowitz, 2006: 19–20; McNally, 2006: 375). In their struggle to satisfy their needs, the rank and file of the left-indigenous movements came increasingly to recognize their common interests and become conscious of their own social power; through their self-activity they came to see themselves as subjects capable of altering the structures of Bolivian society as well as changing themselves in the process through self-organization and self-activity from below.

The events of the first two weeks of October set the stage for the final mass mobilizations that would topple Sánchez de Lozada's government on October 17. The new strength of middle-class protest at this stage helped set the agenda of what would come after. A massive march on October 16, led by FEJUVE and COR, descended once again from El Alto into La Paz, converging with the congregated masses in the Plaza San Francisco. Over three hundred thousand protesters gathered (Hylton and Thomson, 2007: 116). Evo Morales reiterated the position of the MAS in support of a constitutional exit. "This is the moment to rescue Bolivia from the economic, political and social crises," he told the media. "We are not going to negotiate as long as Gonzalo Sánchez de Lozada continues as President and we support the constitutional succession of Carlos Mesa" (*Opinión*, 2003). Mesa himself reappeared on television ratifying his decision to distance himself from the government without rescinding his position as vice president of the country; thus his succession to the presidency in the event of Sánchez de Lozada's resignation was becoming a clearer possibility. Mesa's rhetoric appealed to the middle class. "I am not with the philosophy that reasons of state justify death," he told the nation. "But neither am I with the radical banners that the moment has arrived to destroy everything in order to construct a utopia that nobody wants or knows where it is going" (Rohter, 2003).

The position of the oppositional sectors of the middle class, the MAS, and Carlos Mesa gathered momentum and, with no clear political alternative to the left of this new coalition, Mesa, the MAS, and the oppositional middle class were able to establish sway over the popular movement. The intervention of the middle classes had shifted the balance of social forces in favor of merely presidential resignation and constitutional succession. The masses were united in their absolute resistance to the neoliberal state. They were able to paralyze that state but had no alternative project with which to replace it. Thus the stage was cast for Mesa to take up the minimum program of the insurgent indigenous proletarians and peasants—resignation of Sánchez de Lozada, constituent assembly, and a new hydrocarbons law—without challenging the fundamental precepts of the neoliberal order (García Linera, 2004: 33–66).

Roughly four hundred thousand protesters filled the streets of downtown La Paz on October 17. Sánchez de Lozada was forced to resign and flee to Miami. Carlos Mesa became president according to constitutional procedures in the event of a president's resignation at 10:30 p.m. All the political parties with representation in Congress supported the constitutional succession.

The May–June 2005 Gas War

The son of two of Bolivia's most highly regarded mainstream historians, Mesa was a film critic in the late 1970s and early 1980s, publishing *La aventura del cine boliviano* in 1985. Later he became a radio journalist before turning to television journalism, where he became well known and well respected in middle-class circles. Mesa also established credentials as a historian by cowriting with his parents a thick general history of Bolivia. Throughout the 1990s, his fame grew as a television journalist and political analyst on the program *De Cerca*, or *Up Close*. Mesa had never been a member of the Movimiento Nacionalist Revolucionario (Revolutionary Nationalist Movement, MNR), even after agreeing to run as Sánchez de Lozada's vice presidential running mate in the 2000 elections. He utilized this stature as an independent intellectual without party affiliation to distance himself from a regime in which he had in fact played a key role as vice president.

Upon assuming the presidency, he pledged to piece together independent forces in the government and to restore the credibility of the political class in the eyes of the Bolivian population. In response to the popular October Agenda for which left-indigenous forces had struggled, he promised a referendum on natural gas, a constituent assembly, and modification of the hydrocarbons law. While the constitution established that his mandate ought to last until August 6, 2007, Mesa argued that Congress could convene elections as soon as it deemed it reasonable to do so. Mesa requested a grace period in which social movements would withdraw from mass actions and let him study their demands and proceed with governing the country peacefully. In the midst of the jubilation surrounding the fall of Sánchez de Lozada, Mesa was initially well received by the key sectors that had mobilized in September and October 2003. That would soon change. Mesa, as president at that specific historical moment, is perhaps best considered a Bonapartist mediator between two polarized social blocs (Marx, [1852] 1981; Tapia, 2005).[8] He initially forged tenuous but important ties with popular left-indigenous movements by promising reform and adopting the rhetoric of change. As president he offered cosmetic changes on the fringes of the neoliberal economic model while fundamentally wedding his government to the perpetuation of the basic structure of the political, economic, and social system introduced to the country in 1985.

For the duration of Mesa's government (October 17, 2003 through June 6, 2005), Bolivia was characterized by a deepening political polarization along the axes of class, race, and region. Two social blocs emerged. On the one hand, a left-indigenous bloc, rooted primarily in the most heavily indigenous departments of La Paz, Cochabamba, Oruro, Potosí, and Chuquisaca, was solidified on the basis of a similar alliance of popular classes and indigenous organizations as in the first Gas War in 2003. This bloc's demands were known as the October Agenda because they were essentially carried over from the unfulfilled promise of the October 2003 Gas War. Naming it the October Agenda, moreover, commemorated the martyrs and wounded of the earlier insurrection. The principal collective-action frame of May and June 2005 was again the nationalization of gas; however, the call to convene a constituent assembly was also central to the second Gas War and more important than it had been in the first. The principal social organizations of the left-indigenous forces were the FEJUVE, the COR, the COB, the FSTMB, rural and urban teachers, FUDTCLP-TK, CSUTCB (Quispe), and the coordinator of gas.

The other constellation of social forces to consolidate itself between October 2003 and June 2005 was an eastern bourgeois bloc, led by the regional bourgeoisies of the hydrocarbons-rich departments of Tarija and Santa Cruz, as well as their allies in Beni and Pando. Collectively, these departments are known as the *media luna*.[9] Although led by bourgeois forces and embracing a political project that protected the interests of dominant regional capitalists, the eastern bourgeois bloc nonetheless enjoyed considerable support from the popular rural and urban classes of these departments. While the hegemony of neoliberal ideas had been crushed—at least temporarily—in the departments where the left-indigenous bloc was strongest, they continued to resonate in those of the *media luna*.[10]

The capitalist class of the eastern lowlands had enjoyed direct access to the highest reaches of the state between 1985 and 2003. They held important ministerial positions and dominated the traditional neoliberal parties—the MNR, MIR, and ADN—that governed through a series of pacted coalitions over this period. The October 2003 insurrection, even if it did not fulfill the revolutionary objectives of many in the left-indigenous camp, did defeat Gonzalo Sánchez de Lozada and cut out in this way the direct and unmediated access to the state apparatus enjoyed by bourgeois forces in the east. The fortunes of the three key neoliberal parties tumbled still further in the December 2004 municipal elections, in which their performances were abysmal.

The eastern bourgeois bloc thus sought strategically to entrench itself in the regions where it was able, knowing that establishing hegemony at the national level was not plausible in the short to medium term given the balance of social forces in society at that juncture. This quintessentially defensive strategy expressed itself in the January Agenda of 2005, which was meant to counter the left-indigenous October Agenda of 2003. The January Agenda—so designated in the aftermath of a large mobilization of over three hundred thousand supporters in the city of Santa Cruz in January 2005—was based on an ideological commitment to "free-market" capitalism, openness to foreign direct investment, and bitter racism toward the indigenous majority of the country. It was articulated more precisely through the demand for departmental autonomy for the four departments of the *media luna* within the Bolivian state. Autonomy, in this context, meant, "(1) regional control over natural resources (e.g., land, timber, gas, and oil), (2) the right to retain control over two-thirds of all tax revenues generated in the department, and (3) authority to set all policies other than defense, currency, tariffs, and foreign relations" (Eaton, 2007: 74).

Mesa attempted to mediate between two polarized social blocs (Tapia, 2005). He initially forged tenuous but important ties with popular left-indigenous movements by promising reform and adopting a rhetoric of change. As mentioned, he offered cosmetic changes at the fringes of the neoliberal economic model, but ultimately defended the principal interests of the dominant economic classes, transnational capital operating in Bolivia, and the key international financial institutions, particularly the IMF. In rhetoric and practice, he was forced to take a softer approach to his advocacy of neoliberalism than had Sánchez de Lozada. The particular historical circumstances that allowed him to become president in the first place, and the latent mobilization capacity of the left-indigenous bloc, always just beneath the surface, could not have allowed him to do otherwise.

Mesa therefore choreographed a sophisticated dance between the two social blocs until the beginning of 2005 (Cáceres, 2005). In the ensuing months, however, growing discontent with Mesa's insufficient concessions to the October Agenda reignited popular mobilizations of left-indigenous movements. These, in turn, fostered countermobilization by the autonomist movement of the *media luna* (Chávez, 2005b; Chávez and García Linera, 2005; Lora, 2005). The back-and-forth spiral provided oxygen to the hardest currents of each side. By March 2005, Mesa, underestimating the strength of the left-indigenous bloc, opted for an open realignment with the eastern bourgeois bloc, throwing the country into a pivotal face-off situation that eventually played itself out in Bolivia's second Gas War of May–June 2005.

It is also essential to understand that there were two other groups that effectively dangled between the two blocs in the country—sections of the urban middle classes, especially outside the departments of the *media luna*, and the MAS party, under the leadership of Evo Morales. Their distinct actions at different intervals helped to reinforce one bloc or the other. Because Mesa was not a member of the MNR and because he had betrayed Sánchez de Lozada in the closing weeks of the October 2003 Gas War, he did not have a predictable and loyal base of support in either the Chamber of Deputies or the Senate. The MAS, as the second-largest party in Congress after the MNR, was consequently an important potential ally. From the perspective of the less radical elements within the MAS, tangible benefits would accrue to their own party as well through an alliance with Mesa. Hoping to deepen the reform in Mesa's softer neoliberalism, Evo Morales entered into an unofficial alliance with the executive power that lasted from October 2003 until March 2005, ensuring the political survival of the president. The alliance eventually fell apart during debate over the depth of reforms to be incorporated into the new hydrocarbons law. In the wake of this breakdown, Mesa shifted markedly to the right, and the MAS—hesitatingly and inconsistently—forged new alliances with the reignited radical sectors of the left-indigenous bloc (Chávez, 2005a).

The middle class—that second swing group—played a different role than they had in October 2003. In the first Gas War, the urban middle classes engaged in hunger strikes in support of the left-indigenous overthrow of Sánchez de Lozada. They were responding in part to the brutal repression of civilians orchestrated by the regime. In March 2005, however, when Mesa shifted to the right, the middle classes went with him. Indeed, many went so far as to mobilize actively against the left-indigenous bloc from March until June 2005.

The country became increasingly polarized along race, class, and regional lines throughout the Mesa presidency, but accelerating sharply in January 2005 with a Water War against privatization in El Alto and the emergence of the January Agenda of the autonomist movement in the *media luna* departments of Santa Cruz, Tarija, Pando, and Beni (Spronk, 2007; Spronk and Webber, 2007). The advancing social polarization between January and March 2005 laid the basis for Mesa's ultimately unsuccessful attempt to align himself more closely with the eastern bourgeois bloc and Morales's efforts to build closer ties between his party and the more radical social movements of the left-indigenous bloc. Neither Mesa nor Morales were able to fully overcome the contradictions of their new allegiances by the end of March.

Thus by early April 2005, the polarization of left-indigenous and eastern bourgeois blocs persisted, but in an altered form. Mesa's reunion with the eastern-lowland right wing after his first "resignation" speech in March was short lived.[11] He dangled once again between the blocs, but his position was dramatically more tenuous given the breakdown of his alliance with the MAS. The MAS had shifted to the left out of necessity, but it did not abandon its hopes for coming to office through elections in 2007, or earlier if elections were pushed forward. The party thus committed itself to extra-parliamentary activism to promote a modest change to the tax regime on hydrocarbons (as distinct from the call for full nationalization coming from other social movements). There were, then, two hard blocs on the left and right, and between the two, a fluid, shifting middle ground. A lull in protests set in by the beginning of April 2005. The underlying contradictions, however, had not been resolved. They rose to the surface in mid-May with the approval of a new hydrocarbons law that fell short of the MAS proposal for 50 percent royalties and made a mockery of the more radical demand of nationalization coming from the left-indigenous bloc. The result was the May–June 2005 Gas War, in which the radical left-indigenous bloc rose up in street protests, road blockades, and enormous marches to the capital, all of which had massive popular support and forced Mesa's resignation on June 6, 2005.

Two important theoretical and historical conclusions ought to be drawn from the experience of left-indigenous insurrection between 2000 and 2005 in Bolivia. First, this wave of struggle amounted to an authentic revolutionary epoch, in which fundamental structural transformation of the state, society, and economy was the demand surging from below. Álvaro García Linera, vice president in the Morales government, has eloquently recognized this historical fact:

> It was Marx who proposed the concept of the "revolutionary epoch" in order to understand extraordinary historical periods of dizzying political change— abrupt shifts in the position and power of social forces, repeated state crises, recomposition of collective identities, repeated waves of social rebellion—separated by periods of relative stability during which the modification, partial or total, of the general structures of political domination nevertheless remains in question. . . . The present political period in Bolivia can best be characterized as a revolutionary epoch. Since 2000, there has been a growing incorporation of broader social sectors into political decision-making (water, land, gas, Constituent Assembly) through their union, communal, neighborhood or guild organizations; there has been a continual weakening of governmental authority and fragmentation of state sovereignty; and there has been an increasing polarization of the country into two social blocs bearing radically distinct and opposed projects for economy and state. (García Linera, 2006: 82)

Second, questions of state power and the relevance of revolutionary parties— themes addressed explicitly by Claudio Katz elsewhere in this volume—were raised directly. Despite its impressive capacity to mobilize and its far-reaching anticapitalist and indigenous-liberationist objectives, the left-indigenous bloc in 2003 and 2005 lacked a revolutionary party that might have provided the leadership, strategy, and ideological coherence necessary to overthrow the existing capitalist state and rebuild a new sovereign power rooted in the self-governance of the overwhelmingly indigenous proletarian and peasant majority. As a consequence, the fallout of the extraordinary mobilizations and profound crisis of the state witnessed during the second Gas War was not a revolutionary transformation but a shift in popular politics from the streets and countryside to the electoral arena as elections were moved up to December 18, 2005.

This shift and the victory of the MAS in the December elections dampened the immediate prospects for socialist and indigenous-liberationist revolution growing out of the revolutionary epoch of 2000–2005. This was because of the modestly reformist nature of the MAS party, the relative decline in the self-organization and self-activity of the popular classes after the election of Morales, a president who seemed to represent their interests, and the common phenomenon of social movements losing their transformative energies, organization, and capacity to build popular power when they adopt a preeminently electoral focus. Given the performance of the MAS during the Mesa period, it should have been no surprise that the Morales regime continued to exhibit, in its first years in office, major continuities with the neoliberal model of political economy it inherited from antecedent governments.

Reconstituted Neoliberalism, 2006–2011

As noted, Evo Morales was elected president of Bolivia on December 18, 2005, with a historic 54 percent of the popular vote, and was reelected to a second term in December 2009 with 64 percent. Morales is the first indigenous president in the republic's history, a particularly salient fact in a country where 62 percent of the population self-identified as indigenous in the last census in 2001 (INE, 2001). The 2005 and 2009 elections catalogued the demise of traditional neoliberal parties in Bolivia and popular rejection of their political and economic legacies. Unfortunately, given its changing class composition, ideology, and strategy over the few years leading up to those elections, the party the masses elected into the state apparatus had moderated dramatically since its origins.

The election of Evo Morales signified a historic blow against informal apartheid race relations in the country and was rightfully celebrated domestically and internationally as a major democratic step forward for the country. But it was also true, and harder for many to come to terms with, that the MAS had long since abandoned the perspective of simultaneous liberation from class exploitation and from racial oppression of the indigenous majority. Rather, the party had shifted ideologically and programmatically from its original character in the late 1990s. By roughly 2002 the MAS had committed itself to a crude model of revolutionary stages, according to which a thin cultural decolonization of race relations was possible immediately, whereas socialism was deferred to a distant future.

It should perhaps have been less surprising than it was for many, therefore, that the first year of the Morales government saw only modest breaks with the inherited neoliberal orthodoxies—limited essentially to foreign relations with Cuba and Venezuela and the International Monetary Fund, and domestic policy in the hydrocarbons sector. At the same time, while popular movements had struggled for a revolutionary constituent assembly to refound the country, the actual assembly established by the government in 2006 was a poor substitute, indeed more reminiscent of the proceedings of the existing liberal congress than a participatory and revolutionary rupture with the status quo.

If the first year of the Morales administration was characterized by steady movement away from rebellion and toward reform, the next three years (2007–2010) consolidated that turn in the form of reconstituted neoliberalism, a political economy closely approximating what this volume has referred to as the *izquierda permitida*. The new model abandoned features of neoliberal orthodoxy but retained its core faith in the capitalist market as the principal engine of growth and industrialization. Government revenue spiked, but international reserves were accumulated at record levels, while social spending decreased as a proportion of GDP. Budget surpluses were tightly guarded, as were inflation rates. Rates of poverty and levels of social inequality showed little alteration. Precarious and flexible labor conditions persisted. Indeed, they were encouraged in many ways. Workers were denounced as "counterrevolutionary" when they attempted to organize independently against these trends and for other improvements in their living standards and working conditions. It should be recalled that as far back as the campaign for the December 2005 elections, when García Linera was first selected as Morales's vice presidential candidate, the former became the spokesperson for "realistic" economic moderation, while the latter continued to deploy rhetoric in sync with the radical lineage of the MAS party's history. García Linera's line was, unfortunately, more in tune with the actual development plan the MAS developed for the campaign and subsequently instituted once elected.

Previous to the election of 2005, García Linera began, of course, by positing the impossibility of socialism in Bolivia for at least half a century, and perhaps a full one. In lieu of a socialist project, the MAS promoted something the vice president called "Andean-Amazonian capitalism." This model claimed that a stronger capitalist state could drive a petty bourgeoisie into a future national bourgeoisie of a size and significance unprecedented in Bolivian history. The new national bourgeoisie would be of indigenous heritage—

Andean-Amazonian—as a consequence of the "democratic-cultural" reforms of indigenous liberation, as conceived by the MAS as a process separate from any fundamental socioeconomic transformation of the class structures of Bolivian society. Parallel to the enduring theoretical postulations of the Stalinist Bolivian Communist Party of the 1930s, García Linera envisioned this intermediary stage of prolonged capitalist industrialization as a necessary transition between today's mode of production and the socialism that might be possible in a century's time. The vice president soon after refined these formulations in his conceptualization of "Evismo." Indigenous, democratic, and cultural change, on this view, did not imply radical economic transformation of the inherited neoliberal model nor any revolutionary change in political structures of domination and oppression. Instead, modifications to the existing political institutions of the state, arrived at through negotiation with the elite of the eastern lowlands, would be sufficient to ensure an expansion of indigenous cultural rights and the sort of decolonizing, democratic revolution envisioned by the MAS under Morales.

One of the ways the MAS sought ideologically to overcome the apparent contradiction of promoting simultaneously democratic indigenous revolution and neoliberal continuities in various political and economic power structures was to separate the anticolonial indigenous revolution against racist oppression from the socialist revolution to end class exploitation. Whereas many participants in the social movements of the insurrectionary period between 2000 and 2005 believed that the racist oppression and class exploitation of the majority of indigenous workers and peasants were organically linked and therefore had to be overthrown simultaneously in a combined liberation struggle, the MAS advocated indigenous cultural revolution immediately, with socialist transformation a mere possibility in the distant future.

During the first several months of the MAS administration, the state played its role of reproducing the conditions for accumulation through an array of policies that guaranteed healthy profits for private investors. The broad parameters of neoliberal financial policy inherited by the Morales government were also perpetuated, symbolized not least by the sanctification of Central Bank independence and repeated commitments to extremely low levels of inflation. Through fiscal austerity guarantees and Central Bank independence, the Morales regime set aside from the outset any possibility of enacting economic policies privileging specific popular classes in a new development model. Instead, under the cloak of technical economic policy neutrality, the continuation of neoliberalism ensured that the largest capitalists would continue to enjoy significant profits while the state would reproduce the labor force in their interests. Most other macroeconomic policies, including legislation on the labor market, corresponded with such a conclusion during the first year of the MAS administration.

The Plan de Desarrollo Nacional, 2006–2010 (National Development Plan, PDN), released on June 16, 2006, was predicated on the continuation of extractive capitalism, rooted in the export of primary natural resource commodities—hydrocarbons and minerals—under the principal control of imperialist capital, but with substantial rents going to the state through royalties and taxation. Moderate reforms were introduced in the hydrocarbons sector, as well as in relations to the International Monetary Fund, in the wake of the plan, and these undoubtedly violated the precepts of market fundamentalism. At the same time, these reforms at the margins of the economic model were designed to maintain the basic foundations of neoliberalism in a context of its profound crisis of legitimacy as a development model in Latin America (Orellana Aillón, 2006).

An examination of the political economy of the Morales government over the next three years (2007–2010) reveals the deepening and consolidation of the initial trend toward a reconstituted neoliberalism. The first thing to point out is that prior to the worldwide economic crisis, the fallout of which began to hit Bolivia in late 2008 and early 2009, Bolivia's economy under Morales grew very quickly. As table 7.1 indicates, after relatively slow growth in the early 2000s, the country rode the region's commodity boom of recent years to registered rates of gross domestic product (GDP) growth between 4 and 5 percent in 2004, 2005, 2006, and 2007. This trend peaked at 6.1 percent in 2008, before dropping to an expected 3.5 percent in 2009, the highest projected rate of growth that year of any country in the hemisphere. Since Morales came to office in January 2006, then, average GDP growth has been 4.8 percent. Between 2003 and 2008, Latin America and the Caribbean as a whole grew consistently at above 3 percent, reaching 5.7 percent in 2007 (ECLAC, 2008: 13). This period was the region's highest rate of sustained economic expansion in four decades.

The basic composition of Bolivia's economic structure has not changed profoundly in the last several years. Drivers of GDP growth between 2004 and 2008 included firm demand and high prices in the international market for hydrocarbons and minerals, as well as a modest uptick in private consumption (EIU, 2008: 21). Oil and gas extraction rose from 4.5 to 6.9 percent of GDP between 1999 and 2007 (EIU, 2008: 17). In subsequent years, the hydro-

TABLE 7.1
Bolivia Gross Domestic Product, 2000–2009

Year	2000	2001	2002	2003	2004	2005	2006	2007	2008	2009*
GDP	2.5	1.7	2.5	2.7	4.2	4.4	4.8	4.6	6.1	3.5

Source: Derived from ECLAC, 2010a: 140.
*Figures for 2009 are preliminary.

carbons sector has fallen modestly as a percentage of GDP but remains a massively important source of government revenue. Since 2004 total government
revenue expanded by almost 20 percent, mostly as a consequence of the new
tax regime in hydrocarbons established by Morales in 2006. Between 2004
and 2008, government revenue from hydrocarbons accelerated dramatically.
The state's take increased by roughly $3.5 billion over these years. Hydrocar-
bon revenue as a percentage of GDP went from 5.6 to 25.7 between 2004 and
the fourth quarter of 2008, after which it fell slightly to 21.1 percent by the
second quarter of 2009 (Weisbrot, Ray, and Johnston, 2009: 6–12). Natural
gas exports accounted for 41.3 percent of Bolivia's total exports in 2007, with
Brazil being the country's largest export market by far. A twenty-year supply
agreement was also signed with neighboring Argentina in 2006. Construction
of an important gas pipeline to Argentina, which would expand the volume
of Bolivian gas exports significantly, is also currently under construction,
although Argentina is increasingly investing in its own gas fields as a way of
reducing dependence on Bolivian supply (EIU, 2008: 22–23). Mining, too,
experienced a resurgence beginning in 2005. Indeed, mineral extraction increased from 3.5 percent of GDP in 2005 to 5.1 percent GDP in 2009 (Weisbrot, Ray, and Johnston, 2009: 6). Taken together mining and hydrocarbons
accounted for 12.1 percent of GDP, up from 11 percent in 2004. In the first
half of 2009, Bolivia's GDP grew by 3.2 percent, with metallic and nonmetallic
mineral extraction outpacing all other sectors at 14.4 percent growth. This is
mainly attributable to the intensification of production at the San Cristóbal
mine. Despite being the leading sector, however, metallic and nonmetallic
mineral mining was still down relative to its 63 percent growth over the same
period in 2008. Meanwhile, crude oil and natural gas contracted by 13.1 percent during the first half of 2009, mainly as a consequence of the sharp decline
in demand from Brazil (ECLAC, 2010a: 92).

Agriculture—including forestry, game, and fishing—shrunk by close to
1 percent of GDP between 2006 and 2007, while preliminary data shows it
shrinking still further to 10.4 percent in 2008, before rallying to 12.3 percent
in the first half of 2009 (ECLAC, 2009: 6). Much of this agricultural activity
is rooted in the commercial production of sugarcane, soya, maize, and sun-
flower, among other oil-bearing seed crops (all of which witnessed a rising
world demand until recently) in the department of Santa Cruz (EIU, 2008:
21). Manufacturing has stayed relatively even as a contribution to GDP, hit-
ting a peak of 18.8 percent in 2007. This sector is dominated by the production of nondurable consumer goods, with products "such as food, beverages,
tobacco, detergents, textiles, leather goods and shoes" constituting close to
one half of all manufacturing. The rest is largely taken up by "artisan crafts,

jewellery and intermediate goods, such as processed soya, refined metals, timber products and petroleum refining" (EIU, 2008: 23).

The Morales government has continued to be remarkably austere in its fiscal policy. In contradistinction to the budget deficits of the 2000–2005 period, Morales registered significant fiscal surpluses between 2006 and 2008, accruing at the same time massive increases in international reserves (EIU, 2008: 13). The right-wing opposition has nonetheless made a consistent uproar about inflation levels at different times, with the obvious political aim of conjuring up public fear of a return to the hyperinflationary crisis of the early 1980s. It is true that inflation rose from just under 5 percent at the close of 2006 to 14.1 percent in March 2008. It is also true, however, that the bulk of this trend can be traced to external shocks in food and energy price increases on the international market. Once these two factors are removed, core inflation hit a high of only 9.2 percent in December 2008, and subsequently fell back to 2.4 percent by November 2009 (ECLAC, 2009: 10). Moving into 2009, overall cumulative inflation hit 0.2 percent by October 2009 or 0.8 percent in year-on-year terms. These figures were among the lowest in all of Latin America and signified 11 and 13 percent drops respectively compared with rates in the same periods in 2008 (ECLAC, 2010a: 92). The drop is traceable to declines in international commodity prices, especially food, and an increase in supply domestically as a consequence of improved weather patterns.

Public investment, mainly in infrastructure, accelerated from 6.3 percent of GDP in 2005 to 10.5 percent in 2009. This is a priority for the government, given that transportation costs are estimated to be roughly twenty times as high as in neighboring Brazil (Weisbrot, Ray, and Johnston, 2009: 25). The railways run to only 3,700 kilometers, divided into two unconnected networks, some sections of which are no longer in use owing to neglect and disrepair. Road building has been privileged by the Morales government. This predilection for road building mirrors previous governments' priorities, with the percentage of roads with paved surfaces rising to 33 percent in 2005 from 20 percent in 2000. Two major highway arteries are now under construction, linking Santa Cruz to the Brazilian border of Puerto Suárez, in one case, and La Paz to the Brazilian border of Guayaramerin, in the other (EIU, 2008: 14–15).

Social Spending and Fiscal Stimulus

Social spending, particularly for a government transitioning toward "communitarian socialism" has been remarkably low. Adjusted for inflation, social spending in real terms rose by only 6.3 percent between 2005 and 2008, and *declined* as a percentage of GDP from 12.4 to 11.2 over the same period

(Weisbrot, Ray, and Johnston, 2009: 19). One report, published in December 2009 by a group of sympathetic social democratic economists, put it mildly: "Given the size and needs of Bolivia's poor population . . . and the increased resources that the government has accumulated in the recent years, it would seem that social spending for poverty alleviation and basic needs such as food, health care, and education should be increased" (Weisbrot, Ray, and Johnston, 2009: 19). Some relatively new initiatives in social spending—essentially cash transfers based on hydrocarbon revenues—may begin to partially reverse this trend. These include $29 U.S. per month, per young child, provided to families through the Bono Juancito Pinto program initiated in 2006. So long as children attend school, the cash transfer is distributed as an incentive for children to complete primary school up to grade six. Additionally, there is Renta Dignidad, an initiative kicked off in 2008 that provides roughly $344 per month to low-income citizens over sixty years of age. And, finally, Bono Juana Azurduy (or Bono Madre Niño Niña) was established in May 2009. It provides modest cash transfers to uninsured mothers in an effort to increase the likelihood of their seeking medical care before and after pregnancy. "New mothers receive 50 bolivianos each for four pre-natal medical visits, 120 bolivianos for the childbirth, and 125 bolivianos for each medical appointment until the child's second birthday. Mothers must show that they have the required medical visits in order to receive the funds" (Weisbrot, Ray, and Johnston, 2009: 15). The extent of the coverage for Bono Juancito Pinto and Renta Dignidad is outlined in table 7.2.

In response to the impact of the worldwide crisis on Bolivia, the Morales government introduced a sharp fiscal stimulus between the end of 2007 and 2009, leading to a shift from a surplus of 5 percent of GDP in the first quarter of 2008 to a deficit of 0.7 percent of GDP in the first quarter of 2009. This signified a substantial turn of almost 6 percentage points of GDP (Weisbrot, Ray, and Johnston, 2009: 13). Between the first half of 2008 and the first half

TABLE 7.2
Bolivian Coverage for Bono Juancito Pinto and Renta Dignidad, 2006–2008

	Number of Beneficiaries		Percent of Population Covered	
	Juancito Pinto	Renta Dignidad	Juancito Pinto	Renta Dignidad
2006	1,085,360	487,832	61.8%	76.9%
2007	1,323,999	493,437	75.1%	75.4%
2008	1,681,135	687,962	95.9%	101.8%

Source: Derived from Weisbrot, Ray, and Johnston, 2009: 16.

Note: Relevant populations are students enrolled in primary school, for Bono Juancito Pinto, and residents over age sixty, for Renta Dignidad. Enrollment is available through 2007; for 2008, enrollment is estimated as the average of the prior five years. Population estimates are from projections made by Instituto Nacional de Estadística based on the 2001 census and may result in coverage rates over 100 percent.

of 2009, exports declined by $853 million U.S., or 27.3 percent, as a result of declining hydrocarbon prices, lower demand in Brazil, and trade sanctions from the United States. Remittances from Bolivian laborers working abroad, meanwhile, dropped by 7.4 percent, or $39.4 million U.S., over the same period (ECLAC, 2010a: 92). In this context, the stimulus package was "probably the most important policy move that helped Bolivia avoid the worst effects of the downturn, relative to most of the rest of the region," analysts have pointed out. "It is worth noting that this would not have been possible without the control that the government gained over its natural gas production and revenues" (Weisbrot, Ray, and Johnston, 2009: 13).

Figures on poverty and living standards do not indicate a break with neoliberal social policy, much less the start of a revolutionary transition toward communitarian socialism. Drawing on data from Bolivia's National Institute of Statistics, table 7.3 charts poverty and extreme poverty trends up to 2007, the latest available figures. Note that since 2005 there has been only marginal change in the poverty rate, and that this change has been slightly upward, from 59.6 percent of the population in 2005 to 60.1 percent in 2007.[12] Levels of extreme poverty increase from 36.7 to 37.7 percent over the same two-year period. At the same time, other categories relevant to living standards highlighted in table 7.3, such as household density and access to electricity, running water, and sewage systems, all show modest improvements between 2005 and 2007. It is possible that poverty levels have improved since 2007, and it should also be noted that these figures do not take into account improvements in the social wage of workers and peasants—that is, any improvements in social services for the poor.[13] But the record on poverty nonetheless shows that there is little to celebrate.

Inequality, likewise, remains a huge barrier to achieving social justice in the Bolivian context. Between 2005 and 2007, income inequality, as measured by the Gini coefficient, declined from 60.2 to 56.3 (Weisbrot, Ray, and Johnston, 2009: 18). This hardly represents a revolutionary transfer of wealth, or even effective structural reform, as is perhaps more clearly demonstrated in the figures for the distribution of Bolivian national income, depicted in table 7.4. Here we see that the poorest 10 percent of the Bolivian population received 0.3 percent of national income in 1999 and still received only 0.4 percent by 2007, the last available figure. Meanwhile, the richest 10 percent of the population took home 43.9 percent of national income in 1999 and precisely the same percentage in 2007. If we broaden our perspective, to compare the bottom and top fifths of the social pyramid, we reach similar conclusions. The poorest 20 percent of society took in a mere 1.3 percent of national income in 1999 and in 2007 a still-paltry 2 percent. The richest 20 percent of the population pocketed 61.2 percent of national

TABLE 7.3
Bolivian Poverty and Living Standards, 1997–2007

	1997	1998	1999	2000	2001	2002	2003/2004*	2005	2006	2007
Poverty										
Poverty	–	–	63.5	66.4	63.1	63.3	–	59.6	59.9	60.1
Extreme Poverty	–	–	40.7	45.2	38.8	39.5	–	36.7	37.7	37.7
Household Amenities										
No more than three people per bedroom	42.5	51.6	67.4	67.4	68.0	59.7	60.2	60.6	69.5	71.5
Electricity	67.3	71.3	70.9	70.0	69.3	64.0	66.5	68.3	76.2	80.2
Access to running water**	82.6	85.4	81.5	84.5	84.7	82.3	83.3	85.1	84.3	86.0
Sewage systems***	38.3	43.1	42.6	42.2	41.4	40.7	40.4	45.9	41.9	50.8

Source: Derived from Weisbrot, Ray, and Johnston, 2009: 16.

*Data for 2003–2004 correspond to the Encuesta Continua de Hogares survey that took place between November 2003 and November 2004.

**We classify as having running water those homes with piped or well water (based inside or outside the home, individually or community based). We classify as not having access to running water households that access water via rivers, lakes, and trucks.

***We classify as having sewage systems households with septic tanks or sewage system connections. We classify as not having sewage systems households with outhouses or with no bathroom facilities.

TABLE 7.4
Distribution of Bolivian National Income,
Urban and Rural Areas, 1999–2007

Geographic Area	Year	Quintile 1 (Poorest)		Quintile 5 (Richest)	
		Decile 1	Decile 2	Decile 9	Decile 10
National	1999	0.3	1.0	17.3	43.9
	2007	0.4	1.6	17.0	43.9
Urban	1999	1.3	2.6	16.7	38.9
	2007	1.5	2.6	16.6	38.9
Rural	1999	0.4	0.8	17.3	48.8
	2007	0.2	1.2	18.7	45.4

Source: Derived from ECLAC, 2010a: 67.

income in 1999 and 60.9 in 2007. In other words, there has been almost no change on either end of the scale in terms of the redistribution of income, never mind the redistribution of assets. Abolishing such obscene concentrations of wealth—which are among the worst in Latin America, which is, in turn, the most unequal region of the world—ought to be a fundamental priority for the Morales government. Thus far, it has not been.[14]

There are many who continue to believe that the process of reform has run more deeply than I have suggested. The above sections illustrate that such claims of deep structural transformation do not correspond with the empirical record. Nonetheless, the radical trajectory of the government in its first term is frequently proclaimed, and the current moment, relatively shortly after Morales's decisive victory in the December 2009 elections, is seen as beckoning still further progress in the revolutionary transformation of the country's state, society, and economy. "This revolutionary movement," Frederico Fuentes suggests, for example, "with indigenous and peasant organizations in the forefront, has pushed the traditional Bolivian elite from power through a combination of electoral battles and mass insurrections. It has begun the struggle to create a new 'plurinational' Bolivia—based on inclusion and equality for Bolivia's 36 indigenous nations." Even outside narrow cultural conceptions of indigenous liberation, change is said to have occurred in the economy as well. "The Morales government has reclaimed state control over gas and mineral reserves and nationalised 13 companies involved in gas, mining, telecommunications, railways and electricity," Fuentes argues, drawing on official figures. "This increased state intervention means the public sector has increased from 12% of gross domestic product in 2005 to 32% today." For Fuentes, and many other likeminded observers, "this government is the product of a new anti-imperialism whose roots lie in previous nationalist movements. It surpasses previous nationalist experiments because, for the first time, it is not military officers or the urban middle classes leading the project, but indigenous and peasant sectors" (Fuentes, 2010a).

For Pablo Stefanoni, similarly, the current process of change under Morales evokes a certain popular nationalism similar to that of the postrevolutionary 1950s, however with a novel indigenous nucleus to the project's social base and ideological statements. "The MAS, although it denies it," Stefanoni suggests, "has resumed the policies and rituals of 1952," with the "indigenous military marches, the nationalization of natural resources, and the multiclass alliance of the 'people,' military nationalists, and 'patriotic' capitalists" (Stefanoni, 2010a: 5, 14). But both Fuentes and Stefanoni are confusing the rhetorical commitments of the government to state-led industrialization with actual substantive movement toward that end, as well as superficial rhetorical similarities to the 1952 revolution with the much more limited extent of reforms actually introduced in the Morales era compared to those enacted throughout the earlier epoch. Stefanoni is correct to point out that, today, it is increasingly apparent that the MAS has recreated the legacy of nationalist populism in a new mélange fit for the twenty-first century. The government has indeed incorporated some of the language of indigenous liberation developed by the earlier popular struggles, but it has separated its indigenous focus from the material reality facing indigenous people and has not proposed economic reform anywhere near the levels of the mid-twentieth-century nationalist-populist epoch in Bolivia. A glance at the late 1960s, for example, demonstrates that levels of state employment were massively higher than they were after four years of the MAS administration, and the state's proportion of total investment in the country in the late 1960s was 52 percent, by conservative estimates, as compared to the maximum claims of 32 percent today, with ultimate official goals of only 36 percent state participation in GDP (Malloy and Gamarra, 1988: 16).

Fuentes refers to thirteen nationalized companies. If we focus for a moment simply on mining, we start to recognize that a more incisive and careful dissection of the realities on the ground is important. First, the two nationalizations—of the Huanuni mine and the Vinto smelter—were a consequence of concerted struggles from below, by the mine workers and community allies, which forced the Bolivian government to act. They can hardly be seen as part of the government's overarching agenda. Second, important as these struggles were, it remains true that the overwhelming majority of active mines in Bolivia are owned and operated by transnational mining capital, principally Indian, Korean, Japanese, Canadian, American, and Swiss capital at the moment, with the possibility of French and Russian involvement soon through lithium development (Guachalla, 2010: 14–15). It is now abundantly clear, furthermore, that the presidential decree announcing the nationalization of natural gas in Bolivia on May 1, 2006, did not result in the actual nationalization of the industry but rather signaled a moderate reform to the regime of royalties and taxes owed to the Bolivian state by multinational oil and gas companies. The state now receives a considerably larger share of the profits than it had in the preceding regime (Webber, 2009). The modest reform appeared more radical than it was due to the fact that it coincided with a spike in the international price of natural gas and therefore generated a significant increase in state revenue.

In summary, the first year of the MAS administration witnessed many continuities in political-economic policy and structure in comparison to past regimes. These trends were deepened and consolidated on a number of different levels over the next three years (2007–2010). These observable tendencies toward reconstituted neoliberalism are real and ought to be recognized and acknowledged, even if it is similarly important not to treat them as immutable laws. They are relatively contingent structural processes subject to potential change under altered dynamics of domestic and regional class struggle, imperialism, and global capitalism in the near- to medium-term future.

It should also be clear that, prior to the 2008–2009 stimulus spending spurred by the reverberations of the global crisis in Bolivia, the first term of the Morales government is best understood, in economic terms, as one of high growth and low spending. Government revenue increased sharply with high prices for natural gas internationally and a reformed tax regime, but little of that money was redirected into social spending or job creation. The social consequences of reconstituted neoliberal austerity have included almost no change in levels of poverty and inequality during the years under Morales for which data is available. "Flexibility," or rather precariousness, has been reproduced systematically in the labor market. Such patterns have begun to generate conflict, however, as popular classes begin to confront the chasm between government promises and their lived material realities.

Fissures in Reconstituted Neoliberalism

Class contradictions inherent to the reconstituted neoliberal development model are slowly generating cracks and conflict, expressed in episodic strikes and other social movements that are growing in intensity and scope. These may signal the renewal of collective action from the left of the MAS, something that could very well grow in the near future so long as the Morales administration continues to pursue an economic model based on reconstituted neoliberalism.

One of the earliest major conflicts occurred in the mining zones of the western *altiplano* when private cooperative miners violently confronted state-employed miners for control of the Huanuni mine in October 2006. The MAS government initially backed the cooperative miners, against the promises they had made for nationalization of mines in their December 2005 electoral campaign. The strength of the state-employed miners eventually forced through a series of modest reforms in the industry and led to the resignation of the first minister of mines in the Morales government, but the violence led to sixteen deaths before a deal was struck. It was clear as early as 2006 that basic gains for the popular classes would not be forthcoming from the Morales regime without significant struggle from below (Webber, 2008).

A second challenge to the MAS administration from the left occurred in Cochabamba, beginning in late December 2006 and coming to a gradual close by the end of January 2007. Urban and rural popular forces, many of them the same sectors that led the Cochabamba Water War of 2000, rebelled against the department prefect, or governor, of Cochabamba, Manfred Reyes Villa. The spark was Reyes Villa's plan to hold a second referendum on "autonomy" for the department when one had just been held. This was seen by popular sectors as a plan to wed Cochabamba formally to the right-wing autonomist movement of the eastern lowland departments. As the movement gathered steam, the call went out for Reyes Villa's resignation. The MAS government unequivocally sided with Reyes Villa on this score, opening up another breach between social movements and the government (Webber, 2008).

Another in a series of possible examples of emerging class struggles from below took place in May 2010. A series of relatively small, but nonetheless important, sectoral strikes were carried out, and the first call for a general strike was made by the Bolivian Workers' Central (COB) since Morales first came to office in 2006.[15] The strikes were led by miners, factory workers, urban teachers, and health-care workers. Low-ranking members of the police force and their families also expressed collective discontent early in the month. All sectors were fighting for salary increases that would have merely kept pace with inflation. The only sector to win measurable gains in the course of the struggle turned out to be the miners, and the call for a general strike did not mature into mass working-class pressure on the government to deepen reforms. This has led to casual dismissal of the significance of workers' actions taken in May by some on the international left. The dominant account in the mainstream Bolivian press is comparable (Fuentes, 2010b; Stefanoni, 2010b).

A more reasonable assessment might be that these conflicts potentially mark the beginning of growing conflicts from below with the MAS government over the contradictions of the development model it is pursuing and the government's failure to meet pressing social needs of the majority of the population. The events of May also illustrate, however, the ideological and political aggressiveness with which the Morales government is prepared to encounter popular sectors that take a position to the left of its official stance. García Linera intimated that the United States and the domestic Right were behind the call for a general strike, which he compared to earlier (authentic) right-wing destabilization campaigns that the Morales government had endured. "Those who have been a part of union struggles know that general strikes have a political content; general strikes are declared to overthrow governments," García Linera argued. He said that right-wing groups since 2006 "have tried coup d'états, assassinations, and now they are attempting [destabilization] from within; the Right uses these measures, and I wouldn't doubt that behind this there also could be North American functionaries" (*La Razón*, 2010). Morales, who was in New York at the time, bizarrely told CNN that those union leaders behind the protests were "leaders that come from the dictatorships [of the past], who want to be instruments of neoliberalism, and don't represent all the workers, much less the [popular] indigenous [sectors] or peasants" (*La Razón*, 2010). "They use the language of the Left," García Linera assured Bolivians, "but their objective is to strengthen the Right, the counterrevolution" (*La Razón*, 2010). This is only one piece of many in the puzzle of structural and political obstacles standing in the way of building working-class and peasant independence from the MAS government as a means of applying real pressure for serious confrontation with capital and imperialism, and the beginning of authentic structural reform to the country's political economy.

In July and August 2010 another conflict between social movements and the state broke out, this time in the department of Potosí. By mid-August, the streets of the city of Potosí, six hundred kilometers southeast of the capital of La Paz, were desolate, distended with the uncollected garbage of weeks of a general strike and popular revolt against poverty. Over seven hundred vehicles were trapped in road blockades at Villa del Carmen, Betanzos, Chaqui, Dan Diego, and elsewhere, separating Bolivia's poorest department from its neighboring territories, as well as from Argentina and Chile. Stores were closed, and public and private institutions boarded up, along with schools, markets, and banks. Cash machines were out of money, food and fuel supplies were low, and inflation was lifting the prices of remaining basic commodities into the clouds. Only vehicles authorized by Potosí's Civic Committee—the umbrella organization through which the protests had been organized—were permitted to navigate the streets, although some Potosinos, as residents of this city of 160,000 are known, made their way on bikes and motorcycles through the few internal streets that remained passable. The dynamite of miners was set off from time to time to remind people that this was a city in revolt, even if negotiations with the government—after six aborted efforts—had finally begun in the neutral city of Sucre.

Throughout July and August, the avenues and alleyways of Potosí were adorned with red and white—the colors of the department—and roughly five hundred blue tent stations were scattered in different locales, providing shelter for possibly one thousand people on hunger strike, including the governor, who was a member of the ruling party but who had temporarily broken ranks under grassroots pressure. Two MAS congresspersons also joined the hunger strike initially but were then successfully pressured into abandoning that route by higher-ups in the party. At the peak of the protests, over one hundred thousand people took to the streets in marches. Peasants from nearby Jatun Ayllu Yura (an independent indigenous community) physically occupied the hydroelectrical station that supplies power to the biggest mine in the department, San Cristóbal, run by a Japanese multinational and the site of major worker and peasant disputes earlier this year. San Cristóbal lost $2 million U.S. per day in exports, and $500,000 U.S. was simultaneously lost daily from the cooperative mining sector. Tourism died in Potosí, at the peak of its season.

The protests began on July 30, 2010, with a forty-eight-hour general strike to drive home popular disaffection with the government's failure to respond to a series of electoral commitments made to the destitute department. These agreements had first been outlined in a petition delivered by the Civic Committee to Morales back in 2009. The forty-eight-hour strike was extended to an ongoing action without a definite end when the government's response was silence. Although this conflict with the government was eventually dissolved, its depth and scope signified a number of new political developments. The poorest department in the country (where life expectancy is dramatically below the national average), which gave roughly 80 percent support to the MAS in the last elections of December 2009, rose up in a protest against neoliberal continuity and the failure of basic responses to endemic poverty (Webber, 2010).

The events in Potosí laid the basis in many ways for the *gasolinazo*, or uprising over gas, that occurred in December 2010. "At the end of December," noted radical sociologist Raúl Zibechi (2011), "the first popular uprising in the region against a government of the left took place in Bolivia. It was caused by an excessive increase in the price of fuels." Of course, an increase in basic fuel prices amounted to a tax hike on the poor and a dramatic reduction in their real wage. Protests, strikes, and demonstrations reverberated throughout the country but were particularly strong in the very regional zones in which the MAS draws its key support. "The event demonstrates the difficulties of entering into a truly alternative mode of development," writes Zibechi (2011), "but it also reveals the limits of the Bolivian government's stated effort to re-establish and decolonize the state. . . . The Ipsos Institute released a survey showing that the popularity of President Evo Morales fell from 84% in 2007 to 36% in January of 2011. The results are worse for Vice President Alvaro García Linera whose level of approval fell from 46% in November of 2010 to 29%." The government was eventually forced to revoke, at least temporarily, the hike in fuel prices. However, the damage to the government's legitimacy has not been easily reversed.

The violence in the mining zones, the Cochabamba conflict, the workers' strikes of May 2010, the rebellion of the poor in Potosí in July and August 2010, and the December 2010 *gasolinazo* are merely exemplary snapshots of sectoral disputes between the popular classes and the Morales government and therefore hardly exhaust the list of political disputes and contention that have arisen under the Morales administrations (Mokrani Chávez and Uriona Crespo, 2011). Taken together, however, these do appear to represent signs of growing discontent to the left of the MAS in the tradition of left-indigenous insurrection from below witnessed between 2000 and 2005. The contentious moments thus far have remained fragmented and dispersed with no sociopolitical articulation of a left alternative to the MAS. However, at the level of ideas at least, the discontent is beginning to cohere in venues for left critique of the government. We see this, for example, in the emergence of the prominent indigenous-liberationist journal *Willka* in 2008 and the revolutionary left journal *El Manifiesto* in 2011, which includes several high profile figures from different revolutionary traditions on its editorial board.

Conclusion

Bolivian popular movements have been at the cutting edge of resistance to neoliberalism in Latin America in recent years. Latin America, in turn, has been the region of the world most militantly opposed to the social depravities of neoliberalism. Radical left-indigenous movements rose up in an insurrectionary cycle with a breadth and intensity unparalleled in the Western hemisphere in the first five years of the current century. The popular upheavals of the Water War against privatization in 2000 turned the tide against the previous fifteen years of right-wing assault.

This was followed by the Aymara peasant uprisings of 2000 and 2001, the antitax revolt of February 2003, and the ousting of two neoliberal presidents in the Gas Wars of 2003 and 2005 through mass extra-parliamentary insurrections—Gonzalo Sánchez de Lozada and Carlos Mesa, respectively, were tossed out in the course of these street battles. All this laid the basis for Evo Morales's successful bid to become the country's first indigenous president, as leader of the MAS, in the December 2005 elections. He then consolidated this position four years later, with 64 percent of the popular vote in December 2009 on a 90 percent voter turnout.

What becomes clear through an honest appraisal of the historical record is that the left-indigenous insurrectionary period between 2000 and 2005 did indeed amount to a revolutionary epoch, even if its main protagonists have not yet achieved a social revolution. As politics shifted from the streets to the electoral terrain after the May–June 2005 revolts and the lead-up to the December 2005 elections, we witnessed the common turn toward a dampening of revolutionary possibilities, and social movements demobilized as a moderate political party came to office—a turn, in other words, from the Radical Left to an *izquierda permitida*. While the popular classes demonstrated an extraordinary power to mobilize in 2003 and 2005, they lacked a revolutionary party that might have been able to cohere the disparate insurrectionary forces and respond to the question of state power. In the power vacuum that arose in the absence of such a party, the MAS filled the void.

Since Morales came to office in January 2006, the government has implemented a political economy rooted in a reconstituted neoliberalism. The combined liberation struggle for indigenous liberation and socialism that was witnessed in the country between 2000 and 2005 was diverted into a process of distinct "revolutionary" stages—a thin indigenous liberation today, separated from the socialist revolution, a vague possibility put off until many years into the future. The model of reconstituted neoliberalism, however, has begun to generate increasing mobilization from popular classes situated increasingly to the left of the government. The hope for Bolivia's future remains with the overwhelmingly indigenous rural and urban popular classes, organizing and struggling independently for themselves against combined capitalist exploitation and racial oppression, with visions of simultaneous indigenous liberation and socialist emancipation guiding them forward, as we witnessed on a grand scale between 2000 and 2005.

Notes

1. Natural gas exports increased significantly in 1999 when the new gas pipeline to Brazil was finished, making hydrocarbons much more important to the Bolivian economy.

2. It should be noted that many scholars have called into question the veracity of World Bank figures on poverty. Just as important, poverty figures say nothing about the rate of exploitation of labor by capital.

3. It should be recalled that Bolivia was already the poorest country in South America and one of the most unequal countries in the most unequal region of the world. By 2000, out of all Latin American and Caribbean countries, only Brazil and Chile registered worse Gini coefficients.

4. While this method tends to bias the occurrence of these sorts of contentious episodes in capital cities, the data nonetheless acts "as a useful proxy for social discontent with the policies of the state or with political actors of different time periods" (Gray Molina and Chávez, 2005: 86).

5. During conflicts between peasants and the state over this period, nine peasants were killed between the *cocaleros* of the Chapare and the Aymara highland roadblockers, while approximately 127 were injured (García Linera, Chávez León, and Costas Monje, 2005: 123).

6. It is not clear if the "arms" were symbolic wooden rifles or old Mausers. What is important, as Aymara sociologist Pablo Mamani Ramírez has carefully pointed out, is that this photo, circulated through various media throughout the different departments of the country, became an image of a region in revolt, a self-conscious indigenous rebellion pitted against the state (Mamani Ramírez, 2004: 53).

7. FSTCLP-TK is affiliated to but often acts autonomously from the CSUTCB.

8. "Bonapartism," as used here, refers to a sociopolitical phenomenon that may occur following a revolutionary situation in which the oppressed classes, although massively mobilized, lack the political confidence or power to achieve full victory over the ruling class, which is no longer capable of ruling directly. In this situation, a leader may emerge who seems neither to belong to the ruling class nor to the oppressed masses—who seems to stand above the class struggle. The surface image of this leader's rule is best represented in the adoption of modest reforms to deradicalize and mollify the masses while continuing to act largely in the interest of the old ruling class. A Bonapartist interregnum is inherently unstable, lasting only until either the ruling class or the oppressed masses have developed sufficient confidence and power to impose their leadership on society as a whole. Karl Marx famously discussed these issues with reference to Napoleon I and Napoleon III in France. In the preface to the second edition of *The Eighteenth Brumaire of Louis Bonaparte*, Marx (1981 [1852]: 8) described "how the *class struggle* in France created circumstances and relationships that made it possible for a grotesque mediocrity to play a hero's part." In early twenty-first-century Bolivia, the oppressed rose up to oust President Gonzalo Sánchez de Lozada in the October 2003 Gas War only to have Carlos Mesa, a "grotesque mediocrity," take the helm in a hero's guise.

9. Bolivia is divided into nine departments, or states. In local parlance they have been separated traditionally into those of the *altiplano* (La Paz, Oruro, and Potosí), the valleys (Cochabamba, Chuquisaca, and Tarija), and the eastern lowlands (Pando, Beni, and Santa Cruz). In the contemporary period, the term *media luna* (half moon) has gained political currency as a way of describing Pando, Beni, Santa Cruz, and Tarija. The *media luna* departments are also frequently called the "eastern lowlands" today despite Tarija's traditional positioning in the valley departments and Pando's location in the northwest of the country.

10. This is not to say that neoliberal hegemony, even in Santa Cruz, Tarija, Beni, and Pando, was without contradiction or free from opposition.

11. Mesa threatened to resign in March 2005 but quickly retracted this threat when it seemed that a possible alliance with the eastern bourgeois bloc could be constructed, provided Mesa break all ties with the MAS. The MAS was thus expelled from the tacit government coalition by Mesa in March, but the president's alliance with the Far Right never took hold properly.

12. It ought to be noted here that poverty figures from ECLAC do not correspond with the figures discussed here. The latest ECLAC publications provide national figures for 1999 and 2007, and claim that there has been a downward shift in Bolivian poverty from 60.6 to 54 percent poverty between these years (ECLAC, 2010b: 65).

13. Again, however, social spending has actually *declined* as a percentage of GDP under Morales, even as it increased in real, inflation-adjusted terms.

14. An analysis of agrarian reform remains beyond the scope of this book, but others have pointed out that in this area, too, reform has been wildly disappointing. See Ormachea Saavedra, 2009, for example.

15. It should be noted that the call for a "general strike" is used quite loosely in Bolivian labor movement politics, and for the last twenty-five years it has rarely meant a genuine general strike in the sense commonly understood elsewhere in the world.

References

Albro, Robert. 2005. "'The Waters Is Ours, Carajo!': Deep Citizenship in Bolivia's Water War." In *Social Movements: A Reader*, ed. June C. Nash, 249–71. Hoboken, NJ: Basic Blackwell.

APDHB et al. 2004. *12–13 de Febrero 2003: Para que no se olvide.* La Paz: Plural Editores.

Arze Vargas, Carlos. 2000. *Crisis del sindicalismo boliviano: Consideraciones sobre sus determinantes materiales y su ideología.* La Paz: CEDLA.

Assies, Willem. 2003. "David versus Goliath in Cochabamba: Water Rights, Neoliberalism, and the Revival of Social Protest in Bolivia." *Latin American Perspectives* 30 (3): 14–36.

Cáceres, Sergio. 2005. "El Discurseador: Carlos Mesa." *El Juguete Rabioso*, June 23.

Chávez, Walter. 2005a. "El otro indeciso: Evo Morales." *El Juguete Rabioso*, May 29.

———. 2005b. "Un recorrido histórico: Las luchas por la autonomía cruceña." *Barataria* 1 (3): 60–65.

Chávez, Walter, and Álvaro García Linera. 2005. "Rebelión Camba: Del dieselazo a la lucha por la autonomía." *El Juguete Rabioso*, January 23.

Crabtree, John. 2005. *Patterns of Protest: Politics and Social Movements in Bolivia.* London: Latin America Bureau.

Crespo Flores, Carlos. 2000. "Continuidad y ruptura: La 'Guerra del Agua' y los movimientos sociales en Bolivia." *Observatorio Social de America Latina* 2:21–28.

Eaton, Kent. 2007. "Backlash in Bolivia: Regional Autonomy as a Reaction against Indigenous Mobilisation." *Politics and Society* 35 (1): 71–102.

ECLAC. 2008. *Economic Survey of Latin America and the Caribbean, 2007–2008.* Santiago: ECLAC.

———. 2010a. *Preliminary Overview of the Economies of Latin America and the Caribbean, 2009.* Santiago: ECLAC.

———. 2010b. *Anuario Estadístico de América Latina y el Caribe, 2009.* Santiago: ECLAC.

EIU. 2008. *Bolivia: Country Profile 2008.* London: Economist Intelligence Unit.

Espinoza, Claudia. 2003. "19 de Septiembre ¿Comienza otro ciclo?" *Pulso,* September 19.

Espinoza, Claudia, and Gonzalo Gosálvez. 2003. "Bolivia arrinconada en la azotea de su historia: Levantamiento popular del 12 y 13 de febrero en La Paz." *Observatorio Social de América Latina* 4 (10): 29–36.

Fernández Terán, Roberto. 2003. *FMI, Banco Mundial y Estado neocolonial: poder supranacional en Bolivia.* La Paz: Plural Editores.

Finnegan, William. 2002. "Leasing the Rain." *New Yorker,* April 8.

Fuentes, Frederico. 2010a. "Bolivia: Between Mother Earth and an 'Extraction Economy.'" *Bullet,* Socialist Project E-Bulletin, May 17.

———. 2010b. "Bolivia: When Fantasy Trumps Reality." *Green Left Weekly,* May 22.

García Linera, Álvaro. 2002a. "El ocaso de un ciclo estatal." In *Democratizaciones plebeyas,* ed Raquel Gutiérrez et al., 147–76. La Paz: Muela del Diablo.

———. 2002b. "La formación de la identidad en el movimiento indígena-campesino aymara." *Fe y pueblo* 2 (4).

———. 2004. "La crisis de estado y las sublevaciones indígeno-plebeyas." In *Memorias de Octubre,* ed Álvaro García Linera, Raúl Prada, and Luis Tapia, 29–86. La Paz: Muela del Diablo.

———. 2006. "State Crisis and Popular Power." *New Left Review* 37:73–85.

García Linera, Álvaro, Marxa Chávez León, and Patricia Costas Monje. 2005. *Sociología de los movimientos sociales en Bolivia: Estructuras de movilización, repertorios culturales y acción política.* 2nd ed. La Paz: Oxfam and Diakonia.

García Mérida, Wilson. 2003. "Democracia boliviana: Bajo la bota militar." *El Juguete Rabioso,* February 16.

Gray Molina, George, and Gonzalo Chávez. 2005. "The Political Economy of the Crisis in the Andean Region: The Case of Bolivia." In *Political Crises, Social Conflict, and Economic Development: The Political Economy of the Andean Region,* ed Andrés Solimano, 73–113. Northampton: Edward Elgar.

Guachalla, Osvaldo. 2010. "La exacerbación de la política extractivista del M.A.S.: Privatización con fachada nacionalista." *El Observador* 4 (8): 14–15.

Gutiérrez, Raquel, and Álvaro García Linera. 2002. "El ciclo estatal neoliberal y sus crisis." In *Democratizaciones plebeyas,* ed Raquel Gutiérrez et al., 9–24. La Paz: Muela del Diablo.

Hylton, Forrest. 2003. "Working Class Revolt in Bolivia: The Sudden Return of Dual Power." *Counterpunch,* February 15.

Hylton, Forrest, and Sinclair Thomson. 2004. "The Roots of Rebellion: Insurgent Bolivia." *NACLA Report on the Americas* 38 (3): 15–19.

———. 2005. "The Chequered Rainbow." *New Left Review* 35:40–64.

———. 2007. *Revolutionary Horizons: Past and Present in Bolivian Politics.* London: Verso.

INE. 2001. *Anuario estadístico.* La Paz: Instituto Nacional de Estatística.

Kohl, Benjamin. 2003. "Restructuring Citizenship in Bolivia: *El Plan de Todos.*" *International Journal of Urban and Regional Research* 27 (2): 337–51.

Kohl, Benjamin, and Linda Farthing. 2006. *Impasse in Bolivia: Neoliberal Hegemony and Popular Resistance.* London: Zed Books.

La Razón. 2010. "Bolivia: Principal syndical obrera desafía a Evo Morales con huelga general," May 7.

Lebowitz, Michael. 2006. *Build It Now! Socialism for the Twenty-first Century.* New York: Monthly Review Press.

Lora, Miguel. 2005. "Hacendados armados en el norte de Santa Cruz." *El Juguete Rabioso,* May 15.

Malloy, James, and Eduardo Gammara. 1988. *Revolution and Reaction: Bolivia, 1964–1985.* New Brunswick, NJ: Transaction Books.

Mamani Ramírez, Pablo. 2004. *El rugir de las multitudes: La fuerza de los levantamientos indígenas en Bolivia/Qullasuyu.* La Paz: Aruwiyiri.

———. 2005. *Microgobiernos barriales: Levantamiento de la ciudad de El Alto (octubre 2003).* La Paz: Centro Andino de Estudios Estratégicos.

Marx, Karl. [1852] 1981. *The Eighteenth Brumaire of Louis Bonaparte.* New York: International Publishers.

McNally, David. 2006. *Another World Is Possible: Globalization and Anti-Capitalism.* 2nd ed. Winnipeg: Arbeiter Ring Publishers.

Mokrani Chávez, Dunia, and Pilar Uriona Crespo. 2011. "Bolivia—Construcción hegemónica o monopolización de la política: el Movimiento al Socialismo y las posibilidades del proceso de cambio." *Observatorio Social de América Latina* 29:111–27.

Olivera, Oscar. 2004. "A Political Thesis." In *¡Cochabamba! Water War in Bolivia,* ed Oscar Olivera and Tom Lewis, 117–28. Cambridge, MA: South End Press.

Opinión. 2003. "Opositores, COB y COR El Alto respaldan sucesión constitucional de Vicepresidente." October 17.

Orellana Aillón, Lorgio. 2006. "Oligarquía capitalista, régimen de acumulación y crisis política en Bolivia." *Nómadas* (25):261–72.

Ormachea Saavedra, Enrique. 2009. *Soberanía y seguridad alimentaria en Bolivia: Políticas y estado de situación.* La Paz: CEDLA.

Patzi, Felix. 2005. "Rebelión indígena contra la colonialidad y la transnacionalización de la economía: Triunfos y vicisitudes del movimiento indígena desde 2000 a 2003." In *Ya es otro tiempo el presente: Cuatro momentos de insurgencia indígena,* ed Forrest Hylton et al., 199–279. La Paz: Muela del Diablo.

Peredo, Arturo. 2003. "La policía salvó a Bolivia del impuestazo." *El Juguete Rabioso,* February 16.

Quispe, Felipe. 2005. "La lucha de los *ayllus* kataristas hoy." In *Movimiento indígena en América Latina: resistencia y proyecto alternativo,* ed Fabiola Escárzaga and Raquel Gutiérrez, 71–75. Puebla: Universidad Autónoma de Puebla.

Rivera Cusicanqui, Silvia. 1991. "Liberal Democracy and *Ayllu* Democracy in Bolivia: The Case of Northern Potosí." *Journal of Development Studies* 25 (4): 97–121.

Rohter, Larry. 2003. "Bolivian Leader Resigns and His Vice President Steps In." *New York Times*, October 18.

Schultz, Jim. 2005. *Deadly Consequences: The International Monetary Fund and Bolivia's "Black February."* Cochabamba: Democracy Center.

Spronk, Susan. 2007. "Roots of Resistance to Urban Water Privatisation in Bolivia: The 'New Working Class,' the Crisis of Neoliberalism, and Public Services." *International Labor and Working-Class History* 71 (1): 8–28.

Spronk, Susan, and Jeffery R. Webber. 2007. "Struggles against Accumulation by Dispossession in Bolivia: The Political Economy of Natural Resource Contention." *Latin American Perspectives* 34 (2): 31–47.

Stefanoni, Pablo. 2010a. "Bolivia después de las elecciones: ¿a dónde va el *evismo*?" *Nueva Sociedad*, no. 225: 4–17.

———. 2010b. "Huelga general indefinida, con pocas perspectivas." *Il Manifesto*, May 10.

Suárez, Hugo José. 2003. *Una semana fundamental: 10–13 octubre 2003*. La Paz: Muela del Diablo.

Tapia, Luis. 2000. "La crisis política de Abril." *Observatorio Social de América Latina* 2:3–6.

———. 2005. "El presidente colonial." In *Horizontes y límites del estado y el poder*, ed. Álvaro Gacía Linera et al., 77–110. La Paz: Muela del Diablo.

Webber, Jeffery R. 2008. "Dynamite in the Mines and Bloody Urban Clashes: Contradiction, Conflict and the Limits of Reform in Bolivia's Movement towards Socialism." *Socialist Studies/Études Socialistes* 4:79–117.

———. 2009. "From Naked Barbarism to Barbarism with Benefits: Neoliberal Capitalism, Natural Gas Policy, and the Government of Evo Morales in Bolivia." In *Post-Neoliberalism in the Americas*, ed. Arne Ruckert and Laura Macdonald, 105–19. New York: Palgrave Macmillan.

———. 2010. "The Rebellion in Potosí: Uneven Development, Neoliberal Continuities, and a Revolt against Poverty in Bolivia." *Upside Down World*, August 16.

Weisbrot, Mark, Rebecca Ray, and Jake Johnston. 2009. *Bolivia: The Economy during the Morales Administration*. Washington, DC: Center for Economic and Policy Research.

World Bank. 2005. *Bolivia Poverty Assessment: Establishing the Basis for Pro-Poor Growth*. New York: World Bank.

Zibechi, Raúl. 2011. "Bolivia after the Storm." *Americas Program*, March 23.

8

Venezuela

An Electoral Road to Twenty-First-Century Socialism?

Gregory Wilpert

THERE ARE PERHAPS FOUR PRIMARY VIEWS of Venezuela under President Hugo Chávez. First, there are many who simply depict the Chávez government as a typical Latin American strongman or *caudillo* regime that has installed an authoritarian political system and is on its path toward creating a socialist dictatorship. Those who make this claim include the outgoing Bush administration and most of Venezuela's opposition. The second view is slightly more sophisticated and was expressed recently in an article by political scientist Javier Corrales in *Foreign Policy* (Corrales, 2006). Corrales claims, "Chávez has refashioned authoritarianism for a democratic age." The third position, common among both moderate supporters and moderate opponents of Chávez, is that he is merely reestablishing Venezuelan social democracy, which, for some, is an important achievement in a time when neoliberalism has been the dominant political and economic philosophy.[1] This third view of the Chávez government, while generally a minority position in analyses of Venezuela, most closely resembles the *izquierda permitida* or "good left" conception of the Latin American Left. Finally, the fourth perspective is that the Chávez government is embarking on something new, perhaps even revolutionary, because it is in the process of developing what has been called "twenty-first-century socialism."[2] Such an interpretation places the Chávez government, and the process of the Bolivarian Revolution more generally, squarely within the *radical Left* of the so-called pink tide that made its way through much of the region over the course of the last decade. In what follows, I want to explore the latter two perspectives on Venezuela to see to what extent it is justified to say that Venezuela is heading toward something more than "mere" social democracy or the politics of the *izquierda permitida*. To explain this, we will have to look not only at the current policies of the Chávez government but also at the government's origins and trajectory over time.

History and Origins of the Bolivarian Revolution[3]

It was in a context of Venezuelan economic decline and the deterioration of public institutions in the late 1970s and early 1980s that a young soldier by the name of Hugo Rafael Chávez Frías became politicized. Chávez was born during the Marcos Pérez Jiménez dictatorship, in 1954, and grew up in Venezuela's poorest state in a lower-middle-class family during the country's boom years. He had joined the military mainly because it was one of the few avenues for upward social mobility, which allowed him to receive a higher education. Venezuela's military was rather unusual in Latin America because it allowed ordinary soldiers from poor backgrounds to rise through the ranks to the highest levels and gave them a university education, often outside of the military academies. As a result, Chávez and many of his peers were exposed to leftist thought at public universities.

In addition to this rather progressive military education, Chávez came face-to-face with the Colombian civil war and its leftist guerrillas. He experienced firsthand the brutality of this civil war while stationed near the Colombian border. Disturbed by this experience, in 1977, at only twenty-three years of age, Chávez decided to form his own conspiratorial organization— the Ejército de Liberación del Pueblo de Venezuela (Liberation Army of the Venezuelan People, ELPV). The ELPV had only six members at its inception.

Chávez spent several more years in the military, however, before he turned to conspiratorial organizing seriously. During that time, from 1977 to 1982, while Chávez was stationed in Maracay, one of Venezuela's main air bases, the contradiction between the government's effort to create La Gran Venezuela, or the Great Venezuela, and the reality of economic and institutional decline became ever more glaring. The decline of oil revenues and thus also of per capita gross domestic product (GDP) was steady and unprecedented in the world during this period, declining by as much as 27 percent between 1979 and 1999. Despite the generalized debt crisis across the region in the 1980s, no other economy in South America experienced such a dramatic decline.[4] Poverty increased from 17 percent in 1980 to 65 percent in 1996 (Universidad Católica Andrés Bello, 2001). In addition, interest rates for foreign debt soared, so that between 1970 and 1994 total debt rose from 9 percent to 53 percent of gross national product (GNP).

By 1982 Chávez found several likeminded instructors at the academy who sympathized with his rejection of the increasingly corrupt Venezuelan social and political system and founded the EBR-200. EBR, says Chávez, stood for the three ideological roots of the group: Ezequiel Zamora, Simón Bolívar, and Simón Rodríguez. It also stood for Bolivarian Revolutionary Army (Ejército Bolivariano Revolucionario). The 200 stood for the two-hundred-year anniversary of Simón Bolívar's birth in 1783.

Venezuela spent most of the 1980s in a downward economic spiral so that in 1988 former president Carlos Andrés Pérez, someone Venezuelans associated with the country's boom years ten years earlier, was able to get reelected. Although he had campaigned on a platform against neoliberalism, Pérez reversed this position shortly after taking office and implemented a structural adjustment program of price increases and social-program cutbacks, with the full backing of the International Monetary Fund (IMF). The public's reaction was immediate, and poor neighborhoods throughout Venezuela erupted first in protests and then in riots on February 27, 1989. The government, initially taken by surprise, reacted the next day by sending out police and military to suppress the riots. In the end, after four days of shooting, the civilian death toll stood at somewhere between four hundred and more than one thousand. The incident, which came to be known as the Caracazo, left an indelible mark on the Venezuelan psyche—on the poor for the extremes to which a government would go to repress them, and on the better off for the anger of the poor toward their economic situation.

While Venezuela was dealing with the consequences of neoliberal adjustment and social unrest, Chávez began approaching leftist civilians and including them in his group, renaming his EBR-200 to MBR-200, the Bolivarian Revolutionary Movement. On February 4, 1992, the MBR-200 launched its coup against the thoroughly delegitimized Pérez. Ultimately, even though Chávez was able to capture several key military installations, the coup failed, mainly because word of it had leaked to the government shortly before it took place. However, the coup did catapult Chávez onto the national stage and turn him into a folk hero, even though he was imprisoned for two years, after which he was released under an amnesty.

By 1996 Chávez and his closest advisors decided to opt for the electoral route to power. Within the military, Chávez's organization had been practically destroyed, making any renewed coup attempt impossible. A new party, the Movimiento Quinta República (Fifth Republic Movement, MVR), was formally registered on September 23, 1997, and served as the vehicle for Chávez's election to the presidency.[5] The party wanted to found a fifth republic. It identified four republics since Venezuela's independence and argued the fifth would begin with the passage of a new constitution, if Chávez were elected.

The 1998 presidential contest boiled down to an establishment candidate (Salas Römer), supported by AD (Democratic Action), Copei, La Causa R, and a variety of smaller center-right parties, and an antiestablishment candidate (Chávez), supported by his Polo Patriótico coalition of four major leftist parties and many smaller ones. Given the country's disgust with the establishment, it came as little surprise that Chávez won easily, with 56.2 percent of the vote—one of the largest margins in Venezuela's history. Salas Römer got 40 percent, and the former beauty queen Irene Sáez got 2.8 percent.

Chávez and the Venezuelan Left

Later, in the course of Chávez's presidency, analysts critical of Chávez pointed to the fact that various leftist parties dropped out of the pro-Chávez coalition as proof that Chávez is not an authentic leftist. After all, why else would these parties, all of which have a respectable trajectory on Venezuela's left, leave the coalition? The MAS, in 2000, was the first of these parties to eventually leave Chávez's camp. At this juncture, a significant sector of the MAS split off to form a new pro-Chávez social democratic party known as Podemos (We Can, which would eventually also leave the Chavista coalition in 2007). Prominent leftist individuals that jumped ship included Luis Miquilena and Alejandro Armas, who, along with several others, went on to form the party Solidaridad (Solidarity) in 2001. Prominent left-of-center parties that never supported Chávez at all include La Causa R (center-left) and Bandera Roja (extreme left).

A closer look at all of these left-of-center opposition parties shows, however, that, with the exception of Bandera Roja, they were all adherents of moderate leftist politics—the *izquierda permitida*. The reason that they either did not join Chávez or split from him at various times during his presidency is that they disagreed with Chávez's radicalism. For example, Miquilena and the Solidaridad founders left Chávez's coalition when he refused to compromise on the new land reform, fishing, and hydrocarbons laws, which were passed by decree in 2001. Similarly, the principal leader of La Causa R, Andrés Velásquez, and prominent (ex-)leftists such as Teodoro Petkoff and Américo Martín, never supported Chávez because they endorsed large parts of the neoliberal economic analysis of Venezuela.[6] Bandera Roja, a radical Maoist splinter group, is the only party that hasn't supported Chávez because they consider him insufficiently leftist. In any case, Chávez is probably better off without the support of this often violent fringe group.

Finally, another common criticism regarding the political roots of the Bolivarian Movement is that it incorporates right-wing individuals.[7] The first and perhaps most important piece of evidence for this claim is that Chávez appeared to show sympathies for and on occasion met with the expatriate Argentinean right-wing intellectual Norberto Ceresole. Chávez was interested in Ceresole mainly because of his support for progressive military dictators, such as Peru's General Juan Velasco Alverado and Panama's General Omar Torrijos. Also, Ceresole advocated Latin American integration under a type of continental nationalism, more or less as Simón Bolívar did. Ceresole's anti-Semitism, support for the brutal military dictatorship in Argentina (1976–1983), and theory about a postdemocratic and *caudillo*-led society made him a controversial figure in Venezuela. Chávez parted ways with him, though, when he expelled him from Venezuela in 1999.

Also, before Chávez decisively embraced socialism in 2005, he was often ambiguous about just how much of a leftist he was, going so far as to imply that he favored "third way" social democratic politics during his presidential campaign of 1998 (see Jones, 2007: 77).[8] Some individuals who supported Chávez clearly had more in common with the Bolivarian Movement's nationalism than with its incipient socialism. Examples of such individuals are Luis Alfonso Dávila, who was one of Chávez's first foreign ministers, and Jesús Urdaneta and Yoel Chirinos, both part of Chávez's original MBR-200 group. All of these individuals, though, stopped supporting Chávez once it became clear that he wanted to steer a socialist and anticapitalist course.

While Chávez was still ambiguous about his real political intentions during his 1998 presidential campaign, several sectors of Venezuela's capitalist class decided to support him. The most important sources of support came from the Latin American media mogul Gustavo Cisneros, who owns one of Venezuela's largest TV stations, Venevision (among many other things), and from the left-of-center newspaper *El Nacional*. Also, Chávez's campaign manager, Luis Miquilena, had extensive ties to Venezuela's business community and convinced various businesses to support Chávez's campaign (this would later lead to an accusation that Chávez received a substantial illegal campaign donation from the Spanish banking group Banco Bilbao Vizcaya). Later on, though, these supporters abandoned Chávez, so that his main base within the capitalist class came from the small-business sector, particularly as represented in the chamber of small industries Fedeindustria.

Reformist and Transformative Policy Formulation[9]

How are we to distinguish the Chávez government from the politics of *izquierda permitida* evident in Lula's and Roussef's Brazil and Bachelet's Chile, among other countries in the region? What, exactly, were the policies that caused various moderate supporters to split from the Chávez coalition? Given that, at heart, the Bolivarian Revolution sought to bring about dramatic change in Venezuela's political and economic landscape, it is useful to employ André Gorz's distinction between reformist and nonreformist reform as we attempt to explain the gradual radicalization of the Chávez administration over time (see Gorz, 1964).[10] Reformist policies are those that improve the lives of most people but basically leave the political and economic system intact. Reformist policies may even demobilize those who were fighting for the changes because they see the improvement and no longer feel any urgency for further progressive change. Nonreformist reform, or transformative policies as I prefer to call these, not only improve people's lives but also work toward changing the political and economic system and set the stage for making more progressive change possible. An examination of the Chávez government's policies in the areas of governance, economics, and social and foreign policy will further clarify this distinction.

Governance Policy

Changes that the Chávez government initiated in Venezuela's polity cover at least four broad areas: constitution, judiciary, military, and participatory democracy. Of these four, the most transformative policy has been the effort to create a participatory democracy since this effort affects a wide variety of other policy areas. The creation of participatory democracy was enshrined in a new constitution, which Venezuelans passed by referendum in 1999 following a very broad societal discussion. That is, the new constitution provided for a wide variety of new mechanisms for citizen participation in governance, such as citizen-initiated referenda, local planning councils, citizen assemblies, and civil-society participation in the nomination of members to various branches of the state (judiciary, electoral council, attorney general, etc.). Taken together, the new constitution sowed the seeds of a participatory democracy in Venezuela. This represents transformative policy because increased citizen participation opens the door to further progressive change toward increasing social inclusion and social justice. That is, citizens can use the tools of participatory democracy, such as the citizen-initiated referenda, to implement more far-reaching changes.[11]

Within the wider shift toward participatory democracy, perhaps the most transformative initiative has been the creation of communal councils. These councils, which are based on direct democratic citizen assemblies outlined in the 1999 constitution, bring together a wide variety of citizen groups that had already been created in response to the government's social policies. For example, the public water company urged neighborhoods that had inadequate access to drinking water and sewage disposal to form "technical water committees" that would negotiate with the water company to improve service. Similarly, for the implementation of the community health program known as Barrio Adentro (Inside the Barrio), communities were asked to create health committees that would help institute this program. The urban land reform program, which aimed to give land titles to people who lived in shanties built on illegally occupied land, required communities to form urban land committees. These different types of community committees have come to constitute the pillars of the communal councils. Between 150 and 400 families in a contiguous neighborhood form each communal council and elect spokespersons during a citizen assembly. While the approximately thirty thousand councils have been formed mostly in poor neighborhoods, they have also been formed in many middle-class neighborhoods, particularly since everyone is interested in taking advantage of government funding for neighborhood improvement projects.

The reason the communal councils have the greatest transformative potential is that they organize communities. This has proven to be an effective tool in overcoming poverty because organized citizens are in a better position to improve their own neighborhoods or demand government services. More than that, citizens become actively engaged in a learning process whereby they become more effective citizens. Finally, the communal councils are also stepping stones for broader participation beyond the immediate neighborhood, as the government plans to bring contiguous councils together to form what are known as "communes." According to government plans for creating "Bolivarian socialism," these communes, organized on the scale of a small city, will also become more involved in the economic functioning of their areas. They will take responsibility for major public employers in their territory by playing a role in the management of these companies. At the time of writing (May 2011), several dozen communes were in the process of being formed.

Another important change that Chávez launched via the new constitution was the creation of two new branches of the state, in addition to the usual three of executive, judiciary, and legislature. The two new branches are, first, the so-called moral power—essentially an independent prosecutorial branch of the state, including the attorney general, the comptroller general, and the human rights ombudsperson—and, second, the electoral power, in the form of the National Electoral Council (CNE). The fact that these new branches are independent of the executive, in that the executive has no power to appoint or dismiss their members, creates a powerful check on executive power—of course, only if and when members of these branches are inclined to exercise their power.[12]

The changes that the Chávez government introduced in the judiciary and in the military were generally more reformist than transformative in orientation. That is, the government launched an extensive campaign early in Chávez's presidency to get rid of rampant corruption within the judiciary. Also, following the 2002 coup attempt, in which a slight majority of Supreme Court judges refused to prosecute four key coup organizers, the pro-Chávez-dominated National Assembly expanded the Supreme Court from twenty to thirty-two judges, largely to guarantee that there would no longer be a coup-supporting majority on the Supreme Court. In the end, the reform effort within the judiciary has not improved it much, relative to the pre-Chávez years, meaning that corruption and influence peddling remain serious problems.

Reforms of the Venezuelan military, though, went slightly further toward transforming this institution, in that Chávez moved to bring civilian and military life closer together under the doctrine of "civil-military union." Here the idea was to counter the Latin American tendency to isolate the military from civilian life. All too often in Latin America, the alienation of militaries from wider society enabled them to repress civilians. By having the military carry out more civilian tasks, such as distributing food to the country's poor and helping with the rebuilding of homes, and by vastly expanding the country's military reserve by turning it into more of a militia, the military has developed closer ties with civil society. Also, the 1999 constitution declared that guaranteeing food security is a national security issue, thereby justifying the military's involvement in a variety of food-distribution tasks.

Economic Policy

The Chávez government's economic policies can be divided into the three general categories of oil policy, macroeconomic policy, and social economy. Changes in the first two tend to be more reformist in that they improve the lives of Venezuelans but do not alter the economic system as such. The creation of a social economy, though, if greatly expanded, could eventually lead to the creation of a new and different economic system. Of course, if the social economy ends up encroaching on the more reformist macroeconomy and oil sector, then these latter two could also end up being transformed.

Saying that the Chávez government's oil policy is reformist does not mean to imply that it has not led to a dramatic shift in the way the government runs the oil industry. On the contrary, when Chávez first came into office in 1999, the oil industry—despite having been technically nationalized in the mid-1970s—was run almost completely independently of the government. Its management was still guided by the same business culture as when transnational oil companies owned it. This meant that the state oil company, Petroleos de Venezuela, SA (Petroleum of Venezuela, PDVSA), often undermined official government policies when it came to abiding by quotas of the Organization of Petroleum Exporting Countries (OPEC) and was actively attempting to circumvent government efforts to collect oil revenues. Also, parts of PDVSA had already been partially privatized by the time Chávez became president, mainly via the subcontracting of key functions of the industry to transnational oil companies.

This process of creeping privatization and circumventing revenue collection had gone so far that while in 1981 the industry paid 71 percent of its revenues to the Venezuelan state and kept 29 percent for its operating costs, by 1998 this relationship had been almost reversed, so that merely 39 percent of revenues were passed on to the state and 61 percent were needed for operating costs (Mommer, 2003: 137). There are many reasons for this decline in the proportion of oil revenues that the state captured, such as declining oil price and the declining quality of oil wells. However, another crucial aspect was that PDVSA actively tried to transfer profits outside of Venezuela by selling discounted oil to its own refineries abroad and imported costs by making unprofitable purchases, such as refineries that did not refine Venezuelan oil. It also entered into contracts with transnational oil companies that were very unfavorable to the Venezuelan state, requiring a mere 1 percent royalty for the extraction of extra-heavy crude in the Orinoco Oil Belt and allowing private companies to overcharge for their oil production activity.

One of the first things the Chávez government did, with the passage of the 2001 Hydrocarbons Law, was to change the royalty rates that private companies had to pay, first increasing some from 1 percent to 16 percent, in the case of Orinoco Oil Belt extra-heavy oil, and doubling royalties for all other oil production from 16.6 percent to 33 percent (in addition to an oil tax of 50 percent). The PDVSA management, though, opposed these changes and also continued to resist the imposition of OPEC quotas. As a result, the conflict within PDVSA came to a head in December 2002, when the management, engineers, and administrative employees organized a two-month shutdown of the oil industry. It was only once this shutdown was defeated, with the help of blue-collar oil workers and by bringing in supportive foreign and retired oil engineers, that the Chávez government finally asserted control over its own oil industry.

The defeat of the old oil management brought about further changes in oil policy, such as requiring all operating agreements with private oil companies to be turned from a subcontracting arrangement into a joint venture arrangement, whereby PDVSA would maintain a minimum 60 percent share in the project. In this way private companies would no longer have an incentive to inflate costs, and the interests of PDVSA and the private companies would be more in alignment with each other.

All of these changes that the Chávez government's oil policy brought about were dramatic, considering the history of Venezuela's oil industry, in that they represented a "renationalization" of this sector of the economy. However, the reforms remained within the existing paradigm of state versus private control and the maximization of oil revenues, regardless of what this might mean for oil industry workers and for the environment. Ordinary Venezuelans certainly reap greater benefits from the policy, in the form of better-funded social programs and greater investment in infrastructure, health, and education, among other things, but it does not transcend the paradigm of market competition or central state control.

Furthermore, despite the effort to diversify the economy, these macroeconomic and oil policies fail to overcome what is known as the "Dutch Disease," whereby the massive influx of oil revenues into the economy causes inflation and stifles domestic production because imports are cheaper under the fixed exchange rate. While domestic agricultural production has increased in Venezuela on a variety of fronts,[13] consumption has increased faster, causing imports to increase by 287 percent in the first ten years of Chávez's presidency.[14] So far, it seems, the government has not been able to overcome this "Dutch Disease," a problem typical of countries that predominantly rely on one export product.[15]

It is only with the creation of a social economy that the Chávez government is planting the seeds of a transformative alternative in Venezuela, an alternative that closely corresponds to the characteristics of a *radical Left* as identified by Jeffery Webber and Barry Carr in the introduction to this volume. This social economy involves a wide variety of policies, the most important of which are the promotion of cooperatives and industrial comanagement, the cooperation between communal councils and socialist enterprises, and the pursuit of endogenous development.

As of late 2008, the Chávez government had helped launch over one hundred thousand cooperatives,[16] which represents a more than a hundredfold increase over the number when Chávez came into office. Since each of these cooperatives employs a minimum of five members, this means that at least five hundred thousand Venezuelans are employed in the cooperative sector. This is a relatively small portion of the overall workforce, but is a significant number nonetheless.

The number of Venezuelans employed in comanaged factories, endogenous development projects, and socialist enterprises is far smaller. These projects have received a lot of attention because of their symbolic importance. Over fifteen factories have been taken over by workers in Venezuela during the Chávez presidency, according to FRETECO (Revolutionary Front of

Workers in Occupied and Comanaged Enterprises, Frente Revolucionario de Trabajadores de Empresas en Cogestión y Ocupadas), and are now either self-managed or comanaged with government representatives. The government is also in the process of implementing a plan to create over two hundred social-ist enterprises, including some of the country's largest, such as the mining and metal industries grouped in the CVG, which would be comanaged not only by workers but also by the communities in which they operate. While the social economy probably represents no more than 10 percent of total em-ployment in Venezuela and an even smaller percentage of GDP, the Chávez government intends to increase that proportion so that it is more or less equal in size to the public and the private sectors (Ministerio del Poder Popular para la Comunicación y la Información, 2007: 52).

If one considers that the capitalist economy is based on three main pillars of private ownership of the means of production, competitive market ex-change, and a capitalist state to support the other two pillars, then Venezuela is indeed on a gradual path toward transcending capitalism. That is, coopera-tives and social ownership contribute toward overcoming private ownership, state planning and community-enterprise cooperation contribute toward overcoming market allocation, and a state that supports these two processes would overcome the capitalist state. However, Venezuela's embeddedness in the capitalist world economy will continue to present an obstacle to such a socialist transformation, unless international economic relationships are transformed as well, which is something Venezuela is working on and which will be discussed in the section on foreign policy.

Social Policy

One of Chávez's top concerns after coming to power was to address Ven-ezuela's crushing poverty. The poverty rate had been rising steadily between 1975 and 1995, from 33 percent to 70 percent, according to one study.[17] In the early years of Chávez's presidency, financial resources were relatively scarce and so social programs were relatively limited. However, once the oil industry shutdown of December 2002 to January 2003 was defeated and oil produc-tion recovered to normal levels in March 2003, oil prices began to rise again. As revenues increased, the government was able to introduce one new social program after the other. These programs, though, were instituted outside of the ministries that would normally be responsible for such programs because they were deemed to be too slow and bureaucratic. To signal their unusual character, Chávez called these new programs "missions."

The first missions were dedicated to literacy training (Mission Robinson), high school completion (Mission Ribas), university scholarships (Mission

Sucre), community health care (Mission Inside the Barrio), and subsidized food markets for poor communities (Mission Mercal). Many more were added over the following years to cover issues such as vocational and cooperative training (Mission Che Guevara), indigenous land demarcation (Mission Guaicaipuro), energy conservation (Mission Energy), reforestation (Mission Tree), land reform (Mission Zamora), aid to single mothers (Mission Mothers of the Barrio), and the fight against homelessness (Mission Negra Hipolita), among others.

These social policies are characterized by two main elements. First, they are redistributive in the sense that programs such as the land reform or the social missions are designed to provide state resources, such as land or oil revenues, first and foremost to the country's poor. Second, they tend to incorporate participatory elements in that the land reform and the missions actively seek out the participation of the affected communities in their implementation. These two general characteristics have their roots in Venezuela's 1999 constitution, which states that the Venezuelan state is one based on a participatory democracy and that it guarantees social and economic rights, such as health and education, in addition to the usual political rights. As such, the government's social policies represent a significant advance with respect to those of previous governments, where social rights were not recognized and social policy was based more on charity. Also, the implementation of social policies rarely involved community participation historically, whereas in today's context they are highly participatory.

The redistributive aspect of the social programs and policies is actually not something particularly radical when compared with earlier Venezuelan governments or other government social programs around the world. Earlier Venezuelan governments, particularly in the 1960s and 1970s, gradually built up a significant welfare state in Venezuela. Advances made along social democratic lines during that period included free health care, free education, and broad social-security coverage. That Chávez is reintroducing such programs now, following the dismantling of Venezuela's welfare state in the 1980s and 1990s, makes the policies appear radical to younger poor Venezuelans, who did not experience the country's boom years.

The innovative and transformative component of the social programs is not their mere existence, but the way they are being implemented. That is, rather than being implemented in a top-down fashion through the extremely bureaucratic ministries, they are being implemented with the close participation of the communities of beneficiaries. The land reform, educational, health-care, and mothers of the barrio missions are all being implemented in conjunction with committees from the communities that have a substantial say over exactly how and where the missions should be organized. This means that in many cases the missions are creating a parallel structure alongside the ministries that either complement (as in the case of the educational programs) or practically supplant (as in the case of the housing mission and the health-care mission) the work of the old state ministries.

However, there are two serious limitations in the implementation of the government's social policies. First, social policies, while guaranteed by the constitution, are generally not guaranteed by law. That is, many social policies, such as the educational missions, the Bolivarian University, Misión Mercal, and the urban land reform, are not guaranteed by laws but by presidential decree. This means that they can easily disappear from one day to the next, as has been the case with past social policies whenever the oil revenues suddenly dried up, or they can be implemented capriciously as part of a political patronage system. The practical implication of such a lack of entitlement (other than in the form of the general formulations in the constitution) is that the programs could disappear at any time, and those who are selectively excluded from certain social policies would have a difficult time challenging their exclusion in court.

This problem of lacking legal guarantees (or entitlement) is closely related to the second problem, which is precisely that these programs often appear to be related to partisan or patronage interests. For example, in some of the educational programs, the land reform, and some of the microloan programs, accusations have been made that programs primarily benefit Chávez supporters. Certainly, Chávez supporters are more likely to seek participation in these programs since they come mostly from the country's poor majority. However, as long as vocal opponents have difficulty participating, these programs will not lose their patrimonial character.

Ultimately, though, it is fair to say that these social programs have benefited Venezuela's poor tremendously. In the eleven years of Chávez's presidency, hundreds of thousands of Venezuelans have become literate,[18] over one million Venezuelans have benefited from the land reform, inequality dropped by 20 percent (from a Gini coefficient of 0.485 to one of 0.39), poverty dropped from 50.5 percent to 23.8 percent, infant mortality dropped from 21.4 to 13.9 per one thousand live births, and the human development index, after stagnating for the previous ten years, rose from 0.77 to 0.84. This last statistic puts Venezuela in the category of "high development" according to the United Nations Development Program (UNDP).[19]

Critics of the Chávez government correctly point out, though, that these improvements are much easier to achieve when the price of oil is constantly rising, as was the case between 2003 and 2008. The real challenge and test for the Chávez government's social policies come now, during the world financial crisis, when the price of oil has plummeted from around $140 per barrel in mid-2008 to around $40 per barrel in early 2009.

Foreign Policy

The Chávez government's foreign policy is oriented around two primary objectives. First, it seeks to promote Latin American integration, and second, it seeks to promote the creation of a "multipolar" world so that there are many centers of global power instead of just one, as is currently the case. The pursuit of such a foreign policy has meant consistent Venezuelan opposition to global U.S. hegemony and alliances with many controversial governments around the world. While opposition to U.S. hegemony is undoubtedly necessary for a transformative left project, the alliances this has meant, though, are of a much more questionable value for progressive politics.

With the election of leftist governments throughout Latin America in the early 2000s, Venezuela has faced very favorable conditions for advancing its project of Latin American unity. The Chávez government has done this on a wide variety of economic and political fronts. Chávez has promoted political integration and cooperation primarily via the Bolivarian Alliance for the Peoples of Our America (Alianza Bolivariana para los Pueblos de Nuestra América, ALBA).[20] Current members are Venezuela, Cuba, Bolivia, Ecuador, Nicaragua, Honduras, and the island nations of Dominica, St. Vincent and the Grenadines, and Antigua and Barbuda. The main purpose of this alliance is to develop trade relations that are based on the principles of solidarity and cooperation rather than competitive free trade.

Energy agreements are another avenue through which the Chávez government has promoted Latin American integration. Here the main new institutions are PetroCaribe and PetroSur, which provide Venezuelan oil to a number of Latin American and Caribbean countries with low-interest financing and the option to pay for a portion of the oil bill with in-kind goods and services. The third main integration vehicle has been Venezuela's participation in Mercosur and in Unasur. Mercosur (Common Market of the South) is a traditional customs union to which Argentina, Brazil, Paraguay, and Uruguay belong. All South American countries launched Unasur (Union of South American Nations) in 2005 and formally constituted it as a new regional association in May 2008. Currently, Unasur's main profile is as a political body, with the aim to create a greater political and economic integration along the lines of the European Union. Its main economic projects are the creation of the Bank of the South and of a single currency.

This tremendous push for regional integration that Venezuela has supported with all its might has meant greater progress for such integration in recent years than at any other time since Simón Bolívar's dream of a united Latin America. However, this process has also faced several obstacles, the most important of which have been the recurrent conflicts between Venezuela and the far more conservative governments of Colombia and, less frequently, Peru. Some critics of this integration process have also claimed that Chávez's own ambition to be a regional leader has gotten in the way of authentic solidarity and cooperation across borders.

Venezuela's challenge to U.S. hegemony and efforts to develop a multipolar world have also meant challenging U.S. client regimes, such as Colombia and Israel, and the building of strong alliances with U.S. "enemies," such as Cuba and Iran. The challenge to Colombia has been extremely tricky for Venezuela, though, because Venezuela and Colombia depend on each other to an extremely high degree. For example, Colombian exports to Venezuela have increased by more than sixfold in the past ten years, from around $1 billion in 1999 to over $6 billion in 2009.[21]

Venezuela's challenge to Israel has of course opened it up to false claims that the Chávez government is anti-Semitic, something to which its close relations with Iran have only aided. Moreover, Venezuela's close relations with the right-wing regime of Iran is riddled with ideological contradictions. In the end, though, there is little doubt that Venezuela's foreign policy is one that has been admired by many around the world (particularly in Arab countries), mainly because it represents a consistent thorn in the side of U.S. hegemony.

The Venezuelan People, the Bolivarian Movement, and Chávez

President Chávez clearly has enjoyed an exceptional string of successes during his twelve years as president, decisively winning fourteen out of fifteen national electoral contests. This has allowed him increasingly free rein to pursue the policies described above. What is it, though, that enabled him to be so successful in the electoral arena? Analysts who are opposed to Chávez provide a variety of reasons. The most far-fetched arguments by the radical opposition suggest Chávez rigs elections and makes freedom of speech and assembly impossible for his opponents. However, not even Human Rights Watch, which appears to have been consistently biased against the Chávez government and which has been studying the situation in Venezuela quite closely, makes such extreme claims.[22]

The far more sophisticated argument, presented by more moderate Chávez opponents, is that Chávez's success is due to a combination of demagoguery, populism, and the provision of reward and punishment.[23] This argument is difficult either to prove or refute, though, mainly because its terms are rather vague. Indeed, according to some definitions of populism, Chávez can certainly be labeled a populist. He clearly appeals to ordinary Venezuelans in opposition to the country's elites. But then again, this by itself does not explain a politician's popularity. More important is the opposition argument that Chávez has carefully calibrated rewards and punishments so that people are more likely to support than oppose him. The evidence for this is quite flimsy, however, and is similar in character with the criticisms of the Chávez government offered by Human Rights Watch (HRW), almost all of which can be thoroughly debunked (Wilpert, 2008).

For example, HRW claims that it is general Chávez government policy to fire public employees who do not support the government or who go on strike. However, their main piece of evidence is the politically motivated strike of managers and professional oil industry employees when they attempted to shutdown Venezuela's oil industry for two months in late 2002. To claim that this was a legitimate (apolitical) strike and the firings of its participants illegitimate, as HRW does, has no basis in reality.

Given that Venezuelans regularly rate their democracy far more positively than the citizens of almost any other country in Latin America (except Uruguay), one can argue that Chávez's electoral success must be sought elsewhere, namely, in the fact that the government's policies have benefited the vast majority of Venezuelans, both materially (as can be seen in the positive indicators sited in the previous section) and politically (in terms of political inclusion, as measured by the Latinobarómetro polls [Latinobarómetro, 2007: 88]).[24] Further, Chávez's undeniable personal charisma (instead of populism or demagogy) also plays a crucial role. That is, Chávez's uncanny ability to connect with poor Venezuelans, mainly because he strongly identifies with them and they with him, is the reason that so many poor Venezuelans have stuck with him even through the toughest times, such as during the 2002 coup attempt and the 2002–2003 oil industry shutdown and subsequent recession.

The existence of a national Bolivarian Movement (and party) further fortifies this direct link between Chávez and the Venezuelan people. However, until recently the Bolivarian Movement, mostly as organized in the MVR, was a vehicle for Chávez's mobilizations and his rather frequent electoral contests. In other words, the MVR did not provide a forum for policy debates or for the development of new leadership and, as a result, functioned solely to strengthen Chávez, making the Bolivarian Movement and the things it stands for more dependent on him.

Following his resounding reelection victory in December 2006, Chávez began to organize a new political party, the United Socialist Party of Venezuela (PSUV), which was intended to unify the coalition of parties supporting him and provide better internal organization, with real innerparty democracy and a serious discussion of issues. Chávez had clearly realized that one of the Bolivarian Movement's greatest weaknesses was its dependence on him and that one way to lessen this dependence would be to create a strong democratic party for "twenty-first-century socialism." In the two years following the party's launch, the PSUV has for the most part lived up to its promise by bringing more people under the party's umbrella than was ever the case with the MVR, democratically electing its leadership, and encouraging broad debate about its political program. While there has been some deserved criticism that the PSUV is not as democratic as it claims to be, it is still undoubtedly the only democratically governed party in Venezuela.

Meanwhile, parallel to the PSUV, there are countless smaller organizations, such as small parties, labor unions, community groups, peasant organizations, and community media, among many other types of civil-society associations, that constitute an important part of the overall Bolivarian Movement. It is in these more peripheral groups that new leadership and real discussion evolved, at least until the formation of the PSUV. However, because of their fragmentation into hundreds of independent organizations, they are not sufficiently organized to have a significant impact on policy making or on leadership development. These various organizations are crucial, though, for providing the Bolivarian Movement with a far broader base than it would otherwise have.

Chávez is the glue that brings together this Bolivarian Movement, and, as such, the movement is very dependent upon him, despite the PSUV's recent formation. The key question for the next period of the Bolivarian Revolution (2011–2012, at the end of which the next presidential election will be held) will be whether the movement manages to reduce its dependence on Chávez and eventually stand on its own. As long as this dependence continues, the movement will not only be vulnerable to Chávez's assassination (or sudden illness) but will also have problems developing unconstrained debate and self-criticism. In the current situation, any questioning of Chávez or his government can threaten the government's stability since the government depends on Chávez to such a large degree. The Bolivarian Movement thus faces the contradictory task of freeing itself from Chávez's shadow and doing so without endangering its own hold on state power.

An Electoral Road to Socialism?

The 2008 election of Barack Obama as president of the United States appeared to provide a better international political climate for Venezuela than it did under Bush. However, as Chávez pointed out during his 2009 address to the UN, the change in Washington is more of rhetoric than of practice. On the one hand, Obama says that he wants an equal partnership with the countries of Latin America. On the other hand, the Obama administration has not only failed to undo key Bush administration policies such as the reactivation of the Fourth U.S. Navy Fleet now patrolling the coasts of Latin America, it has also authorized the expansion of U.S. military presence in Colombia and has not stood firmly with the rest of Latin America in opposing the July 2009 coup in Honduras. The United States thus continues to represent a challenge to the Bolivarian Revolution, even though the Obama administration is less "hawkish" than its predecessor.

The second major challenge facing the Chávez government's effort to implement "twenty-first-century socialism" is the global financial crisis, which cut the price of oil to less than half between 2008 and 2009. This has forced the government to cut back its 2009 budget by 10 percent relative to the previous year and also forced it to borrow up to $10 billion (Rosales, 2009; Suggett, 2008). The impact was an almost immediate reversal in economic growth, which had been remarkably high between 2004 and 2008, out of which the government is emerging only in 2011.[25] The fact that the world financial crisis and the ensuing oil price decline affects Venezuela highlights the fact that the country still has an economy that is inextricably tied to the global capitalist market. Any effort to move toward a socialist alternative is caught in a web of contradictions. Government moves away from capitalism have been completely dependent upon the health of the international oil industry and global capitalism.

Aside from the external threats—such as economic crisis and U.S. interference—and a sometimes violent domestic opposition, Venezuela's effort to forge an electoral road to socialism now faces the crucial and contradictory hurdle of how to create socialism as a participatory, bottom-up project, all the while being extremely dependent on one leader for its continued success. This contradiction was perhaps most clearly on display in the February 2009 constitutional amendment referendum, in which Venezuelans voted to amend the constitution so that Chávez (and all other elected officials) would be allowed to run for office for more than just two consecutive terms. For the second time in Venezuela's fifty-year democratic history, citizens were asked whether they wanted to change their constitution, but the primary motivating factor was to enable the leader of the Bolivarian Revolution to run for reelection in 2012, precisely because he continues to be so indispensable for this revolution. In other words, as was argued in the section analyzing the government's policies, the government is gradually and partially transforming Venezuela into a socialist economy and a participatory democratic polity, but it is doing so with enormous dependence on one individual's leadership. Chávez has been crucial for uniting a broad-based and otherwise fractious Bolivarian socialist movement.

Notes

1. Tariq Ali (2008) seems to be representative of the positive version of this perspective.

2. This view has been expressed by myself in Wilpert (2007), by Michael Lebowitz (2006), and by D. L. Raby (2006), among others.

3. For a full account of Chávez's life story, see Jones (2007).

4. Real per capita income (real GDP chain per equivalent adult, in 2000 constant dollars) declined from $11,869 in 1979 to $8,675 in 1999 (data from the Penn World Table, version 6.1, Center for International Comparisons at the University of Pennsylvania [CICUP]; see Heston, Summers, and Bettina, [2002]). Over this period only Peru suffered a decline, of 17 percent, while Argentina, Bolivia, Brazil, Colombia, and Ecuador increased their per capita GDP. Venezuela's real GDP per worker declined far more dramatically, by 36 percent (compared to 27 percent for Peru), indicating that inequality also increased during this time period.

5. The "V" in MVR is the Roman numeral five, which, when spelled out in Spanish, sounds very similar to the letter *B*, thus making MVR and MBR nearly indistinguishable in their pronunciation.

6. Petkoff and Velásquez both supported President Rafael Caldera's neoliberal economic measures in 1996.

7. This is an argument that the analyst Alberto Garrido has made in several of his books on the Bolivarian Movement (see Garrido 2002a, 2002b).

8. "Third way" social democracy refers to the centrist type of politics of Bill Clinton in the United States, Tony Blair in Britain, and Gerhard Schröder in Germany, which accepts the basic postulates of neoliberalism but tries to soften them by maintaining some basic welfare-state provisions.

9. A far more detailed analysis of the issues covered in this section can be found in my book *Changing Venezuela by Taking Power* (Wilpert, 2007).

10. This distinction has also been elaborated more recently by Michael Albert (2003) and Robin Hahnel (2005).

11. For a fuller discussion of participatory democracy in Venezuela, see Wilpert (2010), Bruce (2008), and Martinez, Fox, and Farrell (2009).

12. Critics of the Chávez government like to argue that there is no independence of the different branches of the state from the executive because all branches are controlled by Chávez or his supporters. Such an argument, though, misunderstands the nature of branch independence, which merely requires that the members of the different branches are able to act against the other branches if they are inclined to do so, not that they are necessarily opposed to each other. It is merely due to opposition errors and their unpopularity that they do not control any of the branches of the state, not due to illegal or illegitimate use of executive power. It is well known, for example, that the opposition boycotted the 2005 National Assembly election, which then led to Chávez supporters having a supermajority in the National Assembly, enabling them to appoint Chávez supporters to the judicial, electoral, and prosecutorial branches of the state.

13. According to government data, agricultural production in Venezuela has increased by 24 percent in the ten years of Chávez's presidency. Corn production increased by 205 percent, rice by 94 percent, sugar by 13 percent, and milk by 11 percent between 1998 and 2008. (See Suggett, 2009a.)

14. For more details, consult the Banco Central de Venezuela (2012).

15. Ninety-three percent of Venezuela's export earnings came from oil exports in 2008, when the price of oil had reached a temporary all-time high (Banco Central de Venezuela, 2012).

16. This number comes from Sunacoop, the National Superintendency of Cooperatives (interview with its director, Juan Carlos Baute, September, 2008). Sunacoop does not have an exact figure because tens of thousands of cooperatives formed during this time have ceased operations. They are in a process of recertifying all cooperatives so as to get an exact figure.

17. According to the income-based poverty line used by the Poverty Project of the Catholic University Andrés Bello (Riutort, 1999).

18. The government's figure is 1.5 million, but it is reasonable to believe that this is merely the number of individuals who participated in the program, not the number of people who actually became literate given that the figures provided by the government's own statistics institute show a lower level of literacy following the program's implementation. For a debate on this issue, see Rosnick and Weisbrot (2008).

19. All these figures are taken from the Ministry of Planning (www.mpd.gob.ve) and the Ministry of Communication and Information (www.venezueladeverdad.gob.ve).

20. The acronym ALBA has gone through several transformations as to what it stands for. For a long time it was known as the Bolivarian Alternative for Latin America and the Caribbean.

21. This number dropped again dramatically when Venezuela and Colombia broke diplomatic relations toward the end of Colombian President Uribe's term in office in mid-2009. Trade and diplomatic relations picked up again in early 2010 upon the election of Juan Manuel Santos.

22. For a detailed discussion of Human Right Watch's analysis of Venezuela's human rights situation, see Wilpert (2008).

23. The opposition blogger Francisco Toro (at www.caracaschronicles.com) provides the most sophisticated version of this argument. See also the previously mentioned Corrales (2006) and Corrales and Penfold (2011).

24. The Latinobarómetro report is issued on an annual basis, and each has more or less consistently shown that Venezuelans' regard for their democracy during the Chávez era is among the highest in the region. For a summary of the 2006 report on Venezuela, see Wilpert (2006).

25. The Venezuelan economy declined by 3.3 percent in 2009 and by 1.4 percent in 2010. It began recovering in late 2010, though, growing by 0.6 percent in the last quarter of 2010 (Banco Central de Venezuela, 2012). See also Suggett (2009b).

References

Albert, Michael. 2003. *Parecon: Life after Capitalism*. London: Verso.

Ali, Tariq. 2008. *Pirates of the Caribbean: Axis of Hope*. London: Verso.

Banco Central de Venezuela. 2012. "statistical Information." http://www.bcv.org.ve/ EnglishVersion/c2/index.asp?secc=statistinf.

Bruce, Iain. 2008. *The Real Venezuela: Making Socialism in the 21st Century*. London: Pluto Press.

Corrales, Javier. 2006. "Hugo Boss." *Foreign Policy*, January–February 2006.

Corrales, Javier, and Michael Penfold. 2011. *Dragon in the Tropics: Hugo Chávez and the Political Economy of Revolution in Venezuela*. Washington, DC: Brookings Institution Press.

Garrido, Alberto. 2002a. *Documentos de la Revolución Bolivariana*. Caracas: Ediciones del Autor.

———. 2002b. *Testimonios de la Revolución Bolivariana*. Caracas: Ediciones del Autor.

Gorz, André. 1964. *Strategy for Labor: A Radical Proposal*. Boston: Beacon Press.

Hahnel, Robin. 2005. *Economic Justice and Democracy: From Competition to Cooperation*. New York: Routledge.

Heston, Alan, Robert Summers, and Bettina Aten. 2002. *Penn World Table Version 6.1*. Center for International Comparisons of Production, Income, and Prices at the University of Pennsylvania, October.

Jones, Bart. 2007. *¡Hugo! The Hugo Chávez Story from Mud Hut to Perpetual Revolution*. Hanover, NH: Steerforth Press.

Latinobarómetro. 2007. "Informe Anual 2007." *Corporación Latinobarómetro*, November 2007. http://www.latinobarometro.org/latino/LATContenidos.jsp.

Lebowitz, Michael. 2006. *Build It Now! Socialism for the Twenty-first Century*. New York: Monthly Review Press.

Martinez, Carlos, Michael Fox, and JoJo Farrell. 2009. *Venezuela Speaks: Voices from the Grassroots*. Oakland, CA: PM Press.

Ministerio del Poder Popular para la Comunicación le Información. 2007. *Líneas Generales del Plan de Desarrollo Económico y Social de la Nación 2007–2013*. Caracas: Ministerio del Poder Popular para la Comunicación y la Información, 2008. http://www.minci.gob.ve/libros_folletos/6/443184/?desc=lineas_generales_de_la_nacion20080613-1159.pdf.

Mommer, Bernard. 2003. "Subversive Oil." In *Venezuelan Politics in the Chávez Era: Class, Polarization, and Conflict*, ed. Steve Ellner and Daniel Hellinger, 131–46. Boulder, CO: Lynne Rienner.

Raby, D. L. 2006. *Democracy and Revolution: Latin America and Socialism Today*. London: Pluto Press.

Riutort, Matias. 1999. "El Costo de Eradicar la Pobreza." In *Un Mal Posible de Superar*, 37–42. Vol. 1 of *Resúmenes de los Documentos del Proyecto Pobreza*. Caracas: Universidad Católica Andrés Bello.

Rosales, Arturo. 2009. "In Address to the Nation, President Chávez Introduces New Measures to Deal with the Global Economic Crisis." *Axis of Logic*, March 23. http://axisoflogic.com/artman/publish/article_29942.shtml.

Rosnick, David, and Mark Weisbrot. 2008. "'Illiteracy' Revisited: What Ortega and Rodríguez Read in the Household Survey." Center for Economic and Policy Research, May 2008. http://www.cepr.net/documents/publications/literacy_2008_05.pdf.

Suggett, James. 2008. "Venezuela's 2009 Budget Plans Increased Social Spending and Stable Growth." *VenezuelAnalysis.com*, October 24. http://www.venezuelanalysis.com/news/3896.

———. 2009a. "U.N. Food and Agriculture Organization Says Venezuela Prepared for World Food Crisis." *VenezuelAnalysis.com*, February 27. http://www.venezuelanalysis.com/news/4254.

———. 2009b. "Venezuela Completes 22 Quarters of Consecutive Economic Growth." *VenezuelAnalysis.com*, May 21. http://www.venezuelanalysis.com/news/4460.

Universidad Católica Andrés Bello. 2001. *Un Mal Posible de Superar*. Vol. 1 of *Resúmenes de los Documentos del Proyecto Pobreza*. Caracas: Universidad Católica Andrés Bello.

Wilpert, Gregory. 2006. "Poll: Venezuelans Have Highest Regard for Their Democracy." *VenezuelAnalysis.com*, December 20. http://www.venezuelanalysis.com/news/2146.

———. 2007. *Changing Venezuela by Taking Power: The History and Policies of the Chávez Government*. London: Verso.

———. 2008. "Smoke and Mirrors: An Analysis of Human Rights Watch's Report on Venezuela." *VenezuelAnalysis.com*, October 17. http://www.venezuelanalysis.com/analysis/3882.

———. 2011. "Venezuela's Experiment in Participatory Democracy." In *The Revolution in Venezuela: Social and Political Change under Chávez*, ed. Jonathan Eastwood and Thomas Ponniah, 99–130. Cambridge, MA: Harvard University Press.

9

Ecuador

Indigenous Struggles and the Ambiguities of Electoral Power

Marc Becker

O N SEPTEMBER 27, 2009, THE CONFEDERACIÓN de Nacionalidades Indígenas del Ecuador (Confederation of Indigenous Nationalities of Ecuador,
CONAIE), an umbrella group of Indigenous organizations, led a mobilization against a proposed water bill in Congress that would allow transnational
mining corporations to appropriate water reserves in violation of the 2008
constitution that outlawed the privatization of water. The water bill was part
of what activists interpreted as broader governmental moves to privatize the
country's natural resources, with a particular focus on oil extraction and
large-scale mining projects that were located largely on Indigenous lands. The
protests included marches and demonstrations as well as blocking roads with
rocks, tree trunks, and burning tires. The demonstrations grew intense in the
eastern Amazon as the Shuar and Achuar blocked highways with barbed wire.
Seemingly in an echo of protests in June 2009 in the Peruvian Amazon that
left dozens dead, the Ecuadorian demonstration also grew deadly with the
shooting of Shuar schoolteacher Bosco Wisum (Rénique, 2009).

Rather than confronting a conservative and neoliberal government, as had
repeatedly been the case over the previous two decades, the target of this mobilization was Rafael Correa, Ecuador's president, whom many saw as part of
a red tide sweeping across Latin America. In response to the demonstrations,
Correa denounced Indigenous movements as infantile environmentalists
and for being in alliance with political conservatives who sought to undermine his leftist government. "We are not allied with the Right," Humberto
Cholango (CONAIE, 2009), a longtime Indigenous activist elected president
of CONAIE in April 2011, retorted. "Our struggle has always been loyal to

and consistent with the Ecuadorian people, with the organizations, and with the most poor and humble sectors of our country." Rather than seeking to undermine democracy, Indigenous peoples and nationalities in Ecuador "want to bring the neoliberal oligarchical model to an end, to terminate the injustice under which we have been living." Cholango demanded instead a "true agrarian reform," one that would redistribute land as well as "recuperate and renationalize natural resources." The Indigenous leader denied that social movements had a hidden agenda; rather, "our aspirations and struggles are authentic, and in favor of Ecuador recuperating its dignity." Cholango pledged to keep fighting until the neoliberal model was destroyed. "We will not allow this process of change to be truncated, stopped, or remain half completed," he declared.

Correa emerged as the president of Ecuador at a point at which popular movements had created a new correlation of forces in Latin America. Supporters greeted Correa's election as "a revolution from below, a popular awakening that is challenging the traditional political parties and demanding a new system of governance that responds to the interests and needs of the popular classes" (Burbach, 2007: 9). Correa, however, did not emerge out of popular organizing efforts (he was an economist and college professor before becoming president). Social-movement leaders questioned whether Correa was ideologically committed to their leftist political agenda. Was he, activists worried, merely a populist who would opportunistically exploit social-movement rhetoric to gain election only to rule in favor of the oligarchy once in office? Given Ecuador's long history of populist leaders from José María Velasco Ibarra to Abdalá Bucaram, this was a very real and serious concern. Or could his populism, as Ernesto Laclau (1977) posited, create a critical juncture that would open up the political system and move society in a more radical and leftist direction, as arguably happened in Venezuela under Hugo Chávez? Was Correa part of what the radical Argentine economist Claudio Katz (2007: 37) caustically termed the "modern and civilized left" as symbolized by the governments of Luiz Inácio Lula da Silva in Brazil or Michelle Bachelet in Chile, or a "left nationalist or radical reformist" trend led by Chávez and Evo Morales in Bolivia?

Ecuador's radicalized Indigenous movements celebrated the ascendancy of Chávez and Morales, but challenged the inclusion of Correa as a part of a move away from political and economic exclusion and toward social justice. At the end of January 2009, Correa joined Chávez, Morales, and Paraguayan president Fernando Lugo in a conversation with social movements at the World Social Forum in Belém, Brazil. Correa contrasted capitalism with socialism and appealed to what has become a common Indigenous call to "vivir bien, no mejor," to live well, not better. "We are in times of change," Correa concluded. "An alternative model already exists, and it is the socialism of the twenty-first century" (Becker, 2009). Three days later, however, at the closing of the space where Indigenous peoples debated their agenda, longtime leader Blanca Chancoso asked the forum to join her in condemning Correa for pursuing resource-extractive enterprises that violated the rights of rural communities.

While Correa may be part of an emergent *izquierda permitida* that divides and co-opts leftist challenges to power, social movements with Indigenous organizations in the lead proffered a more radical vision of fundamental structural challenges to empire, neoliberalism, and free-trade agreements. While both Correa and competing Indigenous organizations opposed imperialism and capitalism, social movements were more aggressive than the president in supporting the oppressed and exploited classes, not merely through redistributive mechanisms but also by encouraging the popular capacity to self-organize, to enhance their collective social power from below. Organized social movements often found themselves in positions significantly more radical than those Correa was willing to embrace. Growing struggles between Correa and social movements pointed to important underlying issues. What was the role for state power in leftist political projects? Were these political projects better achieved through street mobilizations or electoral participation? What obstacles existed in building counter-hegemonic movements? Would Correa's left-populist proposals cater to the needs and desires of popular movements that had placed him in power, or were they merely ploys to maintain his power?

Historical Context

Ecuador is one of the most politically unstable countries in Latin America, undergoing frequent and often extra-constitutional changes of power during its almost two hundred years of republican history. During the twentieth century, Ecuador only experienced three periods during which a sequence of presidents peacefully passed power to an opposing politician. All three occurred in the midst of the expansion of export booms, the first with cacao at the beginning of the century, the second with bananas at midcentury, and finally the longest in the aftermath of a 1970s oil boom. Neoliberal reforms in the 1990s, including raising transportation and cooking gas prices and replacing the local currency with the United States dollar, reintroduced extreme political instability, with social movements competing with their counterparts in Bolivia for the record of the number of neoliberal presidents removed from office. Sociologist Leon Zamosc (2004: 131) blames elite attempts to impose a neoliberal agenda for making Ecuador "one of the most, if not *the* most, unstable country in Latin America." During the decade from 1997 to 2007, ten different chief executives held power.

Popular movements in Ecuador became quite adept at pulling down governments that ruled against their interests, but they faced a much more difficult task in constructing positive alternatives. This was a consistent problem throughout the twentieth century. For example, in 1938, at what was perhaps the height of the Left's strength in Ecuador, socialists handed power back to the liberals from whom they had just wrestled control when they could not agree on a consensus candidate for president. Several years later, socialists once again largely controlled the 1944–1945 constituent assembly that wrote what up to that point was the most progressive constitution in Ecuador's history. Rather than placing someone from their own ranks into the presidency, they handed power back to the perennial populist president José María Velasco Ibarra, who abrogated their work and in 1946 rewrote the constitution into a much more conservative form. It is not without reason that popular movements have a learned distrust of charismatic leaders such as Correa who come from outside their ranks.

Ecuador's experience with populist leaders reveals that, because of the strong power of social movements, conservative candidates cloak themselves in a progressive discourse in order to win elections. Once in office, however, they reveal their true colors and rule on behalf of the oligarchy. Abdalá Bucaram (1996–1997), Jamil Mahuad (1998–2000), and Lucio Gutiérrez (2003–2005) all campaigned with the support of grassroots movements before turning on their bases after they won an election. Indigenous militants feared that Correa would similarly co-opt and monopolize their initiatives as other populist leaders had done before him. Rather than a revolutionary like Chávez, Correa appeared to radicalized social movements to be a reformer who represented a continuity of the problems that Ecuador historically had faced. Social movements needed to mobilize to defend their interests in the face of government policies.

Rafael Correa

Correa first gained national attention during a short-lived stint in 2005 as finance minister under his predecessor, President Alfredo Palacio. Correa, who has a PhD in economics from the University of Illinois at Urbana-Champaign and wrote a dissertation attacking the Washington Consensus from a Keynesian perspective, was a strong opponent of free-trade agreements with the United States. As finance minister, he advocated poverty-reduction programs and closer relations with Chávez's government in Venezuela. After four months Correa resigned under pressure from the United States, but he left office with the highest approval ratings of any official in the administration.

Once out of Palacio's government, Correa's name became commonly forwarded as a prospective candidate for the 2006 presidential elections. His candidacy raised questions among social-movement activists as to whether they should support someone from within their ranks or ally with someone with broader popular visibility and appeal. Particularly for the strong and well-organized Indigenous movements that had played leading roles in toppling several presidents over the previous decade, Correa was a controversial and divisive candidate. A devout Catholic, he had worked for a year in a Salesian mission in Zumbahua, Cotopaxi, and spoke the Indigenous Kichwa language. But he was not an Indigenous person nor had he been involved in their social movements. In particular, the Indigenous-led Movimiento Unidad Plurinacional Pachakutik (Pluri-national Pachakutik United Movement, MUPP, commonly known as Pachakutik) felt leery of entering into an alliance with someone who had not emerged out of a social movement. This was a learned response. On January 21, 2000, Indigenous activists had collaborated with dissident junior military officers, including Colonel Lucio Gutiérrez, to remove Mahuad from power after he had implemented unpopular and damaging neoliberal economic policies. After the failed coup, Gutiérrez successfully campaigned for the presidency with Pachakutik. Once in office, Gutiérrez turned his back on his former allies and ruled in favor of the elite. Pachakutik paid dearly for joining his government. Even more damaging, the former colonel exploited clientelistic networks to gain strong support in rural communities. Gutiérrez had deeply divided Indigenous movements, and activists feared that working with Correa would have similarly negative consequences for their bases (Mijeski and Beck, 2011).

Leading up to the 2006 elections, Correa and Pachakutik discussed forming an alliance. Some observers dreamt of a shared ticket between Correa and a historic Indigenous leader such as Luis Macas. Indigenous activists wanted to put their leader in the presidential slot, but Correa refused to consider running as vice president. Some grassroots activists argued in favor of joining a ticket, even as a junior partner, that had strong popular appeal and stood a strong chance of winning. They thought it would be a serious strategic mistake to pass on this opportunity. Others questioned whether Correa was ideologically committed to Pachakutik's center-left agenda of creating a more inclusive and participatory democracy based on ethical, socioeconomic, educational, and ecological changes. They compared Correa to Gutiérrez, complaining that his actions were dividing Indigenous communities, repeatedly reminded Correa "that any revolution and change in Latin America will never be able to be carried out without the participation of Indigenous nationalities and peoples" (CONAIE, 2008: 5). They urged Correa to set aside his arrogance and to foster harmonious relationships with Indigenous and other social movements. Otherwise, the historical opportunity "to carry out a true change and revolution" in Ecuador would be lost.

In response to Indigenous criticisms, Correa closed off dialogues with Pachakutik and subsequently would harbor a certain amount of resentment toward organized Indigenous movements for refusing to support his candidacy. Pachakutik, in turn, ran Macas as its candidate, although he only polled in the low single digits. His dismal showing led Correa to denigrate CONAIE as an insignificant political force. According to an analysis by Kenneth Mijeski and Scott Beck (2008: 53), only about a quarter of the Indigenous population voted for Macas, whereas almost half voted for Gilmar Gutiérrez, who was running in place of his brother Lucio with the centrist Partido Sociedad Patriótica (Patriotic Society Party, PSP), largely because of his skill in using patronage in rural communities to garner votes. Correa polled even worse in Indigenous communities (which comprised about a third of the population) but gained much more support among the majority *mestizo* (people of mixed Indigenous and European heritage) population, which gave him the margin necessary to become a competitive candidate. Correa's strongest base of support was the urban, middle-class academic, and nongovernmental organizational world from which he emerged, rather than the working classes or rural Indigenous communities.

In the first round in the 2006 presidential elections, Correa came in second place to the conservative banana magnate Álvaro Noboa, Ecuador's richest man. Fearing a conservative Noboa government, Pachakutik cast their support to Correa in the second round, thereby helping him win by a comfortable margin. Militant Indigenous activists cheered Correa's victory, embracing his triumph as a blow against neoliberalism. They hoped that it would open up possibilities for a more participatory democracy. "Correa coincides with our struggles," Cholango (2007: 2) stated. "We ask him to deliver on the changes he promised in his campaign." Despite earlier hesitations, it initially appeared that their political interests would coincide.

In his January 15, 2007, inaugural address, Correa denounced "neoliberal globalization that would turn countries into markets, not nations," and called for an end to "the culture of indebtedness" (*Latin American Weekly Report*, 2007a: 4). Correa emphasized that his government would fight against corruption, oppose neoliberal economic policies, and promote regional integration. He refused to sign agreements with the International Monetary Fund (IMF) and resisted free-trade pacts with the United States. He repeatedly attacked the business oligarchy, pledged reforms that would benefit the country's poor, and promised to work to create a more just society. He promised to leave the "long neoliberal night" behind and replace a market with a solidarity economy that empowered the grassroots and responded to local needs rather than distant, wealthy corporations (León, 2008: 31). His government, Correa assured supporters, would be "of the exploited, not the exploiters" (*Andean Group Report*, 2008b: 14). His rhetoric seemed to be in line with that of popular movements.

With traditional political parties discredited and the opposition in disarray, Correa proceeded to consolidate his political control over the country. Contentious divisions within Correa's coalition, however, indicated that a new correlation of forces was emerging, not as a conservative opposition but as an expression of popular movements, Indigenous peoples, and other leftists who felt marginalized by Correa's political project. Indigenous leader and former Correa communication secretary Mónica Chuji (2008) complained of the antidemocratic tendencies in Correa's party and Correa's insistence on following old-style politics that included an emphasis on extractive enterprises that threatened the environment. She accused Correa of presenting "a rehashed neoliberalism with a progressive face" and questioned whether a leader with authoritarian tendencies could lead a participatory revolution moving toward twenty-first-century socialism. Economist Alberto Acosta, a former energy minister, similarly broke from Correa and became highly critical of the president's policies for not being sufficiently radical and for his critical attitudes toward social-movement activists. A series of high-profile defections and repeated challenges from social movements and leftist political parties took the shine off of the apparent value of Correa's victory.

Correa's electoral success was due in part to his ability to consolidate power in the hands of the executive through constitutional and other reforms. But a key question was what he would do with that power. George Ciccariello-Maher (2007: 42) argues in favor of a revised version of Lenin's concept of "dual power" in which "the revolutionary transformation of existing repressive structures" of the state occurs simultaneously through the actions of a centralized state power from above and through the popular initiatives of people from below. Ciccariello-Maher points to the emergence of communal councils in Venezuela as a positive example of the possibilities of autonomous, alternative power structures and the checks they provide against top-down manifestations of power. While Chávez welcomed and embraced these popular initiatives, Correa felt threatened by them and tried to squash them or bring them under his control. Indigenous movements distanced themselves from Correa's government, and it appeared that these divisions would never be bridged.

While some Ecuadorians believed that the country needed a stronger executive to solve continual problems of instability, many activists were concerned that this would be a dangerous move. They feared that heightened state power handed to a sympathetic president could just as easily be used against them if conservatives regained power. Correa, they worried, may have unwittingly laid the ground for a new round of authoritarian governments that would lead to disastrous results for popular movements. Broad executive mandates were not necessarily in the best interests of social movements. Pachakutik congressional delegate Ramssés Torres complained that Correa wanted a "submissive and obsequious congress that would not monitor his government" (*Andean Group Report*, 2007: 6). They threatened to launch another uprising if Correa continued to pursue his extractive policies. "Rafael Correa does not want to see us united," Macas declared. "If you think just because he is tall and has green eyes he will be our leader, you are mistaken" (Meléndez, 2008). Even though Correa denied that he was engaging in a cult of personality, from the perspective of social movements the consolidation of power in the hands of a strong and seemingly egotistical executive meant that they would lose access to the spaces necessary to press their own agendas (Lucas, 2007b: 232). Correa's personal charisma and left-populist discourse demobilized the Left, leaving popular movements in a worse situation than before he took power.

Neoliberalism

Indigenous movements in Ecuador had long played a major role in leading opposition to neoliberal economic policies. CONAIE called for "recuperation of popular sovereignty in the running of the economy." This was necessary because Ecuador had "lived for twenty-five years with an economic model that much more than concentrating wealth also promotes dispossession, inequality, and the handing of sovereignty to large foreign monopolies." The goal of the economic system, CONAIE argued, should not be profit but human welfare, the *sumak kawsay*. Bolivia's foreign minister David Choque-huanca pressed sumak kawsay as a Quechua concept of living well, not just living better (CONAIE, 2007: 2). It included an explicit critique of traditional development strategies that increased the use of resources rather than seeking to live in harmony with others and with nature. Economist Pablo Dávalos (2008) terms *sumak kawsay* as "the only alternative to neoliberal discourse of development and economic growth." It builds on "a vision of respect" and provides an "opportunity to return ethics to human activities." It was a new way of thinking about human relations that was not based on exploitation.

Despite CONAIE's lead on economic issues, it is a mistake to assume that ethnic-based movements would be necessarily opposed to the neoliberal capitalist system. In fact, neoliberalism is highly capable of accepting and integrating ethnic expressions into its agenda. If Indigenous movements do not extend beyond ethnic demands, they threaten to enable a neoliberal system. "The ethnicization of the indigenous movement," anthropologist Víctor Bretón Solo de Zaldívar (2008: 610) observes, "has prioritized culture and identity politics at the expense of the class-based peasant agenda still very much alive in the mid-1990s, thus hindering the formation of alliances between indigenous groups and other sectors of society." Indigenous intellectual Floresmilo Simbaña (2007) is also critical of those who press ethnic demands to the exclusion of class concerns and thereby inadvertently empower a neoliberal agenda. To be successful, critics argued, activists would have to move well beyond expressions of multiculturalism.

Some scholars have criticized identity-based politics for focusing on limited issues such as ethnic rights while ignoring much larger and arguably more important issues of neoliberalism and economic exploitation. From this perspective, multiculturalism reinforces neoliberalism by misdiagnosing problems facing marginalized peoples. If the problem is an issue of racism rather than class divisions, then the solution is to embrace cultural differences rather than addressing issues of economic exclusion. "As a state-sponsored ideology," José Almeida (2005: 93) notes, multiculturalism "obscures its economic roots and issues of power." As a result, this "neoliberal multiculturalism" reinforces existing inequalities. "Far from opening spaces for generalized empowerment of indigenous peoples," Charles Hale (2004: 16) argues, "these reforms tend to empower some while marginalizing the majority." Hale continues, "far from eliminating racial inequity, as the rhetoric of multiculturalism seems to promise," specific and tokenistic multicultural reforms such as extending language recognition without accompanying structural reforms "reconstitute racial hierarchies in more entrenched forms." Hale terms this phenomenon that of the *indio permitido* (authorized Indian), a term he borrows from Bolivian sociologist Silvia Rivera Cusicanqui, who used it "to talk about how governments are using cultural rights to divide and domesticate indigenous movements." The dominant culture grants certain cultural rights (including to specific individuals) that pose no threat to the dominant neoliberal economic model with the understanding or hope that marginalized peoples will not then make additional anti-neoliberal demands that link these cultural rights to the material interests of the rural and urban poor and dispossessed.

In Ecuador, Indigenous leader Nina Pacari received a good deal of criticism for accepting the position of second vice president in the 1998 congressional assembly. While supporters cheered placing an Indigenous woman in such a high legislative position, leftists complained that this came at the cost of entering into an alliance with a conservative, neoliberal governing coalition. An advance for a single person, even though that person comes from a (doubly or even triply) historically marginalized group, does not alter the exclusionary structures that originally placed them in a marginalized position. Simply placing individuals in high positions of power was meaningless if it was not accompanied by deep, fundamental socioeconomic and political changes. Otherwise, the result would be growing individual Indigenous presences in the public sphere but without an increased empowerment of marginalized and excluded peoples in material terms. The socioeconomic structures that reproduce the economic exploitation and dispossession of the Indigenous poor are left intact under neoliberal multiculturalism. Hale argues that the issue becomes not a struggle between individual and collective rights, nor between cultural and economic demands, but rather over how this creates structural limitations to Indigenous empowerment. "Neoliberal multiculturalism permits indigenous organization," Hale (2004: 16) states, "as long as it does not amass enough power to call basic state prerogatives into question." Neoliberalism, then, embraces multiculturalism while limiting the possibilities of it as a political project.

Donna Lee Van Cott (2006), however, argues quite convincingly that while multiculturalism may facilitate neoliberalism in areas of weak social mobilization (such as in the Guatemalan context against which Hale writes), in countries like Ecuador with strong histories of Indigenous mobilizations the opposite is true. Instead, movements for Indigenous rights can provide an effective vehicle for building left-wing coalitions that challenge neoliberalism. Keith G. Banting and Will Kymlicka (2006: 19) contend that confronting oppression is not a zero-sum game, and increased attention to race and culture do not necessarily translate into diminished concern for class and economic interests. Rather, an enhanced sensitivity to one social injustice can lead to more sensitivity to others.

Despite these academic arguments, Indigenous activists in Ecuador continued to agitate against multicultural neoliberalism. For example, the Indigenous think tank Instituto Científico de Culturas Indígenas (Institute for Indigenous Sciences and Cultures, ICCI) (2001) strongly criticized the World Bank's work with the Proyecto de Desarrollo para los Pueblos Indígenas y Negros del Ecuador (Development Project for Indigenous and Black Peoples of Ecuador, PRODEPINE), which embraced the government's neoliberal policies while dividing, fragmenting, weakening, and ultimately neutralizing an alternative Indigenous project. Robert Andolina, Nina Laurie, and Sarah Radcliffe (2009) termed its approach one of "social neoliberalism," providing market-oriented solutions to poverty. Rather than multiculturalism, ICCI argued for fundamentally refounding the state based on the principles of pluri-nationalism. For CONAIE's highland affiliate Ecuarunari (2007: 4), "pluri-nationalism means building a strong and sovereign state that recognizes and makes possible the full exercise of collective and individual rights, and promotes equal development for all of Ecuador and not only for certain regions or sectors." It represented "a democratic rupture that permits the organization and social control over public goods and the state, and in this way surpassing the neocolonial system that marginalizes and subjects people." Pluri-nationalism would "strengthen a new state through the consolidation of unity, destroying racism and regionalism as a necessary prerequisite for social and political equality, economic justice, direct and participatory democracy, communitarianism, and interculturality" (Ecuarunari and CONAIE, 2007: 5) Indigenous ally Alberto Acosta (2009: 17–18, 15) notes that "the challenge is to see pluri-nationalism as an exercise of inclusive democracy," as something that opens the door to the process of a continually deepening democratic tradition. "The construction of a pluri-national state," he argues, "is not only a challenge but a necessity." Many Indigenous militants share his perspective.

Correa's Social and Economic Policies

On many key issues, Correa's policies corresponded with those of social movement activists. For years, activists campaigned against the United States' presence at the Manta air base, complaining that it was a violation of national sovereignty and needlessly dragged Ecuador into social conflicts in neighboring Colombia. In office Correa announced that he would not renew the ten-year lease when it expired in 2009. This provision was written directly into the new 2008 constitution with the declaration in Article 5 that "Ecuador is a land of peace" and would not permit the establishment of foreign military bases in its territory (Republic of Ecuador, 2008). As a result, in September 2009 the United States withdrew its troops from the base. "The capitalist elites no longer set the entire region's agenda with impunity," Katz (2007: 29, 30) writes in reference to political developments in Latin America over the last decade. "The dominant classes can no longer rely on their strategic neoliberal compass; the popular movement has recovered its street presence; and U.S. imperialism has forfeited its capacity to intervene." The new constitution also codified much of what popular movements had long demanded, including reasserting governmental control over oil, mining, transport, telecommunications, and other economic sectors that previous governments had privatized. Whether the government complied with its promises would in large part depend on the abilities of social movements to press for the implementation of these commitments.

Given Correa's background as an economist, logically some of his most concrete proposals emphasized financial reforms. For example, Correa blamed the Central Bank for subjugating the country to foreign and neoliberal interests, and he sought to eliminate its autonomy. He also pledged to raise taxes on the wealthy and create mechanisms for more effective revenue collection in order to increase funding for education and health services. Correa forwarded a nationalistic economic platform and criticized foreign oil corporations for extracting the majority of petroleum rents out of the country. As he consolidated control over power, he pushed through congressional reforms that increased taxes on windfall oil profits, and he used these funds to provide subsides to poor people to lower their utility costs, expand access to credit, and improve social services (Conaghan, 2008: 55). "Now the oil is everyone's," Correa declared (Saavedra, 2007: 1). He stopped short, however, of nationalizing natural resources. With the industry still largely in private and foreign hands, much of the value of petroleum production would not accrue to the development of the country.

Echoing Chávez's rhetoric in Venezuela, Correa spoke of introducing socialism for the twenty-first century into Ecuador. Nevertheless, like Chávez, Correa remained vague on the details of what this socialism would look like. Often both Chávez and Correa defined it in terms of what it is not. This new form of socialism "differs totally from the idea of state control over the means of production and traditional socialism," Correa said (*Latin American Weekly Report*, 2007b: 4). Other than ambiguous comments about curtailing the power of Congress, depoliticizing the judiciary, expanding government control of natural resources, and democratizing the media, this type of socialism generally lacked concrete proposals as to what it would do. Furthermore, Correa opportunistically allied himself with Chávez when it seemed to serve his purposes but distanced himself when the association might prove to be a political liability. One example was Correa's initial refusal to join Chávez's Alternativa Bolivariana para América Latina y El Caribe (Bolivarian Alternative for the Americas, ALBA). Even when he finally joined in June 2009, analysts wondered whether he finally felt he had the domestic support to radicalize his domestic policies, or whether he was seeking to solidify support from regional allies in case he needed their assistance later.

Over time, Correa began to curtail his incendiary rhetoric, positioning himself as a moderate. The *Andean Group Report* (2008a: 14–15), a business-oriented monthly newsletter, observes "that although Correa is radical and often overreacts to criticism, he is probably not dogmatically leftwing." During a January 2009 trip to Cuba, Correa said, "we cannot continue to sustain dogmas history has defeated." These "dogmas" included "the class struggle, dialectical materialism, the nationalization of all property, the refusal to recognize the market" (*Latin American Weekly Report*, 2009: 3). Discarding key elements traditionally associated with socialism while failing to identify alternative visions further underscored doubts as to whether Correa could legitimately lay claim to leftist credentials. Although he did not directly speak of a "third way" between capitalism and communism as some populist leaders did in the 1960s, his emphasis on "the people" while continuing to embrace elements of capitalism led him in a similarly conservative direction. Indigenous activists complained that his social policies were neither revolutionary nor socialistic (ICCI, 2007: 6). "Any policy that indefinitely postpones the anti-capitalist goal ends up reinforcing oppression," Katz (2007: 38) argues. "Socialism requires preparing and consummating anti-capitalist ruptures." Correa's handouts to the poor did not alter the structures of society, and critics suspected that they were merely designed to shore up his political base of support.

Given the realities and traditions of the Ecuadorian political system, it remained an open question as to whether Correa would implement fundamental social changes without resorting to clientelistic practices of using public funds to garner popular support. "Correa is a little better compared to other presidents," Federación Indígena y Campesina de Imbabura (Indigenous and Peasant Federation of Imbabura, FICI) president Maria Tamberla said. "But we're not convinced that he will defend the people, especially the indigenous people" (Riofrancos, 2008). Even while appearing to drift rightward, Correa's government took some steps that gained him broader popular support. On July 8, 2008, for example, he expropriated 195 companies belonging to the Isaías Group in order to recover some of the assets their customers had lost when their bank, Filanbanco, collapsed in 1998 due to corporate corruption. Conservative opponents complained about the attacks on private property, but Correa's supporters applauded the subjugation of private property to the public good. His actions were similar to what Morales had done in Bolivia in nationalizing natural gas and seizing large land holdings, increasing his level of support by distancing himself from the conservative opposition, even though at best the actions represented little more than tepid reforms of a capitalist system (Webber, 2009).

At the same time, Correa has often taken positions that placed him at odds with others on the left. Correa came out of a Catholic socialist tradition, which, for example, meant that his position on topics such as abortion were not the same as those of leftist feminists. Environmentalists opposed his state-centered development projects, which led to significant tensions over mining and petroleum concerns. His agrarian policies favored large-scale agro-industrial development, providing minimal support for small farmers. Much of Correa's base came out of the white, urban, middle-class *forajido*, or "outlaw," movement that had played a key role in the April 20, 2005, street mobilizations that removed Gutiérrez from power, rather than rural the Indigenous community activists who had removed previous presidents. Many of those who took positions in Correa's government were from the world of academia and nongovernmental organizations (NGOs) (*Comercio*, 2008: 7). When a September 30, 2010, police protest threatened to removed Correa from power, it was this urban, professional middle class that came to his defense rather than militant social movements (Torre, 2011). Social movements had been largely excluded from the centers of power, and they mounted growing criticisms of the (negative) influences of NGOs and the depoliticization of their social struggles. Correa's government only deepened those tensions.

ICCI (2008) published an editorial in its newsletter *Boletín ICCI-Rimay* criticizing Correa for not being a true leftist. It contrasted a "social Left" with an "electoral Left." Correa's government, ICCI charged, was not of the Left because instead of governing with and for popular movements, he filled his government with his personal friends, family members, colleagues, opportunists, those expelled from the Indigenous movement, and other confused people. What was missing were representatives of the social Left, those who emerged out of organized social, popular, and Indigenous movements. Correa's government had more in common with twentieth-century social democracies than the ideals of twenty-first-century socialism. Rather than empowering people and popular movements, Correa grotesquely criticized the historical importance of Indigenous and other social movements. Furthermore, he did not provide viable solutions to key problems such as unemployment and low salaries. Correa did not deliver on the fundamental changes for which people in this "deep Ecuador" (*Ecuador profundo*), who were "from below and to the left," had long dreamed.[1] Nevertheless, ICCI's editorial concluded, the Left had elected the government, and the Left needed to engage in the serious task of orienting and pressuring Correa so that he would implement the projects that the social Left desired.

Activists repeatedly found themselves walking a fine line between defending Correa from conservative attacks and pressing him to take more radical positions. Displaying the significant ability of Indigenous movements to mobilize their bases, twenty thousand people joined a March 2008 demonstration in support of Correa's plans to revise the constitution. Journalist Kintto Lucas (2007a: 7) pointed to street mobilization as evidence of CONAIE's continuing relevance. It remained "the social organization with the greatest ability and capacity to mobilize people." The march and a subsequent gathering with officials from Correa's party concluded with a promise to continue meetings between the executive branch and Indigenous representatives to study their demands and proposals. CONAIE also sent Correa a lengthy letter in which they emphasized that Indigenous movements had been in the lead in organizing against neoliberal economic policies that impoverished the majority of Ecuadorians and criminalized social struggles. But rather than just articulating what they opposed, CONAIE emphasized that they also had concrete proposals to move toward a better world. The letter presented a list of twenty-three demands, ranging through issues of opposition to resource extraction and militarism to support for Indigenous rights and institutions. They challenged Correa to embrace their vision for a better world.

Social Movements and Electoral Paths to Power

Sociologist Boaventura de Sousa Santos (2009: 22–23) points to the paradox that social movements face. Confronting the ecological and financial collapse of capitalism that threatens the obliteration of life on this planet, an urgent need exists to act immediately to head off this crisis. On the other hand, Sousa Santos argues, "the transformations that we need are of a long-term nature" that requires altering the fundamental structures of civilization. At first this appears to be part of a long debate on the left between reform and revolution. But, Sousa Santos contends, strategies such as the electoral process that typically have been seen as reformist now, as was apparent in Venezuela, have produced "profound, almost revolutionary, changes," while political ruptures that would typically be perceived as revolutionary end up only proposing tepid reforms. It is as if social movements face the challenge of socialist president Salvador Allende in Chile in the early 1970s to "make haste—slowly," that poverty and inequality require immediate action but the solution requires much deeper changes.

Indigenous movement positioning in the face of Correa's government illustrates the problematic and complicated nature of social-movement engagements with state power. Marta Harnecker (2005: 149) argues that mobilized people will be at the center of political transformations. She writes "that no real change will be achieved without a well organized and politicized popular sector that exerts pressures to advance the process and that is capable of learning from errors and deviations." Some on the anarchist left argue that Pachakutik used a fundamentally flawed strategy in pursuing electoral paths to power. Perhaps most famously, in *Change the World without Taking Power* John Holloway (2002: 19–20) proposes that the world cannot be changed through taking control over state structures. Instead, the revolutionary challenge facing the twenty-first century is to change the world without taking power.

James Petras (2005: 154) favors a revolutionary conquest of power, but he remains very critical of electoral paths to political change. "Direct action class-based sociopolitical movements have been the only political forces capable of resisting, reversing or overthrowing neoliberal regimes and policies," he writes. "There is no evidence that any electoral regime in which the national bourgeoisie plays an essential role has challenged neoliberalism." Petras and Henry Veltmeyer (2005: 216, 137, 174) argue that "electoral politics is a game that the popular movement cannot win, governed as it is by rules designed by and that favor the dominant class, and that compel the movement to settle for very limited change and the illusion of power." It is only a trap designed to demobilize revolutionary movements. "Every single advance of the popular movement," they write, "has been through a strategy of mass mobilizations." Petras and Veltmeyer advise avoiding "electoral politics, the path preferred by the 'political class' because it is predicated on limited political reforms." They condemn Pachakutik for their "serious political mistake to seek state power from within the system."[2] From their perspective, social movements ultimately are more effective at making lasting change.

D. L. Raby (2006: 3, 57, 228) states that this "insistence on direct, unmediated popular protagonism is admirable" but ultimately evades "questions of representation, leadership, organisation and structure which are crucial to the success of any alternative movement." The result, Raby argues, is a "romantic but ultimately defeatist approach," and she terms Holloway's attitude as "the ultimate theoretical formulation of negativism." She argues that while history has shown "that revolutionary state power has all too often lost its popular democratic foundations," it is a mistake to assume that it is not possible to construct "a non-capitalist power structure based on social justice." The problem is not an "emphasis on popular autonomy and protagonism" but a "refusal to consider the need for organisation and leadership." Indeed, Raby contends, to rely only on social movements and to fail to engage state power condemns "people to an endless cycle of circumscribed struggles, frustration and disillusionment." Eventually, social movements will need to enter the electoral realm to achieve their objectives.

Katz (2007: 41) confronts the Holloway thesis even more directly. "Not even the most basic democratic changes that we currently see in Latin America are conceivable without the state," Katz writes. "This instrument is necessary to implement social reforms, create constituent assemblies, and nationalize basic resources." Advocates often present Chávez's Venezuela as an example of how harnessing the instruments of state power can lead to successful and deep-seated revolutionary changes. Building on the Venezuelan example, Ciccariello-Maher

(2007: 54) contends that the debate over whether to change the world with or without taking power asks the wrong question. Rather, we need to look at whether forces attempt to perpetuate or dissolve existing exploitative state structures. Indigenous movements in Ecuador, together with much of the political Left in Latin America, no longer see electoral and extra-constitutional paths to power as mutually exclusive. They largely agree with Katz (2007: 39) that "in the face of the false dilemma of accepting or ignoring the rules of constitutionalism, there is a third viable path: to combine direct action with electoral participation." Activists in Ecuador continue to struggle with how to merge electoral and social movement paths to power as appears to be happening in Venezuela.

Correa's relations with social movements point to the complications, limitations, and deep tensions inherent in pursuing revolutionary changes within a constitutional framework. "A regime that limits and at the same time consolidates the power of the oppressors entails a great challenge for the left," Katz (2007: 37) argues, "especially when this structure is seen by the majority as the natural *modus operandi* of any modern society." This new constitutional framework changes the context in which the Left operates and requires rethinking strategies. Katz concludes, "The battle within the current system is not simple because the current institutionalism renews bourgeois domination in multiple disguises." This remained the challenge for Indigenous movements in Ecuador and for social movements in general. The dance between street politics and electoral participation always remains a complicated undertaking, as do ongoing discussions over how and whether to build alliances with popular populist leaders who do not always have Indigenous concerns at heart. Radicalized Indigenous movements, however, remain determined on one point. They are not willing to concede their demands for far-reaching structural changes in exchange for tokenistic recognition or representation. While Correa's government may embody aspects of an *izquierda permitida*, Indigenous activists are not willing to join him on that path.

Notes

Special thanks to Donna Lee Van Cott and Tony Lucero for their helpful comments on an early draft of this manuscript, as well as to the members of my reading group, Hena Ahmad, Jason McDonald, Rubana Mahjabeen, Bonnie Lynn Mitchell, and Daniel Mandell. This essay capitalizes *Indigenous* as a valorization of the ethnic identities the term represents.

1. The reference to *Ecuador profundo* draws on Guillermo Bonfil Batalla's (1996) argument for the importance of the Indigenous roots of a country's culture.

2. Petras (2009) subsequently backed off from these assertions in the face of changes happening in Venezuela. "Venezuela represents the most exemplary case of a sustained effort to democratize electoral politics," he writes. Chávez "represents a unique case of an effort to *combine the democratization of electoral politics with the socialization of the economy*, deepening and extending democratic politics into the sphere of the economy."

References

Acosta, Alberto. 2009. "El estado plurinacional, puerta para una sociedad democrática. A manera de Prólogo." In *Plurinacionalidad: Democracia en la diversidad*, ed. Alberto Acosta and Esperanza Martínez, 15–20. Quito: Abya Yala.

Almeida Vinueza, José. 2005. "The Ecuadorian Indigenous Movement and the Gutiérrez Regime: The Traps of Multiculturalism." *PoLAR: Political and Legal Anthropology Review* 28 (May): 93–111.

Andean Group Report. 2007. "Constituent Assembly to Supercede Congress." RA-07-07 (July): 6.

———. 2008a. "Nebot Leads Massive Protest in Guayaquil." RA-08-02 (February): 14–15.

———. 2008b. "Nebot Tries to Rally Opposition to President Correa." RA-08-01 (January): 13–15.

Andolina, Robert, Nina Laurie, and Sarah A. Radcliffe. 2009. *Indigenous Development in the Andes: Culture, Power, and Transnationalism*. Durham, NC: Duke University Press.

Bonfil Batalla, Guillermo. 1996. *Mexico Profundo: Reclaiming a Civilization*. Austin: University of Texas Press.

Banting, Keith G., and Will Kymlicka. 2006. "Introduction: Multiculturalism and the Welfare State; Setting the Context." In *Multiculturalism and the Welfare State: Recognition and Redistribution in Contemporary Democracies*, ed. Will Kymlicka and Keith Banting, 1–45. Oxford: Oxford University Press.

Becker, Marc. 2009. "The World Social Forum Returns to Brazil." *Upside Down World*, February 5.

Bretón Solo de Zaldívar, Víctor. 2008. "From Agrarian Reform to Ethnodevelopment in the Highlands of Ecuador." *Journal of Agrarian Change* 8 (October): 583–617.

Burbach, Roger. 2007. "Ecuador's Popular Revolt: Forging a New Nation." *NACLA Report on the Americas* 40 (5): 4–9, 43.

Cholango, Humberto.   2007. "Editorial." *Rikcharishun* 35 (January): 2.

Chuji, Mónica. 2008. "Señores Acuerdo País y compañeros y compañeras asambleístas." September 15.

Ciccariello-Maher, George. 2007. "Dual Power in the Venezuelan Revolution." *Monthly Review* 59 (September): 42–56.

Comercio, El. 2008. "Las ONG dejan su huella en Ciudad Alfaro." July 6.

Conaghan, Catherine. 2008. "Ecuador: Correa's Plebiscitary Presidency." *Journal of Democracy* 19 (April): 46–60.

CONAIE. 2007. *La CONAIE frente a la asamblea constituyente: Propuesta de nueva constitución—desde la CONAIE—para la construcción de un estado plurinacional, unitario, soberano, incluyente, equitativo y laico (Documento de principios y lineamientos)*. Quito: CONAIE.

———. 2008. "La CONAIE frente al referendun y la nueva constitución." *Rikcharishun* 36 (August–September): 5.

———. 2009. "Pueblos Indígenas del Ecuador rechazan declaraciones del presidente Correa, quien acusó al Movimiento Indígena de ser desestabilizador de la democracia en el país." *CONAIE.org*, January 18. http://www.conaie.org/es/ge_comunicados/20090119.html.

Dávalos, Pablo. 2008. "El 'Sumak Kawsay' ('Buen vivir') y las cesuras del desarrollo, Segunda parte." *Boletín ICCI-Rimay* 10 (June).

Ecuarunari. 2007. "Nuestra propuesta a la Asamblea Constituyente." *Rikcharishun* 35 (August): 4–5.

Ecuarunari and CONAIE. 2007. *"Los Kichwas somos hijos de la Rebeldía": Propuesta para la Asamblea Constituyente*. Quito: CONAIE.

Hale, Charles. 2004. "Rethinking Indigenous Politics in the Era of the 'Indio Permitido.'" *NACLA Report on the Americas* 38 (September–October): 16–21.

Harnecker, Marta. 2005. "On Leftist Strategy." *Science & Society* 69 (April): 142–52.

Holloway, John. 2002. *Change the World without Taking Power: The Meaning of Revolution Today*. London: Pluto Press.

ICCI (Instituto Científico de Culturas Indígenas). 2001 "Banco Mundial y Prodepine: ¿Hacia un neoliberalismo étnico?" *Boletín ICCI-Rimay* 3 (April).

———. 2007. "Uno es el discurso . . . otra la realidad." *Boletín ICCI-Rimay* 9 (December): 2–6.

———. 2008. "Un verdadero gobierno de izquierda." *Boletín ICCI-Rimay* 10 (June).

Katz, Claudio. 2007. "Socialist Strategies in Latin American." *Monthly Review* 59 (September): 25–41.

Laclau, Ernesto. 1977. *Politics and Ideology in Marxist Theory: Capitalism, Fascism, Populism*. London: NLB.

Latin American Weekly Report. 2007a. "Correa's Actions at Odds with Discourse." WR-07-03 (January 18): 4.

———. 2007b. "Correa Reigns over Institutional Chaos." WR-07-16 (April 26): 4.

———. 2009. "Correa Attempts to Define Modern Socialism." WR-09-02 (January 15): 3.

León, Magdalena. 2008. "Ecuador: La búsqueda de un 'nuevo modelo.'" *América Latina en Movimiento* 32, no. 430 (March 2008): 31–32.

Lucas, Kintto. 2007a. "La CONAIE y el Presidente: La necesidad de encontrarse en el camino." *Boletín ICCI-Rimay* 9 (October): 7–12.

———. 2007b. *Rafael Correa: Un extraño en Carondelet*. Quito: Planteta.

Meléndez, Ángela. 2008. "La Conaie lanza advertencia a Correa." *El Comercio*, November 1.

Mijeski, Kenneth J., and Scott H. Beck. 2008. "The Electoral Fortunes of Ecuador's Pachakutik Party: The Fracaso of the 2006 Presidential Elections." *Latin Americanist* 52 (June): 41–59.

——. 2011. *Pachakutik and the Rise and Decline of the Ecuadorian Indigenous Movement*. Athens: Ohio University Press.

Petras, James. 2005. "Latin American Strategies: Class-Based Direct Action versus Populist Electoral Politics." *Science and Society* 69 (April): 152–59.

——. 2009. "Venezuela: Socialism, Democracy and the Re-Election of President Chavez." *VenezuelaAnalysis.com*, January 2009. http://www.venezuelanalysis.com/analysis/4098.

Petras, James, and Henry Veltmeyer. 2005. *Social Movements and State Power: Argentina, Brazil, Bolivia, Ecuador*. London: Pluto Press.

——. 2006. "Social Movements and the State: Political Power Dynamics in Latin America." *Critical Sociology* 32 (February): 83–104.

Raby, D. L. 2006. *Democracy and Revolution: Latin America and Socialism Today*. London: Pluto Press.

Rénique, Gerardo. 2009. "Law of the Jungle in Peru: Indigenous Amazonian Uprising against Neoliberalism." *Socialism and Democracy* 23 (November): 117–35.

Republic of Ecuador. 2008. "Constituciones de 2008." *Political Database of the Americas*. http://pdba.georgetown.edu/Constitutions/Ecuador/ecuador08.html.

Riofrancos, Thea. 2008. "Ecuador: Indigenous Confederation Inaugurates New President and Announces National Mobilization." *Upside Down World*, February 6.

Saavedra, Luis Ángel. 2007. "'We've Balanced Out the Power.'" *Latinamerica Press* 39 (October 17): 1–2.

Simbaña, Floresmilo. 2007 "El movimiento indígena y el actual proceso de transición." *América Latina en Movimiento* 31 (August 20): 21–24.

Sousa Santos, Boaventura de. 2009. "Las paradojas de nuestro tiempo y la Plurinacionalidad." In *Plurinacionalidad: Democracia en la diversidad*, ed. Alberto Acosta and Esperanza Martínez, 21–62. Quito: Abya Yala.

Torre, Carlos de la. 2011. "Corporatism, Charisma, and Chaos: Ecuador's Police Rebellion in Context." *NACLA Report on the Americas* 44 (January–February): 25–32.

Van Cott, Donna Lee. 2006. "Multiculturalism versus Neoliberalism in Latin America." In *Multiculturalism and the Welfare State: Recognition and Redistribution in Contemporary Democracies*, ed. Will Kymlicka and Keith Banting, 272–96. Oxford: Oxford University Press.

Webber, Jeffery R. 2009. "From Naked Barbarism to Barbarism with Benefits: Neoliberal Capitalism, Natural Gas Policy, and the Government of Evo Morales in Bolivia." In *Post-Neoliberalism in the Americas*, ed. Arne Ruckert and Laura Macdonald, 105–19. New York: Palgrave Macmillan.

Zamosc, Leon. 2004. "The Indian Movement in Ecuador: From Politics of Influence to Politics of Power." In *The Struggle for Indigenous Rights in Latin America*, ed. Nancy Grey Postero and Leon Zamosc, 131–57. Brighton, UK: Sussex Academic Press.

10

Crisis and Recomposition in Argentina

Emilia Castorina

For a Serious Country, for a Normal Country

—Néstor Kirchner's 2003 campaign slogan

IN 2001–2002 ARGENTINA WENT through one of the deepest financial crises in the world through a massive (spontaneous) popular upheaval under the slogan *¡Que se vayan todos!* ("Out with them all!"), giving way to a novel and generalized state of social mobilization. The December 2001 insurrection involved a disturbing point of convergence for the guardians of order: a demand for the resignation of every person responsible for the ruling regime as a whole. It didn't take long for the Left—intellectuals, social movements, and political parties that in various ways seek to transform or overthrow capitalism—to declare the official death of neoliberalism in Argentina. Interestingly, everyone from the traditional revolutionary Left (Altamira, 2002; Petras and Veltmeyer, 2004) to supporters of the new social subjects (Dinerstein, 2002; Zibechi, 2003), the "multitude" (Negri et al., 2003; Virno, 2002) and the "anti-power" (Holloway, 2002), shared a common view that a fundamental change had emerged in the way politics was being practiced in Argentina as the bourgeois state was said to be "exhausted." While having deep differences as to which of these new actors was the most appropriate interpreter of such transformations, all assumed that a historic opportunity had opened up to overthrow capitalist society.

The aim of this chapter is to explore the failure of the Left to effectively seize the moment, particularly those expressing extra-parliamentary forms of struggle with an ideological orientation toward autonomist visions of "politics from below." The process of political recomposition in the postcrisis period led to a reinvigorated process of capital accumulation, mainly because the Argentine state showed a remarkable capacity to react to challenges from "below" and proved highly successful in taming them without really giving in to their demands—or threatening the interests of the establishment—for two interrelated reasons:

1. Unlike the optimistic prophecies of the Left assuming "old politics" (Peronism) and the bourgeois state to be "exhausted," the fact is that Peronist politics was revitalized by Néstor Kirchner's government to solve the crisis. While Latin America faces a number of very different exits from the crisis of neoliberalism (Robinson, 2007), Argentina seems like a paradigmatic example of *izquierda permitida* (as defined by Jeffery Webber and Barry Carr in the introduction to this volume). Unlike the more radical cases of Venezuela, Bolivia, or Ecuador, placed in comparative perspective, Kirchner's "solution" to the social and economic contradictions of neoliberalism took more of a reformist shape—that is, not a real threat to capital or imperialism but a different means through which to recompose normal capitalism in the face of mass protests and financial crisis.

2. The new social forces emerging out of the contradictions of neoliberalism proved politically incapable of building a unified, plausible alternative from "below" that could effectively resist co-optation from "above."

From a historical perspective, a Peronist exit to the crisis may come as no surprise. Traditionally, Argentine working (and overall popular) classes have been Peronist, not revolutionary leftist. Since the 1940s, Perón's control of workers was achieved over the heads of preexisting, well-established anarchist-, socialist-, and communist-controlled trade union organizations, and any attempt at establishing relatively autonomous working-class organizations either within or outside Peronism have until today been doomed to failure.[1] This is mainly so because Peronism delivered the most important welfare services to the working classes when it was the governing party and remained a powerful heretical subculture challenging conservative rule when it was banned (1955–1973). Peronism, for the most part, has been an acute mechanism to prevent communist, socialist, or anarchist influence within the labor movement, thus reducing the likelihood of revolution since a key aspect of its doctrine relies on the premises that Peronism represents the end of class struggle and that revolution and the threat of communism can effectively be averted by a systematic state effort to channel social conflict and incorporate subaltern classes to the state—be it in a corporatist form through universal social rights (i.e., a party of workers) or in a neoliberal one through clientelism and targeted state relief programs for the poor (i.e., a party based on social work). As a result, Peronism has been a benchmark not only of developmentalism but also of neoliberalism. One reason for this continuing adaptation to different conjunctures can be found in its charismatic nature (it's always Peronism, Menemism, or Kirchnerism) and striking degree of organizational flexibility—it differs from prototypical working-class parties since it's informally organized and weakly routinized (Levistky, 2003; McGuire, 1997)—thus allowing the movement to pragmatically switch politically and ideologically from the center-left (*izquierda permitida*) to center-right (*derecha permitida*) and vice versa without losing political effectiveness. It also explains the successful adaptation of Peronism to the postcrisis period.

On the other hand, the recent predominance of new visions of power from "below" over those more traditionally revolutionary projects aimed at seizing the state within the Left has its roots in a widespread sense of failure of revolutionary tactics that accompanied the process of democratic transition since 1983. Indeed, as the 1970s was marked by an unprecedented scale of political violence[2] resulting in a brutal dictatorship (1976–1983) that repressed and annihilated thirty thousand young activists, the Left came to be seriously discredited and targeted as a major obstacle for democratization and social pacification. Not only was this a key prerequisite for the "democratic" implementation of neoliberalism in the 1990s by the Peronist party, which faced practically no significant challenge from the labor movement (in fact, the General Confederation of Workers [CGT] cooperated with the reforms) or the remainders of the leftist parties. It also enhanced the idea that social change would come peacefully and without grand structural transformations—something that made the concepts of "new social movements," the "multitude," or "anti-power" so appealing but equally problematic in 2001–2002.

The Crisis of 2001

The neoliberal reforms carried out in Argentina during the 1990s by Carlos Menem were more radical than those of most comparable cases, and so was the crisis of 2001. To some extent, the extraordinary character of the Argentine crisis of 2001 was directly proportional to the speed and depth of the neoliberal reforms of the 1990s. Indeed, according to the Inter-American Development Bank (1997), the Argentine reforms were the second most far-reaching in the world in the 1990–1995 period, and they were faster and more far-reaching than those of Thatcher in England and Pinochet in Chile. The orthodox setting—mostly based on severe restraints on fiscal policy to overcome monetary instability after the hyperinflation crisis of 1989—involved a full-package of structural adjustment programs; an extensive opening to international flows of trade and capital; severe limits under a currency board regime[3] to the capacity of governments to apply "countercyclical" policies; a convertibility plan that fixed the exchange rate (one peso = one dollar) to provide an anchor to the price system while also involving a partial but increasing dollarization of the banking system; massive privatization of public utilities and several deregulatory measures in goods and financial markets; and deregulation of the labor market, particularly through flexibilization policies and the compulsory capitalization of retirement and pension funds.

While the combination of trade opening with an appreciated exchange rate resulted in a chronic trade-balance deficit along with a growing structural deficit caused by debt accumulation, this was offset by substantial net capital inflows. Such a dependence on capital inflows made the Argentinean economy more vulnerable to the demands for "a proper investment climate," which usually translated into an active policy of adapting and adjusting the Argentinean social formation to the needs of global capital in its search for productivity. Menem was more than willing to offer favorable conditions for business in the form of flexibilization of labor, reduction of corporate taxation, and cuts in public spending and wages, among other measures, as the economy desperately needed the investment. Given the economy's external vulnerability, financial crises occurring in other parts of the world severely affected Argentina's macroeconomic performance. In addition, Argentina became even more dependent on International Monetary Fund (IMF) loans to meet its obligations and, by the same token, on the IMF's requirements and conditions—mainly that debt servicing could only be met through budget adjustment, that is, through the people's welfare conditions: education, health, and salaries.

The "market friendly" economic setting provided by the convertibility regime, while functional in protecting the value assets held by foreign creditors and investors (as well as the foreign assets held by wealthy Argentineans), soon proved to be a disaster for subaltern classes: full-time employment fell, and the unemployment rate rose to 18.3 percent—with a peak of 22 percent in 2002. This points toward deep social transformations—particularly for a country that by 1980 had the lowest record of unemployment in Latin America. The general impoverishment of society is revealed by data on regressive income distribution. According to the National Statistics and Censuses Institute Permanent Survey of Households (EPH-INDEC), before 1974 income distribution in Argentina was similar to many developed countries, and in the area of Great Buenos Aires alone, the share of the richest 10 percent was 12.7 times more than that of the poorest 10 percent. As the market-led strategy of growth evolved, this gap widened: in 1991 it was 22.1; by 1999 it was 32.9; and by 2001 the share of the richest 10 percent was 51.9 times more than that of the poorest 10 percent. While in 1991, 16 percent of the population was below the poverty line, by 2002 it reached a peak of 54.3 percent, which means that more than half of the Argentinean population fell below the poverty line.

Social contradictions began to be evident by 1996–1997 when the growing unemployed sectors mobilized a contentious repertoire of fragmented struggles across the country. The *piqueteros* movement—mass organizations of unemployed based on direct action (roadblocks or pickets), community organizing, and popular assemblies at neighborhood and other levels—became a prominent actor on the political scene, unraveling the social contradictions of neoliberalism. *Piquetes* (road blockades) and *puebladas* (town insurrections) soon became a new model of social protest for the unemployed, public employees, teachers, rural workers, and all those who began to challenge neoliberal policies in Argentina by organizing outside and against the institutional frameworks of the state, traditional unions, and organized leftist parties. The cycle of protests that began in 1996–1997 signaled the beginning of a process of articulating new collective practices—new social movements associated with new forms of organization, struggle, and identities emerging in response to the realities imposed by neoliberal policies.

The emergence (1996–1997) and consolidation (1999–2002) of the *piqueteros* movement represented the first attempt at departing from patronage politics, clientelism, unions, and party politics, collectively known as "old" politics (Schuster and Scribano, 2001; Svampa and Pereyra, 2003). Abandoned by national compensatory programs or universal measures of inclusion and mainstream unionism, the unemployed were ready (or left with few options but) to mobilize and engage not only in direct action in the streets but also in the creation of new territorial organizations—community-based organizations of social needs. The expansion of the *piquetes* and the increasing institutionalization of the demands for state relief programs throughout the country, particularly in the province of Buenos Aires in 2000–2001, proved the power of *piqueteros* to impose their conditions to a rapidly deteriorating government (that of Fernando de la Rúa).[4]

By 2001 the impossibility of maintaining the parity between the peso and the dollar and maintaining debt servicing became clear (external debt rose from $ 7.8 billion U.S. in 1976 to $128 billion in 2001). The increasing loss of confidence of financial investors fuelled the country risk, the drain of banking deposits, and a massive flight of capital. In order to prevent the bankruptcy of major banks after a run against them at the beginning of December, the government implemented the *corralito* (the freezing of banking savings of the

Argentinean population). It is important to point out that the exodus of cash took place only days before the government froze all withdrawals, leading to a widespread belief that the banks—unlike regular Argentineans, who were taken by surprise—had been tipped off that the freeze was imminent.

Far from solving the problem, the *corralito* triggered social unrest all over the country. Looting spread everywhere and so did police repression that resulted in several deaths. During the evening of December 19, the president announced the imposition of an *etat-du-siege* (state of emergency), which did not tame protest but rather catalyzed a spontaneous massive insurrection (the so-called *cacerolazo*, the massive banging of pots and pans) against the government, the economic program, banks, and the *etat-du-siege* as well. With the slogan *¡Que se vayan todos!* (Out with them all!), Argentinean citizens took to the streets, attacked banks (the main targets were the foreign banks like Citibank), and marched to the House of Government. The following day, police fiercely repressed the people in the streets, adding further to the death toll. Both the rebellion and the repression lasted until the evening of December 20, when President De la Rúa resigned. Over the following days, the country went through five consecutive presidencies and a default of its $95 billion debt, the largest default in history.

The New Prophesies from "Below"

After the events of December 2001, a novel process of grassroots political engagement indeed took place. In downtown Buenos Aires alone, 250 neighborhood assemblies filled the streets and plazas with meetings where people (mostly of the middle classes and without any previous political experience) planned, organized, and voted on different matters. While many of the first assemblies were more like group therapy than political meetings, they soon began to plan for something else: solidarity, another kind of economy, and even a new form of direct democracy. Soup kitchens were opened and trading clubs (Club del Trueque) were formed. Between 130 and 250 factories, bankrupt and abandoned by their owners, were taken over by their workers and turned into cooperatives and collectives. Decisions about company policies were now made in open assemblies, and profits were split equally among the workers. They soon began to network among themselves to plan for an informal "social economy" or "solidarity economy." The continuing assaults carried out by small savers on private banks that had confiscated their savings filled the streets of Buenos Aires's financial district for days. *Piquetes* by the unemployed intensified throughout the country, growing from 1,381 in 2001 to 2,336 in 2002 (Epstein, 2003).

This so-called Argentinazo came to be viewed in the international arena with concern by the "guardians of order"—MIT's famous monetarist economist and former adviser to many Latin American finance ministers and Central Bank presidents Rudi Dornbusch, for instance, said in the aftermath of the events of December 2001, "The excluded are deploying a *class struggle* and institutions have completely collapsed." Conversely, it was greeted with hope by antiglobalization activists as the first national revolt against neoliberalism. For instance, "You are Enron, we are Argentineans" was soon adopted as a chant outside trade summits (Klein, 2003). There seemed to have been a converging vision across the political spectrum about the crisis: it was said to have opened up space for the formation of *autonomous* publics (i.e., with no attachment to traditional political mediations) vis-à-vis an exhausted or declined/collapsed state. This idea was soon translated into a new conception of power from "below," which for the most part proposed a series of new prophesies about "running away from the state."

A new version of anarchist/autonomist discourse gained momentum (locally and internationally) within the emerging grassroots politics, which Alberto Bonnet (2004) ironically defined as "holophobic" (being phobic to holistic thinking) and "microphilic" (having an attachment to small and marginal micropolitics). According to Antonio Negri and others (2003), the Argentinazo was an example of the "multitude"—a force that negates any forms of state representation that emerges within the structures of empire and neoliberalism, an example of the possibilities that emerge when the nation-state "vanishes." For Paolo Virno (2002), the Argentinean revolt was connected to the "multitude in action" that mobilized at Seattle and Geneva because of its "anti-state" and "anti-political" nature. Throughout 2002 the Left (new and old) was actively and extensively debating this concept and its relevance for revolutionary purposes, not only in the media and the newspapers but also in a growing industry of studies on new social movements.

The new experiences of political participation taking place after December 2001 were generally described by their protagonists as autonomous—as a way to distinguish themselves from the state and other hierarchical institutions like unions or leftist political parties, but also as a way of identifying themselves with a politics of self-organization, *autogestión, horizontalidad,* and direct, democratic participation (Sitrin, 2006). These autonomous actors (whether in recuperated factories, neighborhood assemblies, or *piquetero* organizations) were putting their energy into how and what they organized in the present, taking to heart John Holloway's mantra to "change the world without taking power."[5] For instance, at the neighborhood assembly of Colegiales, an activist argued, "Let's reinvent new organizational forms and reinvent society . . . to transform the rejection, *que se vayan todos,* into constructive practices of new sociability and new forms of organization, not ones like the state, but new forms." An unemployed worker from the MTD (unemployed workers movement) in Almirante Brown stated, "We're breaking away from organizing in vertical ways, the way that the system and government work. We are basically starting from scratch. Our movement started because of concrete needs. . . . Now each of us has a voice and a vote." An activist from Tierra del Sur (a neighborhood assembly located in an occupied building and community center) said, "We don't need anyone to impose a new Communist Manifesto on us. . . . The good thing is we have no program. We are creating tools of freedom." An activist at a GLTTB (Gay, Lesbianas, Travestis, Transexuales y Bisexuales) collective similarly argued, "The concept of taking power is archaic. What does it mean to take power? Power over what? The social movements are thinking of a different kind of power that's distinct from the power of dominance, the power of transforming daily relations" (Sitrin, 2006: 41, 44, 160).

Yet the idea that the "old politics" (i.e., the politics of politicians, institutional politics anchored in the state, clientelism, patronage, and machine politics) gave way to a "new politics" (i.e., politics of social movements) was based on a series of problematic assumptions. To begin with, as Iñigo Carrera (2006) argues, there is an illusion that the apparent increase in the political awareness of the Argentine people will per se engender a radical change in the overall process of capital accumulation. Second, the idea that "horizontal" organization represents an effective way of challenging traditional "vertical" forms of organization obviously takes for granted that popular organizations have indeed replaced vertical forms with horizontal ones. Third, the idea that bourgeois democracy has become a "parody" or an "empty shell" is questionable given the capacity of subsequent electoral processes to effectively process social conflict and reproduce political domination.[6]

Prophecies from "Above"

The process that evolved from mid-2002 onward proved all these assumptions to be wrong. To begin with, what the Left called "old" politics—that is, the politics of Pernonism, clientelism, and patronage—was far from exhausted. In fact, it was the key vehicle for political recomposition since taming and harnessing social movements was a fundamental condition for stabilizing the economy. Social movements, intellectuals, and activists endlessly debated the significance of the rise of the multitude or the antipower, autonomy and horizontalism, as well as the need to expand productive self-managed projects and gardens—to experience or perform catharsis in the streets. Meanwhile, the provisional government of Eduardo Duhalde (probably the most important promoter and organizer of political clientelism and patronage politics during the 1990s in the province of Buenos Aires) was promoting catharsis by way of the supposedly vanished or exhausted institutions of the state passing a series of laws and "rescue plans" for the banks and the capitalist class overall. While the Left was debating the end of capitalism and neoliberalism, the ruling class was seizing the opportunity to build new businesses. Indeed, the devaluation of the currency produced an immediate depreciation of salaries, and the "pesification" of bank deposits mainly favored sources of big local capital by allowing them to smooth their debts.[7] For many of Argentina's richest business sectors, this was a highly profitable arrangement; in fact, the banking fiasco and devaluation have actually made them richer than they were before: they now pay their employees, their expenses, and their debts in devalued pesos, but—thanks to the banks—their savings are safely stored outside the country in U.S. dollars.

While the state seemed to have been robbed of its importance by the new prophets of the multitude and antipower, it ended up being remarkably refurbished by reformist forces. Indeed, the "withdrawal from the state" promoted by the new Left ironically coincided with the reassertion and empowerment of the state as a site to roll back challenges from below and reintegrate the poor and excluded within the state apparatus. Indeed, in 2002 Duhalde's government launched a massive state relief program for the poor and unemployed that reached almost two million beneficiaries. Plan Jefes y Jefas de Hogar (Male and Female Heads of Household Plan, JyJDH) involved a cash transfer of $150 in exchange for some form of community work. This program was similar (although bigger as it covered close to 20 percent of the Argentine households) to previous social programs applied in the 1990s following the World Bank's prescriptions of targeted programs to alleviate poverty—in other words, this was "assistance" without any form of social security instead of substantive universal measures of income distribution.

The intention behind the JyJDH was to enable Peronism to recover the territory it had lost to new social forces at the grassroots level—most notably the *piqueteros* (Svampa, 2008). In fact, only 10 percent of these resources were allocated by unemployed organizations, while the rest was distributed by the Peronist machine. According to some research, the program ended up financing part of the operations of the Peronist machine through the "tolls" that brokers (*punteros*) collected for granting access to the program (Auyero, 2007; CELS, 2003). Crucial in this respect is the fact that mayors kept control of the on-the-ground administration of the program. Mayors throughout the country have de facto veto power regarding who is and who is not a welfare recipient (Weitz-Shapiro, 2008). In this way the JyJDH became a key state resource that circulated within the Peronist problem-solving networks and oiled the operations of the Peronist machine (Auyero, 2007).

In addition, the JyJHD contributed to further accentuation of the divisions within the various *piquetero* fractions, who came to struggle and compete for a share in the administration of the program. The *piqueteros* are divided into countless organizations, which can be grouped into three main streams: (1) The larger and more numerous fractions, located in La Matanza, such as the Federación Tierra y Vivienda (Federation of Land and Housing, FTV), have a unionist tradition and a *reformist* vision of power. They use road blockades to bargain with the state and consider "politics" and political alliances with the government as viable resources for political purposes, so they take part in electoral processes. (2) A *revolutionary* or a more "radical" line organized around leftist political parties (Trostkysts, communists, and some nationalist leftists), such as the Polo Obrero (Workers Pole), Barrios de Pie (Standing Neighborhoods), or Movimiento Socialista de Trabajadores (Movement of Socialist Workers, MST), are more critical about the state and tend to be more confrontational (even insurrectional) than the reformist fractions. They don't bargain or form alliances with state power, but they do participate in elections, and the ultimate aim of these organizations is to seize state power and establish a popular government. (3) There are also *autonomous* organizations completely detached from elections and more concerned with local and micro–social work, such as the Coordinadora Anibal Verón, MTD Solano, and other MTDs (Movimiento de Trabajadores Desocupados, Unemployed Workers' Movement). These groups are not interested in creating social and political broader alliances, nor in political parties, much less a "revolutionary vanguard party." At the core of this conception there is a different notion of politics inspired by the Mexican Zapatista movement that is not aimed at seizing state power or other political apparatuses but rather at building autonomous spheres of counterpower.

The government and the media introduced a distinction between "good" *piqueteros* ("moderates" or *dialoguistas*) and "bad" *piqueteros* ("hard liners" or *combativos*) depending on their propensity toward bargaining and dialogue with the government. Critically, only the "good" ones (FTV) were chosen by Duhalde from the entire *piquetero* movement to officially participate in the Consejo Consultivo Nacional (Local Consultative Council), the central body charged with managing the JyJDH, along with various non-*piquetero* organizations. Excluded from such an influential role on this strategic body, the hard-liners resented this official favoritism and began to see the *dialoguistas* as rivals who had "sold out" to the government (Epstein, 2003).[8] The bargaining process ended with the assassination of two *piqueteros* and the subsequent call for national elections.

The presidential election of 2003, however, marked a fundamental rechanneling of social struggles within the boundaries of formal democracy. While most prophets of the new Left expected high absenteeism and spoiled ballots to predominate, as a manifestation of the supposedly popular advance beyond institutionalized, representative democracy, or at least some form of protest against the lack of legitimate political representation, this turned out not to be the case. Spoiled ballots fell from their 20 percent peak in the 2001 elections to 1.6 percent in 2003; electoral absenteeism even went down compared to 2001; blank ballots went down to the smallest figures registered since the 1946 elections; and the number of annulled votes was negligible (Bonnet, 2006; Calvo, 2003; Carrera, 2006). Despite the peculiarities of the election, the Peronist party—a prime example of "old politics"—got an overwhelming majority of votes if the three Peronist candidates are taken together. This is not to mention that Menem, whose ten-year rule of harsh structural adjustment had made him the paradigmatic target of *¡Que se vayan todos!*, led in the first round with no less than 24 percent of the votes. Kirchner (Duhalde's candidate) finished second with 22 percent, but seeing that a second runoff would give Kirchner an overwhelming victory, Menem decided to drop out of the race.

The Peronist Partido Justicialista (Justicialist Party, PJ) victory emptied many of the political initiatives emerging out of the events of December 2001 as hopes for a reordering of political life "from below" gave way to demands for a return to order (Svampa, 2008). Kirchner's electoral campaign sought to capture this message with his slogan, "For a Serious Country, for a Normal Country." The elections of 2003 thus proved the inability of the new social actors and movements emerging out of the crisis to translate the sentiments behind December 19 and 20 into a concrete political platform or alternative project. Naively, many new social movements decided not to participate in elections, thus bringing the electoral process down to a choice between two symbols (Menem or Kirchner) of the "old" politics. Those who did participate either made a very poor electoral showing—like the traditional leftist parties (Izquierda Unida, United Left)—or faced increasing co-optation by supporting Kirchner—like the bigger *piquetero* fractions (FTV) and the independent unions (mainly, the CTA).

The electoral victory of the Peronist demand for a return to a "normal country" probably redefines the meaning of the events of December 2001, away from radical change and toward a more conservative logic of class recomposition. As Eduardo Gruner argues, "when the middle class takes to the streets to demand the return of its private property [bank deposits], when the unemployed demand jobs, what they are saying is: 'We want to be serious class subjects again'" (2002: 159). Moreover, for many low-income people made desperate by the crisis, the notions of autonomy, *autogestión*, or antipower were really unclear, as it is not the history of exclusion (as with the Zapatistas Movement) but the memory and experience of former inclusion that shaped the dynamic of mobilization among the Argentine unemployed. For this reason, autonomous organizations became unable to compete with promises of social integration as put forward by the PJ.

The 2003 electoral campaign proved Peronist clientelism to be more effective on the ground than the new social movements; it was more appealing in terms of selective incentives and material rewards. As an unemployed activist from MTD in Allen notes,

> The elections have sucked in a lot of *compañeros*. They went to the municipality to work for the campaign. What happens is that the party hacks come to the neighborhoods and they buy them. They offer a bunch of money and some—including some that were really valued and respected—end up going along. Verónica is an example of this. She was deeply involved—even speaking in front of thousands of people on behalf of the movement—and then went to work on a political campaign [. . .] and this is the way a number of *compañeros* went. We lost their contributions to the movement, and many of the productive projects suffered—all because of the drainage of *compañeros*. (Sitrin, 2006: 103–4)

Contrary to the mythology that asserts that the events of December 2001 radically changed the way politics is practiced in Argentina, the electoral campaign of 2003 further revitalized the clientelistic penetration of lower-class social networks. Research by Valeria Brusco, Marcelo Nazareno, and Susan Stokes (2004) points to the fact that poverty—and in this case, widespread poverty immediately created by the crisis—turned low-income voters into clients. Their study shows that 44 percent of low-income respondents reported that parties gave things out to individuals during the campaign. The most common item mentioned was food, but also medicine, clothing, mattresses, milk, construction materials, money, blankets, and other materials. Forty-five percent admitted they would turn to a party operative (*puntero*) for help if the head of his or her household lost a job. More than one in five low-income voters did turn to local political brokers or patrons for help during the previous year—the most pressing moment of the crisis.

Kirchner Era: Center-Left Neoliberalism?

Practically unknown in the national political scene, Kirchner came to prominence in the midst of a serious institutional crisis. A governor and *caudillo* of the Patagonian province of Santa Cruz since 1991, and at that time a supporter of the privatization of the national oil company (YPF), Kirchner had in the 1970s been a member of the Juventud Peronista, a left-Peronist youth movement. Contrary to predictions about a weak mandate and low legitimacy due to his low 22 percent of votes cast, Kirchner's capacity to lead and reorganize a divided PJ enabled him to politically recompose the conditions for economic recovery. Given the extraordinary institutional (and ideological) flexibility of Peronism, under Kirchner the PJ was able to depart from its previous commitment to the Washington Consensus and present itself as a left-of-center, anti-neoliberal force.

To some extent, the Argentinazo had moved Argentinean society to the left in the political spectrum, and Kirchner learned how to exploit this for a politics of reinstitutionalization. The new administration expropriated politically the demands of *¡Que se vayan todos!* by turning them into the basis of an effective reconstruction of capitalist state power by addressing the long-neglected moral and political concerns of progressive sectors. This was done by (1) appointing a new Supreme Court, as the previous one has been closely linked to Menemism; and (2) annulling laws (Obediencia Debida and Punto Final) that prevented the military from being prosecuted for crimes against humanity during the dictatorship, thus allowing dozens of members of the armed forces finally to be brought to trial.

In the social context of *¡Que se vayan todos!*—expressing the citizens' rejection of the entire body of politicians and a sharp decline in public confidence in fundamental democratic institutions—Kirchner presented himself as a man who was an outsider in the political system, an antiparty president, even alienating and infuriating some key Peronist leaders. But far from changing "old politics," this was an opportunity for Kirchner to build his own populist power. Indeed, neoliberal populism is characterized by a top-down state-centered strategy of wielding political power based on appealing to the excluded and attacking the "political class" (Weyland, 1996). By definition, populist leaders need a clear enemy in order to build their leadership and unify their followers in the classic "us" versus "them," so Kirchner targeted the "nineties," Menemism, and the IMF as a way to build another support coalition incorporating *piqueteros*, select trade unions, human rights groups, and nonparty leftists. By attacking the "political class," Kirchner resorted to rule by decree instead of congressionally mandated laws (despite having a parliamentary majority) to promote his agenda. He used Executive Decrees of Necessity and Urgency sixty-seven times in his first year in office, surpassing Menem's record of sixty-four. In a few months Kirchner gained an impressive popularity rating—90 percent in August 2003 and an average of 77 percent over his first two years in office—probably indicating a continuation of citizens' "delegative" tendencies in Argentina rather than a fundamental change in political culture, as approval ratings for political institutions as governmental power and political parties were much lower than Kirchner's (Epstein and Pion-Berlin, 2006).

It would not be off the mark to argue that the Argentinean ruling class needed a Bonapartist leader (or for that matter, a pragmatist Peronist) to resolve the crisis, someone able to play "progressively" while reconstructing the conditions for political domination at the same time. It was in this precise sense that Kirchner lined up with Fidel Castro, Hugo Chávez, and Luiz Ignácio Lula de Silva while continuing to implement labor flexibilization, or strongly criticizing the IMF while promptly paying debt service in cash, or defending and promoting human rights policies while repressing adversaries (specially anti-Kirchner *piqueteros*). Overall, as Robinson (2007) argues for the "pink tide" governments, Kirchner's administration involved (1) no significant redistribution of income or wealth, and indeed, inequality may still actually be increasing; and (2) no shift in basic property and class relations despite changes in political blocs, discourse in favor of the popular classes, and mildly reformist or social-welfare measures.

The new phase of economic expansion—based on securing discounts on the defaulted foreign debt (given the impossibility of receiving fresh funds from foreign creditors); an extractive, export-driven model of agribusiness, mining, and energy; import substitution; and the extension of state relief programs for the poor and unemployed[9]—reproduced an even more effective combination of income concentration and social inequality than did the 1990s. Despite an extraordinary average of 8 percent growth rate since 2003, income has been distributed unevenly. According to Claudio Lozano (2005), a comparison between the levels of economic activity in 1998 and 2005 shows that they are similar, suggesting that there has been significant recovery since the crisis of 2001. However, in 2005 there were 30 percent more unemployed, the average income was 30 percent lower, and there were five million more poor people than in 1998. Whereas the gap between the incomes of the richest and poorest 10 percent of society was on average a factor of twenty in the 1990s (17.3 in 1992 and 28.3 in 1999), it is presently a factor of thirty-five. Poverty grew by 96 percent and indigence by 300 percent in the same period of time. Moreover, capitalist concentration increased between 2003 and 2007 as the same ten large corporations that accounted for 37 percent of gross domestic product in 1997 came to account for 57 percent in 2007.

The economic recovery involved a decrease (yet rates are still very high) in unemployment (from 22 percent in 2002 to almost 14.4 percent in 2006) and poverty (from 57 to 32 percent). It was expected that sustained economic growth and the improvement of the taxation system would be continuously translated into job creation and the formalization of work. However, high levels of unregistered employment persisted: only a minority of workers, that is 3.4 million, were registered as waged, and another 3.3 million workers were registered as "unwaged." By the end of 2004 there were five million workers with no legal rights or social security, not to mention the expansion of child labor and child homelessness reaching 1.5 million (data from MTEy SS and UNICEF, cited in *La Nación*, May 9, 2005). According to Lozano (2006), between 2003 and 2005, although 2.5 million paid jobs were created, 1.8 million of these were informal, 70 percent of the total. By mid-2007 informal labor accounted for 43.2 percent of all jobs. This points to the fact that the real basis for the economic recovery—as neoliberal economies prove—mostly lies in the precariousness of labor. Only a few formal workers of the private sector receive a real wage that is higher than precrisis rates; the rest of the working class is characterized by a notoriously low wage level (Dinerstein, 2007).

Therefore, Kirchner's governing strategy can best be described as an alternative formula to the one applied in the 1990s to pull the country out of the recession/crisis and at the same time to prevent—or manage more effectively—social and political unrest, an approach that does not involve a fundamental departure from the social bases of the 1990s. This was mostly based on an extraordinary rise in fiscal surpluses and state resources, giving shape to a system of power in which Kirchner came to have almost absolute control over the distribution and allocation of state resources. According to the Argentine system of fiscal co-participation, it is the national government not the provinces that collects taxes. Unlike Menem, whose administration was characterized by deep fiscal deficits, the new fiscal bonanza gave Kirchner the chance to create a system of political loyalties with the governors based exclusively on cash transfers. With the crisis of 2001–2002, the sanction of a series of "emergency bills" gave extraordinary powers to the national executive to discretionally decide the spending of the national budget—an attribution commonly known as the "superpowers." The distribution of social spending to the provinces thus became a key disciplinary mechanism, forcing governors to support Kirchner in order to guarantee governability in their own territories, and overall it reinforced the PJ's machine politics and clientelism. Indeed, the new state resources allowed Kirchner to claim control of the Peronist machine and to sideline most of his political opponents within and outside the party.

The expansion of clientelism came hand in hand with Kirchner's massive rollout of social programs, which reproduced neoliberal forms of Peronist penetration of lower classes. Indeed, during the 1990s, Peronism created new mechanisms for absorbing and reintegrating lower classes into the state that departed from the old populism in no longer being based on corporatist integration and universal social rights but on targeted programs. As Steven

Levitsky argues, in a context of high rates of unemployment, "clientelist organizations are better suited than unions to appeal to the heterogeneous strata of urban unemployed, self-employed, and informal sector workers. . . . A territorial organization, and especially one based on the distribution of particularistic benefits, can be more effective in such a context" (2005: 195). Moreover, as Kenneth Roberts (1996) explains, the provision of more selective, targeted material benefits to specific groups, which can be used as building blocks for local clientelist exchanges, have a more modest fiscal impact than universal measures, but their political logic can be functionally equivalent, as both attempt to exchange material rewards for political support.

> Besides their lower cost, targeted programs have the advantage of being direct and highly visible, allowing government leaders to claim political credit for material gains. By allowing leaders to personally inaugurate local projects or "deliver" targeted benefits, selective programs are highly compatible with the personalistic leader-mass relationships of populism. As … selective incentives provide more powerful inducements to collective action than do public goods, selective benefits may create stronger clientelist bonds than universal benefits, especially politically obscure ones like permanent price subsidies and exchange controls. (Roberts, 1996: 91)

To some extent, Kirchner has been even more effective than Menem in using this form of disciplining and social control. While Menem's Planes Trabajar were not enough to prevent the rise of mass unemployed organizations, Kirchner was able to demobilize, divide, and co-opt the unemployed sectors through the extension of the JyJHD and the creation of new assistance programs. Kirchner was particularly successful at institutionalizing and depoliticizing issues around poverty and unemployment by surprisingly co-opting the language and material framework of the so-called new politics from "below" and the "social economy." The peculiarity of Kirchner's new social policy—mirroring the World Bank's new trends of "incorporating the voice of the poor"—was to take on board the communitarian and solidarity practices underpinning the implementation of productive projects and other forms of collective action of the unemployed organizations and NGOs since the second half of the 1990s, and to provide them with technical and financial support in the form of social capital funds, microcredits, and various forms of technical assistance to several self-managed productive projects.[10]

The real effect of this social policy was to disempower organizations of the unemployed—not only by institutionalizing their social activities, which are an essential constituent of their politics, but also by making them more dependent on state resources and the way in which they are allocated—therefore making them more vulnerable to clientelistic penetration since local political bosses from the PJ ultimately decide who is and who is not to be a recipient of these resources. Moreover, the extension of these assistance programs led to more individualistic types of work with the explicit aim of disarticulating many collective projects. Overall, social programs became an exquisitely attuned vehicle for disciplining unemployed organizations, rewarding "loyal" *piqueteros* with social programs and state offices for their leaders[11] and isolating (repressing and prosecuting) those that are more critical toward the government. In this way, Kirchner has reshaped (and divided) the *piqueteros* map along the lines of "K" and "anti-K" *piqueteros*.[12]

These focused programs of poverty alleviation have also helped Kirchner create a popular political constituency for electoral success. The overwhelming victory of Kirchner's candidates—both in the 2005 parliamentary elections and the 2007 presidential elections—among the less well-off sectors of society is partly explained by the fact that almost 40 percent of poor households in Argentina have come to depend on state relief programs for their basic survival. Having a large number of voters depending on receipt of a public income, a public salary, a pension, or a subsidy provides a huge advantage to whoever is in power. In this sense, it is important to understand how Peronist domination is constructed daily in the enclaves of poverty.

The Peronist problem-solving networks—where webs work as exchange mechanisms, brokering direct flows of goods, information, and services from their political patrons to their clients, and flows of political support (in the form of attendance at rallies, participation in party activities, and votes) from their clients to their patrons—give shape to a sort of "panoptic" power relation (Auyero, 2007). Political brokers (*punteros*) know the whens, hows, whos, and wheres of the allocation of resources, and they know everything about their clients. In some of his interviews, Javier Auyero (2007) recalls the usage of the term *soguero* to critically describe a powerful local *puntero*; the term refers to someone who throws you a rope (*soga*), someone who gives you a hand. But the same rope (or that same hand, for that matter) can also be used to strangle you. Such "dualism of brokerage as problem solving and naked domination" points to a rather complex form of domination because, while patronage may be based on material exchanges, Auyero warns, it also has a crucial symbolic dimension that is entirely missed by most analysts of clientelism. Indeed, it is quite common for recipients of brokers' patronage, especially those with long-lasting ties to their benefactors, to see them as "friends," "caring neighbors," or "good people" and to think and feel that partisan problem solving is not their "right" but a "favor" performed by helpful and responsible people. Therefore, the exchange of "support for favors" creates a set of durable dispositions (and overall habituation) in beneficiaries or clients that becomes difficult to break.

Conclusions

The Argentine case confirms Gramsci's fears of *transformismo* in times of crisis, when

> the ruling class, which has numerous trained cadres, changes men and programs and, with greater speed than is achieved by the subordinated classes, reabsorbs the control that was slipping from its grasp. Perhaps it may make sacrifices, and expose itself to an uncertain future by demagogic promises; but it retains power, reinforces it for the time being, and it uses it to crush its adversaries and disperse its leading cadres. ([1971] 2003: 210–11)

The remarkable capacity of the Peronist state to control—once again—lower classes from "above" may disprove any naive leftist presumptions about the inevitable impact of increases in poverty and social inequality (that "underpin" capitalism) in producing a popular backlash in favor of progressive alternatives. On the contrary, the process of political recomposition that took place after the crisis of 2001 provides some disturbing conclusions for progressive politics: the political reproduction and extension of clientelism and "old" politics achieved *through* political and economic crises. Not only have leftist parties or autonomous projects become unable to compete with the Peronist machine in winning the support of the poor, but the persistence of high levels of unemployment and poverty have tended to reproduce neoliberal Peronist "politics of poverty" as a form of domination.

Overall, the failure of social movements to really depart from clientelism and "old" politics may point to what Carrera (2006) argues: that the current fashionable ideological rejection of seizing state power, or seizing the power of the general political representatives of social capital, does not express the power of social movement to overthrow capitalism. On the contrary, it may express its *impotence* to do so.

Notes

1. Only in 2008, for the first time, did an independent, non-Peronist union (Central de Trabajadores Argentinos, CTA) achieved juridical recognition.

2. By the 1960s, as Peronism was proscribed from the political arena, there was a resurgence of communist and socialist ideals within the labor and student movements and an attempt at building a revolutionary, class-based trade union movement articulated in the Communist Party (PC, Leninist orientation), the Revolutionary Communist Party (PCR, Maoist), and plenty of small Trotskyist groups. Most of them turned into armed strategies—organic Trotskyists formed the ERP (Ejército Revolucionario del Pueblo), the first armed group formally recognized by the IV In-

ternational, and the so-called Juventud Comunista, and other Trostkyists formed the FAL (Fuerzas Armadas de Liberación). By the 1970s many of them switched to Montoneros, a group of young Peronists encouraged by Perón from his exile to work for his return—the fusion between leftist groups and leftist Peronists gave birth to FAR (Fuerzas Armadas Revolucionarias). Peronism also armed right-wing factions—including the infamous Triple A—encouraged by Perón to tame Montoneros and other leftist organizations once he was back in power in 1973.

3. The Central Bank was obliged to keep full banking of the monetary base at the adopted parity. This involved strict limits on the ability of the bank to act as a lender of last resort to the financial system. It also closed the access of the public sector to Central Bank financing of its public deficits.

4. This was particularly clear in two long road blockades that took place in June and November of 2000, concluding with the adjudication of 6,400 Planes Trabajar (unemployment subsidies of $150) and 2,000 more, 5,000 "bonus" plans, 2,500 *segunda oportunidad*, and almost 7,000 kilograms of food. The words of a prominent leader, Luis D'Elia, were illustrative of this:

> This road blockade was historical because it was made by all the organizations. Also it was a completely new experience: 5000 people blocked the road and in less than 24hs the government came, assumed compromises and conceded to all our demands; they wanted to finish everything very quickly. That was great because up until then there were only unorganized *estallidos* in Cutral-Co y Tartagal. The big difference now in La Matanza is that we have thousands organized. From the very beginning the road blockade was massively organized and saying: we want this, this and that. (quoted in Massetti, 2004: 26)

5. John Holloway is a critical Marxist whose work is closely related to the Mexican Zapatista Movement. His contention that revolution does not involve seizing the state apparatus but daily acts of abject refusal of capitalist society–antipower—has been the object of renewed debates between Marxist, anarchist, and anticapitalist movements.

6. Bourgeois democracy may be a "parody" when measured against radically anticapitalist conceptualizations of the term, but the way autonomists frame it underestimates the capacity of institutional democracy to recompose itself out of the crisis and to reestablish old forms of clientelism together with novel elements.

7. When the exchange rate was freed to float, the government decided to convert to pesos most of the domestic debts contracted in dollars at a one-to-one rate, thus neutralizing most of the effects of relative price changes on the debtors' balance sheets. In contrast, bank's deposits originally denominated in dollars were "pesificated" at 1.40 pesos per dollar.

8. The *piquetero* bargaining flourished under Duhalde's presidency. Indeed, the number of monthly protests peaked nationally in May 2002, when the state relief program went into effect. The various *piquetero* organizations came to control one hundred thousand places within the program. While the FTV/CCC from La Matanza secured 56 percent of these places (57,000), the rest were distributed among several organizations linked with leftist parties and only one autonomist organization, Coordinadora Aníbal Veron (*La Nación*, November 23, 2002). In explaining this distribution of program places, Edward Epstein argues, "the groups that have been able to

take advantage of the present situation are those that have been most politically adept at using the bargaining opportunity. . . . What particularly distinguishes one from the other relates to the degree of perceived flexibility employed by their leaders in their dealings with the national government" (2003: 27).

9. The formula of Kirchner's economy is quite simple: [(soybean + oil ground rent) x devaluation] + fall of wages (Sartelli, 2007). Given the internationally favorable scenario of the rise in commodity prices, Argentinean recovery came to be based on the exports of soybean (and oil soy) and oil, triggered mainly by the demand for primary goods by China (and other Asian Tigers). The government thus strongly committed itself to preserving of a competitive exchange rate for exports (\$1 U.S. = 3 pesos) by Central Bank intervention in the foreign exchange market. Higher exports had a positive effect for the domestic market, which explains the high rates of growth (8.8 percent in 2003, 9 percent in 2004, 9.2 percent in 2005, and 8.4 percent in 2006, according to INDEC), the fiscal surplus, and the increase in federal monetary reserves thanks to export taxes. What is key in this equation is that fiscal surplus allowed the state to subsidize prices of public utilities and massive state relief programs for the poor, giving Kirchner a remarkable space for building social and political consensus

10. Examples of these programs are the following: Plan Nacional de Seguridad Alimentaria: El Hambre Más Urgente (National Food Security Plan: The Most Urgent Hunger); Plan Familias para la Inclusión Social (Families for Social Inclusion Plan); Plan Nacional de Desarrollo Local y Economía Social Manos a la Obra! (National Plan for Local Development and Social Economy: Let's Work!). Credits and microcredits are also provided by Solidarity Funds for Development (Fondos Solidarios Para el Desarrollo) and Social Capital Funds (Fondos de Capital Social, FONCAP). Grants are offered by the Institutional Strengthening for Socio-Productive Development plan (Fortalecimiento Institutcional para el Desarrollo Productivo, FIDSP).

11. D'Elia, leader of the FTV and the most important agitator in the period 1999–2002, became an open supporter of Kirchner, and it's very common to see him standing next to Kirchner in big public demonstrations. Another clear case of co-optation comes from the leaders of Barrios de Pie, formerly hard-liners who now occupy high-level posts at the Ministry of Social Development. Many "K" *piqueteros* have been accused by Kirchner's opposition of helping the government buy votes in the 2005 electoral campaign by distributing domestic appliances and cash.

12. "It must be said, however, that the *piqueteros* organizations contributed to their own isolation and delegitimation—notably the Trotskyist groups, which . . . failed to recognize Peronism's adaptability. Their calls for continued popular agitation in the end underestimated the vast asymmetry of forces between movements and government, as well as the vulnerability of the sectors they sought to mobilize" (Svampa, 2008: 85).

References

Altamira, Jorge. 2002. *El Argentinazo: El Presente como Historia.* Buenos Aires: Rumbos.
Auyero, Javier. 2007. *Routine Politics and Violence in Argentina: The Grey Zone of State Power.* Cambridge: Cambridge University Press.

Bonnet, Alberto. 2004. "Diciembre en los Pasillos de la Academia: Luchas Sociales y Micropolíticas Posmodernas." *Cuadernos del Sur* 37:128–43.

———. 2006. "¡Que se vayan todos!: Discussing the Argentine Crisis and Insurrection." *Historical Materialism* 14 (1): 157–84.

Brusco, Valeria, Marcelo Nazareno, and Susan Stokes. 2004. "Vote Buying in Argentina." *Latin American Research Review* 39 (2): 66–88.

Calvo, Ernesto. 2003. "Una fuerte participación enterró el voto bronca." *Clarín*, April 28.

Carrera, Iñigo. 2006. "Argentina: The Reproduction of Capital Accumulation through Political Crisis." *Historical Materialism* 14 (1): 185–219.

Castorina, Emilia. 2007. "The Contradictions of 'Democratic' Neoliberalism in Argentina: A New Politics from 'Below'?" In *Global Flashpoints: Reactions to Imperialism and Neoliberalism*, ed. Leo Panitch and Colin Leys, 265–83. Socialist Register 2008. London: Merlin Press.

CELS. 2003. *Plan Jefes y Jefas: ¿Derecho social o beneficios sin derechos?* Buenos Aires: CELS.

Dinerstein, Ana. 2002. "The Battle of Buenos Aires: Crisis, Insurrection and the Reinvention of Politics in Argentina." *Historical Materialism* 10 (4): 5–38.

———. 2007. "The Politics of Unemployment: Employment Policy, the Unemployed Workers Organizations and the State in Argentina (1991–2005)." NGPA Research Paper Number 9.

Epstein, Edward. 2003. "The Piquetero Movement of Greater Buenos Aires: Working Class Protest during the Argentine Crisis." *Canadian Journal of Latin American and Caribbean Studies* 28 (55/56): 11–36.

Epstein, Edward, and David Pion-Berlin. 2006. "The Crisis of 2001 and Argentine Democracy." In *Broken Promises? The Argentine Crisis and Argentine Democracy*, ed. Edward Epstein and David Pion-Berlin, 3–28. Lanham, MD: Lexington Books.

Gramsci, Antonio. [1971] 2003. *Selections from the Prison Notebooks*. Ed. and trans. Q. Hoare and G. N. Smith. New York: International Publishers.

Gruner, Eduardo. 2002. "Interview with Eduardo Gruner." By María Moreno. *Journal of Latin American Cultural Studies* 11 (2): 157–62.

Holloway, John. 2002. "Argentina: Que se vayan todos." *Herramienta* 20 (July): 85–92.

Inter-American Development Bank. 1997. *Latin America after a Decade of Reforms: Economic and Social Progress*. Washington, DC: Inter-American Development Bank.

Klein, Naomi. 2003. "Out of the Ordinary." *Guardian*, November 25.

Levitsky, Steven. 2003. *Transforming Labor-Based Parties in Latin America: Argentine Peronism in Comparative Perspective*. Cambridge: Cambridge University Press.

Lozano, Claudio. 2005. "Los problemas de la distribución del ingreso y el crecimiento en la Argentina actual." CTA, Instituto de Estudios y Formación.

———. 2006. "Clandestinidad y precarización laboral en la Argentina de 2006." CTA, Instituto de Estudios y Formación.

Massetti, Astor. 2004. *Piqueteros, protesta social e identidad colectiva*. Buenos Aires: Editorial de las Ciencias.

McGuire, James W. 1997. *Peronism without Perón: Unions, Parties, and Democracy in Argentina*. Stanford, CA: Stanford University Press.

Negri, Antonio, et al. 2003. *Diálogo sobre la Globalización, la Multitud y la Experiencia Argentina*. Buenos Aires: Paidos.

Petras, James, and Henry Veltmeyer. 2004. "Argentina: entre la desintegración y la revolución." In *Las Privatizaciones y la Desnacionalización en América Latina*, ed. James Petras and Henry Veltmeyer, 5–54. Buenos Aires: Prometeo.

Roberts, Kenneth. 1996. "Neo-liberalism and the Transformation of Populism in Latin America: The Peruvian Case." *World Politics* 48 (January): 82–116.

Robinson, William. 2007. "Transforming Possibilities in Latin America" In *Global Flashpoints: Reactions to Imperialism and Neoliberalism*, ed. Leo Panitch and Colin Leys, 141–59. Socialist Register 2008. London: Merlin Press.

Sartelli, Eduardo. 2007. *La Plaza es Nuestra: El Argentinazo a la luz de la Lucha Obrera en la Argentina del siglo XX*. Buenos Aires: Ediciones Ryr.

Schuster, Federico, and Adrian Scribano. 2001. "Protesta social en la Argentina de 2001: entre la normalidad y la ruptura." *Observatorio Social de América Latina*, no. 5 (CLACSO): 17–22.

Sitrin, Marina. 2006. *Horizontalism: Voices of Popular Power in Argentina*. Oakland, CA: AK Press.

Svampa, Maristella. 2008. "The End of the K Era." *New Left Review* 53 (September–October): 79–98.

Svampa, Maristella, and Sebastian Pereyra. 2003. *Entre la Ruta y el Barrio: La Experiencia de las Organizaciones Piqueteras*. Buenos Aires: Biblos.

Virno, Paolo. 2002. "Entre la desobediencia y el éxodo." *Clarín*, February19.

Weitz-Shapiro, Rebecca. 2008. "Choosing Clientelism. Political Clientelism, Poverty and Social Welfare Policy in Argentina." PhD diss., Columbia University.

Weyland, Kurt. 1996. *Democracy without Equity: Failures of Reform in Brazil*. Pittsburgh: University of Pittsburgh Press.

Zibechi, Raúl. 2003. *Genealogía de la Revuelta: Argentina, Sociedad en Movimiento*. Buenos Aires: Letra Libre.

11

Trade Unions, Social Conflict, and the Political Left in Present-Day Brazil

Between Breach and Compromise

Ricardo Antunes
Translated by Laurence Hallewell

IN THE LONDON MEETING OF APRIL 2009, Brazil's President Luiz Inácio Lula da Silva was universally welcomed by everyone from Obama to Sarkozy, from the World Monetary Fund to the G20, as a statesman of globalization and conciliation. Lula has consolidated his membership of the emergent nations' block, the so-called BRIC (Brazil, Russia, India, and China), and has also strengthened his position as a third force in the struggle for the leadership of Latin America: the alternative to Chávez, Morales, and Correa on the left and to Uribe and Calderón on the right. His true position is nearer that of the moderates, Bachelet and Tabaré Vázquez.

Especially over these last twenty years, Brazil has changed into an important industrial power, with a broadly based domestic consumer market, and the target of enormous capital investment by foreigners and transnational corporations, in addition to possessing a huge geopolitical dimension—factors that give it an outstanding role among the so-called developing countries in today's capitalist world. Although Brazil began to take on this role during the eight years of Fernando Henrique Cardoso's presidency (1995–2003), it was really during Lula's two terms, which stretched from January 2003 to December 2009, that this change became firmly implanted.

What has it been about the course of modern Brazilian history that has led to each genuine achievement by the mass of the nation being transformed into successive victories of the dominant classes, whether through repression—as under the dictatorships of Getúlio Vargas (1937–1945) and the military regime (1964–1985), or through conciliation—as with Juscelino Kubitschek (1956–1961) or Lula's recent two presidencies?

At the summits of imperialist hegemony, especially in the United States and Europe, there has so often been the impression that Brazil has become a "modern" country following a "respectable" path of development, although recognized as having inherited an enormous "social inequality," with the largest disparities of wealth and income in the whole world. But its real history has been quite different when analyzed from the viewpoint of the social classes and of bourgeois domination in Brazil.

What indeed has happened to Brazil over these last decades? What are the principle structural transformations it has been undergoing? How have these changes been affecting its class structure, as much among the dominant classes as in the middling ranks? How has the new labor market been shaped? How have such changes been affecting the working class, its trade unions, and the political parties on the left? What is the outlook for the Left, economically, socially, and politically, after eight years of Lula's social-liberal government? Were there any real advances in the socialist struggle under Lula, or were we, on the contrary, taking one step forward and two back? Why has the ruling classes' domination managed to still block what had been real chances for social transformation?. How come the Brazilian Revolution always ends up being morbidly infected by compromise (Fernandes, 1975; Prado Júnior, 1966)?

Such are the central questions that our article makes no claim to resolve, but rather wishes just to contribute to with some outlines of an answer that is certainly more complicated and difficult.

The Historical Backdrop

Industrial capitalism in Brazil had its origin at practically the start of the twentieth century, when export agriculture based on coffee growing still dominated the economy. It was from the 1930s, during the first Vargas presidency, that industrialization really began to take off through a homegrown process of industrial accumulation with strong state support (Vianna, 1976). The next great leaps in the process of industrialization began in the mid-1950s, and especially in the wake of the army coup d'état of 1964, when the internationalization of the national economy made strong progress thanks to the entry into Brazil of various transnational groups and capital.

One side of the Brazilian economy was based on manufacturing consumer durables, such as automobiles, domestic electrical appliances, and other items, for a limited and selective internal market made up of the ruling class and a significant portion of the middle class, mainly its higher levels. The other side of the economy centered on production for export, not only of agricultural products but also of industrialized consumer products and durable goods. This two-fronted economy turned Brazilian capitalism into the eighth biggest economy in the capitalist world, despite always retaining its dependent structure and its subordination to imperialism.

The post-1964 military dictatorship introduced a policy of strong incentives to the globalization and privatization of the economy, directed toward capitalist expansion with some traces of monopolies and oligopolies, and even retaining some important sectors such as petroleum, telecommunications, and iron and steel under state control. Brazil still kept its character of a dependent economy, subordinate to the hegemonic central poles of capitalism: a sort of state monopoly capitalism that was both dependent and subordinate.

This path also led to profound consequences for the class structure in Brazil. The various sectors of the Brazilian bourgeoisie (industrial, financial, agricultural, and commercial) strengthened and deepened their connections with outside capital; the middle sectors turned increasingly toward salaried employment, suffering a process of proletarianization in some of its segments, such as bank clerks, elementary school teachers, and civil servants; while there was also a significant growth in the industrial working class, which at the end of the 1970s provided the social base of the new blue collar workers' movement, which revived in a particularly vigorous fashion. This then manifested itself in a thoroughly concentrated and united workers' movement, of which the metal workers of the ABC (Santo Andrés, São Bernardo do Campo, and São Caetano) manufacturing zone of the conurbation of Greater São Paulo was an example (Antunes, 1994, 1995).

Following some years of repression and containment under the military regime, a change began from 1978 in the effectiveness of the opposition, leading to a resurgence in powerful strikes that led to the birth, at the end of the 1970s, of a new trade union movement of workers, dubbed the *new unionism*, which was where the workers and their unions began to be led by Luiz Inácio Lula da Silva, the then president of the Metal Workers' Union of São Bernardo do Campo.

After a hiatus of many years, Brazil returned to a really strong fight by the working class, which in some sense signaled a breach with the dominant bourgeois establishment. The country went through a particularly strong outbreak of the class struggle with very many strikes, extensive in size and proportion, unleashed by a wide range of sectors, from factory workers (particularly those on automotive assembly lines), through farm employees (especially casually recruited cutters of sugar cane, the so-called *bóias frias*, or "cold lunch eaters"), and bank clerks, to construction workers.

This wave of strikes was characterized as being *greves gerais por categoria* (nationwide within each group of workers), such as the bank clerks' strikes of

1985 or "sit-in" strikes, such as the occupation of the General Motors plant in
São José dos Campos (also in 1985) or that of the Volta Redonda steelworks of
the Companhia Siderúrgica Nacional in 1989. There were also innumerable
strikes against individual firms, until in 1989 the country experienced a succession of general strikes, such as the one in March that year involving some
thirty-five million workers, the largest and best supported general strike in
the history of industrial relations in Brazil. Thus, while there had been 2,259
strikes in 1987 (for example), around 63.5 million working days had been lost
to strikes in 1988.

There had been at the same time, a huge growth in trade union membership among the middle level of salaried employees and of those in the service
sector, symptomatic of a marked proletarianization of employees such as
bank clerks, teachers, health workers, civil servants, and so on, with a significant growth of unionization among such workers and the formation during
this period of important unions.

By the end of the decade, Brazil had some 9,833 trade unions, a number
that by 1995 was to grow to 15,972, both urban and rural and including associations of both workers and bosses. Urban unions alone numbered 10,779, of
which 5,621 were of blue-collar workers in regular jobs. Besides such impressive numbers of unions of the industrial working class, we were also noticing
increased unionization of middle-income sectors. In 1996 there were 1,335
civil service unions, 461 unions concerned with the so-called liberal profes-
sions, and 571 of the self-employed (Antunes, 2001, 2005).

It was also possible to notice in the countryside a continual advance in
the unionization of rural workers, which had been going on since the 1970s,
leading to a restructuring of the labor organization of the agricultural sector.
There were in 1996 5,193 rural unions, 3,098 of which were of workers. This
development of rural unions owed a lot to the involvement of the progressive
wing of the Catholic Church, which would go on to have such an influence in
the birth of the MST (Movimento dos Trabalhadores Sem Terra, Movement
of Landless Workers).

In the cities, the unions began to associate in federations, such as the CUT
(Central Única dos Trabalhadores, Workers' Unitary Union), founded in
1983, whose creation was inspired by the old state-run united trade union
front, the so-called class-based, autonomous, and independent, but state-
sponsored, unionism.

Heir to the social and workers' struggles of the preceding decades, especially those of the 1970s, the CUT was the product of the coming together
of the new trade unionism, born in the bosom of the old official trade union
system, of which the São Bernardo Metal Workers' Union (Sindicato dos
Metalúrgicos de São Bernardo) was an example, and of the unofficial unions,

the *oposições sindicais*, such as the MOMSP (Movimento de Oposição Metalúrgica de São Paulo, Opposition Metalworkers' Movement of São Paulo) and the Campinas Metalworkers' Opposition, which operated outside the official structure and fought against its state-imposed rivals with their dependent, vertically integrated structure. This new unionism was also strongly supported, right from the start, by the new organizations of rural workers.

Even in this cycle of great advance of the workers' and unions' struggle in Brazil, there was parallel progress in organizing at the plant level, the traditional weakness of Brazilian trade unionism, through the setting up of worker-management committees in individual factories and of other forms of organization at the workplace, such as those at factories in São Paulo's ABC industrial belt, including at the Ford Motor Company, linked to the São Bernardo Metalworkers' Union (Sindicato dos Metalúrgicos de São Bernardo), and the autonomous commissions in Greater São Paulo, like that of workers at the Asama Indústrias Metalúrgicas sponsored by the just mentioned MOMSP (Nogueira, 1998).

At the same time, an important stage was passed in the official trade unions' fight for freedom and independence from the government, both in resisting payment of the *imposto syndical* (the Vargas-era levy on the unions) and in their dislike of top-down management by the corporativist state, the means whereby the state apparatus kept the unions controlled and repressed, especially those with any concern to represent the working class effectively. Although state control of official unions had already weakened, some forms of the old subordination were still being practiced, so that the achievements of the 1980s were still quite relevant.

We can therefore say that the heights attained by the class struggle in Brazil in the 1980s were among the most meaningful in the whole capitalist world. Throughout that decade, there was a framework clearly favorable to the new unionism in Brazil (as far as it was a social movement of the workers, with a strong class basis), which headed in a completely opposite direction from that of unions in other countries, undergoing what was a time of crisis in several advanced capitalist countries. If the dominant classes still talked of the 1980s in Brazil as their "lost decade," one might say that this never applied to the working class, which on the contrary saw significant advances in awareness and organization in just that period.

As Brazil passed from the 1980s into the 1990s, however, new economic, political, and ideological tendencies became evident and were responsible for Brazilian unions being plunged into an oppressive wave of a renewed class struggle caused by both the worldwide restructuring of capitalist production, which seriously impacted on Brazil during the 1990s, and the emergence of the neoliberal program that, following the 1989 election of Fernando Collor de Mello, led to the imposition of wide-ranging changes, during Collor's 1990–1992 presidency, along the lines set out by the Washington Consensus.

This process of restructuring capitalist production required Brazil to adopt a new position within the international division of labor, together with the country's reentry into global capitalist production at a time when finance capital was expanding, seriously affecting the big capitalist economies as much as their subordinates and dependents on the periphery. This was why Brazilian capitalism during the 1980s had begun to undergo the first changes imposed by restructuring production and, its corollary, the neoliberal program that was suddenly unleashed on the country.

Even though the model of capitalist accumulation remained unchanged in essentials, it was possible to notice some changes in organization and technology within the processes of finance, production, and services, at a speed that, although slower than that felt by the central economies, would still have irreversible impacts on the structure of production and of social class in Brazil. This was because, although Brazil had stayed relatively far from the central economies where capital production was experiencing an increasingly rapid restructuring and imposition of the neoliberal program, when these did finally reach Brazil in the in the 1990s, they were introduced in overwhelming force. We sketch the principal aspects of this below.

Brazil's Neoliberal Epoch

It was with the electoral victory of Fernando Collor de Mello in 1989 and the imposition of his neoliberal program, which his eventual successor, Fernando Henrique Cardoso (FHC),[1] would continue, that neoliberalism and the process of the restructuring of production in Brazil became overwhelmingly intensified.

Collor's presidency was cut short in 1992 thanks to the enormous amount of corruption that characterized his government. After less than two years, he was ousted by a vast social and political mass movement, a campaign launched by students but which gradually grew throughout 1992 until it was so strong and widespread that it led to Collor's successful impeachment. In the end this almost Bonapartist adventurer ended in being deposed by a plot orchestrated by the very bourgeois alliance that had created him in the first place to avoid a possible electoral victory for Lula in 1989.

All the same, his short period in power was notable, over and above its corruption, for initiating an antisocial policy of broad-based privatization, founded on neoliberal principles, which was taken up and continued three years later when FHC took on the presidency—although, in his case, not as an adventurer but as one endowed with a clear bourgeois rationalism. He gave Brazil eight more years of neoliberalism (although he himself preferred to label it "social liberalism.")

His administration witnessed an enormous change in Brazil's productive sector, but one also reduced by the privatization of state industry, with a direct impact on iron and steel output, telecommunications, electric power, and banking, among other sectors, upsetting the tripod that had upheld the Brazilian economy with its three sources of capital: national, foreign, and state. The policy of the FHC administration was in perfect synchrony with the Washington Consensus, increasing even more the nation's subordination to international financial interests, in a phase of greater globalization of capital, throwing into chaos the productive model that had endured since the time of Getúlio Vargas.

To have an idea of the implications of this restructuring of capitalist production and of the policy of privatization, we can say that, all through the 1990s, about 25 percent of the gross domestic product moved from the state sector to that of international capital, reshaping and globalizing capitalism in Brazil even further (Oliveira, 2003). Not only did this increase in the internationalizing of capital change the structure and shape of the working class, but it also led to a complete change in the makeup of some sections of the middle class. Almost the whole of that part of the establishment known as the "national upper bourgeoisie" was thoroughly incorporated into globalized capital and the foreign bourgeoisie. The powerful state-owned productive sector, which had played a decisive role in the capitalist industrialization of Brazil, was meanwhile absorbed by international capital through the privatization policy.

With such a thoroughgoing development, the combination of neoliberalism with the restructuring of capitalist production had very profound repercussions and consequences in Brazil for the whole of the working class, the trade unions, and the political Left.

In the world of work and in the productive universe, firms began downsizing, cutting the size of the workforce and increasing its overexploitation. Flexibility of employment, deregulation, and new forms of capital management were introduced on a very large scale, indicating that Brazilian Fordism, although still dominant, was now being mixed in with new methods of production, with flexible forms of accumulation and with elements of the Japanese model, the so-called Toyota approach (Antunes, 2006).

From the 1990s onward, this overexploitation of the workforce, along with certain more advanced models of production and technology, characterized the huge inflow of foreign capital into Brazilian industries. Such investment was (and is) indeed interested in combining the creation of a workforce able to operate microelectronic equipment with its remaining underpaid and subjected to ever greater exploitation, as flexibility of employment is imposed and security of tenure abolished, so combining technological advances with the overexploitation of the workforce, through the lengthening of the working day and a speeding up of the pace of the work, an approach that has always characterized Brazilian capitalism up to the present.

Changes in the productive process and in business structure, undertaken within an often regressive framework, have led to a process of the "deproletariatization" of large sections of the working class, depriving them of regular employment, increasing unemployment, and destroying any security of tenure. The automotive industry has been a very prominent example of this. While São Paulo's ABC factory belt, Brazil's most important manufacturing area and where the main car-making plants are all located, gave regular employment in 1980 to over two hundred thousand car workers, this had gone down by 2008 to under one hundred thousand. In Campinas, the other leading industrial area in São Paulo state, the number of car workers fell from about seventy thousand in 1989 to only around forty thousand in 2008. There was also, thanks to restructuring and technological innovations, a marked decline in the numbers regularly employed in fields such as banking. Whereas the banks had employed eight hundred thousand clerks and tellers in 1989, this had fallen to under half that number by 2008.

This productive restructuring of capital that affected almost every branch of manufacturing and the service industries also brought about important changes in the structure of employment in Brazil. If at the pinnacle of Brazilian manufacturing industry in the 1970s it employed around 20 percent of the entire national workforce, this proportion had fallen within twenty years to less that 13 percent. The economic changes of the 1990s, however, introduced new directions in job opportunities.

As the Brazilian economy was opened up more and more to global competition, it began for the first time since the 1930s to lose the number of its industrial jobs, both absolutely and relatively. Between 1980 and 2000, for example, a million and a half jobs disappeared in manufacturing (Pochmann, 2001).

Matching this decline in factory work, the service sectors increased their relative share of employment between 1980 and 2000 by an average of 50 percent, a large part of this being in the informal economy, which came to embrace large numbers of workers, especially in commerce, communications, and transport.

In 1999 Brazil ranked third in open unemployment worldwide, with 5.61 percent of all joblessness (with its economically active population accounting for 3.12 percent of the world total), a considerable worsening of its comparative situation since 1986 when it had been in thirteenth place, with 2.75 percent of the world's economically active population but only 1.68 percent of all the world's unemployed (Potchmann, 2001).

Increased flexibility of employment, deregulation, outsourcing, new ways of managing labor, and other changes became more and more widespread, showing that, if on the one hand we felt the fall in the size of a workforce that had been stable over successive generations and had characterized the earlier stage of the Brazilian manufacturing industry, we were also seeing the growth of the new proletariat of the service sector that had come out of the enormous increase in privatization of this sector, and of the more general process of erosion of long-term employment nationally.

At the zenith of the "financialization" of money capital, of technological-scientific progress, of a world where time and space were convulsed, Brazil was experiencing a labor change that altered the morphology of labor, with an enormous growth in the informal economy, job insecurity, and unemployment, all structural changes. And this complex and contradictory movement did not happen in Brazil without leading to profound changes in the class struggle.

Transformations in the Class Struggle

This new reality weakened the bellicosity of unions, forcing them onto the defensive. They faced on the one side the rise of a neoliberal unionism, a manifestation of the new right accompaniment of the global wave of conservatism, with the new union confederation, the Força Sindical, created in 1991, as the best example. And on the opposite side, the CUT lost flexibility during the 1990s as it fell under the thrall of its majority, the so-called Expression of Unionism (Articulação Sindical), which moved it closer and closer to the European Social Democratic model of trade unionism. And it is this contractual unionism that, although it presented itself as a possible alternative means of fighting neoliberalism, drew steadily closer to the neoliberal agenda. The CUT, the branch of trade unionism in Brazil that had not begun within social democracy, slowly turned itself, bit by bit, into a late copy of it. This "new unionism" then began to collapse, growing old prematurely. The policy of "agreements," "financial subsidies," and "partnerships" with foreign, especially European, social democratic unions, applied intensely for over a decade, reached its limit in a framework of profound changes, strongly contaminating Brazil's class-based unionism, which, deprived of a class-based policy and ideology, gradually moved toward social democracy, in (it must be remembered) a context of the neoliberalizing of social democratic unionism itself. And this process ended up changing the CUT, which had begun with a proposed independence and with a clear class consciousness, into a confederation ever more bureaucratized, institutionalized, and converted to bargaining.

But if traditional trade unionism had come to a dead end, something quite new burst upon the scene to give a new face to the social struggle in Brazil. It was here that social conflicts in the countryside emerged as the most important social and political movement fighting neoliberalism in Brazil. The Homeless Workers' Movement (Movimento dos Trabalhadores Sem-Teto, MST) recreated and reenergized the fight of workers in the countryside, making itself the center of the political fight, throughout the 1990s in particular. The MST has indeed become the chief catalyst and driver of social struggle in recent times (Petras, 1997).

Its chief importance came from the fact that the MST had had, from its creation, the organizing at ground level of all workers in the countryside. In its confrontations, it did not give priority to institutional or parliamentary action (which it regarded as a side issue and not as its center of attack) but drew its strength and vitality from the social fight at its base. And although it had begun as a movement of peasants [The Landless Rural Workers' Movement (Movimento dos Trabalhadores Rurais Sem Terra, also MST).—Trans.], it had increasingly granted membership to workers driven out of their urban employment and back into the countryside, through the "modernizing of production" in manufacturing, creating a rich synthesis that combined and expressed experiences and forms of solidarity deriving from the world of work in both town and country.

The MST's political and ideological basis comes from its origin as the fusion of two important vectors: the experience of the Roman Catholic Left, linked to Liberation Theology and the Church's Base Communities, and the militancy formed ideologically within ideas and praxis taken from Marxism, associating two of the most important directions of the social struggle in Brazil: the Catholic Left and the Marxist Left. Since then the MST has been developing an important program to educate its members, from youngsters upward, politically and ideologically, which permits it to exist and act in constant opposition to the values and ideas of the dominant bourgeoisie.

Besides all this, the MST has a nationwide structure that gives it dynamism, vitality, and punch, and in this way, it lets the working men and women of the countryside glimpse a daily life that has a direction, in so far as the movement gives them the chance of fighting for something real and tangible, namely, for the takeover of a piece of land through organizing collective resistance, taking direct action: squatting on land and occupying farms, fighting the use of toxic agricultural chemicals, facing up on a daily basis to the power of agribusiness and private land ownership. MST is also fighting for a change in

Brazil's economic policies and is confronting the production of genetically modified crops.

With the strength given it by its social roots, MST has become the most important political movement in the whole country, able to help in the organization of other grassroots movements, such as the *sem-teto* (the homeless) and the unemployed, besides playing an important role in the social struggles in Hispanic America and elsewhere in the world, both through the Via Campesina (the international peasants' movement) and by participating in the World Social Forum and the fight against globalization.

The MST pursued its sweeping efforts to organize squatting on agricultural land under both the Fernando Henrique Cardoso and Lula administrations. While the former's response was to criminalize it, the latter was so beholden to the Workers' Party (Partido dos Trabalhadores, PT) and on support by parties of the right and center that its response to the MST hardly differed in practice from that of its predecessor, particularly as regards preserving the traditional system of large-scale landownership and in its virtual obsession to incentivize agribusiness to develop production of ethanol. Lula's rural policy amounted to driving Brazilian agriculture back to colonial conditions, creating a vast desert of cane fields, with casual day laborers, the so-called *bóias frias*, engaged to cut over ten metric tons of sugar cane during each daily recruitment, and often very much more than this, according to the region where the cane was being cultivated.

In this way what might have been the start of the death knell of neoliberalism in Brazil turned into its exact opposite. Indeed, Lula became the new paladin of social liberalism in Latin America, which is what we shall be discussing in this next section.

Lula and Social Liberalism

In 1989, when Lula made his first run for president, Brazil was experiencing a cycle of fierce struggles by workers, unions, and parties, exemplified by the birth of the PT in 1980, the CUT in 1983, and the MST in 1984, plus a nationwide wave of strikes. But as we have already seen, when Lula was eventually successful in 2002, the picture was quite different, with the PT itself having undergone a marked process of institutionalization and a moderating of its aims (Antunes, 2004).

This was the situation when, with the support (total or qualified) of the chief currents of the Left in Brazil, Lula won the presidential elections, after a period of great social, political, and economic retrogression caused by the implantation of neoliberalism by the Collor and FHC governments. Moreover, his win happened in a national and international context very different from that of the 1980s, when Brazil had been experiencing a significant wave of social struggles.

There were now two contradictory processes going on. This victory of the Left in Brazil was achieved precisely when it was at its weakest, lacking any strong backing by, or anchorage in, the central poles that had originally nourished it (the industrial working class, the lower ranks of white-collar workers, and the agricultural labor force), and at a time when what Gramsci calls *transformism* had changed the PT into what Marx dubbed a "Party of Order." When Lula won, the situation had changed completely from the 1980s. The Workers' Party, the PT, had lost what had been its really strong point at the time of its creation: its real links to what ordinary people had been fighting for. The creative power of the social struggles of the 1980s had been wholly lost. This meant that the 2002 election was a political victory achieved too late. The PT was no longer the same, nor was Lula, nor was Brazil. The country had been forsaken, and the PT had lost its backbone. And Lula had changed into one more instrument of traditional Brazilian-style compromise. One of the most outstanding leaders that the working class in Brazil had ever had had gone from the era of the new trade unionism to becoming a new tool of the ruling classes.

How may we explain this transformism? Why, instead of marking the start of a break with neoliberalism, did the Lula administration, having the PT as its principal political support, follow the easy path of continuity in relation to the previous government, especially in regard to its political policy of encouraging large-scale capital in both finance and production?

The explanations are, certainly, complex, but they can be found, to a great degree, to have been part of the general conditions of the 1990s, where we could witness very broadly based movements, clearly implying a long-drawn-out counterrevolution in Brazil. The main features of this counterrevolution were the following:

1. The enormous spread of neoliberalism throughout all Latin America except Cuba.
2. The collapse of the so-called real socialism and the mistaken acceptance of the thesis that proclaimed the victory of capitalism.
3. The conversion of a substantial part of the Left to social democracy, leading to the high tide of the "social-liberal agenda," the euphemism used to "hide" its real neoliberal nature.

The PT, a party created amid the social, trade union, and left-wing struggles of the late 1970s and which had flourished through repudiating "real socialism" as much as it disdained social democracy, has been swinging since

1990 between resisting neoliberal demolition and accepting the policy of half measures and the imposition of order. At the very time it was struggling against the standard solutions and pragmatism of the neoliberals, it was becoming increasingly subject to the exigencies of the electoral calendar, acting more and more like a traditional political party seeking office through the established path of elections.

Starting from a resistance to capitalist order (stripped, nevertheless, from its earliest days, of political and ideological solidarity, since the upper echelons of the PT openly repudiated both Marxism and any revolutionary program), a party that had been born within the class struggle steadily changed into one that was increasingly a prisoner of the electoral calendar, of "broad" coalitions, to the point where it became a traditional political party. Lula's electoral defeats in 1994 and 1998 increased his belief in transforming the party, as the reasons diagnosed as causing these defeats led to a supposed need to "broaden" the party's electoral appeal to encompass the whole of Brazilian society.

A policy was gradually introduced of forming broader and broader alliances with various sectors of the center and even of the Right, justified by Lula (when not actually imposed by him on the party) as the necessary condition for him to agree to run for a fourth time. And his decisions in support of this new policy found more and more support from the dominant sectors of the party, which tended increasingly to base its support for Lula on what was called "Linkage."[2] Contrary to many of the values that marked its beginnings, the Workers' Party then implanted a policy that definitively consolidated the new phase of full subjection to institutionality. An example is clear enough when, at the end of the FHC presidency in 2002, there was an agreement about "intentions" with the IMF, this international financial agency that follows directions given by Washington, insisting that those running for president should proclaim their agreement with the terms and conditions of the agreement.

This was when Lula's Workers' Party published the "Letter to the Bankers" ("Carta aos Brasileiros"), which made clear its acceptance of the document, witness to his policy of submitting to the IMF and to international finance. To help him win the elections, the Workers' Party had to become a fixed part of the so-called phase of globalization and financialization of wealth, adapting to the globalized world and its overriding imperatives.

As was to be expected, this met with the strong opposition of the grassroots of the PT and its active membership, as well as from social movements, from class-based unionism, and from the Movement of Landless Workers. But the new policy was in the end imposed by the party's leadership and its majority sectors as soon as it was considered to be an inescapable condition for achieving the electoral victory of 2002.

It is worth remembering that Brazil is a country bearing an enormous weight of conservatism, which has always sought to stop the working class from becoming a real alternative political force. At every chance of a breakthrough, the classes in power have responded either with repression or with conciliation. If in 1989 every step was taken to thwart an electoral victory by Lula and the parties of the Left, in 2002 the ruling classes managed to get the major force on the left (the PT) and most of its leadership to accept the demands of capital. This was precisely how the PT metamorphosed into a Party of Order, allowing Lula to enjoy the confidence of the bulk of the ruling classes, including the worlds of finance, industry, and even agribusiness.

We have also to admit that the electoral victory of Lula (and his party) in the elections of 2002 had an enormous significance, both actual and symbolic, since a working-class candidate had, for the first time in Brazilian history, won the presidency, after three earlier failed attempts. But, as we have seen, neither he nor the party were anything like what they had been. What was clear, and confirmed by the first actions of their government, was their intension to go ahead with an open continuance of neoliberalism, albeit under the new name of *social liberalism*. The new government's economic policy, for instance, was (and still is) of clear benefit to financial capital, reiterating Brazil's subservience to the dictates of the IMF.

Lula's administration, during both his presidencies, allowed large-scale rural landholding to continue, and its policies were marked by the total absence of land reform and by the huge incentives conceded to agribusiness. It supported private pension schemes, helping to dismantle social security. It obliged retired workers to pay income tax on their state pensions (a requirement imposed by the IMF and which led to a break with large sections of the trade union movement, those representing civil servants, who began strongly to oppose his government).

His policy of allowing genetically modified crops to be grown in Brazil was a surrender to pressure from multinational corporations such as Monsanto. His monetarist policy of primary surplus was aimed at always being able to reward financial capital. And last but not least, his government was responsible for creating a political structure of corruption that inherited and adopted the situation bequeathed by its predecessors, ensuring an unholy alliance between the administration and its political fabric of support in Congress, using public resources as much as private ones. All this witnessed to Lula's first administration (2002–2006) being much more one of continuing neoliberal policies than of breaking away from them. This tendency was basically maintained in his second administration (2008–2010), albeit with some minor changes. This second mandate was sustained by a range of political forces that widened even more his base of support among those sections of Brazil's traditional right-wing that were directly included in his new administration.

The only meaningful change between the first and second presidencies lay in his reaction to a grave political crisis with the *mensalão* (a monthly bribe paid to congressional deputies from other parties to ensure their voting support), a practice that almost led to Lula's impeachment during his first term. But here it is important to emphasize that, despite the clear political opposition of the center parties, such as the Party of Brazilian Social Democracy (Partido da Social Democracia Brasileira, PSDB), and some on the right, such as the Liberal Front Party (Partido da Frente Liberal, PFL)—which later restyled itself the Democrats (Democratas, DEM)—to the Lula government during the *mensalão* crisis, there was clear agreement among the principal sectors of the ruling bourgeois classes against any impeachment, because his government's economic policy was one of thoroughgoing support of the interests of capital, their guarantee and assurance they would retain their position. Hence he has continued the high levels of profits enjoyed by finance capital, by investment in large-scale production, and by the agricultural export sector.

When he realized that his government had only survived the crisis because of this support from sectors of the ruling class, he concluded that it would be essential during his second term for him to widen his support base, now that he could no longer depend on wide sections of the organized working class, which had been disillusioned by his actions.

Thus it was that his second term began with an important political change. After the total failure of his Zero Hunger program, he broadened the Family Allowance (Programa Bolsa Familia, PBF). This was a grant conditioned on school attendance by children of school age, but it was very extensive, nonetheless, reaching in 2009 some fifteen million poor families (amounting to about sixty million people with low incomes), who received an average monthly allowance worth about $30 U.S. Such a "social policy" of what was really outdoor poor relief was favorably cited by the World Bank and appreciably widened the social basis of Lula's support during his second term, as it was, quantitatively speaking, far more extensive than the similar programs of earlier Brazilian governments, such as that of Fernando Henrique Cardoso, whose analogous schoolchild's allowance (*bolsa-escola*) reached no more than two million families. And it is this appeal to the most impoverished social strata that made up for the support Lula and the party had lost among many sectors of the organized working class.

This is how the Lula administration plied the two prongs of Brazil's traditional savagery. It rewarded, like no other, the various sectors of the ruling classes, and at the opposite end of the social pyramid, where we find the most unorganized and impoverished parts of the population, dependent on state handouts just to survive, it proffered an outdoor relief system, without really impacting in the slightest degree either of the two pillars holding up the Brazilian tragedy.

The great popularity that had accrued to the Lula government by 2008 was due then to the fact that its social program had an inclusiveness never before attained by its conservative predecessors from the ruling classes. And, paralleling this broadening of its focused program of social assistance, it was guaranteeing the highest profits in Brazil's recent history to large-scale financial capital (banks and pension funds) and to large-scale industrial capital (iron and steel, heavy metals, agribusiness, etc.).

And as if this were not enough, his government still had the support of a large section of trade union bureaucracy, still dependent for its income on the public treasury and so tied to the government. The former rivals CUT and the Força Sindical now live side by side in the same ministries of the Lula government. As regards Lula's leadership, it has to be said that he exercises it rather as if he were a reincarnation of Getúlio Vargas, the demagogic dictator of the mid-twentieth century. He keeps up his "direct" empathy with the masses, as their charismatic, almost messianic, referee. At two historic moments, in 2002 and 2006, when none of the rival parties of the ruling class could be sure of winning the presidency, he became the spokesman of a government that could talk to the poor, enjoy the benefits of power, and even ensure the welfare of big capital. A sort of half-Bonaparte (to echo the jibe of Engels and Trotsky), politely effacing before the power of high finance while craftily managing his popular support, who has been easing away from dependence on organized labor toward dependence on the more downtrodden and impoverished levels of those who receive the Family Allowance.

Distancing himself from his working-class beginnings, immersed in the new myth of the "middle class," climbing ever higher steps on the social scale, all this has been changing Lula into a variety of José Samargo's "Double" who has come more and more to admire the examples of those who come from "the lower orders" while achieving success within society. His new existence has created an inverted understanding of his past and a present that dazzles him.

The consequence of this metamorphosis and this "transformism" is that his government, without facing up to any structural element that accounts for the misery in this country and ensures its continuance, has, on the other hand, demonstrated a wondrous ability to divide workers in private employment from those working for the state. Were it only not so tragic, one could joke that the party and its leader, born out of the class struggle, have transformed themselves into stirrers up of a struggle within the working class.

The most important party on the left in the last quarter century, and which raised so many hopes in Brazil and in so many other parts of the world, has grown into, as far as its leadership is concerned, a copy of Old England's New Labour. It has exhausted its chances of transforming the established social order, in order to become an agent of the great vested interests that rule this country. It has turned itself into a party dreaming of capitalism with a human face, putting together a policy of privatizing public wealth that serves both the interests of business associations (greedy for control of pension funds) and those of the financial system that effectively controls his government's economic policy.

For at least six years Lula was able to govern during the most favorable of international economic circumstances. At the start of his second term, he was able to stimulate a return to economic growth that reached around 5 percent in 2008, with a consequent fall in the previously high rates of unemployment. But with the deepening of the capitalist system's structural crisis, which began in the United States in 2007 and then spread to Europe and Asia, its effects began seriously to impact employment and growth levels in Brazil at the end of 2008. This started to show the weakness of economic growth in Brazil and its dependence on external factors. It has been the result, on the one hand, of investments by finance capital that enjoy the world's highest interest rates and, on the other, of the increase in commodity prices, driven by China's enormous growth. But this scenario, it seems, began to change in the second half of 2008.

The Lula administration, which might have at least begun the first challenge to neoliberalism in Brazil (expecting anything else would have been exaggerated if not unfounded), allowed itself to be taken prisoner, adopting a sort of social liberalism that strengthened the pillars of bourgeois domination in Brazil, rather than pulling them down. He who in the mid-1970s presented himself as the symbolic expression of the possibilities of such a break was, just three decades later, becoming the chief instrument of the reconciliation of the classes in Brazil. Once more, he was marching in reverse, taking two steps back for every one he took forward.

Lula and the Class Reconciliation

Although Lula recovered support from several different levels of society during the early years of his second term, reaching new heights of popularity, there was also becoming visible the broadening of social and political discontent among a variety of movements that refused to be co-opted by the policy of government handouts. The Movement or Landless Workers, although it has made no frontal attack on the Lula government but has often given him qualified support, has not desisted from its policies of squatting on landholdings and challenging agribusiness and genetically modified crops. The growth in discontent among its grassroots shows a change in its relations with the Lula administration.

The overall picture has also quite changed in the field of trade unionism. Those who wanted to fight openly for their demands but were defeated by the Lula government's fierce drive to coopt them have since been trying, through their left wing, to create new poles of organization, resisting and confronting the government, gathering together the more definitely socialist and anticapitalist wings of unionism into the National Coordination of Struggles (Coordenação Nacional de Lutas, CONLUTAS) and the INTERSINDICAL.

CONLUTAS was created quite recently as the embryo of a new federation of unions, breaking with the CUT and having as its main political force the United Socialist Workers' Party (Partido Socialista dos Trabalhadores Unidos, PSTU), plus including parts of the Socialism and Freedom Party (Partido Socialismo e Liberdade, PSOL) and other sectors of the independent Left. CONLUTAS proposes to organize not only the unions but also the social movements outside the unions and has been growing in importance in recent times, increasing its opposition to the Lula administration, struggling to regain the workers' lost rights and to organize a wide range of social forces that are currently outside existing organizations.

INTERSINDICAL derives likewise from disillusioned sectors that have broken away from the CUT and can count on the support of militant unionists from the PSOL, former militants of the PT, and other sectors of the independent Left. INTERSINDICAL comes somewhat closer to being an orthodox trade union, aimed at reorganizing working-class unionism. Both organizations, CONLUTAS and INTERSINDICAL, sought to react against the conversion of CUT into a top-down organization dependent on the state.

In the field of left-wing unionism, despite its support of the Lula government, we have the recently formed Trade Union Federation of Working Men and Women of Brazil (Central dos Trabalhadores e Trabalhadoras deo Brasil, CTB), which grew out of the Working Class Union Current (Corrent Sindical Classista), linked with the Communist Party of Brazil (Partido Comunista Do Brasil, PCdoB), which left the CUT in 2007 to create its own federation of unions.

In the field of center-right unions, we have the already-mentioned Força Sindical, which combines elements of neoliberalism with the old trade unionism that "modernized" itself, plus various smaller federations such as the General Union of the Workers of Brazil (Central Geral dos Trabalhadores do Brasil, CGTB), the General Union of the Workers (União Geral dos Trabalhadores, UGT), and Nova Central, all with a low number of member unions to represent, and all in some way or another heirs, more or less, of the old state-dependent unionism.

As may be inferred, there are, since the defeat by the CUT of was then called the new unionism, very many challenges that have to be faced before a new reorganization can be brought about of grassroots class unions in Brazil.

The growing individualization of labor relations and the tendency of corporations to try to break down the spirit of solidarity and class consciousness and disorganize workers within the workplace even more are decisive challenges. Fighting the mistaken idea that workers have ceased to be employees and are now "associates," something that firms fall back on more and more to hide the fundamental divergence of interests between the workers as a whole, on the one side, and of capital as a whole on the other, is another fundamental step in this process of reorganizing left-wing unionism. The struggle against the elimination of rights and the end of job security also remains a central day-to-day concern. It suffices to say that, in producing sugar cane for ethanol, the life expectancy among workers in some regions of northern Brazil is less than it was in the nineteenth century under slavery, forcing unions of rural workers to fight against the degradation of the slavelike conditions of labor in the countryside.

Beyond this, there lies the very much here-and-now fight for self-government, freedom, and independence of the unions vis-à-vis the state. Quite recently, in 2008, the Lula administration took a decision that even increased state control over the unions, decreeing that trade union federations would start receiving the Trade Union Tax, created under Vargas's semifascist Estado Novo at the end of the 1930s. In a recent government-approved measure that took the positive step of legalizing the union federations, it also gave them the right to levy the Trade Union Tax.[3] This means that they can if need be exist on their income from this government-levied tax without having to have their members agree to pay dues. It is worth recalling that when the CUT was started it was definitely opposed to the Trade Union Tax. The Força Sindical, on the other hand, has always been in favor of the tax, seeing that it was created by a mixture of a revived *peleguismo* (the control of unions by government stooges) and the spreading influence of neoliberalism among some union leaders. Nowadays, however, the CUT and the Força Sindical pursue similar policies and act in very similar ways.

Besides all this is the fact that there were during Lula's two terms hundreds of former trade union officials receiving big salaries and commission payments to sit on the boards of state-owned industries (and some newly privatized ones), plus countless jobs in ministries and commissions set up by the government, co-opting former union leaders, who found themselves part of the state apparatus, compromising their independence and hitching them up ever closer to those in power.

Brazil's political parties on the left stretch across a broad spectrum. Many are pursuing policies and making alliances in open opposition to Lula's government. Such are the United Socialist Workers (Partido Socialista dos Trabalhadores Unificado, PSTU), the [Formerly Stalinist.—Ed.] Brazilian Communist Party (Partido Comunista Brasileiro, PCB), which is undergoing reorganization, and the recently created Socialism and Freedom Party (Partido Socialismo e Liberdade, PSOL), an attempt to reply to the PT's conversion into a "party of order"—that is, one supporting the status quo. At the other end we have the [Historically Maoist.—Ed.] Communist Party of Brazil (Partido Socialista do Brasil, PCdoB), which has been participating directly in the Lula government and giving it its full support.

All the same, in the contemporary mosaic that characterizes the Left in Brazilian society, its unions, and its politics, and particularly those sectors with a clearly socialist inspiration, there is a long road to be run, if not indeed a need to start all over again. The major challenge is to try and create a basic social and political pole that will seek to offer the country a program of anticapitalist changes, fighting the real historical causes that maintain the social and political structure of the ruling class in Brazil. And, in this way, it can join in the social and political struggles of all Latin America, facing and helping solve the great dilemma of the twenty-first century, which forces us, yet again, to reopen the question of socialism.

Notes

1. Vice President Itamar Franco acted as president from the impeachment of Collor until the accession of Cardoso, October 2, 1992, through December 31, 1998.—Trans.

2. In its 2002 electoral campaign, the PT made some alliances on the left, including the [originally Maoist] Communist Party of Brazil (Partido Comunista do Brasil, PCdoB) and some smaller groups, but its alliances stretched much further toward the center and right, including the Liberal Party (Partido Liberal, PL) a small political grouping on the center-right that chose as Lula's running mate for the vice presidency an important businessman from Minas Gerais, strengthening the moderate, multiclass tendency that dominated the summit of the PT.

3. Every employee of a private firm has a day's wages compulsorily deducted each year by the state, which retains a fraction of it but passes the rest on to the individual unions and groups of unions, and now also to the union confederations (*centrais*).

References

Antunes, Ricardo. 1994. "Recent Strikes in Brazil: The Main Tendencies of the Strike Movement of the 1980's." *Latin American Perspectives* 21 (1): 24–37.

——. 1995. *O novo sindicalismo no Brasil.* Campinas: Pontes.

——. 2001. "Global Economic Restructuring and the World of Labor in Brasil: The Challenges to Trade Unions and Social Movements." In "Urban Brazil," special issue, *Geoforum* 32 (4): 449–58.

——. 2004. *A desertificação neoliberal no Brasil: Collor, FHC e Lula.* Campinas: Editora Autores Associados.

——. 2005. "Una radiografia dele lotte sindacali e socieli nel Brasile contemporâneo e le principale sfife da afrontare." In *Lotte e regimi in América Latina,* ed. M. E. Casadio and L. Vasapollo. Milan: Jaca Book.

——, ed. 2006. *Riqueza e miséria do trabalho no Brasil.* São Paulo: Boitempo.

Fernandes, Florestan. 1975. *A revolução burguesa no Brasil.* São Paulo:.Zahar.

Nogueira, Arnaldo. 1998. *A modernização conservadora do sindicalismo brasileiro.* São Paulo: Fundação de Amparo à Pesquisa do Estado de São Paulo.

Oliveira, Francisco. 2003. *Crítica à razão dualista / O ornitorrinco.* São Paulo: Boitempo.

Petras, James. 1997. "Latin American: The Resurgence of the Left." *New Left Review,* no. 223 (May–June): 17–7.

Pochmann, Marcio. 2001. *O emprego na globalização.* São Paulo: Boitempo.

Prado Júnior, Caio. 1966. *A revolução brasileira.* São Paulo: Brasiliense.

Vianna, Luiz W. 1976. *Liberalismo e Sindicato no Brasil.* São Paulo: Paz e Terra.

12

Neoliberal Authoritarianism, the "Democratic Transition," and the Mexican Left

Richard Roman and Edur Velasco Arregui

Mexican Exceptionalism?

THE GROWTH OF INEQUALITY, poverty, and economically compelled emigration has been a widespread phenomenon throughout Latin America in the age of neoliberalism. As well, many Latin American countries, including Mexico, have been experiencing organic crises. While the Left in much of South America has been able to form national popular blocs, so dense that they have been able to absorb a good part of the energy of the social movements that preceded them, the Mexican Left has been frustrated in finding a national reformist solution to the crisis of neoliberalism in the first decade of the twenty-first century. Mexico, so close and so far from the rest of Latin America, finds itself trapped in its singular labyrinth.

The last four presidential elections in Mexico have seen the triumph of the new conservative-neoliberal power bloc. They have been able to "win" in spite of the devastation wrought by neoliberalism, devastation comparable to that experienced by the rest of Latin America before the rise of center-left governments in several Latin American countries. The Mexico case would seem to be a counterexample to the experience of most of Latin America, where neoliberal devastation has led to a variety of major left and left-nationalist electoral victories in opposition to the human costs of neoliberalism. The contrast becomes even stronger when we see that in the first decade of the twenty-first century these countries with center-left governments, such as Argentina and Brazil, have experienced notable economic dynamism in comparison to the stagnation of gross domestic product (GDP) per capita in

Mexico, albeit within the limits of nationalist capitalism (CEPAL, 2010: table 2.1.1.2) How can we explain the mystery of Mexico's divergence from the Latin American pattern?

Mexico's divergence from the general leftward trend in Latin America is related both to characteristics of the regime and its contradictory processes of change as well as to characteristics of the Left. Mexico has been undergoing a threefold process of transformation: (1) the constrained growth of electoral competition and the development of a multiparty Congress; (2) the neoliberal transformation of the economy and society, which involves the destruction of many of the social rights of citizenship; (3) the transformation of the regime into an even more repressive, militarized, and exclusionary one. The context for the democratic left forces is not that of a democratic state but rather the development of an increasingly repressive state with constrained electoral processes. The new regime, given the balance of forces and the efforts at legitimation, has had to allow some space, within significant constraints, for the growth and participation of middle-class civil society but little and diminishing space for popular forces of protest.

While neoliberal policies and continental integration have destroyed millions of Mexican jobs and sources of rural livelihood, emigration to the United States has provided alternative sources of employment, albeit poorly paid and often with unsafe working conditions. This precarious emigration to the United States has also provided important sources of income to families and communities that have allowed them to survive. This safety valve for potential urban and rural discontent is threatened by the U.S. economic crisis.

Mexico's stalemate is even more surprising given both the vibrancy of revolutionary rhetoric and traditions in Mexican popular culture and the hopes raised by the "democratic transition." Mexico's recent popular insurgencies—the Zapatistas, the Oaxaca Commune, and the mass antifraud movement of 2006—have echoed Mexico's long history of insurgency (1810, 1861, 1910). But the extra-electoral movements have not been able to translate their struggles into significant victories or the building of durable national organizations. The electoral Left, in a complex way to be discussed below, has made inroads electorally, but nevertheless, the Far Right has "won" the last two presidential elections (2000 and 2006). But these struggles—both electoral and extra-electoral—and the regime's fear that the seething popular discontent may yet explode nationally have so far helped block the fulfillment of the whole neoliberal agenda.

Mexican exceptionalism, however, is not exclusively rooted in the constrained, repressive, and frequently fraudulent character of the electoral liberalization. It is also rooted in characteristics and limitations of the Mexican Left. The more than seventy years of PRI domination has left deep legacies of *caudillismo*, clientelism, co-optation, and corruption that has affected and corroded almost all political parties and social movements. While this political culture is not unique to Mexico, it is deeply rooted there. This political culture involves the patrimonial administration of government subsidies, lack of rank-and-file control over formally democratic institutions, and clientelism. In respect to the electoral Left, these characteristics are deepened by the massive state subsidies to officially registered parties and the consequent pressure to play by the rules of the constrained parliamentary game. In respect to the extra-parliamentary Left, it has contributed to the co-optation of many initially solidly based popular movements seeking to make or maintain gains for their members, gains that generally require state action or acquiescence to be consolidated. This inherent dilemma of *all* revolutionary movements in non-revolutionary moments has combined in the case of Mexico with the legacies of PRI culture to undermine popular movements, attenuating their cohesion and the links of the base to the leaders. Alongside and intermixed with Mexico's long revolutionary traditions, then, are powerful traditions that undermine the democratic and participatory character of popular movements.

Both the electoral Left and the extra-electoral Left are politically and regionally fragmented. The parliamentary Left is, in fact, a complex coalition of regional forces; none of the left parties is a national party or movement with a shared program and significant degree of cohesion. And the two most important extra-parliamentary movements—the Zapatistas and the Oaxaca Commune—are also basically regional movements. And while they have had a diffuse ideological influence nationally and, in the case of the Zapatistas, internationally, they have not been able to build either a national or an international movement, except in a very thin and scattered manner. The Left is extremely divided and has very limited capacity to mount an offensive against the regime.

Left Electoralism, Neoliberal Authoritarianism, and the "Democratic Transition"

The fluid and intersecting paths of electoral and extra-electoral, institutional and extra-institutional, gradualist and revolutionary strategies of change have been a perennial source of tension for the Mexican Left. The student protests of 1968 stimulated one of the most powerful movements of democratic insurgency in twentieth-century Mexican history. The brutal government repression—the massacre of hundreds and the jailing of thousands on October 2—gave a dramatic impetus to student activism and also led to the development of a number of guerrilla movements among those who lost hope in nonviolent gradual change, movements also inspired by the examples of Cuba and Vietnam. The loss of legitimacy and the growth of guerrilla struggles led the regime to seek to regain some legitimacy by liberalizing the political system in the 1970s and 1980s. The struggle for democratizing the system came to be energized by the discontent of the popular sectors and sections of the party with neoliberalism and the hardships it imposed, as well as by its betrayal of "revolutionary nationalism." These dynamics, combined with the struggle for presidential succession in 1987–1988, produced the most important split and crisis of the ruling party since its foundation and the emergence of mass neo-*Cardenismo,* which will be discussed below. And the Zapatista rebellion further increased the pressure for democratization.

The insurgency and repression of 1968 deepened and spread a socialist-oriented radicalism that was able to permeate those areas of the country where popular movements had already developed incipient roots in the 1960s. While its epicenter was Mexico City, its influence has extended toward the south and southeast of the country—to states such as Tabasco, Chiapas, and Oaxaca. The schisms in the ruling party in 1987, the exciting election campaign of 1988, and the fraud in that presidential election led to the development of a left electoralist opposition. The institutionalist route seemed to be validated when it appeared that the Zapatistas' mass mobilization in support of indigenous rights in 2001 would lead to constitutional change. When that door was slammed in their face, the Zapatistas retreated to reevaluate their strategy, as will be discussed below. While for most Mexicans the institutional electoral route seemed to be validated by the 2000 presidential election, the continuation of repression, neoliberalism, and massive electoral fraud has brought that into question.

Electoralism and the Mexican Left Then and Now

The Left has always had divisions over the issue of participation in elections. In the past, Mexico's one-party regime sharply restricted the possibilities of the electoral route and made left electoralism a somewhat moot question. But when the regime deliberately opened up the electoral system in the 1970s as a way of pushing the Left away from revolutionary paths, the Left, understandably, had diverse responses. Although they were fully aware that they could only gain a token electoral presence, the majority of the Trotskyist movement and the Partido Comunista Mexicana (Mexican Communist Party, PCM) and its successor organizations chose the electoral route. They saw it as an opportunity to speak to the masses and expand their base, while continuing their other political work. But, at the same time, these parties maintained their independence and, having no hope of winning more than token representation, were not faced with the danger of electoral opportunism. Until 1987–1988, these disputes continued to take place in a context of a ruling party that was intact.

The emergence of neo-*Cardenismo*, first as a popular electoral alternative, then as a mass anti-electoral-fraud movement, and finally as a new party, Partido de la Revolución Democrática (Democratic Revolution Party, PRD), created a qualitatively new situation and posed new dilemmas. Major portions of the revolutionary Left were drawn to this party because it was challenging the one-party system, expressing strong opposition to aspects of neoliberalism, and mobilizing millions of workers and *campesinos*. Those who chose to participate were hopeful that the presence of a strong Left alongside the mass anti-neoliberal base of this new party would push it to the left in spite of its moderate leadership. Much of the revolutionary Left joined the new party with these hopes but, in the process, forfeited much of their independent existence. The seduction of electoral opportunism now began to take hold—though not in a context of a genuine transition to democracy but in the context previously described, that is, of constrained electoral liberalization and increased repression.

The 1988 Crisis, the Formation of the PRD, and the Absorption of the Left

The development of the PRD was based on more than a split of an important current within the official PRI party and the adhesion of a number of left groups. It was also based on a rising discontent with austerity programs and neoliberalism and a process of the dissolution of the PRI into its regional forces that had already begun. Some of these forces returned to their traditional "revolutionary nationalist" perspective, in some cases going back to their roots in the 1920s. This was the case, for example, with the liberal nationalist groups of the state of Veracruz and, in a certain sense, with some of the anticentralist social forces of northern Mexico. This was the basis for the constitution of the neo-*Cardenista* bloc that sustained the PRD.

These regional forces had found expression within the "revolutionary nationalist" project throughout the 1920s and 1930s. But they had become submerged within the authoritarian party during its long period of rule, losing their dissident profile. They began to reconstitute themselves as forces with their own organic structure after Mexico's turn to neoliberalism and especially following the election of Carlos Salinas in 1988. Their development was facilitated by the successive political reforms that allowed them to constitute themselves outside the PRI.

In order to understand the PRD, we have to understand the depth and power of the ideology of revolutionary nationalism. Neo-*Cardenismo* represented symbolically and in its political leadership the notion of restoring revolutionary nationalism, restoring the Mexican Revolution to its "true" path, which to the left revolutionary nationalists implies the most left interpretation of radical populism and even, to quite a few, some notion of socialism, or at least a transition to socialism. This restorationist notion and the currents promoting it were not new phenomena. The debate about the meaning of the revolution and post-revolution has been as continuous as the government's claim, only dropped in 1985, that the revolution had never ended. Many on the left felt that the revolutionary process had reached its highest, most progressive moment during the presidency of Lázaro Cárdenas (1934–1940). But after 1940, Mexico took a sharp turn to the right with capitalist development trumping social justice and egalitarian concerns. The split in the ruling party in the mid-1980s and the campaign of Cuauhtémoc Cárdenas, the son of the revered Lázaro Cárdenas in whose presidency revolutionary nationalism had reached its highest point, electrified the nation and revived many dormant, demoralized revolutionary nationalist currents.

Neo-*Cardenismo* and the PRD were born of these long-existing mass revolutionary nationalist sentiments as well as the elitist-populist culture and traditions of the left of the PRI. The ambiguous legacy of revolutionary nationalism had remained strong among the masses and sections of the middle classes. It embodied hopes for reforms that would spread well-being and enhance the dignity of the humble and of the nation. Its ambiguity had given the political elites great maneuverability to continue to reproduce their reformist Bonapartism, while seeking to maintain an equilibrium in the class struggle that helped sustain their autonomy. Revolutionary nationalism, in the new context, challenged key aspects of the neoliberal onslaught while not being anticapitalist. Revolutionary nationalism had never been an ideology that stood for worker or peasant power but rather for an equilibrium of power between the peasant, the worker, and the "popular" sectors (the middle class; small business) on the one hand and capital on the other, mediated, shaped, and controlled by the "revolutionary nationalist" political elite.

The PRD has been the most important expression of the left electoralist opposition. It has articulated a defense of nationalized industries and democratic rights, as well as concern for the growing inequality and poverty in Mexico. It has also strongly opposed PAN proposals to deal with Mexico's fiscal crisis by regressive taxes on food and medicines and called for taxing the big corporations, which now pay almost no taxes.

Setting the Limits on Left Electoral Power via Ongoing Exclusion and Fraud

The key to understanding the electoral hegemony of the conservative-neoliberal bloc is to probe not only how the bloc succeeds in adding and subtracting votes, but also how electoral participation has been reduced to less than half of potential voters through systematic exclusion. Each of the last four presidential elections (1988, 1994, 2000, and 2006) has been followed by four successive electoral reforms, each time recognizing the inequities and irregularities of the previous election. And each time, in acts of exceptional cynicism, the conservative-neoliberal bloc has successfully invented new tricks and maneuvers to elude popular will and to emerge victorious, whether it is with the acronym of the PRI or the acronym of the PAN. In either case, the neoliberal project continues.

The massive number of Mexicans who migrate internally and to the United States in search of work are systematically excluded from voting by government policy that has continued from the days of PRI one-party rule through the PAN presidencies. Those living in the United States face a variety of costs and obstacles in their attempt to vote, and those without legal documentation are highly unlikely to engage in a process that could make them more visible and vulnerable to U.S. authorities. Ecuador is also a country with a high rate of emigration, but its policies facilitate emigrants voting from abroad. In the 2006 elections, only 1 percent of the Consejo Nacional de Población 's estimate of Mexicans abroad voted.[1] Compare that to the 63 percent of Ecuadorian emigrants who voted in their November 26, 2006, election (Abogados del Ecuador, 2007: 2). A meager 40,876 Mexicans out of approximately ten million abroad voted (CONAPO 2010: 102).[2]

As well, voting opportunities are denied to most of Mexico's internal migrants—estimated to have been fifteen million people between 1995 and 2010 (INEGI, 2011: 19)—by making voter registration difficult for people without stable addresses as they have to register at least six months before the election.[3] The simple device of setting up a dramatically insufficient number of special polling stations[4] that are only permitted to have 750 ballots each effectively excludes millions from voting. Many internal migrants with voting credentials in hand were turned away in 2006 when that meager number of ballots was rapidly exhausted. Thus many of this massive number of internal migrants are de facto excluded from voting rights.

In addition to exclusion—and heavy use of patronage—various and changing mechanisms of fraud play a very important role in the blocking of a possible victory for the presidency by the PRD. Paving the way for sanctioning and executing fraud, the Fox government in 2003 increased PAN-PRI control over the election process itself when, in alliance with the PRI, it destroyed the autonomy of the Instituto Federal Electoral (Federal Electoral Institute, IFE), so hard to come by in years of struggle, by appointing political allies to the IFE rather than independents as required by law and previously done (Albarrán 2007: 11). It also sought to judicially disqualify the popular PRD candidate, Andrés Manuel López Obrador, only backing down in the face of massive protests. There was a last-minute substitution of electoral officials at numerous voting stations (carried out by the SNTE,[5] the national teachers' union, to support Calderón), a related massive falsification in the counting of votes that produced great and perhaps decisive incongruencies in the overall voting results (Crespo, 2008: 48, 94; López Obrador, 2007: 234; Raphael, 2007: 288–89), and a failure of the electoral monitoring institutions (IFE and the Tribunal Electoral del Poder Judicial de la Federación [Electoral Tribunal of the Judicial Power of the Federation, TEPJF]) to follow the law (Código Federal de Instituciones y Procedimientos Electorales [Federal Code of Electoral Institutions and Procedures, COFIPE]) in recounting votes at polling stations with significant errors (Crespo, 2008: 94). There was neither transparency nor equity in the course of the 2006 electoral process.

Electoralism, Fraud, and Mass Protest: 2006

The 2000 presidential election had seen the defeat of the old ruling party and an end to the one-party rule of the presidential regime. But the attempts of the government of Vicente Fox (2000–2006) to impose a second generation of neoliberal reforms had been frustrated by popular resistance and the related congressional stalemate. As the 2006 presidential election approached, with the strong prospect of a left victory, democracy was cast aside for the safety of capital, domestic and foreign, and for a renewed push for a second generation of neoliberal restructuring.

Confronted by the electoral fraud of 2006, the Obradoristas organized one of the most important popular insurgencies in recent Mexican history, centered especially in Mexico City: the antifraud mobilizations of the summer and fall of 2006. Their goal was to use mass pressure as a tool for forcing the electoral processes back onto an honest track. But they neither wanted to lose control of the movement nor bring about a brutal state repression. They therefore deliberately constrained the emerging popular energies.

The experience of the antifraud movement illustrates both the potential of the movement and its limitations. Hundreds of thousands of people protested the fraud of July 2, 2006, in unprecedented street mobilizations that lasted for weeks and took the form of a new organization, the Convención Nacional Democrática (National Democratic Convention, CND), that had great grassroots participation but was carefully controlled from above by the López Obrador leadership. All supporters who participated were called "delegates," but they were neither elected to represent anyone nor did they have a decision-making role. Their only voice was ratifying resolutions proposed from above at mass, plebiscitarian rallies with no opportunity for discussion or for the proposal of alternatives. López Obrador's popularity was too strong and the Left too weak for an alternative conception of the CND as a tool of mass struggle to triumph. The mass mobilizations remained contained within the bounds of plebiscitarianism and elite bargaining strategies, and the CND gradually petered out.

López Obrador has ceaselessly toured Mexico in the years since the 2006 presidential election, visiting small towns and large cities alike, laying the groundwork for a mass movement that could prevent another fraudulent presidential election in 2012 as well as one that could fight the deepening antipopular offensive in the interim. This movement was formalized in the creation of the Nuevo Proyecto de Nación y al Movimiento de Regeneración Nacional (New Project of the Nation and the National Regeneration Movement, MORENA) in January 2011. It is organized along the geographical lines of the electoral districts and is creating a mass network that could monitor the elections as well as mobilizing the voters to fight the anticipated fraud. According to López Obrador (Hernández Navarro, 2011), 29,000 of Mexico's 65,000 electoral districts already have active committees, involving one million people. The character of this movement/organization will be shaped by the lessons drawn from 2006, the dynamics of the combination of social movement/electoral organization, the tensions between the democratizing energies from below and the traditions of top-down leadership from above, and the character of the electoral campaign and the subsequent vote count. This is not simply an electoral organization but also a social movement that expands and contracts depending on the political conjuncture.

Opposition or Accommodation: Which Future for the Electoral Left?

The sharp divisions between the main currents in the PRD have led to bitter infighting and even mutual accusations of electoral fraud in internal elections. The fraud in the 2006 presidential elections led to sharp divisions over the "realist" necessity of accepting the presidency of Felipe Calderón or continuing, at least symbolically, to declare him "illegitimate" both within and outside of Congress. The approaching 2012 presidential and congressional elections have divided the party sharply over analogous issues in the peculiar approach of the accomodationist currents, especially the Nueva Izquierda (New Left , NI), popularly known as the "Chuchos," with the support of the smaller Alternativa Democrática Nacional (National Democratic Alternative, ADN),[6] to advocate a joint candidate with the right-wing party of the president against the old state party, the PRI. The fight over running an independent center-left candidate or a joint candidate with the neoliberal and clericalist right has led to a bitter battle for control of the party.

While there are also other important strategic as well as ideological differences among the currents, it is important to note that the main currents in the PRD are broad alliances of minor currents often held together more by pragmatic considerations (nominations, party positions, and the spoils of office) than by ideological concerns. As well, there are several other left parties, the Partido de Trabajo (Labor Party, PT) and Convergencia (Convergence), as well as the new movement MORENA, that need to be viewed as part of the organizational ecology of the electoral Left.

The major accomodationist current, the Nueva Izquierda, led by Jesús Ortega and Jesús Zambrano, takes what they view as a realist perspective about the "inevitability" of neoliberalism. They see themselves as a responsible pressure group within the neoliberal regime and, in exchange, want to be rewarded with political positions and government funding for their party and the jurisdictions governed by them. Their bureaucratic approach to politics requires more and more paid staff, which itself depends on winning votes to be eligible for the quite lucrative governmental funding of political parties.

The main opposition to the NI is another broad front of currents, called the Izquierda Unida (United Left, IU), whose main public face is Alejandro Encinas. It is an even more heterogeneous and less cohesive front than NI. The component currents range from radical left to moderate left but generally share variations of the perspective of revolutionary nationalism. López Obrador has positioned himself within and outside of the PRD, building MORENA outside but remaining close to these left currents inside. These left currents recently defeated the "Chuchos" over the issue of running a PRD candidate or a PRD-PAN candidate in the very crucial state of México. Encinas was the PRD candidate in the 2011 election for governor of the state of México, the largest state by far in terms of population and also with a significant presence of industry.

In addition to the dispute over an electoral coalition with the Right, the main other differences between NI and IU are over (1) the privatization of energy natural resources (oil, water, minerals, coastal areas) and public services, (2) tax and federal budgetary policy, and (3) indigenous rights. NI is willing to consider privatization on a pragmatic basis, whereas IU is opposed, in principle, to privatization of natural resources or public services. NI supported the neoliberal fiscal policy in the budget adopted in November 2009, whereas the currents in the IU camp vociferously opposed them, pointing out their class bias and their exemption of large corporations from any taxes. NI members of the Senate voted in 2001 and 2002 with the PRI and PAN to defeat the indigenous rights legislation proposed in the San Andrés Accords, whereas the left currents that later formed the IU supported and continue to support those demands. The instrumental and *caudillista* mode of operation of PRD currents makes it difficult to clearly delineate them ideologically, as ideology is often subordinated to the struggle for funds and office. There is, however, a great difference between the bureaucratic political style of the NI and that of the IU currents, which operate in a more populist and plebiscitarian manner and are more open to social movements and to engaging in extra-parliamentary activity.

Though the PRD remained dominant in state and local governments in their areas of long-term strength (Mexico City, Michoacán, and Guerrero), they lost power in 2010 in Zacatecas and Baja California Sur, leaving them without any state governments in northern Mexico. These cases show that the PRD is stronger when pressured to articulate a more coherent, redistributive, and popular public policy and more fragile when reproducing the old PRI cacique practices, which form a part of its DNA. Social movements are strong and exert a great influence on the PRD in the DF, Michoacán, and Guerrero. The party is forced to assimilate demands from below, whether they like it or not. There are strong reciprocal influences and linkages in these states between the *izquierda no permitida* and the *izquierda permitida*. This is also true in Oaxaca, though its recent expression has been in relation to a broad electoral coalition and not to a PRD state government. On the other hand, in states where the social movements are weak (Zacatecas and Baja California Sur), the PRD governments have been more authoritarian and less accountable to their political base. The top-down processes of these PRD state governments and their lack of embeddedness in popular movements has made them more vulnerable to challenges from the right as they lack the popular roots that the party has in other states.

The most important jurisdiction governed by the PRD is the Federal District, or DF, held by PRD mayors since elections were first held in 1997. The DF, with a population of nine million people, 8 percent of the population of Mexico, is the financial, cultural, and economic heart of Mexico. One-fifth of the GDP of Mexico comes from the DF. This wealth has been the basis for the largest subnational budget in the nation and provides the material basis of the social benefits that the PRD governments have provided. These governments have created a more modern and efficient administration of public services, reduced everyday corruption, improved accountability, and acted on their commitment to public works and to funding for the social wage—cheap public transportation, health, and education. The experience of governing the DF, given its size and political, cultural, and economic centrality within Mexico, has given the PRD great legitimacy among the popular sectors and important parts of the middle classes in the DF and some other parts of Mexico.

In 2011 the Left of the PRD, a diverse coalition of eight different currents, broke the absolute control of the PRD apparatus by its most accomodationist current. The coalition of left currents defeated the Chuchos' proposal to run a joint candidate with the PAN for governor of the strategic state of México by carrying out a massive campaign in favor of the PRD, running its own candidate, the leftist Alejandro Encinas. The Left also won the election of the second most important post in the party, that of national secretary, won by the militant Dolores Padierna. The strength of López Obrador within the PRD has increased with the recent victories of the Left in the party. His leadership, however, is not uncontested, as he is being challenged for the PRD's 2012 presidential candidacy by Marcelo Ebrard, the mayor of Mexico City. Ebrard represents both a more institutional approach (*una transción sin ruptura*—a transition without a rupture) and is more friendly to big business, whereas López Obrador is for a rupture with the old power sectors, is for strengthening the state sector within a market economy, and seeks to mobilize the middle and popular classes in extra-parliamentary actions to oppose electoral fraud and energy privatization.

Extra-parliamentary Movements

The south of Mexico has been the scene of both of the country's major extra-parliamentary uprisings, one starting in Chiapas in 1994, the second in Oaxaca in 2006. These are two of the states with the greatest poverty and highest percentage of indigenous population. The Zapatista revolt was centered in rural areas of the southern state of Chiapas, with its influence coming to radiate out to various parts of Mexico and the world; the Oaxaca revolt was an urban-based uprising in the capital city of Oaxaca, with its influence radiating out strongly to other parts of the state of Oaxaca, somewhat to the rest of Mexico, and very little internationally. These revolts, as well as the antifraud mobilizations of 2006, are indicators of the explosiveness of the Mexican situation. They also point to the complexity and ambiguity of the relationship between reform and revolution in a not-quite-revolutionary situation, a situation where the belief in nonrevolutionary change has not been exhausted and in which the repressive power of the state has remained relatively intact. And they show the limits of uprisings in the economic and geographical periphery of a predominantly proletarianized and urbanized country.

The Zapatista Insurgency

The changing character of the Zapatista strategy and goals and their metaphorical rhetoric has made them difficult to define. They are a guerrilla organization rooted in communities in the far southern periphery of Mexico.

They hoped their armed uprising in Chiapas on New Year's Eve, 1994 would spark a national rebellion. The uprising induced widespread sympathy and massive mobilizations in support of their cry for social justice but little support for a national insurrection. Faced with possible annihilation by the federal army and a tremendous popular outcry for peace and negotiation, the Zapatistas made a dramatic change of direction. They began a long process of dialogue and fluid alliances with elements of Mexican and international civil society to struggle as a social movement for community survival and the transformation of all of Mexico.

Their class character (Brass, 2005; Collier and Lowery Quaratiello, 1994; Wolf, 1971) has received much less attention than the indigenous character of their social composition, the latter often taking on an essentialist character. The Zapatista movement, the EZLN, developed from a fusion of a small focoist guerrilla group with a vibrant movement of indigenous agrarian petty commodity producers. These were not traditional peasant indigenous communities but new communities of colonists, people who had been displaced by earlier capitalist development and political oppression in their regions of origin. Most of these new communities in Chiapas were developed without legal sanction on public lands that were considered economically marginal at the time. The settlers hoped to eventually gain legal ownership through Mexico's agrarian reform legislation. The state paid little attention to them for several decades, allowing the development of a significant degree of community identity and autonomy. But when President Salinas ended land reform through changes to Article 27 of the constitution in 1992, he ended all hope of legalization and security of tenure for these communities. As well, the richness in resources—oil and hydro power—made powerful interests covet these areas, previously considered marginal. Their very survival was threatened. These relatively new communities, already with significant degrees of autonomous community organization, had already been significantly politicized by the influences coming from liberation theology religious organizations, governmental sponsored organizations seeking to contain them, and left groups. Some of these vibrant organizations felt that nonviolent, institutional paths of redressing their grievances had now been exhausted and fused with the Zapatistas to form the EZLN.

The Zapatistas have carried out several national mobilizations in the attempt to use moral suasion and popular pressure to achieve fundamental changes in law and governmental policy. The most important was the Caravan for Indigenous Rights (2001), a large caravan that traveled the country holding rallies in a great number of small towns and large cities with the local population to show support for pending congressional legislation. The various mobilizations were very successful in getting popular support and raising consciousness but failed to achieve any progressive change in government legislation or practices. Nor did they lead to the development of a national movement. The EZLN retains popular sympathy, but it is neither a mass nor a national movement. Its great moral-political influence of the mid-1990s within Mexico has been greatly diminished by the failure of these various national mobilizations to produce any significant change or build an ongoing national movement. As well, they've alienated many on the left by their Other Campaign, which was launched as an alternative to the national election campaign of the PRD during 2005 and 2006. They directed their harshest criticism at the PRD at a moment in which major sectors of the popular classes saw their hopes in a victory of López Obrador.

The culture and practice of corruption and co-optation in the electoral process made the Zapatistas wary of any engagement in general, including in relation to the PRD, some of whose local and state governments had attacked and repressed the Zapatistas and other indigenous movements. The unanimous vote of the PRD senators for the government's alternative to the indigenous rights legislation proposed in the San Andrés Accords was justly viewed as a betrayal.[7] The legislation denied the central demand for formal recognition of indigenous communities as subjects of public law within the constitution. It was a slap in the face of the hopes and demands of the Caravan for Indigenous Rights, one of the most impressive national mobilizations in Mexican history.

The combination of this defeat with the liberalization of the one-party authoritarian state put the Zapatistas in a very difficult situation. On the one hand, some of the major forces pushing for a democratic transition and sympathetic to the Zapatistas came to ignore the key role of the Zapatista rebellion and consequent mobilizations in the breakdown of the old authoritarian state. These more institutional fellow travelers used their new positions to marginalize and undermine the bases of the insurgent indigenous movement through the clientelistic use of new economic and political resources. This was especially the case with the PRD government of Salazar Mendiguchía in Chiapas (2000–2006), a PRD governor who had just left the PRI. The political transition came to be the point of departure for a new political offensive against the independence and autonomy of indigenous communities nationally. "Civil society," that diffuse urban, educated opposition to the old regime, put their own agenda first and distanced themselves from the insurgent communities of Chiapas.

As well, there developed a bifurcation between the paths of the indigenous movement and its more institutionalized urban popular allies that neither side was able to bridge. The Zapatista movement had received support not only from many urban popular organizations but also from unions and even formal support from universities as institutions. While many of these organizations and institutions found space to expand their social and political influence in the new political ambiance, the insurgent indigenous communities faced a new deception, a new betrayal, a new oblivion.

The reaction of Zapatismo was to turn inward, to remake itself with the Juntas de Buen Gobierno, in order to resist the "democratic siege," the attempt at co-optation of insurgent communities through patronage and clientelism. These attempts at co-optation were often accompanied by the strategic use of violence against communities that refused to barter away their rights. Zapatismo and indigenous rights were thus pushed off the national agenda.

The focus on building at the local level does not mean that the Zapatistas have renounced returning to the national arena to challenge their old and new adversaries. Confronted by a new and unfavorable political scenario in 2003 when the PRI regained control of the Chamber of Deputies,[8] they resolved to wait and resist, repeating the mantra that they would never again allow themselves to be manipulated in battles among the political elites. While the strength of their resistance to cooptation helped preserve their movement, the vehemence with which they expressed it also increased their isolation from much of the urban popular movements.

The Supreme Court's pardon in August 2009 of the paramilitaries who carried out the Acteal massacre ten years earlier is an ominous sign. The protracted low-intensity war against the Zapatistas could become all-out open warfare again. Given these circumstances, the Zapatistas have to be prepared for war. They have been patiently and quietly reaching out to hundreds of communities, rural and urban, communities that are as fed up with the official lies and policies as are the indigenous communities. The survival of the Zapatista movement will depend on their effectiveness in knitting together a web of resistance to overcome the isolation that makes them especially vulnerable to an all-out government offensive.

In 2011 the Zapatistas emerged from their relative isolation. They broke their silence of almost five years and have assumed a central role in the campaign against the brutal violence[9] and militarization of the country, thus linking up with a vast network of new and old social movements.

The Oaxaca Rebellion

The Oaxaca rebellion of 2006 was an urban insurrection in one city that created grassroots forms of popular government that controlled the city for over five months (Roman and Velasco Arregui, 2008). As with the Paris Commune in 1870–1871 and the Russian Soviets in 1905 and 1917, the new organization that emerged, the APPO (Asamblea Popular de los Pueblos de Oaxaca, Popular

Assembly of the Peoples of Oaxaca), was both an organ of struggle against the Oaxacan state government and an embryonic government. The APPO ran the city of Oaxaca and some outlying areas of the state for close to half a year. The brutal repression of a teachers' strike on June 14, 2006, had triggered a massive spontaneous uprising that drove the police and the governor out of the city. The breadth of support for the uprising produced a plethora of demands and a diversity of hopes and expectations. The unifying demand was the removal of the especially unpopular PRI governor of the state.

The movement had widespread support from almost all sectors of the population, but its core was working class. The Oaxaca section of the teachers' union (Section 22), a seventy-thousand-member dissident section of the national authoritarian teachers' union, provided cadre and organizational strength to the movement, though, at times, there were important tensions within the union and overlapping tensions between the union and the APPO. This movement was insurrectionary in form and potentially revolutionary in implications, but its fundamental—and nonnegotiable—demand was not revolutionary. It was simply the replacement of the governor of the state; something that had happened previously in Mexico when the federal senate declared the state to be in a situation of *ingobernabilidad* (ungovernability). This demand was directed at the national government, specifically the Senate, which had the constitutional authority to remove the governor. This was political bargaining by local insurrection.

There was a profound ambiguity between the unavoidable bargaining with the national government and the radical, participatory, and self-governing character of the movement's dual government. The rebellion manifested many aspects of a revolutionary process but, its territorial limitations precluded it from developing into a threat to the national state.

The electoralist leadership of the López Obrador coalition generally kept its distance from insurrectionary movements for a series of reasons. In spite of a radicalized rhetoric after the 2006 fraud, it was continually concerned to reassure society and capital, domestic and foreign, that they were only using extra-parliamentary struggle as a method of making parliamentary struggle honest. The APPO on the other hand, while having revolutionary elements and revolutionary rhetoric, continued to bargain from June to November 25 with the national government that had carried out the July 2 electoral fraud and toward which the antifraud movement directed its wrath. Although there was great sympathy among the rank and file for each other's struggles, there was great uneasiness and suspicion between the leadership of the two movements. And the Zapatistas only interrupted their Other Campaign to join the protests against the repression in Atenco. They chose not to engage in Mexico's two mass and quasi-insurrectionary movements of 2006. They expressed support for the Oaxaca struggle and solidarity with the rank and file of the antifraud movement, but they made no significant political interventions in relation to either struggle. The political and geographical divisions of the Left facilitated the survival of the government in the face of two major mass insurgencies occurring at the same time in 2006.

The attempt of the APPO to become a national movement through the creation of the Alianza Popular de Pueblos de México never got off the ground. The APPO's development was shaped by Oaxaca's strong traditions of collective struggle and an especially odious governor that united broad sectors across the political spectrum. Although many of these conditions and traditions are shared throughout Mexico, they were not able to translate their strategy of negotiation by insurrection into national terms, especially because of their political differences and tensions with the mass antifraud movement.

The APPO as a vibrant mass movement, an organ of struggle, and an embryonic government disappeared after its defeat in October 2006. While a shell of the APPO remains, its component movements and mass base have returned to their own organizational forms with their own agendas that, in a very fluid process, sometimes coalesce. The APPO as the unifying center of diverse popular struggles and energies no longer exists.

These movements joined with a great variety of political forces to form an electoral coalition to defeat the corrupt and murderous PRI machine of Oaxaca in the state elections of 2010. The popular forces viewed this as a great victory even though it was based on a broad coalition from left to right behind the gubernatorial candidacy of Gabino Cue, a moderate dissident and member of the modernizing sector of the local elites. The new state government has not and is not likely to carry out socially progressive changes, but it has dislocated the old network of political control of the PRI cacique and paramilitary structures. It has changed the terrain of class struggle. The tensions between unions and communities and the new state government have returned but, at least for the moment, in a context of some civility, and not one of persecution and massacres, so common over a long century of PRI rule in Oaxaca.

The Underground Left in Mexico

Guerrilla forces have been present in Mexico throughout the twentieth century. Even "the dirty war" of the 1970s and the successive reforms aimed at "institutionalizing" the radical Left failed to eliminate them. The decline of the PRI and its loss of the presidency in 2000 seemed to open up the possibility of an accord with the guerrilla forces that would reflect the new situation. However, the treatment received by the Zapatistas pushed these forces away from their flirtation with moving from armed to open, institutionalized struggle. The state security organs also lost significant capacity for reading what was happening in the political underground of Mexico with the decline of the PRI and its historic links to the grassroots.

On the surface, it appeared that the end of PRI rule and the "democratic transition" would lead to the slow dissolution of clandestine armed forces. However, these movements came to be nourished with new recruits from two sources. One was the growing discontent in the rural zones due to the deteriorating economic conditions in the first nine years of the government of alternation, as well as the endemic corruption and violence by the government and local elites. The other source of new recruits for guerrilla movements—as well as for the drug cartels—was the thousands of desertions from the armed forces related in complex ways to the demise of the state party's local and regional networks. The influx of these new recruits began to revive these dormant guerrilla organizations, which had been undergoing serious divisions and disarticulation. It is estimated that, as of 2009, there are at least seven guerrilla groups with stable operating capacity in Mexico.[10]

These guerrilla forces, out of view since 1996, have reemerged from the shadows in relation to the discontent over the 2006 electoral fraud and the repression in Oaxaca. The return of these forces to front stage was symbolized by the sabotage of the gas pipe lines of PEMEX in July 2007. Although still small in numbers, these guerrilla movements have a presence in over half of the states of Mexico and a notable military technical capacity, as was demonstrated in various armed actions after 2006.

The guerrilla movements have focused traditionally on rural areas. But they have recently shifted their work to also include the poor barrios of many of the new medium and large cities, those two hundred urban zones of over one hundred thousand people. This urban embeddedness is a development that the counterinsurgency of the 1970s always sought to avoid and has important implications for the next upsurge of popular struggle.

The guerrilla groups, in general, believe that institutional methods of struggle have no viability and that the legitimacy of the electoral alternative will decline further. That belief is coupled with the belief that Mexico is heading in a catastrophic direction that will lead to a social explosion and brutal repression. The need of people to defend themselves against repression, they feel, will create a basis for the growth of armed struggle in the cities as well as the countryside, not in a focoist sense or as an alternative to mass struggle, but as part of mass struggle. Their shift of emphasis to the cities represents this perspective.

Streams of Resistance

The Mexican regime's two-pronged strategy of control—constrained electoral liberalization and terror (deliberate and incidental to the "War on Drugs")—has run aground of two major contradictions. First, the two parties of the dominant class were never able to modernize their collusion; their ideological disagreements, their different cultures of authoritarianism, one secular, one clericalist, and their competition for positions and patronage shredded the attempt at a civil electoral process and alternations of power. They decided to try to annihilate one another, triggering an unanticipated instability in the political-economic transition. Secondly, Mexican society has a deeply rooted and dense tangle of networks of resistance, formal and informal, old and new, that have presented a continuing obstacle to the consolidation of a neoliberal regime.

The Mexican Left can be seen as divided into three broad and diverse streams. One stream is a network of state and local governments, small and limited to a few cities, but with a real margin of autonomy from the centers of power in the country. The second is the mass civil movement, the National Regeneration Movement of López Obrador, with tens of thousands of small electoral committees that are spread throughout the country. And the third is a vast network of social movements that includes workers from unions destroyed by privatization, farmers devastated by free trade, and the Zapatistas and other underground forces. Many of these social movements have come together in the new movement against violence and militarization.

Workers play an important role in all three streams of resistance. Yet they've only spoken in their own voice in a very limited way, in spite of the fact that Mexico is an urban country (64 percent of Mexicans live in cities with over one hundred thousand people—73 million of a total population of 115 million), most of the economically active population is waged or salaried (75 percent or 32 million of an economically active population of 43.8 million) (INEGI, 2008), and almost all have experienced decades of deterioration of wages and working conditions, now made even more acute by the recent economic crisis.

The decades of deteriorating wages and working conditions as well as the weight of the urban working class in the population would seem to create a significant potential for workers to emerge as actors in their own right, as a leading element of broader movements like happened in Oaxaca in 2006, rather than simply as members of or a base for these broader movements. But the development of this potential has been thwarted by massive repression as well as the long-standing institutions of labor control carried over into the neoliberal period (Roman and Velasco Arregui, 2006). The vast majority of the working class lacks genuine unions through which to build effective resistance to the neoliberal offensive. And the union movement has not yet developed an effective strategy for building its own movement in the face of these obstacles.

Yet the Mexican working class has the potential for great strategic leverage given its double integration into the U.S./North American production system. Industrial production in Mexico is an integral part of North America's integrated production systems, and Mexican workers make up a significant part of the working class within the United States. Working-class insurgency in Mexico would immediately impact production in the rest of North America, and it is highly likely that most Mexican workers in the United States would be allies of the struggles of their class within Mexico. Continental integration, promoted by big business in all three countries of North America, has multiplied the potential ramifications of class and political struggles in Mexico. As well, a renewed working-class movement would force social content onto the front burner of Mexico's popular struggles rather than constituting demands that could be sacrificed in the course of struggle. How this dynamic unfolds in the explosive context of the July 2012 elections will be crucial in determining the content, durability, and effectiveness of the struggle against the regime. The overlap between the Mexican and U.S. 2012 electoral processes, including likely postelection struggles in Mexico, has important implications. The debate over immigration is already a hot issue in U.S. politics. Intensified sociopolitical struggles in Mexico, a civil war or an "Egypt" on the border of the United States, would have a dramatic impact on the U.S. presidential and congressional elections. A crucial year in the Mayan calendar, 2012 could be a crucial year for the future of North America.

Notes

1. Mexican citizens abroad as well as those living out of their areas of voter registration within Mexico are only eligible to vote in the presidential election.

2. There are an estimated ten million Mexicans living in the United States, not counting the children of Mexican nationals born in the United States and entitled to dual citizenship. In the sixteen years since the start of NAFTA, the National Population Council (CONAPO) estimates that seven million Mexicans have emigrated from Mexico, many of them probably having been previously registered as voters in Mexico (CONAPO 2010: 102).

3. The expulsion of people by intensified violence is sharply increasing internal migration (Najar, 2011).

4. The special polling stations are for citizens living outside the locality in which they are registered to vote on the day of the presidential election.

5. The SNTE (Sindicato Nacional de Trabajadores de Educación, National Union of Education) is an authoritarian union previously connected to the state party and now an ally of the PAN and a key cog in the conservative-neoliberal power bloc. The major dissident sections, such as Section 22 of the state of Oaxaca, face repression by both the government and their own national union.

6. The ADN is a small current that has strength in Ciudad Nezahualcoyotl and in the state of México and is strongly corporatist in structure.

7. Most of the PRD members in the Chamber of Deputies voted against this legislation.

8. The PRI had never lost control of the Senate.

9. In the first five years of the Calderón presidency, the number of murders and executions in the War on Drugs (more aptly called a War for Drugs given the complex interlacing of state actors and institutions with the drug cartels) reached forty thousand, almost as many as U.S. deaths in Vietnam and twice the number of disappeared in Argentina's dirty war.

10. The most important are the Ejército Revolucionario del Pueblo, the Fuerzas Armadas Revolucionarias del Pueblo (FARP), the Ejército Revolucionario del Pueblo Insurgente (ERPI), the Comando Jaramillista Morelense 23 de Mayo, the Ejército Villista Revolucionario del Pueblo, and the Tendencia Democrática Revolucionaria-Ejército del Pueblo (TDR-EP).

References

Abogados de Ecuador. 2007. *Informe de las Elecciones: Padrón de Electores de Ecuador en el Exterior*. Quito: Ministerio de Relaciones Exteriores del Ecuador.

Albarrán, Daniela. 2007. "Las Revolución en Mexican y el proceso de 2006." *Revista Nuevos Mundos*, January 25.

Brass, Tom. 2005. "Neoliberalism and the Rise of (Peasant) Nations within the Nation: Chiapas in Comparative and Theoretical Perspective." *Journal of Peasant Studies* 32, nos. 3–4: 651–91.

CEPAL (Comisión Económica para América Latina). 2011. *Anuario Estadístico de América Latina*. Santiago de Chile: CEPAL.

———. 2010. *Anuario Estadístico de América Latina y el Caribe*. Santiago de Chile: CEPAL.

Collier, George A., and Elizabeth Lowery Quaratiello. 1994. *Basta! Land and the Zapatista Rebellion in Chiapas*. Oakland, CA: Food First.

CONAPO (Consejo Nacional de Población). 2010. *La Situación Demográfica de México*. Mexico City: CONAPO.

Crespo, José Antonio. 2008. *2006: Hablan las actas; Las debilidades de la autoridad Mexicana*. México City: Random House Mondadori.

Hernández Navarro, Luis. 2009a. "La Asamblea Nacional de Resistencia Popular." *La Jornada*, October 27.

———. 2009b. "Las remesas a México cayeron 36% en octubre, frente a 2008." *Wall Street Journal*, December 1, Spanish edition.

———. 2011. "López Obrador a fortalecer el Morena." *El Universal*, May 1.

INEGI (Instituto Nacional de Estadística y Geografía). 2008 *Anuario Estadística*. Mexico City: INEGI.

———. 2011. *Censo de Población y Vivienda, Resultados Básicos*. Mexico City: INEGI.

López Obrador, Andrés Manuel. 2007. *La mafia nos robó la Presidencia*. Mexico City: Grijalbo.

Najar, Alberto. 2011. "México: Más de doscientos treinta mil desplazados por la violencia." *BBC en Español*, March 29.

Raphael, Ricardo. 2007. *Los socios de Elba Esther*. Mexico City: Planeta.

Roman, Richard, and Edur Velasco Arregui. 2006. "The State, the Bourgeoisie, and the Unions: The Recycling of Mexico's System of Labor Control." *Latin American Perspectives* 33 (2): 95–103.

———. 2008. "The Oaxaca Uprising: Implications for Mexico." In *Global Flashpoints: Reactions to Imperialism and Neoliberalism*, ed. Leo Panitch and Colin Leys, 248–64. Socialist Register 2008. New York: Monthly Review Press. Also available as "The Mexican Crisis and the Oaxaca Commune." *Socialist project E-Bulletin*, no. 99 (April 23). http://www.socialistproject.ca/bullet/bullet099.html.

———. 2009. "Mexico: The Murder of a Union and the Rebirth of Class Struggle." Pts. 1 and 2. *Socialist Project E-Bulletin*, no. 279 (November 25): http://www.socialist project.ca/bullet/279.php; no. 280 (November 26): http://www.socialistproject.ca/ bullet/279.php.

Wolf, Eric. 1971. *Peasant Wars of the Twentieth Century*. London: Faber and Faber.

13

The Chilean Left after 1990

An Izquierda Permitida *Championing Transnational Capital, a Historical Left Ensnared in the Past, and a New Radical Left in Gestation*

Fernando Leiva

CHILE STANDS OUT IN LATIN AMERICA as the one country where the neoliberal capitalist class project seems to have been most successfully implemented. After a U.S.-supported September 11, 1973, military coup violently ended the Chilean people's attempt at a peaceful road to socialism, the military regime of General Augusto Pinochet (1973–1989) wielded state terror and laissez-faire economics to destroy and replace the model of capitalist development that had existed in Chile since the late 1930s. Under Pinochet's rule, the twinned forces of state terror and the market demolished the social arrangements and institutions of the old state-capitalist import-substitution industrializing model. At the same time, under Pinochet, laissez faire economics cum repression (concentration camps, forced disappearances, summary executions, torture) were instrumental in laying the foundations for a new regime of accumulation based on the export of raw materials with low levels of processing and the hegemony of transnational finance capital over society.

However, what is distinct about the Chilean case is that for two decades the legitimization and institutionalization of this new capitalist order was led and engineered by the center-left coalition known as the Concertación de Partidos por la Democracia, or Concertación. In office as the longest-lasting political coalition in Chilean history (1990–2010), it oversaw a far-reaching process of capitalist expansion and social and cultural transformation. Celebrated throughout Latin America as a success story to emulate, these transformations have also had overwhelmingly "toxic" consequences for Chilean society, most of which the Concertación successfully managed until only recently. Starting in 2006, the elite pact that had anchored capitalist expansion, social quietude, and political stability (as well as the Concertación coalition itself) began to show undeniable signs of exhaustion and crisis. Thus, forty years after the overthrow of Allende, Chilean society starkly embodies—with its profoundly transformed capitalist economy, polity, and culture—the traits, vicissitudes, and challenges of the new transnationalized twenty-first-century model of domination emerging in Latin America. The electoral victory by a right-wing coalition in the January 2010 runoff presidential elections—the first time in fifty years that Chile's Right has taken control of the government via the ballot box—attests to the extent to which two decades of servicing transnational capital by the center-left buttressed bourgeois hegemony over society, even if this always incomplete and contradictory goal has been achieved at the price of the demise of the Concertación itself. Two decades of Concertación governments paved the road so that the economic conglomerates—which already dominated the economy, media, and educational system—can now expand their influence to the direct management of the state's executive branch.

One outcome is that the "cartographies of the past" have become inadequate for accurately mapping the contours and direction of the contemporary Chilean Left (expansively understood here to also include the center-left in government, or *izquierda permitida*). Fifty years ago, Chile could boast the broadest-based Marxist Left in Latin America, mainly structured around two equally powerful socialist and communist parties that, on the basis of an "anti-oligarchic, anti-feudal, and anti-imperialist" program, came together to elect Salvador Allende as president and began the recuperation of national resources from foreign control, democratized Chilean society, and blazed the "Chilean road to socialism." In stark contrast—after seventeen years of dictatorship and twenty years of Concertación administrations—today's Left is an archipelago of vastly dissimilar historical projects. Thus one significant consequence of neoliberal restructuring is that the Chilean Left no longer displays an easily recognizable family resemblance. Today it is composed of (1) an *izquierda permitida* that while in government faithfully championed for over two decades the interests of transnational capital under the veneer of a progressive discourse; (2) a *historical Left* ideologically and politically ensnared in the past, with a weakened social base and a marked incapacity to represent new demands and the new sectors of an increasingly female, young, and flexibilized labor force created by capitalist development, as well as unable to decisively intervene in the social and cultural spaces currently articulating capitalist modernity and daily life; (3) a *new radical Left* being born under the banners of autonomy, horizontality, and bottom-up construction of popular power, which despite important advances within the student movement and other social sectors, has failed so far to emerge on the national scene as a visible political alternative; and finally, (4) a wide range of atomized practices in popular socio-spatial territories that give life to a highly fragmented *izquierda social*, seeking to fill the void left by the market, the state, and party-based solutions to the pressing problems confronted by Chile's popular sectors through mostly microscale localized forms of collective action.

This chapter aims to analytically explore the trajectory of the Chilean Left after 1990 and assess its current dynamics and future prospects. A core organizing notion of this volume is that the *izquierda permitida* divides and co-opts radical leftist challenges, while the *izquierda brava*, the radical Left, offers fundamental challenges to empire, neoliberalism, and capitalism. The Chilean case presented below significantly expands these notions. It shows that the historical role of the *izquierda permitida* extends far beyond merely dividing and co-opting the radical Left; its historical role is much more *generative* in the sense that it produces the rationality, institutions, and social imaginary for regulating conflicts inherent to the new regime of accumulation. In so doing, it provides the necessary legitimacy and furnishes the more or less stable conditions required for expanded capital accumulation. It reshapes relationships between the state, the economy, and society, deploying a new set of policies that increasingly operate at the socio-emotional level and facilitate the colonization of every social interstice by the logic of transnational capital. It is able to do so by acknowledging the importance of non-market-based forms of coordination (the state *and* trust-based networks) and by harnessing and subordinating these to the contemporary requirements of the valorization of capital and capitalist hegemony construction (Leiva, 2008). Thus it is against this broad set of societal tasks—the construction of a new social imaginary, rationality, and mediations between twenty-first-century peripheral capitalist modernity and daily life—that the role of the "progressive bloc" within the Concertación, the paragon of the continent's *izquierda permitida*, must be analyzed. Additionally, this chapter shows that Chile's "other" Left has been shattered not only by the repression of the 1970s and 1980s and almost four decades of "neoliberal modernization," but most significantly by its own inabilities to address the new societal realities and rise to the tasks of the new historical epoch. Thus neither the "historical" nor the "new radical" Left have yet emerged in Chile as effective challengers to the growing power of empire, neoliberalism, and capitalism. Nonetheless, the massive student mobilizations of 2011 and the widespread support that they have engendered suggest that a unique historical opportunity for doing so has opened up in Chile.

Capitalist Transformations of Chilean Society

As four Concertación administrations deepened Chile's dependence on global circuits of capital, this process transformed the country's class structures, social identities, political patterns, and cultural practices. As in other countries, dein-dustrialization; transnationalization of the economy and society; a weakening of the labor movement; the loss of influence by a mostly male urban mining and manufacturing proletariat as capital opts for a younger, female, contingent, and disposable workforce; and an accelerated concentration of wealth in the hands of an increasingly transnationalized capitalist class have been some of the main outcomes. What makes Chile stand out is that capitalist expansion over the 1990–2009 period also increased access to consumer credit and consumer goods across all different social classes. Income per capita in Chile rose by 103 percent or 5.7 percent annually between 1990 and 2008, while it only grew by 38 percent in Latin America during the same period (on the basis of CEPALSTAT data). Despite obvious limitations, this suggests that a new material reality with far-reaching political and ideological ramifications has taken shape after 1990. A poll carried out for the Chile Human Development Report found that 65 percent of all Chileans considered their family better off than ten years ago, a view prevailing across all social strata (PNUD, 2009). Indeed, by July 2008, one out of every five Chilean adults above the age of eighteen (about 2.6 million individuals) was behind by at least thirty days in their consumer debt payments, forcing their creditors to report their names to the Boletín Comercial. And these figures do not include those in arrears in paying their electricity, telephone, and water bills, or the hundreds of thousands of student loans. Even so, each of one these Chileans in arrears had an average of five different unpaid loans totaling $846,000 Chilean, or about $1,714 U.S, each (*Mercurio*, 2008). Massive indebtedness and credit-fueled consumption have contributed to expanding the internal market but have operated both as powerful social control mechanisms (Moulian, 1997) and as fuel for new social demands and struggles, as the 2011 student mobilizations illustrate.

Against this backdrop of a contradictory process of capitalist expansion, we need to explore how changing material and symbolic conditions of existence for Chileans from all social classes have interacted to produce, among other things, the current state of the Chilean Left, widespread support for the Concertación during 1990–2009, as well the reasons why the majority of voters marked their ballots in favor of billionaire Sebastián Piñera and his right-wing coalition.

Thumbnail Sketch of Transformations

The Concertación's status-quo-friendly, center-left policies, inspired by Economic Commission for Latin American and the Caribbean (ECLAC) neostructuralism, consolidated and legitimized the export-oriented regime of accumulation established by Pinochet and the "Chicago boys." Whereas gross domestic product (GDP) growth averaged 2.9 percent a year during the Pinochet regime, during the four subsequent Concertación administrations the economy grew at much higher rates. Despite the 1998 and 2008 global crises, GDP grew at an average of 7.7 percent a year during the 1990–1993 Aylwin administration, 5.4 percent during the 1994–1999 Frei Ruiz-Tagle government, declined to 4.25 percent under the 2000–2005 Ricardo Lagos administration, and fell to 4.1 percent for the 2006–2008 period under Michelle Bachelet. These positive growth rates had important social and political ramifications. On the one had they allowed the Concertación to gain support from the business sector by delivering continuity in economic policies that expanded profitable business opportunities via access to new markets made possible by the signing of over fifty bilateral "free trade" agreements. Positive economic growth rates also allowed the Concertación, particularly during the 1990s, to maintain middle-class and working-class support thanks to the promise and reality of greater access to consumption. Nonetheless, as the data for the period shows, after thirty-five years of existence, the export-oriented model shows evident signs of slowing down, and the steady decline in growth rates since 1990 has opened up a debate about the future paths of the economic model.

Three dynamic poles for capital accumulation have emerged since 1990, each one generating significant volumes of surplus value and rents for the handful of domestic and foreign transnational conglomerates dominating the Chilean economy: (1) the export of natural resources (copper, gold, fruit, fish, lumber) with low levels of processing and produced by a super-exploited and flexible labor force; (2) a financial- and business-service outsourcing platform from which corporations seeking to expand to the Southern Cone and Latin American countries can profitably operate; and (3) an internal demand-driven services and commerce sector (retail, banking, health, financial services, utilities, privately managed highways) highly concentrated in ownership and that, through collusion and oligopolistic practices (cartel behavior, price setting, price gouging, outright usury, false advertising, lobbying and buying off of politicians and ministerial functionaries), excises a modern form of financial tribute from Chilean consumers. In mid-2009 Chile was rocked by a price-fixing scandal among the three major chain pharmacies existing in Chile (Cruz Verde, Salco Brand, and Farmacias Ahumada). Millions of dollars in surcharges were detected through a system called "La canela." Underpaid clerks could make additional income if they pushed certain name-brand drugs instead of generics. A list would be compiled daily, prices agreed upon in the cartel, and clerks when ringing up a sale could see how much commission they would make from the sale of each designated product. Similar arrangements exist in retail, cell phones, internet providers, social security, and the credit industry, all service industries controlled by six or seven large "*grupos económicos.*"

The extraordinary level of surplus extraction going on in Chile is depicted best by copper mining, where private transnational mining corporations control 72 percent of copper production. From 1974 to 2005, a period encompassing more than three decades, total investment in mining reached $19.9 billion U.S. In 2006 alone transnational mining corporations remitted abroad in the form of profits and interests payments $20 billion U.S.! In other words, remitted profits of a single year outstrip foreign direct investment in mining carried out over a period of thirty-two years (Caputo and Galarce, 2009).

Ensuring the continued expansion of each of these nodes of accumulation has sometimes required conflicting sets of policies (most evident in debates around the exchange rate, the level of fiscal spending, and labor flexibility), conflicts which many times have been assuaged because all of the major economic conglomerates (e.g., Luksic, Angelini, Matte) are present in all three nodes. Thanks to the policies of the *izquierda permitida*, these domestic transnational conglomerates have been able to extract high rates of surplus value, rents, and profits. Far from attempting to arrest these trends, Concertación and *izquierda permitida* policies have actively contributed to ensuring the expansion of domestic conglomerates within and across different economic sectors, their ability to invest abroad, and their successful integration with U.S., Canadian, and Spanish banks and transnational corporations (Fazio, 2005, 2006, 2007; Leiva and Malinowitz 2007). The reason—and here is the key point previous studies of the Chilean Left have generally overlooked—is that, as I have argued elsewhere (Leiva 2005, 2006, 2008; Petras and Leiva 1994), there has been a profound ideological conversion so that the *izquierda permitida* now sees transnational capital as the most trustworthy and dynamic agent of progress and modernity. According to the Concertación's *izquierda permitida*, Chile proves, beyond any reasonable doubt, that transnational capital and the market economy, complemented with innovative and progressive social policies, offers the best way forward for Latin America. This conviction born out of a profound ideological realignment, and not the legacy of "authoritarian enclaves" from the military regime, constitutes the fundamental reason why they have favored domestic and foreign transnational capital.

Though quickly rebounding from the 2008–2009 global crisis, Chile's large conglomerates and their foreign counterparts have found a growing number of obstacles limiting their ability to further the processes of proletarianization, commodification, financialization, and rent seeking that have been the basis of their success over the past four decades.

As economic sluggishness becomes more pronounced, and official unemployment climbs over 10 percent, the main mechanisms driving capital accumulation for the past twenty years—namely the intensification of work, expanded productive and speculative investments abroad, a shift from productive to speculative activities, intensified efforts at cost cutting at the expense of workers and subcontracted firms, new alliances with foreign transnational capital, politically mediated socialization of environmental costs, and overexploitation of natural resources in the salmon, fishing, mining, and other key export industries—are now being actively resisted by increasingly mobilized social sectors and communities. The debate over how best to restore profitability and shore up hegemony led the bloc in power to question during 2009 whether their interests could continue being served by the *izquierda permitida*'s administration of the state apparatus. It realized that managing it *manu propia* through Chile's Berlusconi, billionaire speculator Sebastián Piñera, and the right-wing parties spawned under Pinochet would more effectively remove the fetters on capital accumulation.

Social Structure and Social Dynamics

Changes in the economy also modified the country's social structure and class-formation dynamics. Some of the major transformations to note have been the following:

1. *Increased proletarianization.* Of the 2.87 million Chileans who joined the labor force between 1986 to 2008, 2.18 million (or 76 percent) of them did so as waged workers. Yet though wage work in the private sector increased, employment in manufacturing declined as a proportion of the total labor force from 16.1 percent in 1990 to 12.8 percent in 2008. Nonetheless, the 2.4 million wage workers who in 1986 represented 63.3 percent of the labor force increased to 4.6 million, or almost 69 percent, in 2008 (Leiva, 2012).
2. *Feminization of the labor force.* While the rate of labor-force participation for men declined from 73.6 to 72.6 percent between 1990 and 2006, female labor-force participation increased from 31.3 to 42.9 percent over the same period (Reinecke and Valenzuela, 2008). During the 1997–2004 period, when there was a net creation of 372,500 jobs, 252,200 of them were filled by women (OIT, 2004). In establishments employing between one and four workers, the net increase in employment was more or less equal between males and females (around 27,000), but as the size of establishments increases, one observes a marked preference for female labor. Thus, in establishments of five to nine workers, 9,500

males lost their jobs while 8,100 females were hired. In establishments with ten or more workers, the trend was even more acute: 4,500 males were shed, while 108,500 female workers were hired (OIT, 2004).

3. *Tertiarization of the economy and of the labor force.* Over the past decade there has also been a decline in relative terms of the weight of agriculture, mining, and manufacturing employment in the total occupational structure, from 36.2 percent in 1986 to only 26.4 percent in 2008. Though employment in these three sectors increased in absolute terms from 1.4 million to 1.8 million, this loses significance when one considers that the employed labor force went from 3.9 million to 6.7 million during the same period (INE, 2010).

4. *Increase in wages, but below increases in labor productivity.* Although real wages have risen since 1990, these increases have been consistently below increases in labor productivity. For the 1996–2007 period, for example, wages grew by 16.23 percent, while labor productivity did so by almost 24 percent. This has two important implications. First, wage increases are being paid by workers themselves, not employers, as wage increases failed to keep pace over this period with increased labor effort and output per worker. Second, the functional distribution of income became even more unequal. Thus, if in 1996 workers received 38.3 percent of national income, by 2007 their share had declined to only 35.1 percent, further increasing inequality (Miranda Radic, 2008)

5. *Expansion of the petty bourgeoisie.* The type of economic growth, declining public employment, and higher education levels for middle and upper-middle strata have led to the growth of technical and professional strata and small-size entrepreneurs, processes that some authors equate with an expansion of the "middle class," from 26.2 percent of the labor force in 1971 to 37.2 percent in 2000 (Torche and Wormald, 2004: 15).

These changes have been accompanied by other structural transformations that further alter the correlation of forces in favor of capital and against workers, their families, and communities: (1) the transnationalization and financialization of the economy; (2) the drastic commodification in the daily and generational reproduction of labor power; (3) the informalization of labor-capital relations (not to be confused with the informal sector, which has actually declined); and (4) the rapid concentration of income, wealth, and power by an increasingly transnational class of owners of the means of production.

In a nutshell, profound changes in the economy, the occupational structure, and class-formation dynamics have altered the nature of social demands and thoroughly recomposed what before 1973 had been the traditional social base of the Left.

Cultural Change, Meanings, and Identity

Transformations in economic and social structures have also modified how different sectors of Chilean society give meaning to their daily life and construct a sense of who they are. Concertación ideologues (the majority of whom come from the *izquierda permitida*) extol how, thanks to their successful management of the economy and society over the past two decades and to access to new levels of consumption, Chileans have changed not only their living conditions and aspirations but their very relationship to modernity itself. Hence, thanks to the skilled supervision of the *izquierda permitida*, the age-old dream of becoming "modern and developed" held by Latin America's Eurocentric elite is finally about to be realized, or so they claim. Indeed, access to consumption, growing indebtedness, greater Internet access, widespread cell phone coverage, and increased rates of homeownership and households with color TVs and refrigerators have profoundly changed how Chileans interact and construct their identities. But by successfully shepherding Chile's deeper incorporation into global circuits of capital and global markets the *izquierda permitida* has also facilitated the emergence of new modalities through which inequality, spatial segregation, and class differences are produced and reproduced materially and symbolically. Along with the new forms of capitalist exploitation and the valorization of capital, these transformations have established a new terrain for class conflict, social struggles, and collective action. The new identities and subjectivities that have emerged are not the product of market forces alone; they have also been forged under the influence of government policy and state action, especially after 1999, when the *izquierda permitida* assumed a leadership role under the governments of Ricardo Lagos (1999–2005) and Michelle Bachelet (2006–2010) (Schild, 2000, 2007; Leiva, 2008). It is in this period that public policies begin what I have called the "socio-emotional turn." The *izquierda permitida*'s policy wonks (unlike Chile's *izquierda histórica* or new radical Left) have clearly grasped that as a mode of governmentality (govern + mentalities) "neoliberalism operates on interests, desires, and aspirations rather than through rights and obligations; it does not directly mark the body, as sovereign power, or even curtail actions, as disciplinary power; rather, it acts on the conditions of actions" (Read, 2009: 29). By marrying market forces and public policies targeting the socio-emotional realm, the *izquierda permitida*'s entrepreneur/intellectuals (Tironi, Brunner, Correa, Halpern, Navia) have discovered the potent political consequences of articulating the economy, culture, and daily life. Hammered in by the market, advertisers, the media, capitalist employers, *and* the state, their message is simple and repetitive: it is good behavior and responsible job performance, not collective action, that will open the gates to new consumption and credit opportunities. Individual good behavior and responsible job performance are the best paths toward the latest-model TV, sound system, digital gadget, car, or your own home and the status that accompanies these in the eyes of your partner, children, friends, and community (Moulian, 1997). In this way, many labor militants could and have been transformed into "happy consumers" (Stillerman, 1997), and the *izquierda permitida* has continually celebrated this as a hallmark of modernity and progress.

The Chilean Left after 1990

Instead of the usual dichotomist vision of the Left divided into two camps, one acknowledging "democracy as the only possible political regime" (Garretón, 2006: 86) and another not "yet come to its senses," I offer an alternative framework. Against the backdrop of the transformations sketched above, current dynamics of Chile's post-1990 Left are best captured by mapping it onto *four* different segments:

1. An *izquierda permitida* composed of the Socialist Party (PS), Party for Democracy (PPD), and Radical Party (PRSD), members of the Concertación coalition, all of whom underwent a profound conceptual realignment after the mid-1970s, one than extends well beyond the revalorization of democracy *sin apellidos*. With deep conviction, these parties embraced servicing transnational capital as the crucial task for economic development and achieving modernity in the twenty-first century. These three parties obtained 26.1 percent of the vote in the 2008 municipal elections in which the Concertación obtained 44.6 percent of the total votes cast.

2. A *historical or traditional Left* composed of the Partido Comunista (Communist Party, PC) and smaller allies such as the Izquierda Cristiana (Christian Left, IC), a fickle Partido Humanista (Humanist Party, PH), and more recently, a breakaway group from the Socialist Party, the Allendista Socialists, led by former socialist and Concertación minister Jorge Arrate. The PC, the IC, the PH, and the Socialistas Allendistas formed the Juntos Podemos Mas–Frente Amplio electoral alliance for the 2009 presidential elections, initially supporting Jorge Arrate as president. Up until now, its defining trait has been its persistent incapacity to respond to the new historical conditions, develop a social base under the new class basis of Chilean politics, or move beyond top-down institutional and electoral politics. Relying more on growing discontent with the Concertación than systematic grassroots organizing, the historical Left obtained 9.1 percent of the national vote in the 2008 municipal

elections, allowing the PC to elect a handful of mayors and municipal leaders.

3. A *new radical Left* represented by a diverse array of small formations such as the Movimiento SurDa and, to some extent, Fuerza Social y Democratica (Social and Democratic Force, FSD), Generación 80, and a variety of small-scale anticapitalist initiatives, such as the recently created federative Movimiento Pueblos y Trabajadores (MPT). With different ideological backgrounds and representing different generations, these formations have sought to construct new forms of representation based on bottom-up organizing, social mobilization, and autonomy from political parties and the state. Though they have not participated in national-level elections, SurDa and the autonomist current have won many university student elections, capturing before 2010 the leadership of influential university federations such as the University of Chile. In the December 2009 elections, SurDa, supported independent activists linked to social movements in two congressional districts. Likewise FSD's slate Convergencia Sindical, formed mostly by former communist unionists dissatisfied with what they saw as the PC's passivity, lack of internal democracy, and penchant for backroom deals. The PC and current CUT leadership reneged on the promise made at the 2004 CUT Congress to implement democratization and direct election of union leaderships (Leiva, 2012). Convergencia Sindical received 8.6 percent of the votes in the 2004 CUT elections.

4. An *izquierda social* composed of highly atomized and microscale community and local initiatives (such as a neighborhood people's library, youth after-school programs, health groups, cultural centers, etc.). Based on solidarity, collective action, territorial organizing, and efforts to preserve the historical memory of past popular struggles, myriad such initiatives attempt to address daily problems of poverty, discrimination, lack of voice, and participation in the different socio-spatial territories where the urban and rural poor live.

Each of these four currents is engaged presently in a distinctive maneuver, a signature gesture if you will, that captures their current objectives, tactics, and stance vis-à-vis the current historical juncture. These can be described as follows:

- *Izquierda permitida* (PS, PPD, PRSD): From "deepening democracy" to servicing transnational capital while promoting social-protection policies that securitize risk via the private financial system.
- *Izquierda histórica* (PC, IC, PH, Socialistas Allendistas): From "all forms of struggle" to an electoralist "Pacto por Omisión" and political and electoral subordination to the Concertación.

- *New radical Left* (SURDA, FS, Generación 80, MPT): From conceptions of autonomy and bottom-up organizing to animating society-wide
  struggles.
- *Izquierda social*: From the combative antidictatorial popular subject (*sujeto popular*) of the past to overcoming apathy, distrust, and exclusion in
  the midst of governmental cooptation, drug trafficking, and mall culture,
  the shifting terrain of the modern popular subjects and their identity
  (Cabalín, 2008).

The overview presented here underscores the extent to which capitalist
expansion and the Left's own shortcomings have left old and new sectors
of Chile's exploited, oppressed, and dispossessed without adequate political
voice and representation. The current disarray of the Chilean Left is clearly
depicted by the cul-de-sac it found itself in after the December 2009 presidential elections. While the *izquierda permitida* and the historical Left, the
CP and the CUT, called for voting for the Concertación's Eduardo Frei as the
"lesser of two evils," large portions of the radical, historical, and social Left
called for abstention or annulling the votes cast. The net result of these efforts,
however, was the electoral victory in January 2010 of Chile's right-wing coalition, Alianza por Chile (Alliance for Chile, AC), led by billionaire Sebastián
Piñera, the first time in more than fifty years that Chile's reactionary Right
gained control of the state apparatus via elections.

Izquierda Permitida: From "Deepening Democracy" to Servants of Transnational Capital

The change in the "class character" of the PS, PPD, and PRSD has been the
outcome of a complex process that began before 1990 (see chapter 4 in Petras
and Leiva, 1994). The main mileposts in such a metamorphosis have been (1)
the conceptual realignment of these parties with respect not only to "democracy" but more centrally regarding the pivotal role attributed to transnational
capital in forging a twenty-first-century path toward modernity; (2) the upward socioeconomic mobility experienced after 1990 by key *izquierda permitida* leaders as they scaled up from jobs with opposition NGOs and think tanks
in the 1980s to government and ministerial posts in the early 1990s, to be
later recruited to the board of directors of U.S., Spanish, Canadian, and other
foreign and domestic transnational mining corporations, privatized public
utilities, banks, institutional investment funds, private health- and social-se-
curity-management firms (the ISAPRES and AFPs created by Pinochet), and
new corporations granted lucrative concessions to operate toll highways and

the new Transantiago urban bus system; and (3) stints of varying length in the international development and techno-political complex made up by the Inter-American Development Bank, OAS, World Bank, UNDP, ILO, IMF, and ECLAC, all of which have been increasingly staffed at the top by former Concertación ministers and technocrats.

If, thanks to mid-1970s "socialist renovation," these parties finally embraced the centrality of "bourgeois rights," since then both the Socialist Party and the Party for Democracy continued undergoing a major political realignment. The Socialist Party, under the leadership of Camilo Escalona, further shifted to the right, extolling capitalist globalization and modernity and its alliance with the PDC. In a long historical arc, it has gone from defending armed struggle in the late 1960s, to the process of socialist renovation of the 1970s and 1980s (Barros, 1986), to the strategy of "deepening democracy" chronicled by multiple authors (Loveman, 1993; Roberts, 1998), to finally fully embrace transnational capital and global capitalism as the motor force of history. The PPD also went through its own metamorphosis, advancing from a purely instrumental party created in 1987 for the 1988 plebiscite to becoming the political representative of a new cosmopolitan liberal professional class seeking to break Chile's elite-dominated system of status and upward mobility, which to their disadvantage has been traditionally based on family connections rather than academic or professional merit. The links between the PPD and the think tank Corporación Expansiva, denominated as the secret fifth political party of the Concertación, have become closer, and both PPD and Expansiva represent the vision of this new cosmopolitan, sophisticated, and technically savvy professional class (Corporación Expansiva, 2007).

Beyond just co-opting the "other Left," the *izquierda permitida* has played an important generative role. While with one hand it seeks to erase the tradition of critical thinking that, among other things, placed the question of how surplus is produced, appropriated, and distributed at the center of analysis, with its other hand it has sought to produce a new social imaginary and rationality to legitimize and regulate the new regime of accumulation initially structured by laissez-faire neoliberalism. Its ability to engender a project for a new form of governmentality and new forms of subjectivity is where its key historical contribution lies. Over the past two decades, not only has it failed to "touch the capitalist system's inner metabolism through reforms" (Bellamy Foster, 2008: 13), but on the contrary it has facilitated the further expansion and hegemony of transnational capital over society. In this sense, the "success" of twenty years of government by the *izquierda permitida* paved the way for the triumphant return of Chile's right-wing and capitalists to direct control of the state apparatus in 2010.

The Historic Left: From "All Forms of Struggle" to a "Pacto por Omisión" with the Concertación

If the Socialist Party traveled down the long and winding road of political realignment, the same can be said about the PC and its allies in the Juntos Podemos Mas coalition (the IC, PH, and Allendista Socialists).

In the early 1980s, the PC adopted the political line that "all forms of struggle" were valid in the fight against the Pinochet military regime. This decision broke with the PC's historical commitment to the "peaceful road" and endorsed the 1983 formation of the Frente Patriótico Manuel Rodríguez (Manuel Rodriguez Patriotic Front, FPMR). With a leadership composed of an experienced military cadre, many of them graduates from military academies in Cuba and the former GDR and with combat experience in Nicaragua, the FPMR carried out spectacular armed operations against Pinochet. Before 1990 the person in charge of military affairs for the PC was Guillermo Teiller, the current president of the party, elected in December 2009 to Congress thanks to the "Pact of Omission" signed with the Concertación.

During much of the 1990s and early 2000s, the PC sought to conform a broad anti-neoliberal block without really engaging in its own process of self-criticism and renovation of its strategy. Like many of the other political parties of the Chilean Left, during these years the PC was long on rhetoric, quick on ensuring party control of social organizations, and weak on constructing from the grassroots up. Many left the PC during these years, frustrated with its leadership. Those who did not move right to join the PPD moved to the left, into either the Fuerza Social Democrática or independent communist organizations, or became active in social organizations and their communities without formal links to party directives.

Moderate electoral victories (Juntos Podemos [JP] obtained 5.34 percent of the vote in the 2005 presidential elections), a reactivation of the trade union movement and the CUT after 2003, the emergence of combative social mobilizations after 2006, and growing signs of discontent with the Concertación, particularly after the fiasco of reorganizing bus transport in Santiago through Transantiago, gave the PC the impression that its efforts were bearing fruit (Partido Comunista, 2009). These expectations, however, were dashed when the PC and JP negotiated a "Pact of Omission" with the Concertación coalition for the December 2009 congressional elections. Negotiated over many months, the pact stipulated that the Concertación would omit itself from presenting candidates in agreed-upon districts. The "empty" slot would be filled by a JP candidate who in a two person race against a right-wing candidate would presumably also be supported by Concertación votes. Four PC and one IC candidate ran under this formula, and three of the five were eventually elected to Congress. Such an agreement, it was argued, was necessary to overcome the PC's unjust political exclusion sanctioned by the binomial electoral system established by the 1980 Pinochet constitution and endorsed by the Concertación after 1990.

Many political observers, including members of the PC, decried this agreement, pointing out that instead of contributing to an independent left alternative, the PC had ultimately decided to subordinate itself to the Concertación. PC leaders countered that this was just a tactical alliance to end political exclusion (Flores, 2008). Only time will tell whether the PC's gamble paid off and whether sacrificing the Left's autonomy for achieving representation in a discredited and captive Chilean Congress was worth it. Either Teiller and the PC leadership made the correct tactical choice, or, despite assurances to the contrary, the PC has entered into a new level of political subordination to the Concertación, further confirming its inability to envision politics beyond electoralism (Montecinos, 2008a).

A New Radical Left, Still in Gestation

The post-1990 historical context also brought to life new political conceptualizations and practices that can be grouped under the all-inclusive and imprecise category of a "new radical Left." Four very different major streams flow within this sector undergoing rapid changes: the Movimiento SurDa, Fuerza Social y Democrática (FSD), Generación 80 (G-80), and the recently formed Movimiento de los Pueblos y Trabajadores (MPT). Despite differences among them, all share a common assessment that can be summed up as the understanding that previously existing "party-based knowledge has been profoundly undermined by its incapacity to solve with efficacy the challenge of constructing a social base and strength under the new conditions" (Ruiz, 2002: 13). Despite their differences, they all share four characteristics: (1) they are critical of hierarchical or vanguardist strategies for building the Left and the popular movement; (2) they are extremely critical of the Concertación and do not see it as progressive force but rather as the political instrument of the new capitalist bloc in power; (3) though participating in student federation and trade union elections, their strategy is one of building popular power and popular mobilization from the bottom up, through direct action and the activity of social organizations; and (4) they all lack national-level political representation. Despite this commonality, and limited joint actions in the past between SurDa and FSD, no preestablished path of convergence among them currently exists, though the outcome of the January 2010 runoff elections will certainly encourage renewed efforts.

What about the "Old" Revolutionary Left?

Before 1990 three main organizations had embraced a politico-military strategy in Chile. The Movimiento de Izquierda Revolucionaria (Movement of the Revolutionary Left, MIR), founded in 1965, suffered heavy repression under Pinochet and experienced a series of divisions in 1985 from which it never fully recovered. Today "*mirismo*" remains alive in six to eight organizations and collectives that have limited practical, intellectual, or political weight. The second organization was the Frente Patriótico Manuel Rodriguez (FPMR) founded in 1983. The Frente split during the late 1980s into two main wings, the Frente Patriotico Autónomo, which broke with the PC, and the Movimiento Político Manuel Rodriguez, which remained closely linked to the PC for a while. Like "*mirismo*," "*rodriguismo*" is splintered into myriad collectives and fractions, also of limited influence. The last formation was the Fuerzas Rebeldes y Populares Lautaro, an outgrowth from MAPU, which was effectively liquidated during the 1990s by the Concertación-led security forces. In sum, the "old" revolutionary Left has not been able to sum up its historical experience in a forward-looking manner. Nonetheless, some former militants remain active in different types of social organizations, workplaces, and communities. From this praxis, but mostly from the lessons being provided by contemporary social struggles of workers, indigenous people, students, and urban poor, the synthesis of old and new radical strategies, conceptions, and aspirations is taking place. It is from these efforts that the new post-neoliberal radical Left is being forged.

La Izquierda Social

Battling the devastating effects upon daily life of spatial segregation, poverty, and lack of opportunities, these small-scale initiatives (a community library, a youth cultural group, local environmental activism against dumps) keep the utopian dream of social justice through self-reliant collective action alive, reaffirming the construction of a popular identity and dignity in the midst of a vastly transformed society. Increasingly pressured by apathy, consumerism, drug trafficking, and carefully conceived government programs aimed at co-opting local leaders and entrenching a new political culture of market-based self-care, these local initiatives constitute the front lines in the cultural and ideological battle against the dominant ideology. Local activists and leaders, outside of party directives, uphold collective action in many working-class urban and rural communities. Capitalist modernization and government programs have significantly weakened the historical links of solidarity and trust-based networks within communities that in the past created the strong bonds that fueled local social movements, working-class identity, and political radicalization. In addition to government social programs aimed at neutralizing autonomous social organizations, and the growing presence of drugs and narco-trafficking in poor neighborhoods, at least in Santiago, these initiatives face the changes brought about by expansion of new subway and bus transport networks, urban toll highways, and malls that have profoundly deterritorialized and reterritorialized working-class and popular sector sociability and identity construction. Instead of hanging out in the street corners of their *población*, where in the past localized identities and solidarities were constructed in a bounded territory, new developments such as the metro, large supermarkets, nearby malls, and high-speed highways have shifted the places of socialization. Even for working-class and poor urban youth, who before lived in relatively isolated socio-spatial territories, now access to the mall, the video arcade, or the local cyber stall have come within reach. In the process, identity is not constructed just on the basis of demands for housing or better wages and working conditions, but increasingly "the popular historical-political subject, initially constituted on the basis of demands to occupy a place in the city, today is a subject that makes claims to occupy a space in society and the market in equal conditions as the rest" (Cabalín 2008: 67).

Concertación spokespersons proudly tout access by the poorest sectors of society to new forms of consumption as proof positive of the success of their project of globalized modernity. What all these changes have brought about is the fracturing of the old forms of identity construction and consciousness and the establishment of new ones (Cabalín, 2008). While the *izquierda histórica* has not fully come to terms with this process, and the new radical Left at least is aware of the new basis for identity construction, the only presently existing antidote to these effects is the disjointed initiatives deployed by the broad *izquierda social*. Without a broader political project within which to frame such initiatives, the efforts by the *izquierda social* continue to remain local and testimonial in character, with limited counter-hegemonic scope. Nonetheless, in neighborhoods such as La Victoria, La Bandera, El Bosque, and La Pincoya, and in many rural communities throughout Chile, the inexhaustible capacity of people for self-organization and collective struggle still survives.

Fissures in the Foundations

Despite the hagiography, the facade of Latin America's "most successful transition" shows deepening crevice lines spidering across its economic, political, and ideological foundations. The Chilean model (as well as much of the previous scholarship on the Left) is showing its shortcomings. The most significant of these fissures are:

1. The profusion of objective and subjective indicators attesting to the growing crisis of legitimacy of the political system based on Pinochet's 1980 constitution embraced by the *izquierda permitida*.

2. A persistent slow-down in the rate of economic growth and fragility of the most dynamic export sectors of the current regime of accumulation.

3. The falsification of official poverty statistics and failure of the *izquierda permitida* to reduce ever more extreme levels of inequality.

4. The appearance of massive and combative extra-institutional social mobilizations after 2006, displaying a growing autonomy of social organizations from state-sanctioned forms of co-optation and political control by Concertación political parties.

5. A society-wide crisis of political representation, most seriously evident in the case of the younger and more exploited and oppressed sectors of society.

6. The end of the Concertación's and *izquierda permitida*'s own political cycle—the exhaustion of its political imaginary and political discourse, prefigured by the coalition's plummeting ability to ensure loyalty, internal cohesiveness, and discipline in the lead-up to the December 2009 elections. In the course of 2008–2009, important Concertación political figures jumped ship and abandoned the coalition. On the right, Senator Fernando Flores and former deputy of the PPD Jorge Schaulson created a stillborn Chile Primero and joined the right-wing Alianza por Chile; Senator A. Zaldivar from the PDC also left the coalition to run as an independent; Senator Carlos Ominami, former minister of economics under Aylwin, and his son, deputy Marco Enríquez Ominami, both from the Socialist Party, abandoned the PS and ran as independents. At the same time, other socialist leaders—Jorge Arrate, former minister of labor under Eduardo Frei Ruiz-Tagle, and Senator Alejandro Navarro—abandoned the Socialist Party to run as separate leftist presidential candidates. The broader exhaustion of the political cycle is also evidenced by the lack of generational renewal in the political class, who chose the same depleted, dog-eared and unappealing standard-bearers for the 2009 presidential elections as Eduardo Frei Ruiz-Tagle and Sebastián Piñera.

By themselves, these elements certainly do not configure a generalized crisis in the system of domination, but they do indicate that the old forms that worked so well to engender the "intellectual, political and moral leadership over society" by the bloc in power are rapidly loosing efficacy and must be replaced. Hence, a new period has opened up marked by increased jostling and competition among the different political actors, each of them testing new imaginaries, discourses, and programs to see which are best capable of gaining elite endorsement, middle-class allegiance, and working-class acquiescence.

The election of Sebastián Piñera and the right-wing coalition that supported Pinochet in the January 2010 presidential runoff elections will not prevent these six crevices from expanding or eliminate the urgent need for shoring up capitalist hegemony over society. Elite negotiations and the ability of existing politics and political parties to contain and eventually repair these six fissures will define the repositioning of the different components of the Chilean Left for the next decade. The negotiation for a new social and political pact that will unfold in 2011—to replace the exhausted pact crafted at the end of the 1980s between the military, the bourgeoisie, and the civilian political class, which laid the foundations for a transition to a civilian regime after 1989—will further reveal the class allegiance of Chile's *izquierda permitida*. Though a full account of how each of these fissures will develop and interact with one another is beyond the scope of this chapter, a brief sketch shows the magnitude of the challenge that the Chilean ruling classes, its political system of representation, and Chile's exploited and dispossessed will face in the coming years.

A Crisis of Legitimacy of Political Institutions

Measured by public opinion surveys, subjective indicators reveal high rates of disapproval and distrust of institutions like Congress and political parties, and weak support for democracy as "the best system of government under any circumstances." Objective indicators such as extremely low and decreasing levels of participation in elections especially among younger potential voters, as well as the rising number of purposefully annulled and blank votes cast, are also dire warning signs of political malaise and loss of legitimacy of the main political institutions of the country.

The gap between the population entitled to vote and those officially registered to vote, for example, rose from 1 million in 1990 to 3.1 million in 2005. A political scientists linked to the Socialist Party and the liberal technocratic Corporación Expansiva remarks,

> It is useless to point out that in 2009 this gap is even more dramatic. . . . When one takes into account as an indicator of disaffection that those who have not registered to vote, along with those who annul their vote or vote blank, in addition to those who abstain, represented back in 2005 57.42 percent of those registered in the electoral rolls, this becomes an alarming figure that assesses with rigor the legitimacy of election events. Naturally, today, these figures are even more insufferable. (Joignant, 2009)

In the 2008 municipal elections, the number of annulled and blank votes reached 12.33 percent, a number larger than the number of votes cast for many of the main political parties, including the PRSD, PPD, and PS, and very close to what the PDC, the largest party in the Concertación, individually obtained (Montecinos, 2008b). In the presidential and parliamentary elections of 1989, 35 percent of young adults in the eighteen to twenty-nine age group voted; by 2005 this proportion had fallen to 8.95 percent (*Revista Qué Pasa*, 2009). Overall, 30 percent of Chileans eligible to vote have not registered.

The country's key political institutions for channeling citizen decision making, Congress, the Judicial power, and political parties, consistently receive extremely negative assessments. Polls carried out by Universidad Diego Portales, El Mercurio Opina S.A., and FLACSO show that Congress and the Judidical power have a credibility rating below 17 percent, while political parties rate below 9 percent. The crisis of legitimacy has escalated over the past decade, despite the *izquierda permitida*'s best efforts and its newfound respect for "bourgeois rights."

Exhaustion of the Regime of Accumulation

Thirty-five years after the start of Chile's neoliberal counterrevolution, Chileans remain convinced that the state must play a leading role in the economy and society. In its Fourth National Survey carried out in 2008, the Universidad Diego Portales found that 70% of respondents want a greater role of the State in the ownership of banks and public utilities. Of those polled, 71.6 percent want the state to own public utilities and 65.7 percent want a state-owned social-security management firm (AFP). Likewise, 58.1 percent believe public transport should be state-owned, 52.3 percent support universities being publicly owned, and 51.9 percent endorse the idea of state-owned supermarkets (*Nación*, 2008). Mystified by the "statism" of Chileans, some newspapers reporting these results emphasized the "growing gap between Chileans and the political class" (Rebolledo, 2008).

Fraudulent Success in Poverty Reduction, Inability to Combat Inequality

A central claim by the *izquierda permitida* over the past two decades has been that in the proper dosage, the mix of market-friendly pragmatism with innovative social policies have been extraordinarily successful in reducing official poverty from 38.6 percent in 1990 to 13.7 percent in 2006 (MIDEPLAN, 2007), a rate much lower than OECD member Spain. As *izquierda permitida* policy makers have gloated *urbe et orbi*, "We are uncertain if there is another experience where the poorest people had had such progress over the last 14 years" (Ottone and Vergara, 2004: 3). Allegedly, such historical exceptionalism is the product of Chile's dynamic export growth cum government-sponsored social programs so that "new bridges of social inclusion have been created for those who have less, specially through the *Chile Solidario*" (Ottone and Vergara, 2004: 3).

Yet serious questions about the government's poverty figures have emerged, and the "historical exceptionalism" of Chile's poverty reduction seems to have statistical feet of clay.

Some have called for the need to recalculate the official poverty line, raising it from two to three and half times a minimum food basket used in official calculations. If the official poverty line is raised from a monthly income of around $43,500 Chilean (approx $65 U.S.) to $115,000 ($184 U.S.) as some authors suggest, the percentage of the population living in poverty would rise to over 70 percent of Chile's population (Claude, 2002). In fact, the Chile office of the International Labor Organization, using a poverty line set at $250,000 ($575 U.S.) as defined by the government-appointed Consejo para la Superación de la Pobreza (Council for Overcoming Poverty), calculates a much more realistic figure for actually existing poverty: if only household work income is considered *41.8 percent of all Chilean households are below the poverty line!* When all sources of monetary income are considered (including government transfers), *33.2 percent of Chilean households are below the poverty line*, exactly three times higher than MIDEPLAN's official 2006 figures of only 11.3 percent (Reinecke and Valenzuela, 2008).

The fraudulent methods used by government and ECLAC statisticians to misrepresent actually existing poverty rates by directly manipulating indicators have been denounced by former Instituto Latinoamericano de Planificación Económica y Social (Latin American Institute for Economic and Social Planning, ILPES) researcher Juan Pablo Moreno. According to him, statistical manipulation also misrepresents the real levels of existing inequality. The dispute about Chile's real level of poverty is not only methodological. The most serious challenge to government figures on poverty has come from Juan Pablo Moreno, a former professor and researcher at ECLAC and the Latin American Institute for Social and Economic Planning (ILPES), precisely the institution subcontracted by the Chilean government to process the data from MIDEPLAN surveys. Moreno has accused that the Finance Ministry, MIDEPLAN, and ECLAC have purposely and blatantly manipulated data to present a much rosier picture. The fraud involved a two-step operation. First, eliminating the richest five thousand families from official calculations, notwithstanding that these receive 37 percent of monetary income. Then, co-efficients for the item "income from property and capital" in the Banco Central matrix were undervalued by 99.88 percent ($34.8 billion U.S.) (Moreno, 2008). Regarding the 10/10 inequality index that estimates the ratio between the income of the richest and the poorest 10 percent of families, instead of showing a decline to only 31.3 times as the government claims, Moreno and others contend that if undistorted figures are used the decline in inequality vanishes. Income inequality in Chile has not declined but increased, and the ratio between the income of the richest 10 percent of families to the poorest 10 percent climbed to 80.2 times under the governments of the *izquierda permitida*.

Massive Social Mobilizations after 2006

In November of 2008, forestry workers led by the Confederacion National de Trabajadores Forestales blocked access and occupied four industrial plants in Horcones, Cholguán in Yungay, and Nueva Aldea belonging to Bosques Arauco, all in Chile's southern Bio Bio region. Their main demand is a minimum wage of $250,000 Chilean per month ($460 U.S. at today's exchange rate) "for all workers regardless of how modest their job might be" at the same time that the conglomerate owning the plants called on the government to "restore the rule of law in the region" (*Tercera*, 2009). With Piñera and the former collaborators of the Pinochet dictatorship in office, such calls will be much more expeditiously answered than under Bachelet.

This mobilization by forestry workers is but the latest in a string of ever more militant and massive forms of collective action that have emerged after 2006. These protests involving workers from both the private and the public sector, high school and university students, indigenous communities, and urban dwellers share at least two traits that trigger a growing concern among Chile's elites and the political class in its service: (1) they have become more "political" in the sense that they link specific demands to denounce the overall economic and political model existing in Chile; and (2) they have gained an important level of independence from the Concertación, the *izquierda permitida*, and even political parties of the historical Left. Thus mobilizations by high school and university students and forestry, salmon, and copper workers, along with the growing rebellion and coordination by Mapuche indigenous communities, have caught the political class and the business elites by surprise. One of Piñera's main campaign promises was to put an end to such "lawlessness" and restore a favorable investment climate and entrepreneurial values throughout society. Not only have these mobilizations evidenced the emergence of new forms of consciousness and collective action, but they have also shown themselves to be initially impervious to the social-control strategies deployed by the *izquierda permitida* and Piñera governmental apparatus. Long gone are the days of 1990, when Labor Minister René Cortázar could boast that the allegiance of over 80 percent of all social leaders to the Concertación assured the government's ability to deliver social quietude.

Though they have achieved limited political victories so far, these mobi-lizations demonstrate to other sectors that combative collective action can be effective for achieving immediate economic demands. Furthermore, the high school student mobilizations of 2006 and 2007 (colloquially known as *la revolución pinguina*), those of subcontracted copper workers, the ongoing struggle of Mapuche communities against landowners and lumber companies in southern Chile, and the massive high school and university student mobi-lization of 2011 demanding a quality public education and the elimination of the profit motive in the educational system all prove how truly utopian and ideologically driven were the claims of *izquierda permitida* intellectuals who in the late 1990s decreed that Chile's modernization had forever banished such "antiquated forms" of participation. In their Eurocentric and modernist fantasy, protests, demonstrations, mass assemblies, rallies, and mass occupa-tions, been historically replaced by more modern forms "of being in society" such as consumption, trawling the internet, or watching CNN (Brunner, 1996; Tironi, 1997). They also indicate that despite the shortcomings of the political parties and the Left, the mass movement has been on the ascent and will continue this upward flow at least for the immediate future.

Crisis of Representation

As the late Nelson Gutiérrez, a historic leader of the MIR, stated in 2005, "Wage earners, workers, Chile's poor and excluded have neither the right nor the possibility of entering into those areas where real political power is contended. Political struggle is an affair that corresponds only to bourgeois exclusivity" (Gutiérrez, 2005: 13). The majority of the population is de jure and de facto excluded from intervening in national decision making regard-ing policies that determine the production, appropriation, and distribution of economic surplus. Though periodically invited to choose among a list of candidates narrowly limited by Chile's binomial electoral system and fully committed to ensure the continuity of the current system, the Chilean people don't even have the consolation prize of tokenism. No peasant, no worker, no union leader, or member of indigenous peoples is a member of Congress. No housewife, no urban youth, no informal-sector workers, or retired person has had access to a seat in Chile's legislature. As one commentator put it, "We have the honor of being at the top of the list of countries with one of the most classist Congresses in the world" (Pefaur, 2008).

The Exhaustion of the Concertación's Historical Cycle

The final crack in the political economic foundations of the current order is that, after twenty years of Concertación administration, the coalition finally ran out of gas. What gave it its wings, credibility, and coherence—the epic narrative about its role in the conflict between dictatorship and democracy (which conveniently erased the role played by the Chilean popular resistance and its combatants)—no longer resonates. "The cement that we had at the birth of Concertación has shattered" (Joignant, 2009). The result has been increasing political disarray, confusion, and petty battles among party dinosaurs over congressional spoils and slots, with the enhanced personal influence and status they offer. All of this encased a recalcitrance of Jurassic proportions by the old generation to step out of the limelight and give space to a younger leadership.

Before the January 2010 electoral defeat, *izquierda permitida* pundits suggested relaunching the Concertación, no longer aligned along the dictatorship-democracy axis but upon a new *idée force*. The trouble was that they could not seem to find the right one. Some suggested the healing powers of the "citizenship society" banner that Michelle Bachelet attempted to unfurl at the beginning of her administration. Others argued for "a democracy of proximity," or "circuits of acknowledgement," as a way of relaunching a refurbished "politics of recognition" (Águila, 2005; Díaz-Tendero, 2005; Joignant, 2009), while making every effort to further distance themselves from any notion that could be misconstrued as a return to the "prehistoric" politics of redistribution. All proved to be nothing more than vain attempts akin to rearranging deck chairs on the Titanic. The Concertación and the *izquierda permitida* have entered into a terminal crisis. The fundamental reason for their demise is that instead of merely symbolic or cosmetic adjustments, Chilean society needs to find a way to construct a real participatory democracy and economy, something that, given their embrace of transnational capital's modernizing allure, the Concertación and the *izquierda permitida* have shown themselves incapable of providing, even after twenty years in office.

Conclusion

Chile starkly illustrates how the conditions of existence of recomposed working classes under the new regime of accumulation have been successfully institutionalized with the active participation of the *izquierda permitida*. In Chile, as under Lula's Brazil and Vázquez's Uruguay, the *izquierda permitida* has contributed to consolidating the new system of domination. Yet, despite their best efforts, the economic and political foundations of the Chilean model have begun to crumble, showing the limits of symbolic politics and the inherently contradictory character of contemporary Latin American capitalism.

A new round of elite negotiations to restore profits and economic growth as well as renew capitalist hegemony over society is at hand. The election of Sebastián Piñera in Chile's January 2010 runoff election indicates that Chile's transnationalized capitalist class will direct this process *manu propia*, relieving the *izquierda permitida* with a pat on the back and the acknowledgement of a "mission accomplished."

In such a context, forty years after his death, Salvador Allende's political stature looms ever larger. Whatever his political shortcomings, he remained to the very end true to his commitment to Chile's working-class and popular sectors and a staunch anti-imperialist. A 1972 speech still rings out the unfinished tasks of Chilean society: "We must strengthen the definitive presence of the working class in the management of public affairs, and establish new institutions, so that Chile advances according to its own social and economic reality. So that the people are able to understand for the first time that it is not from the top that a new Constitution will give them their existence as a sovereign people with dignity. This must rise up from the roots, from working people's own convictions" (Allende, 1992: 479). This task, like his hope voiced in his last speech on September 11, 1973, moments before the Air Force bombed the Moneda presidential palace where armed with an AK-47 he resisted the coup, will have to remain on hold until a new Left and a new popular social subject can fulfill his dream that "Mucho más temprano que tarde, se abrirán las grandes alamedas por donde pase el hombre libre, para construir una sociedad mejor."[1]

Note

1. "Much sooner than later, the broad avenues will open up so that a free people can build a better society."

References

Águila Z., Ernesto 2005. "Una refundación ciudadana de la política: Igualdad, identidad y reconocimiento." In *Los desafíos del progresismo: Hacia un nuevo ciclo en la política chilena*. Ernesto Águila Z., 124–40. Santiago: Catalonia.

Allende, Salvador. 1992. "Una Constitución más democrática: Discurso ante los dirigentes de la Unidad Popular." In *Obras Escogidas*. Santiago: Editorial Antártica.

Barros, Robert. 1986. "The Left and Democracy: Recent Debates in Latin America." *Telos* 68:49–70.

Bellamy Foster, John. 2008. Foreword to *The Challenge and Burden of Historical Time: Socialism in the Twenty-First Century*, by Istvan Mészáros. New York: Monthly Review Press.

Brunner, José Joaquín. 1996. "Participación y Democracia: Viejos y Nuevos Dilemas." Santiago: Ministerio Secretaría General de Gobierno, División de Organizaciones Sociales.

Cabalín, Cristián. 2008. "Identidad del sujeto popular y el impacto de los medios de comunicación en la población La Bandera." Master's thesis, Universidad de Chile, Santiago.

Caputo, Orlando, and Graciela Galarce. 2009. "La desnacionalización del cobre profundiza la crisis de la economía chilena." *Rebelión*, July 11. http://www.rebelion. org/noticia.php?id=88312.

CEPALSTAT. n.d. *Base de Datos y Publicaciones Estadísticas de la Comisión Económica para América Latina.* http://websie.eclac.cl/infest/ajax/cepalstat. asp?carpeta=estadisticas.

Claude, Marcel. 2002. *Determinación del Nuevo Umbral de la Pobreza para Chile: Una Aproximación desde la Sustentabilidad.* Santiago: Fundación Terram.

Corporación Expansiva. 2007. *Somos más, queremos más, podemos más: Innovación institucional y convivencia para el progreso de Chile.* Santiago: Corporación Expansiva.

Díaz-Tendero, E. 2005. "Iluminismo democrático versus ciudadanía sectorial: La nueva matriz social chilena y los desajustes de la acción política institucional." In *Los desafíos del progresismo: Hacia un nuevo ciclo en la política chilena*, ed. Ernesto Águila Z., 141–64. Santiago: Catalonia.

Fazio, Hugo. 2005 *Mapa de la extrema riqueza al año 2005.* Santiago: LOM Ediciones.

———. 2006. *Lagos: El presidente "progresista" de la Concertación.* Santiago: LOM Ediciones.

———. 2007. *Chile en el período de las vacas gordas: Sus grandes beneficiarios.* Santiago: LOM Ediciones.

Flores, Teresa. 2008. "Los responsables de la crisis del Partido Comunista." *Revista Principios* (October). http://revistaprincipios2008.blogspot.com/2008/10/los-responsables-de-la-crisis-del.html.

Garretón, Manuel Antonio. 2006. "La izquierda chilena contemporánea." *Revista Mexicana de Ciencias Políticas y Sociales* 196:85–92.

Gutiérrez, Nelson. 2005. "Balance sumario de la historia del MIR y su papel en la historia de la segunda mitad del siglo XXI chileno." *CorrentRoig.org*, January. http:// www.correntroig.org/IMG/pdf/MIR.pdf.

INE (Instituto Nacional de Estadísticas). 2010. *Compendio Estadístico 2010.* Santiago: Instituto Nacional de Estadísticas.

Joignant, Alfredo. 2009. "La Reinvención: Bases institucionales y estrategias generales para salir del antiguo ciclo." Santiago: Instituto Igualdad.

Leiva, Fernando Ignacio. 2005. "From State Terrorism to the Politics of Participation under the Concertación." In *Democracy in Chile: The Legacy of September 11, 1973*, ed. Silvia Nagy-Sekmi and Fernando I. Leiva, 73–87. Brighton, UK: Sussex Academic Publishers.

———. 2006. "Neoliberal and Neostructuralist Perspectives on Labour Flexibility, Poverty and Inequality: A Critical Appraisal." *New Political Economy* 11 (3): 337–59.

———. 2008. *Latin American Neostructuralism: The Contradictions of Post-Neoliberal Development.* Minneapolis: University of Minnesota Press.

———. 2012. "Flexible Workers, Gender, and Contending Strategies for Confronting the Crisis of Labor in Chile." *Latin American Perspectives* 39 (3): forthcoming.

Leiva, Fernando Ignacio, and Stanley Malinowitz. 2007. "Financialization in the Americas: Evidence and Consequences." Paper presented at the meeting of the Latin American Studies Association, Montreal, Canada.

Loveman, Brian. 1993. "The Political Left in Chile, 1973–1990." In *The Latin American Left: From the Fall of Allende to Perestroika*, ed Bary Carr and Steve Ellner, 23–39. Boulder, CO: Westview.

Mercurio, El. 2008. "Más del 20% de los mayores de 18 está en el Boletín Comercial." July 12.

MIDEPLAN. 2007. *Serie análisis de resultado de la Encuesta de Caracterización Socioeconómica Nacional (CASEN 2006): No.1 La Situacion de Pobreza en Chile, 2006.* Santiago: MIDEPLAN.

Miranda Radic, E. 2008. "Empleo y Producto 2007." *Estudios Instituto Nacional de Estadísticas.* Santiago: Instituto Nacional de Estadísticas

Montecinos, Hernán. 2008a. "Mi crítica al pacto electoral por omisión entre el Partido Comunista chileno y los partidos de la Concertación." *Critica.cl*, July 9.

———. 2008b. "Reflexiones e ideas en torno a la reciente farsa electoral en Chile." *Rebelión*, November 5.

Moreno, Juan Pablo. 2008. "Encuesta de Caracterización Socioeconómica: Cómo, por qué y quienes la falsificaron." *Rebelión*, February 13.

Moulian, Tomás. 1997. *Chile actual: Anatomía de un mito.* Santiago: LOM Ediciones.

Nación, La. 2008. "Cuarta encuesta de la Universidad Diego Portales, Chilenos quieren mas estado." *Diario La Nación*, December 19.

OIT (Organización Internacional del Trabajo). 2004. *Chile: Informe de Empleo Primer Semestre.* Santiago: Organización Internacional del Trabajo.

Ottone, Ernesto, and Carlos Vergara. 2004. "Chile: A Case of Progressive Development." *Progressive Politics* 3 (3): 1–4

Partido Comunista. 2009. "Sintesis del Informe al Decimo Primer Pleno del Comite Central del PCCH." *PCChile.cl*, March 14.

Pefaur, Jorge. 2008. "¿Es hoy una alternativa el grupo electoral 'Juntos Podemos Más'?" *Rebelión*, April 3. http://www.rebelion.org/noticia.php?id=65470.

Petras, James, and Fernando I. Leiva. 1994. *Democracy and Poverty in Chile: The Limits to Electoral Politics.* Boulder, CO: Westview.

PNUD (Programa de Naciones Unidas para el Desarrollo). 2009. *Informe 2008: Desarrollo Humano en Chile.* Santiago: Naciones Unidas.

Read, Jason. 2009. "A Genealogy of Homo-Economicus: Neoliberalism and the Production of Subjectivity." *Foucault Studies* 6:25–36.

Rebolledo, Javier. 2008. "Encuesta Nacional de la UDP: Patricio Navia 'No sabemos bien por qué los chilenos aparecen tan estatistas.'" *La Nación*, December 21.

Reinecke, Gerhardt, and María Elena Valenzuela. 2008. *Distribución y mercado de trabajo: Un vínculo ineludible.* Santiago: Organización Internacional del Trabajo.

Revista Qué Pasa. 2009. "Paradójas electorales." January 6.

Roberts, Kenneth. 1998. *Deepening Democracy: The Modern Left and Social Movements in Chile and Peru.* Stanford, CA: Stanford University Press.

Ruiz, Rodrigo. 2002. "Ascender a las raíces: Notas sobre el debate actal de la izquierda." *Surda* 9 (32): 22–28.

Schild, Verónica. 2000. "Neoliberalism`s New Gendered Market Citizens: The 'Civilizing` Dimension of Social Programmes in Chile." *Citizenship Studies* 4 (3): 275–305.

———. 2007. "Empowering Consumer Citizens or Governing Poor Female Subjects? The Institutionalization of 'Self-Development' in the Chilean Social Policy Field." *Journal of Consumer Culture* 7 (2): 179–203.

Stillerman, Joel. 1997. "Militant Trade Unionist or Happy Consumer? The Ambiguities of Working Class Identity in Post-Pinochet Chile." Paper presented to the meeting of the Latin American Studies Association, Guadalajara, Mexico.

Tercera, La. 2009. "Forestales del Biobío paralizan actividades por reajuste salarial." September 24.

Tironi, Ernesto. 1997. *La irrupción de las masas y el malestar de las elites.* Santiago: Grijalbo.

Torche, Florencia, and Guillermo Wormald. 2004. *Estratificación y movilidad social en Chile: Entre la adscripción y el logro.* Políticas Sociales 98. División de Desarrollo Social (CEPAL). Santiago: Naciones Unidas.

14

From Guerrillas to Government

The Continued Relevance of the Central American Left

Héctor Perla Jr., Marco Mojica, and Jared Bibler

I N FEBRUARY OF 1990, NICARAGUANS turned out to vote in elections that effectively ended the U.S.-sponsored Contra War against the Frente Sandinista de Liberación Nacional (Sandinista Front for National Liberation, FSLN),
even while ousting the Sandinistas from office. Two years later, on January 16,
1992, thousands gathered in San Salvador's Plaza Cívica to celebrate the signing of peace accords that ended twelve years of fighting between the Frente
Farabundo Martí para la Liberación Nacional (Farabundo Martí National
Liberation Front, FMLN) and the Salvadoran government. Similarly, on
December 29, 1996, representatives of the Unidad Revolucionaria Nacional
Guatemalteca (Guatemalan National Revolutionary Union, URNG) and the
Guatemalan government signed peace accords ending a brutal thirty-six-year
civil war. These transitions came after decades of right-wing dictatorship,
social-movement activism, violent political repression, and revolutionary
armed struggle against U.S.-supported forces. Despite great difficulties and
setbacks, as the twentieth century came to a close these movements' struggles
had helped achieve what once seemed impossible: their countries' political
democratization.

Former bastions of despotic right-wing rule and military dictatorships, the
nations seemed poised for democratic governance that could transform three
of the poorest countries in the hemisphere. Yet instead of bringing change for
the benefit of their impoverished majorities, during the 1990s and first years
of the twenty-first century, Central America's structural transformation was
marked by a pronounced shift toward neoliberal economics. The revolutionary guerrilla-movements-turned-political-parties also struggled to find the

appropriate course for confronting the new brand of transnational capitalism that has dominated globalization.

Nevertheless, following acrimonious internal divisions, the Central American Left has recently begun to make significant inroads in local as well as national legislative and presidential elections. In 2006 Sandinista leader Daniel Ortega was reelected president of Nicaragua. The following year, Alvaro Colom was elected president of Guatemala. Colom had previously been the candidate for a leftist coalition supported by the URNG during its postwar electoral debut. Most recently, the FMLN's candidate, Mauricio Funes, won El Salvador's March 2009 presidential elections. This chapter explores the role that these former guerrilla forces have played in their countries' recent histories. We document their transitions from war to peace, the rise of neoliberal hegemony, the Central American Left's divisions, as well as its recent resurgence.

Izquierda Con y Sin Permiso

The enormous transformations brought about by globalization have occasioned equally momentous changes in the Latin American Left. Thus we are sympathetic to the editors' attempts to understand these changes by creating a typology that categorizes the Latin American Left's evolution in this new era. The editors' adaptation of Charles Hale's concept of the *indio permitido* into an analogous *izquierda permitida* is an important first step in this process.

However, we argue that the *izquierda permitida* concept has important limitations. Analytically, we are uncomfortable with the concept's dichotomization of the Left (i.e., *izquierda permitida* versus *izquierda auténtica*). Within the current administrations in Nicaragua, El Salvador, and Guatemala, there are factions that range from the political center (middle-class reformers) to the Left (socialists and communists). Therefore, forces that could be considered *permitida* and *no permitida* operate within the same parties and movements. Labeling the Sandinistas, the FMLN, or a particular leader, such as Guatemala's Alvaro Colom, as part of the *izquierda permitida* or not provides little analytical leverage for understanding the current configuration of Central America's political economy. Politically, the concept of an *izquierda permitida* lends itself to the divide-and-conquer tactic of right-wing pundits, like Jorge Castañeda (2006), who have promoted the idea of a good left versus a bad left in Latin America. Unfortunately, the *izquierda permitida* concept does nothing to formulate a counter-hegemonic narrative around which center-left and left forces can coalesce for progressive social change.

Finally, the *izquierda permitida* concept can promote an excessive focus on tactical objectives, the immediate practices used by political actors, at the expense of strategic objectives, the long-term goals of these actors. This is not an issue with the editors' formulation, but rather arises from the nature of the concept that they borrow. In the case of indigenous rights, this undue attention was manifested by the legitimation of contentious political mobilization, which was labeled as the authentic *indio* space, while denigrating institutional political participation as the alleged practice of the *indio permitido*. Analogously, for the Latin American Left, the use of the *izquierda permitida* concept could lead analysts to anoint only those that seek to immediately initiate a socialist transition as the *izquierda auténtica*, while potentially mischaracterizing as *izquierda permitida* those parties that view a progressive national capitalist stage as a necessary precursor to socialism, without taking into consideration that both may be tactical decisions made to achieve the same strategic objective (at least by some in that particular constellation of forces) (Katz, 2007).

However, as Hale (2004) noted concerning the *indio permitido*,

> there is no point in trying to neatly classify this experience [participation in government] as either cooptation or everyday resistance; both are blunt conceptual tools, too focused on the practices themselves rather than on the consequences that follow. These consequences will remain unclear, in turn, until the process of Maya rearticulation begins. . . . To occupy the space of the indio permitido may well be the most reasonable means at hand [for that rearticulation]. If so, it will be especially crucial to name that space, to highlight the menace it entails, and to subject its occupants to stringent demands for accountability to an indigenous [or leftist in our case] constituency with an alternative political vision.

In fact, the Central American Left is currently in a process of rearticulation to define how it will govern in the era of globalization. Specifically, this rearticulation revolves around the historical question recently raised by Claudio Katz: Have the productive forces in Latin America matured enough to permit undertaking an anticapitalist transformation immediately, or is a progressive capitalist stage necessary to initiate a socialist process (Katz, 2007)?[1]

This is a particularly pressing question in Central America, which is among the most underdeveloped regions in the hemisphere. The three former guerrilla movements have opted for the latter response.[2] This entails building broad national coalitions with patriotic elements of the bourgeoisie and middle classes against the transnational faction of the capitalist class linked to neoliberal globalization (Robinson, 2003). These efforts are similar to the Central American Left's historical project of forming national fronts (as indicated by the three revolutionary organizations' names).[3]

Nicaragua

Since the FSLN's electoral defeat in 1990, the Sandinistas have witnessed the dismantling of their revolution's socioeconomic achievements, come under heavy criticism for acts of corruption like the *piñata*,[4] and had prominent members leave its ranks. The Violeta Chamorro (1990–1997), Arnoldo Alemán (1997–2002), and Enrique Bolaños (2002–2007) governments introduced neoliberal reforms that reversed most of the revolution's social gains (i.e., health care, agrarian reform, and education), downsized the public sector, and pushed countless Nicaraguans into informal employment.

Throughout the 1990s, the FSLN experienced the disintegration of the coalition that supported it during the 1980s. First, many mass-based organizations (labor, peasant, women, students) central to the Sandinista hegemonic project rejected the party's top-down leadership structure and became independent actors (Vilas, 1991). Second, the neoliberal reforms reduced government spending on social programs and stimulated the growth of nongovernmental organizations (NGOs) to mitigate the impact of the state's retrenchment. But this new state-society relation functioned on the premise that civil society must be independent of political affiliations, leading many organizations away from the FSLN. Third, the Chamorro and Alemán administrations instituted privatization of the public sector and reduced the state through massive layoffs. This created high unemployment rates, mainly among formerly unionized Sandinista state employees whose now-precarious employment situation hindered their political mobilization.

Schisms and Dissent within the FSLN

Also during the 1990s, the FSLN underwent a major split. Debates emerged regarding the type of party the FSLN should be and what type of opposition it should mount in the neoliberal era. Eventually, two antagonistic currents emerged: "the Democratic Left" and the "reformers." The reformers' support came primarily from intellectuals and Sandinista legislators, such as Sergio Ramírez, Dora María Tellez, and Ernesto Cardenal, who advocated transferring the struggle to the National Assembly and from there negotiating neoliberalism's implementation. Their rationale centered on the idea that the FSLN had to become a traditional political party within a democratic electoral system and that globally neoliberalism had changed the rules under which the national economy functioned.

In contrast, the Democratic Left wanted to confront neoliberalism head-on in the streets, organizing the masses to resist it. Its base of support included most social-movement organizations and a minority of the party's National

Assembly delegation. Its leadership included Daniel Ortega, Monica Balto-dano, Victor Hugo Tinoco, Julio López, and Orlando Nuñez. By 1995 the Democratic Left faction became dominant within the party, and the reform-ers split to found the Movimiento de Renovación Sandinista (Movement for Sandinista Renovation, MRS), leaving the FSLN for a brief period with only a small legislative faction in the National Assembly.

Emergence of Daniel Ortega as the FSLN's Top Leader and El Pacto

After the 1995 split, Daniel Ortega was elected as the FSLN's secretary general. But Ortega's leadership was once again questioned after he lost the 1996 presidential election to Arnoldo Alemán and his Partido Liberal Con-stituticionalista (Liberal Constitutionalist Party, PLC). Surprisingly, instead of being weakened by this challenge, Ortega consolidated power through a series of negotiations with his liberal archrival, Alemán, culminating in agree-ments known as *el pacto* (the pact) in 1999. These allowed the FSLN to regain power within state institutions by facilitating the election of its cadres to the Supreme Court, the Supreme Electoral Council, and the Comptroller's Office. However, since Alemán was notorious for his misappropriation of govern-ment resources, Ortega's adherence to the *pacto* led Sandinista opponents, the U.S. government, and former FSLN comrades to criticize Ortega as cor-rupt and authoritarian. [5]

Nevertheless, one of the *pacto*'s main outcomes was the passage of a new electoral law that facilitated the FSLN's return to the presidency. The new law allowed a presidential candidate to be elected outright with a minimum threshold of 40 percent of the vote.[6] Moreover, the new law stipulated that if the top candidate received 35 percent or more of the vote, plus at least a 5 percent advantage over the second-place candidate, then the first-place candi-date wins the presidency. If the top candidate does not reach either threshold, then the top two vote getters must do a runoff.[7]

The 2006 Elections: The FSLN and the Unida, Nicaragua Triunfa Coalition

In the 2006 election, with the new law in effect, Daniel Ortega once again ran for president. Throughout the race the U.S. government and its Nicara-guan allies made every effort to derail a Sandinista victory. Relying on the politics of fear, which they had used successfully in previous elections, U.S. officials and the Nicaraguan Right launched a campaign linking the FSLN to terrorism, the Contra war, the military draft of the 1980s, and *el pacto* to scare voters away from the Frente. Additionally, Ortega's right-wing rivals, liberal dissident Eduardo Montealegre[8] and PLC candidate José Rizo, attacked the FSLN as lackeys of Hugo Chávez.[9] Similarly, U.S. ambassador to Nicaragua Paul Trivelli repeatedly criticized the FSLN and Ortega, stating that their victory would mean "an introduction of a Chávez model here on the isthmus" (Thomson, 2006).

In contrast, Ortega campaigned under the banner of reconciliation. He put together a coalition of personalities and political parties, including former Contras, called the Unida, Nicaragua Triunfa (United Nicaragua Triumphs). Most prominently, Ortega chose Jaime Morales, a former Contra leader, as his running mate, a clear symbol of reconciliation between former enemies. Additionally, Ortega received the support of Cardinal Miguel Obando, who as head of the Nicaraguan Catholic Church was historically known for his anti-Sandinista positions.[10]

Meanwhile, the MRS went from being the FSLN's electoral ally to running its own candidate, Herty Lewites (Telléz 2001). A popular and charismatic former FSLN mayor of Managua, Lewites was expelled from the Frente in 2006 after he challenged Daniel Ortega in the Sandinista primaries. Recognizing Lewites as someone who could draw a significant share of the Sandinista vote away from Ortega, former FSLN leaders like Henry Ruíz, Luis Carrión, and Victor Tirado formed a dissident organization called the Movimiento Por el Rescate del Sandinismo (Movement to Rescue Sandinismo, MPRS), which backed the MRS and Lewites's candidacy (AFP, 2006; EFE, 2006; Lewites, 2006). In the months before the 2006 elections, the U.S. Assistant Secretary of State for Western Hemisphere Affairs Thomas Shannon publicly declared U.S. support for Lewites (AFP, 2006). Knowing that with the liberals divided the new electoral law made a first-round Sandinista victory possible, U.S. support for Lewites sought to divide the Sandinista vote and force the FSLN into a runoff against Montealegre. The strategy failed and Ortega won the election (AFP, 2006).

The FSLN Return to Power: Reconstructing the Revolution

The first decisions made by the new Sandinista government were to reinstitute access to free primary and secondary public education for all children and free health care in public hospitals for poor Nicaraguans (Morel, 2007). This was followed in 2007 with a program to reduce hunger and reactivate the rural economy called Hambre Cero (Zero Hunger). This program provides peasant families with a cow, chickens, a pregnant pig, fruit trees, seeds, and agricultural supplies. With financial support from the World Bank, Taiwan, and Venezuela, this program has benefited 32,709 families and plans to benefit a total of 75,000 families in five years. To keep the program going, each family has to return 25 percent of the investment, which is used to benefit other families (Sandoval, 2007; Taiwan Embassy, 2007). Similarly, in the cities, Ortega created a credit fund for small-business development, called Usura Cero, whose main beneficiaries are poor women (Loásiga López, 2007). Poor urban and rural Nicaraguans have enthusiastically received these programs, which the FSLN views as the reconstruction of the Sandinista Revolution.

However, the global economic crisis of 2008–2009 has limited these programs as the Nicaraguan Central Bank has already announced slow growth in the economy, largely because of decreased exports to the United States. In addition, the government has had to limit its public spending and follow a conservative monetary policy. Also, due to allegations of fraud in the 2009 midterm elections, some international donors (Sweden, Germany, the European Union) have withdrawn monetary assistance used to balance the Nicaraguan budget. Similarly, the United States suspended the disbursement of Millennium Challenge funds for poverty reduction to Nicaragua.[11] Likewise, Ortega's relationship with some civil-society organizations has been tense and confrontational. A network of twenty-four Nicaraguan organizations, known as the Coordinadora Civil, has been highly critical of Ortega's policies. Yet the FSLN has received the support of the Coordinadora Social, a network that includes organizations from different sectors of Nicaragua's civil society, including labor, consumer rights advocates, community and women's organizations, and the Union of Ranchers and Farmers.

In an effort to establish nonconfrontational relations with the United States, Ortega chose Arturo Cruz Sequeira, a former Contra, as his ambassador to Washington. However, Ortega has also reestablished ties with Cuba and Iran, sought closer relations with the Russian Federation, and joined the Venezuelan-led Alianza Bolivariana para las Américas (Bolivarian Alliance for the Americas, ALBA), firmly establishing his independence from U.S. influence. The FSLN has also reconnected Nicaragua to groups such as the Non-Aligned Movement, which allowed the country to obtain the presidency of the United Nation's 63rd General Assembly (2008–2009). Thus the FSLN has shown its capacity to maneuver internationally to maximize economic and political benefits for Nicaragua.

In the last two years of Ortega's presidency, an important question emerged in Nicaragua concerning who would succeed him after his term ended. No one within the FSLN's leadership has nearly as much support among the party's base, except for his wife, Rosario Murillo, who lacks support outside of Sandinista militants. However, Nicaragua's current constitution does not permit consecutive reelection. As a result, the FSLN decided to promote a constitutional amendment that would allow Ortega's bid for reelection. This would require either a two-thirds vote in the National Assembly to change the constitution—something that the opposition stated it would not support—or a ruling from the Nicaraguan Supreme Court that challenged the constitutionality of this electoral restriction. On October 2009, the Supreme Court ruled in Ortega's favor (Reuters, 2009). This ruling prompted the opposition to call his bid illegal and a possible victory "illegitimate." Yet the latest polls placed Ortega in first place with 47.8 percent, followed by the candidate of an alliance of dissident liberals and Sandinistas from the MRS, Fabio Gadea (12.8 percent), and in third place former president Arnoldo Alemán (5.7 percent). It is important to note that 31 percent of the electorate was still undecided (Olivares, 2011).

Additionally, important sectors of civil society, the Catholic church, and the private sector all demanded that the 2011 elections be fair and clean. Meanwhile, the MRPS was challenging the constitutionality of reelection through the electoral council, calling Ortega's bid "illegal, unconstitutional, and illegitimate" (ACAN-EFE, 2011). As a result, the 2011 electoral process marked an important moment for the Nicaraguan Left. After its victory in 2011, the FSLN now dominates the executive, legislative, judicial, and electoral branches of government, leaving very little space for any maneuvering to the fragmented Right, represented in the different liberal currents led by Alemán and Montealegre, among others. While the other Sandinista-identified groups, unable to electorally challenge the FSLN on their own, have either sought alliances with the liberals or are challenging the constitutionality of Ortega's bid.

El Salvador

Unlike the Sandinistas, the FMLN entered the neoliberal era without the benefit of having held state power. But the 1992 signing of the peace accords created huge expectations among its supporters. The FMLN's discourse at the time was triumphalist, as indicated by the way it framed the peace accords, "*¡Ganamos la paz!*" This led many Salvadorans to expect that since the FMLN had "won the peace" conditions would improve quickly. Unfortunately, while conditions in the political realm improved, the social and economic reality did not.

From 1989 to 2009 the Alianza Republicana Nacionalista (Nationalist Republican Alliance, ARENA) party used its control of the Salvadoran executive branch to implement sweeping neoliberal reforms. The structural adjustment of the economy began immediately under the Alfredo Cristiani government (1989–1994) and laid the foundation for how ARENA would govern after the civil war. Shortly after taking office, ARENA's second president, Armando Calderón Sol (1994–1999), declared that he wanted to turn El Salvador into "one big free trade zone" (*Central America Report*, 1995: 1–2). This slogan exemplified ARENA's governing philosophy during the twenty years that it held executive office. In that time, all the banks and most state-owned enterprises were privatized, with unsuccessful attempts to privatize water and health care. Moreover, under the third ARENA president, Francisco Flores (1999–2004), the national currency—the colón—was replaced by the U.S. dollar. As a result, during the administration of Antonio Saca (2004–2009), ARENA's fourth consecutive president, the cost of living skyrocketed.

Divisions among the Left

From 1992 until the first postconflict elections in 1994, the FMLN had no political representation in the National Assembly. The center-left parties that did participate were not representative of the Left's strength and could not block ARENA initiatives. Although the FMLN participated in the 1994 elections and became the country's second largest political force, internal divisions hindered its ability to form a strong opposition. Throughout the civil war, the FMLN had been a coalition of five autonomous parties, each with its own organizational structure.[12] While this compartmentalization had advantages during the conflict, in the postwar era it became a liability. In their first legislative session, seven of the FMLN's twenty-one elected deputies, affiliated to the People's Revolutionary Army (ERP) and National Resistance (RN), immediately split from the party. In exchange for leadership positions in the National Assembly, these legislators gave ARENA the necessary votes to pass its neoliberal reforms. Thus, from 1989 until the March 1997 legislative elections, both the Cristiani (1989–1994) and Calderón Sol (1994–1999) administrations faced no effective obstacles from the Legislative Assembly.

In 1995, to prevent further divisions, the FMLN reformed its internal structure by forging a single party organized around currents of thought, called tendencies. The tendencies that emerged ranged ideologically from left to right: the Revolutionary Tendency, the Socialist Revolutionary Current (CRS), the Reformers, and the Renovators. These did not come into existence at the same time and were not all formal structures within the party. While there was some continuity between the previous parties and the tendencies, they did not overlap precisely. The Revolutionary Tendency (TR) came overwhelmingly from the left wing of the Communist Party (PCS). The Renovators came primarily from the right wing of the Popular Forces of Liberation (FPL). The Reformers were more mixed but tended to come from the FPL as well. The CRS was made up primarily of the PCS and the left wing of the FPL. Despite the reforms, the FMLN subsequently experienced several more divisions.

The next factional dispute came not from the right but from the left.[13] Members of the former PCS, led by Dagoberto Gutiérrez, became disenchanted with the party's excessive electoral focus. While originally a tendency within the party, many of its prominent members left FMLN leadership positions to work in civil-society organizations. The TR has not formed its own political party, nor does it compete in elections. Instead, its members continue to work in many key sectors of society, including unions, universities, and various social-movement organizations. In early 2011 this included launching a Salvadoran citizens' movement for participatory democracy.[14]

The FMLN's most bitter split came to a head around the 1999 presidential elections. The Renovator wing of the party, led by Facundo Guardado, nominated Héctor Silva (former FMLN mayor of San Salvador) as the party's presidential candidate. This was strongly opposed by the CRS and TR. After rancorous and debilitating infighting at successive party conventions, a weak compromise was reached. The compromise allowed Guardado to run as the party's candidate with former guerrilla commander Nidia Díaz as the vice presidential candidate. When the party underperformed, Guardado resigned as the general coordinator. The Renovators eventually left the party following his expulsion in 2002.

The FMLN's latest excision, the Reformers, coalesced around several legislative deputies elected to the National Assembly in 2003. This group proposed running TV news host Mauricio Funes as the party's 2004 presidential candidate. When this failed to materialize, they nominated FMLN mayor Oscar Ortíz. But they became alienated from the party after Schafik Handal, a veteran PCS guerrilla commander, defeated their nominee. They left the party in June 2005 following the expulsion of two legislative deputies who voted for ARENA's national budget, which the FMLN opposed. The Reformers immediately started a new political party called the Frente Democrático Revolucionario (Democratic Revolutionary Front, FDR) taking seven of the FMLN's legislative seats and undermining its ability to stop ARENA's political agenda.[15]

However, the party's base rallied behind the FMLN's historic commanders and CRS leaders, Schafik Handal and Salvador Sánchez Ceren. Strategically, the CRS's short-term goal was to defeat neoliberal capitalism. They argued that this required that the FMLN remain a cadre party committed to political education of its militants, requiring their militants' active mobilization through a network of *comités de base* (base committees) and their integration with social-movement struggles. Tactically, it has meant following a two-track approach of both grassroots social-movement organizing and participation in electoral politics. The 2004 electoral strategy illustrates the CRS's plan in action. Running Handal as its presidential candidate, the FMLN added Dr.

Guillermo Mata, a popular union leader of the anti-health-care-privatization movement as its vice presidential candidate.

Underlying these factional splits, the real fight has been for the FMLN's mission, and especially whose vision of how to respond to neoliberalism would lead the party. The ERP and the RN split in 1994, as well as the Renovators' in 1999, resulted from their belief that the Left had no alternative other than to administer neoliberalism with a softer face because leftist positions were no longer viable. Similarly, the FDR faction represented a move to the right and a reorientation of the party toward an exclusive focus on electoral politics. These factions would have changed the FMLN into a mass party, deemphasized political education and the active militancy traditionally expected of cadres, and sought alliances with center and right-wing forces. Ironically, the Revolutionary Tendency's grievances have resulted from its assessment that the party has already gone too far in these directions.

Electoral Rise of the FMLN

While the confrontations noted above have been heated, they have generated only minimal negative impact for the FMLN in terms of the party's electoral performance. Conversely, the Frente's political offshoots have all "withered on the vine." The ERP and RN factions' Democratic Party failed in their first electoral race to garner the 3 percent vote minimum required by law to continue existence as a legal political party. Its founders, like the Renovators, have faded into a public obscurity broken only by their opportunistic reappearances as pro-ARENA pundits during election campaigns. Lastly, the FDR's electoral aspirations were frustrated in the 2006 elections when they failed to win enough votes to garner even a single legislative deputy, and in the 2009 presidential election the party ended up endorsing ARENA's presidential candidate against the FMLN.

In contrast, beginning with the first postconflict election, the FMLN's vote share has increased in successive contests. In the 1994 presidential elections, the FMLN backed Social Christian leader Rubén Zamora as its coalition candidate, who received 25.29 percent of the vote. In 1999 a divided FMLN grudgingly ran Facundo Guardado as its candidate and garnered 29 percent of the vote. Meanwhile, in the 2004 elections, the FMLN's presidential candidate, Schafik Handal, received 36 percent of the vote. This increase, while visible in relative terms, is even more pronounced in absolute numbers. In the 1994 elections, the FMLN received about 250,000 votes and approximately 350,000 votes in 1999. In 2004 the FMLN received more votes than it had in the previous two elections combined and more than ARENA had received to win either of these contests: over 830,000 votes.

A similar trend is evident at the municipal level. From 1997 to 2009 the FMLN governed San Salvador, the country's capital and largest city. This included electing its first-ever female mayor, Violeta Menjívar. in 2006. Moreover, from 2000 to 2006 FMLN mayors governed municipalities that together included over 50 percent of the country's population (CISPES, 2006). Likewise, in the National Assembly the FMLN's vote shares have increased significantly. The party went from being the second largest political force in 1994, beginning originally with twenty-ove out of eighty-four deputies, to having the largest share (thirty-one) from 1997 to 2006. In 2006, while the FMLN received the largest number of votes for the National Assembly (nearly 800,000), it only received thirty-two deputies.[16]

This increase continued in the January 2009 legislative and municipal elections and March 2009 presidential election. While the FMLN lost San Salvador, reputable observers argue that this was due to fraud.[17] Moreover, this loss does not overshadow the increase in FMLN-governed municipalities (from fifty-nine to ninety-six), many for the first time and in historically ARENA-controlled areas. Likewise, in the National Assembly, the FMLN won thirty-five out of eighty-four seats, giving the party a plurality in the legislative branch (Tribunal Supremo Electoral de El Salvador, 2009). Still, the party faced an uphill battle in the legislature because ARENA, in combination with two small right-wing parties, still held a majority.[18] However, in the first few months of 2010, sixteen ARENA legislators split from the party (leaving ARENA with nineteen in the National Assembly) and founded their own legislative faction, eventually forming a political party called the Grand Alliance for National Unity (Gran Alianza por la Unidad Nacional, GANA). Since then GANA has voted on several occasions with the FMLN against their former party (Escobar, 2011).[19]

The Future of the Salvadoran Left

Following the death of Schafik Handal in 2006, the FMLN's electoral strategy was renegotiated between the CRS and Reformist factions of the party. The decision to run Mauricio Funes as the party's presidential candidate, alongside Salvador Sánchez Ceren as the vice presidential candidate, is a clear example of this compromise. Running Funes as the FMLN's candidate gave the CRS two things they had previously been unable to achieve. First, it gave them the ability to overcome decades of psychological vilification of the former guerrillas, attracting about four hundred thousand new voters. Second, Funes gave the FMLN a figurehead that was not a lightning rod of opposition from Washington.[20] Transnational grassroots efforts by solidarity and Salvadoran American organizations pushing the Obama administration to issue statements of neutrality and willingness to work with an FMLN government, while initially received coolly, were successful in the crucial week before the election.[21] In contrast, the CRS gave Funes and the Reformers something that they did not have: the capability to mobilize the votes of nearly one million FMLN militants committed to major political and economic change.[22]

Once in office, Funes gave clear indications of how he would govern. His administration's first foreign-policy action was to immediately reestablish diplomatic relations with Cuba, while also making it clear that he would prioritize good relations with the United States and not join the ALBA. Domestically, Funes's first act was to make public health care free by eliminating so-called voluntary quotas that prevented many Salvadorans from receiving medical attention. Likewise, in his second week in office, Funes announced a Comprehensive Anti-Crisis Plan, which entailed a $587 million economic stimulus package through several programs. The first program created a social safety net for the poor and elderly. It included building thirty thousand new low-income homes and creating a universal basic pension for forty-two thousand senior citizens without incomes. Second, the Ministry of Education began funding free school meals and providing a free pair of shoes, two school uniforms, and school supplies for 1.4 million poor students from nursery school to ninth grade, which were purchased from small businesses. This reform also included eliminating parents' "voluntary" contributions for their children's schooling. Third, it proposed stimulating job growth through public works projects and private job growth through low-interest loans to micro-, small-, and medium businesses. It also included creating a state bank to stimulate domestic production—especially in the agrarian sector—and establishing a fund for the state to guarantee loans.

However, at the same time Funes declared that he would not try to repeal the Central American Free Trade Agreement (CAFTA), nor seek to reinstate a national currency. In sum, the Funes administration has been characterized by increased social-welfare spending to improve living conditions for the population, but no structural change. As Funes himself explained, "I have come to the presidency of the Republic not to change the system but to change the model of economic and social management, which was largely based on a model that promoted speculative investment rather than productive investment" (Soriano, 2011).

As a result, during the first two years of his administration, tensions have surfaced in the governing relationship between Funes and the FMLN—with the president and party leaders getting into high-profile public disputes. In large part, these disputes have been fueled by the president's authoritarian personal style and pragmatic ideology, but also by the huge international and domestic pressures on him to maintain the country's traditional policies.[23] And at the same time, there are immense desires and demands for revolutionary change from the FMLN's base. To date the latter has only been channeled into social mobilization as a counterweight against right-wing pressure on the new administration in a limited number of instances around key issues (Gutierrez, 2009; Mendez, 2009; Ávalos and Bonilla, 2009).

About eight months into his administration, the conflicts between the FMLN and Funes came to a head. Funes tried to turn the citizen's movement that backed his candidacy, Amigos de Funes (Friends of Funes), into a more institutionalized social movement called Movimiento Ciudadano por el Cambio (Citizens' Movement for Change). It was announced with great fanfare and a huge turnout was expected, with the president himself arriving as the keynote speaker. But it was a major flop, with sparse attendance, indicating that Funes lacks a true social base independent of the FMLN. Since then the FMLN leadership and Funes have agreed to tone down the rhetoric, meet, and coordinate more regularly, and they have achieved a more harmonious modus vivendi—where disputes are discussed privately rather than aired publicly in mutually harmful confrontations (Alegria, 2011).

Partly in response to this situation and to Funes's close ties with the United States, the Obama administration announced a highly publicized visit to the country as part of a regional tour that included only two other countries: Brazil and Chile. Obama's visit was an attempt to create a social base for Funes outside of the FMLN, not only in El Salvador but also in the United States—among Salvadoran Americans, who are now the third largest Latino community in the United States (Pew Hispanic Center, 2011). During his visit Obama announced the introduction of Plan Central America, which links the drug war efforts of Plan Mexico (Merida Initiative) and Plan Colombia. He also announced the Partnership for Growth and the BRIDGE Program, which seek to use remittances to stimulate productive investment.[24]

However, the most interesting development within the Salvadoran political scene in the last two years is the increased growth of the FMLN's autonomous power at different levels of government. This has included their local initiatives for development at the municipal level—which they have leveraged into at least one major international program. The municipalities governed by the FMLN have created a joint enterprise with Petrocaribe, the Petróleos de Venezuela (PDVSA) subsidiary, called Energia Para El Salvador (Energy for El Salvador, ENEPASA), which has begun importing cheaper gasoline into the country to slow down the rising price of gas (Alegria, 2011).[25]

However, the FMLN's most important initiatives have come out of the legislative assembly, where it has astutely managed the splits between ARENA and GANA. They have taken advantage of this split to elect an FMLN legislative leader, Sigfrido Reyes, president of the National Assembly for the first time ever. At the same time, the FMLN has secured GANA's votes on several occasions to pass important laws and reforms. These changes include a law against feminicide and domestic violence and a reform of the tax system to increase revenues by closing loopholes, fighting tax evasion, and increasing taxes on liquor and tobacco.[26] Finally, the FMLN-led legislative assembly passed a law for the protection of emigrants and their families that included input from Salvadoran Americans; it was approved unanimously in the week before Obama's visit.[27] The National Assembly also held a regional forum with the Central American Parliament and members of Central American civil society that issued what was called the San Salvador Declaration on Central American Immigrants Rights. The declaration was handed to the foreign minister for delivery to both President Obama and Funes during their meeting.[28]

In sum, relations between the FMLN and Funes are now developing in a more cooperative manner, despite the fact that this collaboration clearly has limits, as the FMLN maintains its autonomy and vision for the deep transformation of Salvadoran society that Funes does not share. The next five years are potentially historic in that the Salvadoran people are scheduled to go to the polls three times, including in 2014 to elect a new president. Today no other political party is better positioned than the FMLN to win the next few rounds of elections.

Guatemala

On January 14, 2008, Alvaro Colom became Guatemala's first left-leaning president since the 1954 overthrow of Jacobo Arbenz. This was the culmination of a long road to victory for Colom, a journey that included a shift toward the center. However, the implications for the former guerrillas of the URNG remain unclear. The Guatemalan Left has been plagued by years of power struggles and fissures, the results of both political and personal differences. Furthermore, impunity for those involved in the human rights abuses of authoritarian regimes in the past, combined with increasing levels of insecurity and human rights abuses today, continues to challenge the country's democratic institutions and the viability of any political project, especially one committed to social justice.

The URNG's current political standing is intimately tied to the country's civil war. From 1960 to 1996 Guatemala experienced a brutal internal conflict filled with widespread human rights abuses, including over six hundred documented massacres and two hundred thousand (mostly civilian) deaths. The most extreme levels of violence were directed at the majority Maya Indian population, prompting denunciations of genocide (Grandin, 2004: 3). According to Guatemala's Truth and Reconciliation Commission, government forces committed 93 percent of the abuses, while only 3 percent were attributable to the guerrillas (CEH, 1999).

The URNG emerged in 1982, bringing together four political-military organizations: the Revolutionary Organization of the People in Arms (ORPA), the Guerrilla Army of the Poor (EGP), the Armed Rebel Forces (FAR), and the Guatemalan Workers Party (PGT). At the height of the conflict, the guerrillas numbered between six thousand and eight thousand combatants, with tens of thousands of active collaborators (Jonas, 2000: 23). In December 1996, the URNG officially demobilized 2,940 combatants and a 3,000-member international political network (Allison, 2006).

Internal Divisions

After years of armed struggle, URNG leaders were confronted with transforming the organization into an effective political party. Their first obstacle was overcoming the internal divisions that had plagued the wartime coalition and threatened the party's effectiveness in the postwar period. The URNG's second challenge was that it did not hold a monopoly over leftist politics. During the war, various leftist political actors emerged, including individuals such as Nineth Montenegro and Rigoberta Menchú and organizations focused on human rights and ethnic issues such as the Mutual Support Group (GAM) and the Council of Ethnic Communities (CERJ). Despite any connections such movements may have had with the URNG coalition during the war, most emerged from the conflict as independent organizations. A third challenge was redefining the URNG's direction, especially in light of changing global circumstances. By accepting electoral democracy as the new arena for battle, the organization had to adapt its struggle accordingly, while also analyzing how to best confront neoliberal globalization.

Documents published by the former guerrillas underscore the difficulties that its leadership faced in establishing a unified party. In a 1996 document, URNG leaders lamented how wartime divisions among its four factions weakened the organization, and they issued a call for political unity to all URNG members, regardless of prior allegiances. In March 1997, ORPA's founder, Rodrigo Asturias, issued a similar appeal urging members of the organization to support URNG unity (ORPA, 1997).

The URNG's hierarchical wartime command structure became an obstacle to unity in the postwar period. After the war, no internal elections were conducted, nor did the party hold a convention to elect new leadership. Instead, former military leaders Ricardo Ramírez de Léon (who took the nom de guerre Rolando Morán during the war) of the EGP, Jorge Soto (Pablo Monsanto) of the FAR, and Rodrigo Asturias (Gaspar Ilom) of ORPA assumed command of the party (Kruijt, 2008). Without a mechanism for internal deliberation, the party's leadership structure fueled disillusion among younger leaders. Furthermore, disagreements between the three commanders exacerbated the situation, with divisions becoming even more acute following the death of Ramírez de Léon in 1998 (Kruijt, 2008; Sáenz de Tejada, 2007).

The URNG's leadership structure also impeded possible alliances with other social forces on the left. Throughout the 1990s, various organizations emerged that formed the core of the New Guatemala Democratic Front (FDNG). This coalition won six congressional seats in the 1995 elections, while peace agreements were still being negotiated (Allison, 2006; LARR, 1999). The FDNG was made up of widely recognized labor, peasant, indigenous, student, and women's organizations that potentially provided the URNG a strong constituency. However, the URNG failed to incorporate these civil-society activists into their leadership structure (Sáenz de Tejada, 2007). This hindered the URNG's ability to expand its support base and establish itself as the leading expression of the Guatemalan Left.

Electoral Performance

Divisions have impeded the construction of a strong electoral force for the URNG and on the Guatemalan Left more broadly. In an attempt to overcome this lack of unity, various political forces, including the URNG and the FDNG, created the Alianza Nueva Nación (ANN) to compete in Guatemala's first postwar presidential election in 1999, with Alvaro Colom as the ANN's presidential candidate. However, internal disagreements caused the FDNG to break from the ANN before the election. FDNG leaders accused Colom and the ANN of undemocratic practices regarding power sharing among coalition members. Nevertheless, the ANN carried on without the FDNG, winning 12 percent of the vote and finishing third overall (Allison, 2006; LARR, 1999). As part of the coalition, the URNG obtained nine out of 113 congressional seats (Allison, 2006; Sáenz de Tejada, 2007). However, the ANN's success was short lived, and the alliance disintegrated shortly after the election. This remains the URNG's best electoral showing to date.

In 2001 the URNG experienced another split when Jorge Soto, then serving as the secretary general, was defeated in the party's internal elections. Soto's faction, known as the Revolutionary Current, composed of former FAR members, accused the URNG of moving to the center, being complacent in the face of neoliberalism, and losing sight of what the Guatemalan Left should represent (Pico, 2002; Sáenz de Tejada, 2007). URNG leaders maintained that congressional voting did not indicate movement to the center but represented pragmatic decisions within the democratic system. The party leadership blamed the rift on Soto's desire to exercise hegemony over the party, as well as marginalize Rodrigo Asturias due to a history of personal rivalry (Pico, 2002). Failing to gain sufficient support for his agenda, Soto left the URNG and resurrected the ANN together with URNG congresswoman and civil-society leader Ninth Montenegro (Kruijt, 2008; Pico, 2002). Soon thereafter, Rodrigo Asturias became the new face of the URNG.

Both the URNG and the ANN had disappointing electoral turnouts in 2003. Rodrigo Asturias, the URNG's presidential candidate, obtained less than 3 percent of the vote. In the legislative elections the party received 4 percent of the vote, winning just two seats in Congress. Although the ANN did not run a presidential candidate, it faired slightly better in the legislative elections, winning six seats (LARR, 2003; Sáenz de Tejada, 2007). Alvaro Colom, who left the ANN after the 1999 election to form his own party, National Unity for Hope, came in second in the presidential race and won thirty seats in Congress (IFES, 2006). This was a devastating loss for the URNG, which received only seventy thousand votes (Allison, 2006).

The Future of the Guatemalan Left

After the war, when the URNG redirected its energies into the formal political arena, the organization rearticulated its goals. The party presaged this transition even before the war ended when it published a document devoid of the terms *exploitation, oligarchy,* and *agrarian reform,* which had frequented previous publications. The document focused on eliminating corruption, human rights violations, and the militarization of society, while advocating the construction of a new "pluricultural and multilingual nation," with a "viable and just social model" (Guerrero, 1995). Some observers saw this as a major shift to the center. One even quipped that the "comandantes of the last insurgent movement in Central America no longer talk of socialism, but rather of how to improve capitalism" (Guerrero, 1995). However, others posited that such a shift indicated that the URNG was listening to civil-society organizations and was willing to work in a broad-based coalition (Guerrero, 1995).[29]

In truth, the URNG's new agenda echoed many of the same criticisms that it had expressed throughout the war. The main difference is that the peace accords provide the legal framework for changing the system from within (Conciliation Resources, 1997; Jonas, 2000). Human rights have become a rallying point for the URNG and the Guatemalan Left as the country continues to be plagued by violence and organized crime. Approximately fifty candidates and party activists were murdered during the 2007 campaign season, including eighteen from Colom's UNE Party (Logan, 2007). Impunity for political and criminal abusers of human rights is still a major threat to Guatemalan democracy. From January 2008 through December 2010 there were 18,750 homicides in Guatemala, but the fact that less than 4 percent of the cases resulted in conviction speaks to the level of impunity that exists in the country. Furthermore, many ex-military personnel, accused of human rights violations, have become established actors in the democratic process and taken key roles in party politics. Former dictator Efraín Ríos Montt is just one example of an influential politician and congressmen with ties to massive human rights abuses. In 2007 the ANN and the URNG discussed a possible coalition. However, the URNG backed out, refusing to work with ANN's ex-military members with questionable pasts (Kruijt, 2008).

In 2005 URNG leader Rodrigo Asturias died. His death was devastating to both the party and the Guatemalan Left more broadly, as it lost one of its key historical figures. Of the URNG's three top commanders, only Jorge Soto is still alive. Soto ran for the presidency on the ANN ticket in the 2007 election but won less than 1 percent of the vote. The URNG won 2.5 percent, a figure similar to the 2003 elections. Meanwhile, Colom was elected president as a social democrat, pledging to transform Guatemala into a "social-democratic country, but with a Mayan face" (LARR, 2007).

Since his 1999 presidential bid for the left-wing ANN, Colom has shifted to the center, causing many to question his leftist credentials. However, his presidency has highlighted the immense obstacles to fiscal and social reform in Guatemala, two causes of the Guatemalan Left. Colom has introduced tax reforms, advocated increased social spending, and taken steps to combat impunity, but he has met considerable opposition in each area. Ultimately, the administration's ability to increase social spending and effectively combat impunity rests on its ability to reform Guatemala's regressive tax system. And such reforms have been strongly opposed by the powerful private-sector organization the Coordinating Committee of Agricultural, Commercial, Industrial, and Financial Associations (Cacif), whose members have historically benefited from the system, as well as conservative elements in Congress, led by Otto Pérez Molina and his Partido Patriota.

The 1996 peace accords stipulate that the tax intake should be 12.5 percent of GDP, a goal that is already below the current tax intakes of most Latin American nations. However, the intransigence of the private sector and their allies in Congress has resulted in a meager 10.4 percent and 10.5 percent in 2009 and 2010 respectively. In spring 2011 Colom conceded defeat in fiscal reform, admitting that he would abandon his attempts to reform the tax system while in office (*LAWR*, 2010b, 2011b). Guatemala currently has the lowest tax as a percentage of GDP of any Central American country (*LAWR*, 2011b). Furthermore, over 75 percent of the tax collected is indirect taxes on consumer items. Direct taxation on income and assets remains very low, resulting in one of the most regressive tax systems in Latin America (CESR, 2009).

The world economic recession exacerbated the country's bleak fiscal situation with a decline in remittances. This decline has hit the lower class the hardest since an estimated 50 percent of the income of households categorized as poor and extremely poor comes from remittances (PDH, 2009). The devastation caused by the eruption of Volcano Pacaya and Tropical Storm Agatha in May and June 2010 caused an estimated $1.5 billion in damage (*LAWR*, 2011a). These natural disasters disproportionately affected the most marginalized groups in Guatemalan society due to preexisting inequalities in access to food and adequate housing.

While Colom has taken measures to combat impunity, another important initiative of the Guatemalan Left, his efforts have been slowed by accusations of corruption and murder. His actions have also sent mixed messages about the legacy of the military. In February 2008 Colom announced that the military archives would be opened to the public, a move that would potentially provide information concerning the tens of thousands disappeared during the war and other human rights abuses (*LAWR*, 2008a). However, shortly thereafter, Colom announced the expansion of the army to "improve security and reduce violence," a move which contradicts the peace accords and the legacy of the Left (*LAWR*, 2008b). In early March 2009, Colom announced the formation of the Presidential Commission against Impunity to combat drug trafficking, organized crime, and terrorism (CEG, 2009b). A primary role of the commission is to support the UN-backed International Commission against Impunity (Cicig), which has had a mandate in Guatemala since 2007, but both commissions have to operate within the very system they must investigate, a system rampant with corruption, violence, and the powerful vested interests of those who enjoy impunity from past human rights abuses.

The Colom administration came under heavy fire in May 2009 when he and members of his administration were accused of killing attorney Roberto Rosenberg in a corruption cover-up. The accusations came from Rosenberg himself, in a video that had been recorded before his death. Political opponents and members of the private sector called for Colom's resignation. However, Colom maintained his innocence and asserted that Rosenberg's murder was part of an effort to destabilize his government and block much-needed social reforms (*LAWR*, 2009a, 2009b). Cicig's investigation concluded that Rosenberg, blaming the Colom administration for the death of his mistress and her father, orchestrated his own murder in order to inflict the maximum amount of damage to the Colom administration (*LAWR*, 2010a). The findings exonerated Colom, yet raised new questions of corruption within his administration, including first lady Sandra Torres de Colom. Cicig has since opened an investigation on the Social Cohesion Council; a government office responsible for administering social programs, which until recently was headed by the first lady. Critics maintain that the council was not sufficiently transparent in its allocation of millions of dollars of government funds.

In the fall of 2011, Guatemalans will return to the polls to elect local and national leaders. Of the current candidates, the first lady is the only one who professes leftist views. Her relationship to the president prohibited her candidacy, but the first family cleared the constitutional obstacle by getting a divorce (*LAWR*, 2011a). Despite her husband's attempt to move Guatemala toward social democracy, over half the population remains below the national poverty line and nearly 15 percent live in conditions of extreme poverty (CESR, 2009). In this dismal, and often dangerous, political environment, the Guatemalan Left continues to denounce impunity and the ills of neoliberalism while championing the defense of a broad conception of human rights. In February 2011 the URNG entered a broad coalition with sixty-four social and political organizations aimed at social, economic, and political change (CEG, 2011). The 2011 election will demonstrate whether the coalition can cooperate and mobilize an effective constituency.

Conclusion

As Nicaragua, El Salvador, and Guatemala entered the twenty-first century, they did so after enduring extremely turbulent and violent episodes that dominated their recent political history. The Left in these three nations, battered by decades of dictatorship and state-sponsored repression, finally won the hard-fought right to participate freely in legitimate elections. With greater or lesser success the FSLN, FMLN, and URNG have made the transition from political-military organizations to political parties and participants in government. In Nicaragua, while challenged by a sizable number of high-profile ex-Sandinistas, the FSLN continues to maintain the support of the bulk of the party's traditional grassroots base. In El Salvador, despite various splits, the FMLN has consolidated itself and become synonymous with "the Left," finally taking state power in March 2009. Lastly, in Guatemala, the URNG has not fared as well, but it nevertheless continues to occupy a leftist space in the political spectrum. Meanwhile, a social-democratic Left once allied with the URNG now governs the country.

Whether the Central American Left should be categorized as an *izquierda permitida* and will govern as such, or even whether this conceptualization is useful, is debatable. The moves by the United States to impede the FMLN's victory in 2004 and President Obama's hesitance to declare its neutrality in the lead-up to the 2009 elections, along with the Bush administration's 2006 attempts to prevent an FSLN victory, while labeling the MRS as the "democratic" (*permitida*) Left, is an indication that both the Frente Sandinista and FMLN are still seen with suspicion by Washington. It was only after a clear FSLN victory that the United States chose to maintain cordial diplomatic relations with the new Sandinista administration. Likewise, only after a deluge of grassroots pressure by solidarity and Salvadoran American organizations did the Obama administration make clear statements of neutrality and willingness to work with an FMLN government (Gonzales, 2009).

In fact, the Central American Left's rise to power results from a rearticulation of these forces' tactics in new circumstances, which have mobilized various sectors of Central American society, ranging from former enemies on the right to old allies on the left, and are not easily captured by the *izquierda permitida* concept. These tactical shifts, where implemented successfully, have neutralized the intentions of their right-wing adversaries and the U.S. government to impede their victories, by taking advantage of their political rivals' divisions to gain the opportunity to govern their countries. Nevertheless, the June 28, 2009, coup against center-left president Manuel Zelaya of Honduras, as well as the destabilization caused by the Rosenberg affair in Guatemala, both highlight the tentativeness of elite tolerance of even reformist projects and, more importantly, the continued fragility of democracy in the region.

In this sense, the *izquierda permitida* typology cannot fully explain the complexities of the terrain in which the Central American Left now has to maneuver to govern progressively. Therefore, we propose several criteria that future conceptualizations must incorporate to understand the Central American Left in power today. First, it must document and explain the Left's rearticulation to meet its present challenges, including making sense of the fact that within each of these parties there is a range of both strategic objectives and tactical positions coexisting, sometimes in great tension. Second, the concept must be able to differentiate the diverse tactics—formal (domestic and international institutional politics) and informal (national and transnational social movements)—that the Left can use to achieve its historical objective—a more just society with an equitable distribution of wealth and power—from a change in that strategic objective. Finally, a new typology must promote a counter-hegemonic framing of the political landscape that allows left, center-left, and patriotic national factions of the capitalist class to cohere as a viable coalition and alternative to neoliberal capitalism.

Notes

1. Katz argues that Latin America can and should initiate the transition to socialism immediately, without the need of first initiating a progressive stage of national capitalist development (Katz, 2006). We are not staking a position on this question, as it is beyond the scope of this chapter, but rather documenting the ideological debates underlying the political maneuvering taking place in the Central American Left today.

2. This is not uniform across the three movements, and there are left-wing factions within each of them that advocate for the immediate transition to socialism. While at this point those that advocate a transition to socialism through a progressive national unity phase have become dominant, this is a fluid and ongoing rearticulation of the correlation of forces that may shift in the future.

3. In Nicaragua, this was clearly the path taken by the FSLN during the insurrection and the original Junta de Gobierno de Reconstruccion Nacional. Likewise, in El Salvador it is similar to the broad coalition that the FMLN's precursors formed during the electoral contests of the 1970s, known as the Unión Nacional Opositora. Lastly, it is also the type of government that the Arbenz administration initiated during its tenure in office.

4. Prior to the transfer of power in 1990, the FSLN used its control of the legislature to pass Laws 85 and 86, which legalized properties for many Nicaraguans, mostly beneficiaries of the agrarian reform or people who lived in properties for a long time in urban centers without a title. The laws provided a legal guarantee while also compensating the expropriated owners of these properties. However, these same laws also transferred state-owned properties to some Sandinista top leaders. See Booth, Wade, and Walker (2006); Ramírez (1999).

5. During the Enrique Bolaños (2002–2007) administration, an investigation was launched against Arnoldo Alemán for using government funds for personal use. He was charged and found guilt of taking more than $7 million and was sentenced to twenty years in prison. See Equipo Nitlápan-Envio (2000); Prevost and Vanden (2006); Tinoco (2005); Walker (2003).

6. This in effect changed Nicaraguan presidential elections from an absolute majority to a minimum plurality law.

7. In Law 331, Title XI, Chapter 1, Article 145. See the Consejo Supremo Electoral's website, www.cse.gob.ni.

8. Eduardo Montealegre broke with the PLC after Arnoldo Alemán chose another candidate to run in 2006. Disgruntled, he founded his own movement and ran under a different liberal party ticket.

9. The FSLN had negotiated favorable terms for the importation of Venezuelan oil to Nicaragua, donation of fertilizer for peasant farmers, and eye operations for the needy. Ortega's adversaries called Chávez's support interventionist.

10. The support of Cardinal Obando came at the heels of the FSLN voting for a law that made abortions in Nicaragua illegal even if the life of the mother is diagnosed to be in danger. This law has led to confrontations between the FSLN and feminist organizations. See Carroll (2007).

11. Millennium Challenge funds are multiyear agreements between the U.S. government's Millennium Challenge Corporation and an eligible country to fund programs targeted at reducing poverty and stimulating economic growth and are part of the United States' ongoing polyarchy promotion strategy. The concept of polyarchy promotion is developed in Robinson (1996).

12. The five political military organizations that made up the FMLN were the People's Revolutionary Army (Ejercito Revolucionario del Pueblo, ERP), the National Resistance (Resistencia Nacional, RN), the Popular Forces of Liberation (Fuerzas Populares de Liberacion, FPL), the Revolutionary Party of Central American Workers (Partido Revolucionario de Trabajadores Centroamericanos, PRTC), and the Communist Party of El Salvador (Partido Comunista de El Salvador, PCS).

13. The TR is not a true "division" from the FMLN as its members have not publicly come out against the party and many are still militants in the party. Rather, they are a minority faction that disagrees with the party's tactical emphasis on electoral politics.

14. See http://mdp.org.sv/.

15. Not all of the Reformers opted to leave the FMLN. Among those that remained within the party are Oscar Ortíz, Hugo Martinez, and Gerson Martinez. They all continue to occupy prominent leadership roles, especially in the Funes transition team or administration.

16. The country's electoral rules provide smaller parties with residual seats at the expense of larger ones. See CISPES (2006).

17. Héctor Perla Jr.'s personal communication with a very high-ranking member of the Salvadoran Human Rights Ombudsman's Office of Political Affairs, San Salvador, February 18, 2009, and personal correspondence with members of the Salvadoran American National Association (SANA) international observers' delegation.

18. In May 2011 the Salvadoran Supreme Court ordered that these two parties be dissolved because they did not meet the minimum threshold during the 2004 presidential elections, and the subsequent law that the ARENA-led legislative assembly passed to keep them alive was ruled to be unconstitutional. See Rivera (2011): Arauz (2011).

19. For a breakdown of legislative factions, see the Legislative Assembly website on the makeup of the legistature: http://www.asamblea.gob.sv/pleno/representacion/por-grupos-parlamentarios. For information on GANA, see http://www.gana.org.sv/.

20. Héctor Perla Jr.'s personal communication with Congressman Howard Berman, chairman of the U.S. House of Representatives' Foreign Affairs Committee, and the U.S. Embassy in El Salvador.

21. Héctor Perla Jr.'s personal communication with the U.S. State Department, U.S. Embassy in El Salvador, SHARE Foundation, CISPES, and SANA.

22. This is Perla Jr.'s own estimate based on voting statistics from the 2004 presidential election (over 800,000) and both the 2006 (nearly 800,000) and January 2009 (944,000) legislative and municipal elections (as reported by CISPES, FMLN, and the Salvadoran TSE).

23. See, for example, Clinton (2009); Gutierrez (2009).

24. For the BRIDGE program, see U.S. Department of State (2010), and for Partnership for Growth, see U.S. Department of State (2011).

25. As of May 18, 2011, ENEPASA has sixty-five gas stations throughout the country, including municipalities not governed by the FMLN. See the ALBA Petróleos de El Salvador map of stations, http://www.albapetroleos.com.sv/sitio/index.php?option=com_content&view=article&id=74%3Amapa-de-estaciones-de-servicio&catid=41%3Adonde-comprar&Itemid=60.

26. The reform is not as thorough as the FMLN would have liked, and Funes used his line-item veto power to send it back to the legislative assembly, where right-wing parties including GANA have tried to chip away at what was enacted. For details, see http://www.fmln.org.sv/detalle.php?action=fullnews&id=673. For a broader discussion of the FMLN's legislative agenda and its relation to Funes and the Plan de Gobierno, see the interview with Roberto Lorenzana: http://www.fmln.org.sv/detalle.php?action=fullnews&id=678.

27. Importantly, for the first time legislators from all parties jointly visited several U.S. cities to gather input from the Salvadoran American community on how to improve the law.

28. Author Héctor Perla Jr. was an invited participant in these events.

29. For a discussion of how civil-society organizations participated in the peace negotiations, see Koonings (2002).

References

ACAN-EFE. 2011. "Disidentes sandinistas impugnan candidatura de Ortega por 'inconstitucional.'" *La Prensa*, March 21. http://www.laprensa.com.ni/2011/03/21/politica/55503.

AFP. 2006. "Estados Unidos prefiere a Montealegre o Lewites." *El Nuevo Diario*, June 22.

Aizenman, N. C. 2006. "Sandinista Aims for Comeback in Nicaragua." *Washington Post*, July 23.

Alegria, Damian. 2011. Authors' personal correspondence.

Allison, Michael E. 2006. "The Transition from Armed Opposition to Electoral Opposition in Central America." *Latin American Politics and Society* 48 (4): 137–62.

Arauz, Sergio. 2011. "Corte destituye al magistrado del PCN en el Tribunal Supremo Electoral," *El Faro*, May 14. http://www.elfaro.net/es/201105/noticias/4091/.

Ávalos, Jessica, and Alexandra Bonilla. 2009. "Presidente electo dice no estar ligado a la derecha." *La Prensa Grafica*, May 2. http://www.laprensagrafica.com/el-salvador/politica/31052--presidente-electo-dice-no-estar-ligado-a-la-derecha.html.

Booth, John A., Christine J. Wade, and Thomas W. Walker. 2006. *Understanding Central America: Global Forces, Rebellion, and Change.* 4th ed. Boulder, CO: Westview Press.

Carroll, Rory. 2007. "Killer Law." *Guardian*, October 8. http://www.guardian.co.uk/society/2007/oct/08/health.lifeandhealth.

Castañeda, Jorge G. 2006. "Latin America's Left Turn." *Foreign Affairs*, May–June.

CEG (Centro de Estudios de Guatemala). 2009a. "Informe de la PDH califica al año 2008 como el mas sangriente." *Daily Report*, January 22.

———. 2009b. "Presidente propone crear comisión contra la impunidad." *Guatemala Hoy*, March 3.

———. 2009c. "Fueron capturados supuestos asesinos del abogado Rodrigo Rosenberg." *Guatemala Hoy*, September 12.

———. 2011. "Organizaciones presenta Frente Amplio." February 28.

CEH (Comisión para el Esclarecimiento Histórico). 1999. *Guatemala Memory of Silence: Report of the Commission for Historical Clarification, Conclusions and Recommendations*. Guatemala: CEH.

Central, Redaccion. 2005. "MRS proclama candidato presidencial al sandinista Herty Lewites." *La Prensa*, August 21.

Central America Report. 1995. "One Big Free Trade Zone." February 3, 1–2.

Central/EFE, Redaccion. 2006. "Cse Proclama a Autoridades Electas." *La Prensa*, November 22.

CESR (Center for Economic and Social Rights). 2009. "Rights or Privileges? Fiscal Commitments to the Rights to Health, Education and Food in Guatemala." http://www.cesr.org/article.php?id=1039.

Chamorro, Carlos F. 1997. "The Style of an Authoritarian Caudillo." *Envio*, no. 191 (June). http://www.envio.org.ni/articulo/2017.

Chamorro, Xiomara. 2006. "La Democracia Esta En Peligro." *La Prensa*, March 22.

CISPES. 2006. "CISPES 2006 Salvadoran Elections Analysis—March 2006." *CICPES.org*, March 4. http://www.cispes.org/index.php?option=com_content&task=view&id=91&Itemid=29.

Clinton, Hillary. 2009. "'Critical Moment' for the Hemispere." *Miami Herald*, June 1.

Conciliation Resources. 1997. Accords of the Guatemalan Peace Process. http://www.c-r.org/accord-article/accords-guatemalen-peace-process.

EFE. 2006. "Lewites: Soy de izquierda democratica, seria y no confrontativa." *El Nuevo Diario*, May 19.

Equipo Nitlápan-Envio. 2000. "Despues del pacto: La suerte esta echada." *Envio*, no. 214 (January). http://www.envio.org.ni/articulo/985.

Escobar, Ivan. 2011. "Sigfrido Reyes, del FMLN, nuevo presidente de la Asamblea Legislativa." *Diario Co-Latino*, February 1.

Fienberg, Richard, and Daniel Kurtz-Phelan. 2006. "Nicaragua between *Caudillismo* and Modernity: The Sandinista Redux." *World Policy Journal* 23 (2): 76–84.

Gonzales, Alfonso. 2009. "FMLN Victory and Transnational Salvadoran Activism: Lessons for the Future." *NACLA Report on the Americas* (July–August): 4–5.

Grandin, Greg. 2004. *The Last Colonial Massacre: Latin America in the Cold War*. Chicago: University of Chicago Press.

Guererro, Gonzalo. 1995. "Guatemala: Is the URNG Moving to the Center?" *Envio*, no. 168 (July). http://www.envio.org.ni/articulo/1876.

Gutierrez, Dagoberto. 2009. "Carta Al Movimiento Popular." *Diario Co-Latino*, April 27. http://www.diariocolatino.com/es/20090427/opiniones/66175/.

Hale, Charles R. 2004. "Rethinking Indigenous Politics in the Era of the 'Indio Permitido.'" *NACLA Report on the Americas* 38 (2): 16–21.

IFES (International Foundation for Electoral Systems). 2006. "Election Guide." http://www.electionguide.org/results.php?ID=395.

Jonas, Susanne. 2000. *Of Centaurs and Doves: Guatemala's Peace Process* (Boulder, CO: Westview.

Juarez, Lester. 2006. "Condenan Intervencion De Chavez." *La Prensa*, March 4.

Katz, Claudio. 2006. "Socialismo o neodesarrollismo." *LaHaine.org*, November 27. http://www.lahaine.org/index.php?p=18867.

———. 2007. "Socialist Strategies in Latin America." *Monthly Review* 59 (4). http://www.monthlyreview.org/0907katz.php.

Koonings, Kees. 2002. "Civil Society, Transitions, and Post-War Reconstruction in Latin America: A Comparison of El Salvador, Guatemala, and Peru." *Iberoamericana* 32 (2): 45–71.

Kruijt, Dirk. 2008. *Guerrillas: War and Peace in Central America*. London: Zed Books.

Kunzle, David. 1995. *The Murals of Revolutionary Nicaragua, 1979–1992*. Berkeley: University of California Press.

Latin American Caribbean and Central America Report. 1999. "Last-Minute split in left-wing alliance." RC-99-07, August 1999.

LARR (Latin American Regional Reports). 1999. *Caribbean & Central America*. "Last Minute Split in Left-Wing Alliance." August.

———. 2003. *Caribbean & Central America*. "Berger and Colom will contest Guatemala's presidential run-off." November.

———. 2007. *Caribbean & Central America*. "Colom Wins Presidential Run-Off." November.

LAWR (Latin American Weekly Report). 2008a. "Guatemala: Opposition GANA Ruptures." February 28.

———. 2008b. "Guatemala: Colom Announces Army Expansion." September 4.

———. 2009a. "Guatemala: Rosenberg Investigation Moves at Snail's Pace." May 21.

———. 2009b. "Guatemala: Opposition Piles on the Pressure." June 4.

———. 2009c. "Tracking Trends." July 16.

———. 2009d. "Guatemala: Colom Declares National State of Calamity." September 10.

———. 2010a. "Guatemala: Rosenberg Case 'Solved'." January 21.

———. 2010b. "Tracking Trends: Guatemala Tax Take." February 4.

———. 2011a. "Guatemala: Torres Clears Initial Hurdle." April 20.

———. 2011b. "Tracking Trends: Guatemala Tax Take." May 5.

Lewites, Herty. 2006. "Somos de izquierda y somo independientes." *Envio*, no. 290 (May). http://www.envio.org.ni/articulo/3258.

Loásiga López, Ludwin. 2007. "Ortega lanza Programa Usura Cero." *La Prensa*, September 30. http://archivo.laprensa.com.ni/archivo/2007/septiembre/30/noticias/politica/218508.shtml.

Logan, Samuel. 2007. "Governance in Guatemala Increasingly Threatened by Organized Crime." *Power and Interest News Report*, October 19. http://www.samuellogan.com/articles/governance-in-guatemala-increasingly-threatened-by-organized-crime.html.

Martinez, Moises. 2007. "Giro Al Populism: Asume Presidente Daniel Ortega." *La Prensa*, January 11. http://archivo.laprensa.com.ni/archivo/2007/enero/11/noticias/politica/166744.shtml.

Mendez, Raúl. 2009. "No me he movido ni un milímetro hacia la derecha." *La Página*, May 1. http://www.lapagina.com.sv/nacionales/8112/2009/05/01/No-me--he-movido-ni-un-milimetro-hacia-la-derecha.

Morel, Blanca. 2007. "La odisea de la salud y la educación." *El Nuevo Diario*, April 19. http://impreso.elnuevodiario.com.ni/2007/04/19/nacionales/46616.

ORPA (Revolutionary Organization of the People in Arms). 1997. Statement from Rodrigo Asturias. Guatemala.

Olivares, Iván. 2011. "Ortega lidera encuesta M y R." *Confidencial*, April 17. http://www.confidencial.com.ni/articulo/3780/ortega-lidera-encuesta-m-y-r.

PDH (Procurador de los Derechos Humanos). 2009. "Informe Anual Circunstanciado, Tomo I: Situación de los derechos humanos en Guatemala durante 2009."

Pew Hispanic Center. 2011. "Statistical Portrait of Hispanics in the United States, 2009." http://pewhispanic.org/factsheets/factsheet.php?FactsheetID=70.

Pico, Juan Hernandez. 2002. "The Guatemalan Left: In a Delicate State," *Envio*, no. 252 (July). http://www.envio.org.ni/articulo/1596.

Prevost, Gary, and Harry E. Vanden. 2006. "Nicaragua." In *Politics of Latin America: The Power Game*, ed. Harry E. Vanden and Gary Prevost, 527–59. Oxford: Oxford University Press.

Ramírez, Sergio. 1999. *Adiós Muchachos: Una Memoria De La Revolución Sandinista.* Mexico City: Aguilar.

Reuters. 2009. "Nicaragua Courts Open Way for Daniel Ortega Re-election." October 20. http://af.reuters.com/article/worldNews/idAFTRE59J11820091020.

Rivera, Edgardo. 2011. "Inicia proceso para cancelar a PCN y PDC." *El Mundo*, May 17. http://elmundo.com.sv/inicia-proceso-para-cancelar-a-pcn-y-pdc .

Robinson, William I. 1996. "Globalization, the World System, and 'Democracy Promotion' in U.S. Foreign Policy." *Theory and Society* 25 (5): 615–65.

———. 2003. *Transnational Conflicts: Central America, Social Change, and Globalization.* London: Verso.

Rocha, José Luis. 2004. "¿Hacia donde ha transitado el FSLN?" *Envio*, no. 268 (July). www.envio.org.ni/articulo/2168.

Ruiz, Henry. 2000. "Henry Ruiz: The FSLN Has Lost the Strong Ethical Basis That Motivated Us." *Envio*, no. 226 (May). http://www.envio.org.ni/articulo/1422.

Sandoval, Consuelo. 2007. "Banco Mundial apoyará programa 'Hambre Cero.'" *El Nuevo Diario*, February 2. http://impreso.elnuevodiario.com.ni/2007/02/02/politica/40293.

Sáenz de Tejada, Ricardo. 2007. *Revolucionarios en tiempos de paz: Rompimientos y recomposición en las izquierdas de Guatemala y El Salvador.* Vol. 2. Guatemala: FLACSO.

Soriano, Antonio. 2011. "Presidente Funes rechaza que siga modelo neoliberal." *El Mundo*, May 5. http://elmundo.com.sv/presidente-funes-rechaza-que-siga-modelo-neoliberal.

Taiwan Embassy. 2007. "Taiwan ayuda a Nicaragua en su programa 'Hambre Cero.'" August 28. http://www.taiwanembassy.org/ct.asp?xItem=39703&ctNode=2237.

Telléz, Dora Maria. 2001. "La Convergencia es un proyecto con futuro para la nación y para el sandinismo." *Envio*, no. 236 (November). http://www.envio.org.ni/articulo/1119.

Thomson, Adam. 2006. "Ortega's Populism Battles against Long Memories." *Financial Times*, September 14. http://www.ft.com/cms/s/2/a85783c6-442b-11db-8965-0000779e2340.html#axzz1wCPuonAd.

Tinoco, Victor Hugo. 2005. "Esta crisis empezó hace siete años en el FSLN con un pacto contra la democracia y sin ética." *Envio*, no. 280 (July), http://www.envio.org.ni/articulo/2979.

U.S. Department of State. 2010. "U.S. BRIDGE Initiative Commitments with El Salvador and Honduras." September 22. http://www.state.gov/r/pa/prs/ps/2010/09/147549.htm.

———. 2011. "Remarks at the 41st Washington Conference on the Americas." May 11. http://www.state.gov/secretary/rm/2011/05/163025.htm.

Varela, Alejandro. 2006. "Ramirez augura corrupcion y populismo si GANA Ortega." *La Prensa*, January 11.

Vilas, Carlos M. 1991. "El debate interno sandinista." *Nueva Sociedad* 113:28–36.

Walker, Thomas W. 2003. *Nicaragua: Living in the Shadow of the Eagle*. 4th ed. Boulder, CO: Westview.

15

The Overthrow of a Moderate and the Birth of a Radicalizing Resistance

The Coup against Manuel Zelaya and the History of Imperialism and Popular Struggle in Honduras

Todd Gordon and Jeffery R. Webber

THIS CHAPTER CHARTS THE CARTOGRAPHY of recent Honduran political history and its imbrications with the imperial interests of the United States. In the 1990s and early 2000s, as neoliberal economic restructuring was introduced, the fabric of the Honduran social and political lefts—historically, with few exceptions, already the *izquierda permitida* counterpart to neighboring mass-based and revolutionary insurgencies—suffered terribly under the structural transformations of urban labor markets and rural economies. Plebian gang violence, narco-trafficking, mass imprisonment, and state repression were the predominant sociopolitical expressions of neoliberal reform and the poverty and inequality it deepened and extended.

Out of this desolate landscape, Manuel Zelaya, leader of a center-left faction within the traditional Liberal Party, assumed the presidency in 2006. In domestic affairs, Zelaya's limited social and economic reforms fell neatly into the policy agenda of the *izquierda permitida* as described in this volume. In the realm of foreign policy, however, Zelaya's pragmatic relations with Hugo Chávez in Venezuela and formal incorporation into Venezuelan-led regional bodies, Petrocaribe and the Bolivarian Alternative of the Americas (ALBA), signified, at least in the perception of the Honduran oligarchy and North American imperialism, a dangerous embrace of worrying counter-hegemonic trends in the region. On June 28, 2009, Zelaya was overthrown in a coup d'état by Roberto Micheletti, also a member of the Liberal Party. The coup then sought to disguise itself in the frock of democracy with fraudulent elections in late November of the same year. Porfirio "Pepe" Lobo replaced Micheletti as the chief administrator of the coup regime. Repression under the Lobo dictatorship only intensified in scope and depth. One paradoxical element of the regime shift in Honduras toward the authoritarian right, however, has been the emergence for the first time in recent Honduran history of an eclectic, popular movement of resistance, increasingly characterized by radical left ideologies and practices, under the leadership of a coordinated social-movement- and trade-union-based Frente Nacional de la Resistencia Popular (National Front of Popular Resistance, FNRP).

Neoliberal Pacification

With the end of the Cold War, the defeat of the Sandinista revolution in Nicaragua in the 1990 elections, and the ending of the civil wars in El Salvador and Guatemala, Central America transitioned from a period of state terror and guerrilla struggle in the 1980s to an epoch of neoliberal consolidation over the course of the 1990s—what James Dunkerley (1994) has called the "pacification of Central America." With its own particularities, the trajectory of Honduras largely mirrored this regional turn (Flynn, 1984; Gill, 2004; Grandin, 2006; LaFeber, 1993).

The ascendance to the presidency by Rafael Callejas of the National Party in the 1990 elections marked the earnest inauguration of neoliberal restructuring in the country. Callejas, an agricultural economist, banker, and member of one of the wealthiest families in Honduras, headed up a newly hegemonic wing of the National Party dominated by neoliberal technocrats and novel components of the externally oriented fractions of the Honduran bourgeoisie (Robinson, 2003: 127). Callejas introduced the first of three structural adjustment packages (SAPs) implemented in Honduras in the 1990s, agreeing to a range of measures advocated by the International Monetary Fund (IMF), the Inter-American Development Bank, the World Bank, and other foreign lenders. He ushered in an austerity program, consumption tax hikes, liberalization of price controls, privatization of various state-owned enterprises, and tariff reductions. These measures constituted the pillars of a wider orientation in political economy toward free markets, tourism, nontraditional exports, free-trade zones, and *maquila* (assembly plant manufacturing) promotion, an orientation that would continue under successive Liberal and National governments over the next decade and a half (Booth, Wade, and Walker, 2006: 144; Robinson, 2003: 129). The political-economy trajectory established by Callejas was deepened further throughout the course of the 1990s and early 2000s by the next two Liberal presidents, Roberto Reina and Carlos Roberto Flores Facussé, and then the Conservative Ricardo Maduro (Booth, Wade, and Walker, 2006: 145).

Within a few years of the first SAP in 1990, foreign direct investment flooded into five new government-sponsored export processing zones, as well as five privately run industrial parks, in which the majority of workers were cheap, female, and nonunionized. A *maquila* workforce of only 9,000 in 1990 ballooned to 20,000 in 1991, 48,000 in 1994, and 100,000 by the turn of the century (Robinson, 2008: 120). By 2007 value-added export earnings from the *maquila* sector amounted to $1.2 billion U.S., relative to $203.7 million in 1996. This made *maquiladoras* the second most important source of foreign exchange after family remittances flowing in from the United States. Parallel to the *maquila* sector and remittances, tourism revenue increased from $29 million U.S. in 1990 to $556.7 million in 2007 (EIU, 2008: 15–16).[1] Foreign direct investment eclipsed old records in 2007, reaching $815.9 million U.S., the better part of which was directed toward the *maquiladoras*, transport, communications (particularly cell phones), the financial sector, and tourism (EIU, 2008: 24). The same record-breaking year, however, brought with it the slow beginning of a fall in U.S. demand for Honduran-manufactured exports, as well as increased competition from lower-cost producers in Asia. While solid figures for 2008 and 2009 are not yet available, it is fairly obvious that the global economic crisis, and particularly its American dimensions, will "hit the real economy in the form of lower demand for Honduran exports, a fall in income from family remittances and reduced inflows of foreign direct investment" (ECLAC, 2009: 113).[2]

As indicated in table 15.1, in spite of an influx of foreign direct investment and positive appraisals from the international financial institutions regarding the pace and character of neoliberal reform, macroeconomic growth in Honduras over the course of the 1990s only peaked above 4 percent for one year (1997), and the decade was bookended by periods of negative growth. The next decade, though, witnessed a distinct shift in keeping with wider Latin American trends (Ocampo, 2009: 704). Together with remittances, high commodity prices,[3] and primed demand in the United States, Honduras qualified in 2005 for debt relief as part of the Heavily Indebted Poor Countries (HIPC) initiative (ECLAC, 2006: 129). The initiative is scheduled to bring $1.2 billion

TABLE 15.1
Growth of GDP in Honduras, 1980s to 1990s

	1980–1985	1985–1990	1980–1990	1990	1995	1996	1997	1998	1999
GDP	1.5	3.2	2.4	–0.1	3.7	3.7	5.0	3.3	–2.0

Source: Derived from CEPAL, 2000a: 68.

U.S. in debt relief between 2005 and 2015, some of which is supposed to go toward reducing poverty in Honduras as part of United Nations Millennium Development Goals (EIU, 2008: 17).

A brief perusal of table 15.2 will indicate that gross domestic product (GDP) accelerated quite rapidly between 2003 and 2007, surpassing 6 percent in 2005, 2006, and 2007, before tumbling with the onset of the global economic crisis in 2008.[4] In spite of high growth rates, however, social conditions at the end of this period remained abysmal. Of 177 countries listed in the United Nations Development Program's Human Development Index (HDI) for 2009, Honduras ranked 112. Of the Latin American and Caribbean countries, only Bolivia (113), Guyana (114), Guatemala (122), Nicaragua (124), and Haiti (149) registered worse results (UNDP, 2009). Seventy-five percent of the population lived below the poverty line and 38 percent below the indigence line in 1990, the inaugural year of neoliberalism (CEPAL, 2000b: 269). By 2002, just prior to the commodities boom, those figures had in fact risen to 77 and 54 percent, respectively. By 2007, in the wake of the boom and auspicious conditions for improving social conditions, poverty and indigence levels had only receded to 69 and 46 percent, respectively (CEPAL, 2009: 16).

Likewise, the figures of national income distribution depicted in table 15.3 illustrate regression rather than progress since the outset of neoliberalism, in spite of the favorable economic environment for radical redistribution between 2003 and 2007. The marginal drop in the proportion of national income going to the richest 10 percent of the population between 2002 and 2007 was largely passed on to the next highest 20 percent of income earners. The poorest 40 percent of the population still took home less of the national income in 2007 than they did in 1990, and the boom years of the 2000s actually erased some of the extremely modest gains they had made over the course of the 1990s. Even after the boom years, eleven percent of households are overcrowded, one in six people over fifteen years of age is illiterate, and approximately 15 percent of households go without an adequate sewage system (EIU, 2008: 11).

TABLE 15.2
Growth of GDP in Honduras, 2000s

	2000	2004	2005	2006	2007	2008*
GDP	4.1	5.7	6.2	6.1	6.3	3.8

Source: Derived from CEPAL, 2009: 85.
*Projected figures.

TABLE 15.3
Distribution of National Income in Honduras

Year	Poorest 40%	Next 30%	20% Below Richest 10%	Richest 10%
1990	10.2	19.7	27.1	43.1
1999	11.8	22.9	29.0	36.5
2002	11.4	21.7	27.6	39.4
2006	8.8	22.5	29.3	39.3
2007*	10.1	23.5	29.5	37.0

Source: Derived from CEPAL, 2008: 230.
*Projected figures.

Resistance, Repression, and Violent Pathologies in the Neoliberal Era

The rural and urban popular classes resisted the neoliberal assault on their live-lihoods over the 1990s and into the 2000s, but this epoch was also notable for its persistent state repression and punctuated remilitarization of politics under the aegis of the "war on crime" and the "war on gangs." Peasant movements remained an important social force in Honduran politics. Indeed, Tegucigalpa acted as the headquarters for probably the most important transnational peasant movement in the world, the Via Campesina, between 1996 and 2004.[5] Nonethe-less, the collective power of Honduran peasants to resist the reigning power structure at home began to diminish between the mid-1990s and the early 2000s as the political economy of the countryside plunged into precipitous decline. In the labor movement, banana workers—and increasingly *women* banana workers—"struggled to survive plantation closures, new production systems, and other machinations of the banana corporations—not to mention Hurricane Mitch" (Frank, 2005: 58).[6] New women's groups, worker and peasant organiza-tions, and community associations continued to emerge in the dozens over the course of the 1990s and engaged in different modes of struggle (Robinson, 2003: 132). By 2003 urban social movements against the privatization of state-owned utilities and public services were able to draw twenty-five thousand people into the streets (Booth, Wade, and Walker, 2006: 147). All the same, by the late 1990s the overarching character of Honduran political and social life was made manifest not in effective rural and urban class struggle from below but in the emergence of new and violent social pathologies among the poor and dispos-sessed (Cruz, 2010). For example, in 2006 there were 3,108 killings, a yearly av-erage of 46.2 violent deaths per 100,000 people, which exceeds by five times the global average (Mejía, 2007: 27). The gang activities associated with the booming narco-trade helped give rise to the remilitarization of the state, ostensibly as a means to ameliorate plebeian violence, but in reality a coercive guarantee for the preservation of the neoliberal order. It is only against this historical backdrop of state remilitarization that we can begin to understand the relative ease with which Roberto Micheletti organized and orchestrated the violent and repressive coup against democratically elected President Manuel Zelaya in late June 2009.

The Coup of June 2009 and Zelaya's Domestic and Foreign Policy

Early Sunday morning, June 28, masked soldiers stormed Zelaya's home, fired warning shots, and pointed a gun at his chest. They hauled him out of his house and rammed him into a Honduran air force jet destined for Costa Rica). Tanks barreled into the capital and soldiers surrounded the presidential palace, where the de facto regime, under the leadership of Micheletti, had been installed. The Nicaraguan, Cuban, and Venezuelan ambassadors reported that they were detained and beaten by security forces (Rogers, 2009; Thomson, 2009). Radio and TV stations, including CNN and Telesur, were forced off the air (Cano, 2009a). In front of the presidential palace, a celebration of coup supporters was staged. Roberto Micheletti, who had failed three times to become president through the electoral process, had achieved the de facto mantel through military coercion (Cano, 2009b).

Zelaya, a wealthy ranch owner and business magnate in the logging industry, assumed the presidential office in January 2006 as leader of the dissident Movimiento Esperanza Liberal (Liberal Hope Movement) current inside the traditional Liberal Party. His ascension to government took place roughly eight years into a significant social and political shift to the left across large parts of Latin America, and close to a decade into what has proven to be a prolonged legitimacy crisis of the neoliberal model. At the same time, Zelaya's rise to office coincided with the intensification of efforts by imperialism and the Latin American Right to turn back the clock (see Jeffrey R. Webber and Barry Carr in the introduction to this volume).

Zelaya had been a Liberal congressperson for three consecutive terms between 1985 and 1999, and he headed up the World Bank–funded Fondo Hondureño de Inversión Social (Honduran Social Investment Fund, FHIS) between 1994 and 1999. In the presidential campaign of late 2005, he faced off against National Party challenger Porfirio Lobo Sosa. The campaign pivoted almost exclusively around the issue of violent crime and youth gangs, with Lobo Sosa pledging to continue the *mano dura* approach and to reintroduce the death penalty, which had been abolished in 1937. Zelaya, by contrast, opposed the death penalty and the antigang legislation, arguing that this type of repressive framework in the past had actually exacerbated the country's crime problem. Instead, he offered vague promises of new social programs to alleviate high levels of poverty and unemployment, which he believed to be central factors driving youth into the gangs (Thompson, 2005a, 2005b).

Once in the presidency, Zelaya made some modest moves toward progressive social and economic reform. He introduced free school enrolment, raised the salaries of teachers, and made initial efforts to reduce rising fuel costs (EIU, 2008). He also increased the minimum wage by 60 percent, from $6 U.S. to $9.60 per day, apologized for the executions of street children at the hands of security forces in the 1990s, advocated the legalization of some narcotics as opposed to escalating the "war on drugs," and vetoed legislation that would have made the sale of the morning-after pill illegal (Grandin, 2009a). In the domain of natural resource extraction, Zelaya introduced mining legislation for approval by Congress that outlined stricter environmental regulations, including the prohibition of open-pit mines. A new Forest Law passed in September 2007 introduced measures to prevent further ecological collapse, designating 87.7 percent of Honduran national territory as protected area (EIU, 2008: 12). In spite of pressure from business groups and right-wing factions of his own party, the president also refused to privatize the state-owned electricity company, Empresa Nacional de Energía Eléctrica (ENEE), and the telecommunications firm, Hondutel (EIU, 2009).

At the same time, it is easy to exaggerate the leftist turn of the Liberals under Zelaya, which, at least in domestic policy, never escaped the parameters of the *izquierda permitida*. Public spending on education remained at merely 3.8 percent of GDP. In April 2006 Honduras joined the Dominican Republic–Central American Free Trade Agreement (DR-CAFTA) with the United States, an accord meant to abolish tariffs and other trade barriers and establish an environment attractive to foreign direct investment, particularly export-oriented multinational firms with an interest in making Honduras their launching pad (EIU, 2008: 10). Two years later, in April 2008, Zelaya's government signed a standby agreement with the IMF that "commits the government to maintaining macroeconomic stability, lowering current spending (particularly the government's wage bill), achieving a fiscal deficit of 1.5% of GDP, and focusing public expenditure on infrastructure and poverty reduction" (EIU, 2008: 10). What is more, to the extent that Zelaya enacted social reforms, it was in no small part due to consistent and intense pressures exercised from below through increasingly militant trade unions, peasant organizations, and student groups influenced by revolutionary left ideologies and liberation theology. There were no fewer than 722 officially recorded social conflicts over the first thirty-two months of his presidency, against privatization and free trade and for salary increases and subsidies to control the price of the basic breadbasket (Hernández Navarro, 2009).

As noted, Honduras entered a steep economic downturn in 2008 associated with the spiraling global crisis, and particularly the deepening slump in the United States, Honduras's main export market and source of tourists, remittances, and foreign direct investment. It was in this context that Zelaya pragmatically opted for joining ALBA in September of that year. As part of the deal, "Venezuela . . . offered to buy Honduran bonds worth $100m, whose proceeds will be spent on housing for the poor. Mr. Chávez has also offered a $30m credit line for farming, 100 tractors, and 4m low-energy light bulbs (Cuba will send technicians to help to install them, as well as more doctors and literacy teachers)" (*Economist*, 2008a). The international financial press saw this move on the part of Zelaya not as "a matter of ideological association, but rather one driven by financial need" (*Economist*, 2008b).[7]

Nonetheless, as history has indicated, it is hardly necessary for Latin American governments to adopt social revolutionary measures before the traditional elite and conservative military forces feel threatened and act violently in protection of their interests. In the lead-up to the nonbinding referendum to be held at the end of June 2009, tensions sharpened. Zelaya called on the military to distribute the ballots for the referendum after the Supreme Court had ruled that the referendum was illegal.[8] The head of the Honduran armed forces, General Romeo Orlando Vásquez Velásquez, refused to comply. Zelaya dismissed Vásquez as head of the armed forces, and the general went on to play the leading military role in the coup against Zelaya.[9] Once Vásquez had been fired, the minister of defence, Ángel Orellana, resigned and the Supreme Court ruled that Vásquez's dismissal was illegal (*Jornada*, 2009). The majority of Congress, including the right-wing faction of the Liberal party led by Micheletti, turned against the president.[10] A medley of conservative social forces saw their opportunity and converged around the overthrow of Zelaya: "Conservative evangelicals and Catholics—including Opus Dei, a formidable presence in Honduras—detested him because he refused to ban the 'morning-after' pill. The mining, hydroelectric and biofuel sector didn't like him because he didn't put state funds and land at their disposal. The law-and-order crowd hated him because he apologized on behalf of the state for a program of 'social cleansing' that took place in the 1990s, which included the execution of street children and gang members. And the generals didn't like it when he tried to assert executive control over the military" (Grandin, 2009b; see also *Latin Business Chronicle*, 2009).

The Imperialist Assault on Honduran Democracy

The coup against Zelaya provided the United States with an opportunity, as Henry Veltmeyer notes in this volume, to recover some of its influence in the region, which had waned since the 1990s in the context of the reemergence of radical social movements, the election of left-wing administrations, and a foreign policy more absorbed with the Middle East and Central Asia. Part of the reassertion of American power in the region under the Obama administration, tied as this process is to American support for the Honduran coup, is the aim of checking the influence of Venezuelan President Hugo Chávez and the Bolivarian Revolution (expressed through subregional formations like ALBA and Petrocaribe) and ensuring the maintenance of a neoliberal trade and investment regime. This entails an increasingly aggressive foreign policy posture, expressed in a stronger projection of military power (such as the Obama administration's agreement for seven new military bases in Colombia), greater political alignment with stalwart imperial allies with very poor human rights records (such as Colombia and Peru), and support for the extra-constitutional efforts of right-wing forces to violently depose political leaders and repress social movements that are not sufficiently acquiescent to the neoliberal status quo. Thus the Honduran coup, despite its affront to liberal democratic norms, gave the United States an opportunity it was not going to pass up to roll back social and anti-imperial gains (however modest) in that Central American country in particular and the region in general.

In its calculated response to the coup, the Obama administration has been careful not to be seen as openly supporting it while nevertheless undermining Zelaya and the anti-coup resistance at every turn. Brazenly supporting the violent attack on liberal democracy in Honduras, in a context in which even the very moderate governments (what Veltmeyer refers to as social neoliberal regimes) of the region issued sharp condemnations of the coup, would undermine whatever political capital Obama could conceivably muster from his "liberal" credentials in the still-early days of his tenure. But this obviously does not gainsay American aspirations to undermine Zelaya and the reform movement in Honduras. Zelaya may have returned to Honduras (to be imprisoned in the Brazilian embassy), the Tegucigalpa–San José Accord may have been signed by Micheletti and Zelaya at the urging of the Americans and Canadians, and the fraudulent November 29, 2009, elections may have proceeded, but the coup—despite never being explicitly supported by the United States—was successful in truncating Zelaya's presidency and stifling efforts at constitutional reform. The region's progressive forces (leery of suffering Zelaya's fate) and right-wing forces (emboldened by the successes of the coup) will undoubtedly be forced to take notice.

In some ways the American government's position can be gleaned as much from what it has not done as from what it has. Referring on the day of the coup simply to the "detention and expulsion of President Mel Zelaya," Obama merely called on "all political and social actors in Honduras to respect democratic norms, the rule of law and the tenets of the Inter-American Democratic Charter" (White House, 2009). There is neither reference to a coup nor any demand for Zelaya's immediate return, nor are the coup forces singled out for rebuke. Instead, attention is drawn to "all political and social actors," tacitly implicating Zelaya and his supporters as responsible for his forceful removal from power. The Obama administration only declared that Zelaya was the rightful president of Honduras and should be allowed to return home after the OAS, the European Union, the UN General Assembly, and the presidents of Brazil, Argentina, and Chile denounced the coup and demanded Zelaya's return (Cockburn, 2009).

This declaration by the Obama administration did not mark a serious about-face on the part of the United States, however. When the OAS threatened to suspend Honduras following the coup, Micheletti proactively withdrew his government from the body. Instead of leading to stronger reaction by the United States, this action led to the Obama administration, working with Canada, seeking to water down the OAS's resolution suspending Honduras (preventing it from adopting sanctions, for instance) and imposing negotiations—outside the framework of the OAS, where opposition to the coup was stronger—on Micheletti and Zelaya through Costa Rican president cum mediator Oscar Arias. The San José mediation process drew sharp criticism from Latin American leaders, who charged that the negotiations represented an end run around the OAS and provided legitimacy to the coup leadership (ALBA, 2009; Grandin, 2009a, 2009b; Thompson and Lacey, 2009). The talks were not designed to bring a just resolution to the situation, nor could they ever do so. Zelaya, the democratically elected president, was being forced to negotiate his return with a coup plotter, and all the real pressure for a solution was being placed on him. As negotiations faltered, American officials, including Secretary of State Hilary Clinton, would remind Zelaya that he brought the coup on himself because of supposedly reckless and inflammatory behavior as president. At the same time, the proposals put forward by the American-allied Arias and rejected by Micheletti were clearly designed to undermine any strength Zelaya may have had and to render him toothless should he actually return to the presidency. Aside from Zelaya's reinstatement, Arias's proposals included Zelaya's agreement not to pursue constitutional reforms, amnesty for participants in the coup, the establishment of a national unity government including coup leaders, and moving up general elections—and thus shortening Zelaya's already truncated presidency—from the end of November 2009 to the end of October (Mejía, 2009). Even if Micheletti accepted these proposals, Zelaya's modest social-reform agenda would clearly have been defeated.

Thus the Obama administration may have stated that Zelaya was the rightful president of Honduras and should be allowed to return home, but it was evident that Micheletti was not going to make that easy and that the Americans were not going to do anything to strengthen the hands of Zelaya and the anti-coup movement. Micheletti's refusal to allow Zelaya to return, his hard line in the original San José negotiations, and his recourse to repression should not be viewed, therefore, as a misreading of Washington's desires or as exploiting an ambiguous position from the White House. The Obama administration's position on the coup is less ambiguous than right-wing critics, including Republican opponents in Congress and former officials in past Republican administrations, have aggressively suggested. The latter have painted Honduras as an important front in the fight against the spread of Chavism and left-wing populism in the region (Thompson and Nixon, 2009).[11] Point man in Central America during the Regan administration and senior official for both Bush presidencies Otto Reich, for instance, pronounced that "what happens in Honduras may one day be seen as either the high-water mark of Hugo Chávez's attempt to undermine democracy in this hemisphere, or as a green light to the continued spread of Chávista authoritarianism under the guise of democracy" (quoted in Pine, 2010: 20). But this perspective is likely not lost on the Obama administration. While Obama has talked about his "New Partnership for the Americas," his goals of fighting poverty, hunger, and global warming with his Latin American counterparts, and relaxed restrictions on travel and remittances to Cuba, he also attacked during his presidential campaign "demagogues like Hugo Chávez" and "his predictable yet perilous mix of anti-American rhetoric, authoritarian government, and checkbook diplomacy that . . . offers the same false promise as the tried and failed ideologies of the past" (Dangl, 2009). Obama appointments for the region include ambassador to Honduras Hugo Llorens, who held the Andean desk at the National Security Council during the failed 2002 coup against Chávez, and advisor for the Summit of the Americas Jeffery Davidow, who served as ambassador to Chile during the coup against Salvador Allende in 1973 (Ross and Rein, 2009). The Obama administration also announced in the fall of 2009, as noted above, plans to open seven military bases in Colombia, whose tensions with Venezuela are well known.

So the Obama administration may not be as bluntly pro-coup as its Republican critics, but it has no interest in assisting reform-minded leaders or popular movements—and its response to events in Honduras confirms this. As a number of observers have pointed out, the Obama administration could have taken sharper measures against the coup government, and done so more quickly, but chose not to. Two months after the coup, when it was clear that Micheletti was not going to support the San José Accord, and with pressure mounting internationally and in the United States to step up the pressure on the coup regime, Clinton finally announced the United States was cutting aid to Honduras and freezing the visas of coup supporters. But military aid was excluded from this action, and the assets of the individuals behind the coup, which could have been frozen, were not, while only four people initially had their visas revoked (to be expanded in late October) (Grandin, 2009a, 2009b; Joyce, 2010). Thus from July to September the United States condemned the coup, on the one hand, but allowed the coup regime to survive, ensuring the prolongation of Zelaya's exile and the repression of the resistance. Neither Obama nor Clinton spoke out against the violence directed toward opponents of the coup or the censorship of media in Honduras, but instead simply called for both sides to continue negotiating. One State Department official interviewed by Adrienne Pine (2010) actually played down the repression against the anti-coup resistance and suggested that the resistance itself had committed violence. This was a calculated strategy by the State Department to promote the legitimacy of the Micheletti dictatorship as a mere interim government helping to stabilize an otherwise chaotic situation, and thus as a worthy negotiating partner. As Rosemary Joyce (2010: 15) notes, "State Department statements aimed at an evenhanded approach that treated the de facto government as equivalent to the constitutional executive."

As the violence continued and efforts to negotiate Zelaya's return (with powers narrowly circumscribed) stalled, Zelaya would continue to be blamed for his fate. This was made clear in a letter on August 4 to Richard Lugar, senior Republican senator on the Senate Foreign Relations Committee, signed by Assistant Secretary of State for Legislative Affairs Richard Verma, which states that the government is not "supporting any particular politician or individual" and that "Zelaya's insistence on undertaking provocative actions contributed to the polarization of Honduran society and led to a confrontation that unleashed the events that led to his removal" (quoted in Litvinsky, 2009). The coup regime, meanwhile, responded to criticisms of its forceful removal of Zelaya with a public relations offensive, funded by the Business Council of Latin America and employing former lawyer to Bill Clinton and presidential campaign advisor to Hilary Lanny Davis (Goodman, 2009). The work of Davis, along with a number of right-wing think tanks and their congressional allies that dominated debate on the coup in Washington (Pine, 2010), was largely responsible for the inaccurate but politically effective claim, repeated ad nauseam by the media, that Zelaya was removed from office because he was making a power grab (that is, his constitutional reforms were simply aimed at allowing himself to run for president again). This has served to smear Zelaya in the popular North American consciousness, reducing pressure on the Obama government to take more meaningful action to restore democracy in Honduras.

Rather than a reversal of fortunes for coup supporters, the Tegucigalpa–San José Accord and the electoral cycle following it marked another victory against democracy in Honduras. While Zelaya's surreptitious return to Tegucigalpa in September shook the dictatorship and its supporters (both at home and abroad), the repression Micheletti unleashed against the anti-coup movement faced little meaningful objection from the United States, which in turn successfully pushed for the accord. Although the accord should be seen in part as the product of an incredibly resilient anti-coup movement, the United States was also undoubtedly motivated by the knowledge that the November elections—and the Obama administration's policy on the crisis, including its support for the elections—would not achieve legitimacy in the international community without a nominal return to constitutional order, especially with Zelaya back in the country. Of course, the democratic restoration the Americans were seeking was not that for which working-class and poor Hondurans had been fighting.

The Americans presented the accord as a major victory for democracy in Honduras. It is clear, however, that what was signed by Zelaya—under siege in the Brazilian embassy and hoping perhaps that even a weak agreement before the elections would put the coup forces further back on their heels—was in reality a victory for pro-coup forces inside and outside of Honduras. For instance, the accord did not ensure Zelaya's reinstatement but referred it back to Congress; it called for a power-sharing government of Zelaya and coup supporters; it ruled out appeals for the convening of a constituent assembly; and, of course, the settlement came five months after the coup and with only two months left in Zelaya's term. It quickly became clear, however, that the coup regime was not actually going to reinstate Zelaya, and instead it began—and finished—the electoral campaign with him still under siege in the Brazilian embassy. And with the accord in place, the Obama administration proceeded to then reverse its position that it would not recognize the elections without constitutional order being reestablished. Assistant Secretary of the State Thomas Shannon (2009) argued that "the formation of the National Unity Government is apart from the reinstatement of President Zelaya" and that under the accord it is the Honduran Congress that will decide whether to reinstate him or not. Zelaya—who subsequently withdrew his support for the accord, calling it "without value" (quoted in *Latin America Herald Tribune*, 2009)—was again left in the cold. As expected, despite the repression leading up to and during the vote and the questions surrounding the turnout, the United States was quick to recognize the elections as legitimate.

The election has been used by the Obama administration to recognize the Lobo government, claim that the coup is over and the return of constitutional normalcy achieved, and encourage Honduras's reintegration with the international community. Following the election, Clinton argued that "by voting in the November 29 presidential election in Honduras . . . the Honduran people expressed their commitment to a democratic future for their country. They turned out in large numbers, and they threw out, in effect, the party of both President Zelaya and the de facto leader, Mr. Micheletti" (Joyce, 2010: 10). This is of course an obvious misrepresentation of the election and the Lobo government, which, despite token representation from the social democratic Partido Unificación Democrática, is full of pro-coup supporters. Nevertheless, Clinton has continued to press for recognition of the Lobo government, including at the OAS General Assembly in Lima in June 2010, where she asserted that "we saw the free and fair election of President Lobo," who has formed "a government of national reconciliation and a truth commission." "Now it is time," she insisted, "for the hemisphere as a whole to move forward and welcome Honduras back into the inter-American community" (Clinton, 2010). Yet Honduras is still a very dangerous place to organize or speak out against the government or its ruling oligarchy. Between Lobo's inauguration at the end of January 2010 and Clinton's speech to the OAS General Assembly in June, at least eight journalists and six *campesinos*, organizing to reclaim land in Aguán stolen by wealthy landowners during a previous government, have been assassinated.[12] It has been reported by activists in Aguán, furthermore, that Colombian paramilitaries, who observers of Colombia have demonstrated are tied to the Colombian government that is closely aligned with the United States, have helped train local security forces (Bird, 2010; Hristov, 2009). Colombian President Alvaro Uribe and Lobo, in fact, signed a security cooperation agreement following the latter's inauguration, which was followed by a delegation of Honduran mayors and Interior Minister Africo Madrid to Colombia in April to discuss common security concerns and strategies (Fernandez, 2010). This "government of national reconciliation," in other words, is inserting Honduras into a violent security nexus of imperial-aligned forces.

As we have suggested above, however, the United States has not been alone in its support for the coup. Canada has also played an important role, as it works to increase its standing in the region to protect the interests of Canadian capital against the specter of left-of-center governments. The United States is not the only country with extensive capitalist interests in the region, nor is it the only country supporting the forces of reaction in Honduras. Canada is actually one of the largest foreign investors in Latin America in general and in Honduras in particular. It has in fact the largest mining industry in the world, and the ecologically destructive actions of Canadian mining companies, and their general disregard for communities living in mining areas, has been met with well-organized and militant resistance throughout the Americas, including in Honduras (Gordon, 2010; Gordon and Webber, 2008, 2010a; North, Clark, and Patroni, 2006).

There is not space here to fully cover Canada's role in the success of the coup.[13] However, like Hilary Clinton, Canada's minister for the Americas, Peter Kent, has consistently ignored violence against the resistance and blamed Zelaya for his ouster. Canada maintains the November 2009 elections were fair and was quick to recognize the Lobo government. Kent actually visited the new Honduran president in February before Clinton made her first visit, and his meeting with Lobo was followed by that of Ambassador Neil Reeder, who brought with him representatives of Canadian capital, who used the opportunity to push for a new liberalized mining law. Canada's representative at the OAS, Graeme Clark, speaking before Clinton at the General Assembly in Lima, argued as well for Honduras's readmission into the OAS. Support for coup forces comes as Canada has strengthened its relations with Colombia, publicly denounced the Venezuelan government, pressured the Ecuadorian government of Rafael Correa to water down an initial draft of its new mining law, supported the coup against Jean-Bertrand Aristide in Haiti while continuing to play a lead role in that country's post-earthquake neoliberal reconstruction, and generally worked to defend the interests of Canadian capital in the hemisphere (Gordon, 2010).

Cracks in the Empire: A New Honduran Left Emerges

A crucial turning point in the effort of the regime to consolidate the coup took place in the form of fraudulent elections on November 29, 2009, elections designed to construct a democratic guise to the continuation of the coup. Porfirio Lobo won the elections and was inaugurated on January 27, 2010, in the midst of mass resistance protests in the streets of Tegucigalpa and elsewhere. A veritable reign of terror cast its long shadow over voting day on November 29. An atmosphere of military repression and intimidation prevailed. The election was boycotted by the anti-coup resistance movement, offered no candidate opposing the coup, and has not been recognized by most Latin American governments. The official voter turnout figure of over 60 percent provided by the Honduran Electoral Tribunal is almost certainly inflated. One official with the tribunal told the *Real News* that the figure was pure invention. Hagamos Democracia, a nongovernmental organization contracted by the tribunal to provide early reporting, put the turnout at 47.6 percent. Drawing on grassroots reports from across the country, various activists of the FRNP we spoke to claim that turnout was probably closer to 30 percent.

Paramilitary terrorization of the FNRP and its allies has been constant throughout the period since Zelaya's overthrow and has not slowed since Lobo's assumption of office. According to the Comité de Familiares de Detenidos Desaparecidos en Honduras (Committee of Family Members of the Disappeared of Honduras, COFADEH), the country's most prestigious human rights organization, founded in the 1980s, there had been forty-three politically motivated assassinations of civilians associated with the resistance by the end of February 2010. This number is almost surely a low estimate, the human rights organization acknowledges, as community members and the families of those killed are often too afraid to come forward for fear of repri-sal. Many political murders are passed over in the mainstream media as gang killings. As early as January 2010, the FNRP claimed that over 130 activists had been assassinated. By March 5, 2010, COFADEH had documented 250 violations of human rights since Lobo's inauguration on January 27.

After Costa Rica, Honduras had stood out as the Central American coun-try with the longest period of uninterrupted constitutional governments (1981–2009) in recent history (Cálix, 2010: 35). Consequently, the coup of June 2009 was a particularly stunning shock to the country's political system. At the same time, the break in constitutional rule in Honduras may well be a harbinger of things to come in neighboring countries if the fragilities of their electoral democracies continue to reproduce themselves. A number of Latin American scholars situate the Honduran coup in the wider context of narrowly circumscribed, elite-driven transitions to electoral democracy throughout Central America generally in the 1980s and 1990s—transitions that resolutely failed to address enduring problems of inequality and poverty (Rojas Bolaños, 2010: 101; Torres-Rivas, 2010: 53–56). The social chasms in the structure of Honduran society eventually forced Zelaya to take up a series of modest reforms, as we have seen, but these same fissures meant that the tiny oligarchy in whose hands so much of the country's wealth is concen-trated had a tremendous amount to lose if democracy were to begin to extend beyond the attenuated ritual of elections every four years into the areas of in-come and wealth redistribution, not to speak of enduring inequalities in other sociocultural and economic realms. Against this backdrop, Zelaya's cautious shifts in domestic and foreign policy were perceived as a perilous omen of deeper potential challenges to the status quo around the corner, and so the oligarchs, supported by North American imperial powers, orchestrated and consolidated their coup d'état.

However, as an unanticipated consequence of their casual breach of liberal institutions, the coup plotters spurred the emergence of an increasingly powerful popular resistance that has been characterized by ideologies and practices much closer to the radical left of the spectrum than had been the case in most of the modern political history of the Honduran Left (Rojas Bolaños, 2010: 111). The resistance erupted almost immediately. While Micheletti celebrated his triumphal seizure of the presidency, elsewhere in the capital, and throughout the country, an eruption of the popular classes—led by teachers, urban workers, students, indigenous communities, peasants, the urban poor, environmentalists, women's organizations, and others—was taking shape and braving waves of repression. Makeshift barricades were erected in Tegucigalpa, highways were blockaded, tires burned in the streets, clashes between protesters, police, and the military erupted, and graffiti labeling Micheletti a fascist and, better, "Pinocheletti," sprang up on walls throughout the cities.[14] "They want to kick Zelaya out at whatever cost," Rafael Alegría contended, "but the only thing they have achieved is to present our country as savage, where the rules of democracy are not respected. Or do you know of another case in the world in which a poll has originated a coup d'état?" (quoted in Cano, 2009a). Between June 28 and November 29, when the national elections consolidating the coup were held, there were roughly 150 days of continuous resistance activities, with charged pinnacles on July 5—when Zelaya unsuccessfully attempted a return from exile by plane—and September 15— when the FNRP organized a parallel march to the official state celebrations of National Independence Day (Cálix, 2010: 44).

The institutional core of the FNRP consists of different sectors of the labor movement—particularly teachers, banana workers, public-sector workers, and bottling-plant workers. However, it also incorporates an array of social-movement actors, including peasants, women, alternative media groups, indigenous and Afro-indigenous sectors, human rights organizations, and lesbian, gay, bisexual, and transgender (LGBT) activists, among others (Frank, 2010). Delegates from these various social-movement and trade union bases are sent to participate in the central coordinating body of the front as representatives of their sectors. More than simply calling for the return of Zelaya, the FNRP almost immediately began calling for a constituent assembly to fundamentally refound the country on the basis of social justice and equality. In ideology, and through its reliance on direct, mass actions that have built the capacities of popular sectors to organize themselves under dire conditions, the FNRP represents an increasingly radical social Left in the Honduran landscape.

Around this institutional core of the resistance radiates roughly three wider constituencies. First, there are the Zelayistas, Liberal Party supporters of the deposed president who are animated in their support for resistance activities but who remain in many respects still reticent of the radical left program of the FNRP. Second, there are the grassroots activists of the social democratic Unificación Democrática (Democratic Unification, UD) party who have stayed loyal to the resistance, in spite of the betrayal of two of their important leaders, Carlos Ham and Marvin Ponce, who accepted positions in the new dictatorship of Lobo. Third, and finally, there are the largely unorganized, proletarian urban neighborhoods, which—until recently dominated by the antipolitics of gang violence—have supported the struggle against the coup regimes without having integral links to the institutional structures of the FNRP (Frank, 2010).

The authors witnessed the spirit of the resistance most vividly in the streets of Tegucigalpa on Wednesday, January 27, 2010, the date of Lobo's inauguration. It was clear that with the transfer of power from Micheletti to Lobo business as usual would not go uncontested by the FNRP. Despite the black-suited sharpshooters visible on the tower edges of buildings running parallel to the resistance march and the hundreds of military and police troops weighed down with automatic weapons, it was hardly obvious that the protesting masses had more to fear than Pepe Lobo. Indeed, as one popular resistance T-shirt proclaims, *"Nos tienen miedo porque no tenemos miedo" (They fear us because we're not afraid)*.

In a meeting the authors attended in Tegucigalpa on the eve of Lobo's inauguration, Radio Globo journalist Felix Molina suggested that Honduras was entering a fourth moment of the coup. The first phase involved its preparation and execution. The second saw the gathering of domestic elite and imperial forces around the San José Accord. The third carried out that accord. A week before Lobo's inauguration, the forth moment began to congeal. Posters plastered the walls of the capital celebrating the commencement of the new government of "national unity." "This fourth moment," Molina argued, was "about constructing normality, ostensibly with peace and reconciliation. It's about selling a supposed project of national integration. Essentially, the objective is to say that nothing happened here, that coups can be a democratic method to correct a democracy gone awry. The point of this fourth moment is to legalize the coup." As quickly as the state's posters of calm and consensus marked the avenues of Tegucigalpa, graffiti artists of the resistance offered their response— *Fuera golpistas asesinos! (Out with the coupist assassins!).* The corporate media cast Lobo as the "elected president," whereas the *FNRP* repudiated him as the "son of a coup." The corporate media celebrated a national unity government of integration, whereas the *FNRP* refused dialogue with Lobo's regime and denounced it as the latest incarnation of the original coup of June 2009.

This war of words found its material expression in the protesting cascades of hundreds of thousands marching from downtown toward the airport on

January 27. The march paid homage to Zelaya—as he finally escaped four months of sequestration in the Brazilian embassy for exile in the Dominican Republic—and, at the same time, announced that the struggle against the coup regime would continue. We approached the first row of military police and the crowd rang out, urging folks to study and learn so they'll never have to be on the other side of the barricades.

Estudiar, aprender, para chepo nunca ser!

A group of energetic ten-year-olds danced amid the marchers, chanting concordantly for the death of the *golpista* regime. Peasants, trade unionists, feminists, and different left groupings walked arm in arm and cheered ecstatically as cars moved in the other direction honking in solidarity. Teenagers leaned out of the windows of a passing bus, their fists raised in the air.

El pueblo ¿dónde está?
¡El pueblo está en las calles exigiendo libertad!
[Where are the people?
The people are in the streets demanding liberty!]
¿Estás cansado?
¡No!
¿Tienes miedo?
¡No!
¿Entonces?
¡Adelante, adelante, que la lucha es constante!
[Are you tired?
No!
Are you afraid?
No!
So?
Forward! Forward! In constant struggle!]

"The resistance has two principal pillars," Rafael Alegría, a principal peasant leader in the resistance, informed us during the march. "A social pillar for the revindication of the people's rights, in which the resistance accompanies people in their daily struggle, for agrarian reform, for just salaries, and opposition to the privatization of social services. This is the pillar of social mobilization." The other pillar, Alegría emphasized, "is the political arm—to convert ourselves into a militant political force that will work toward taking political power in our country."

We asked Alegría about the constituent assembly, as the crowd around us thundered:

> *¿Qué somos?*
> *¡Resistencia popular!*
> *¿Qué queremos?*
> *¡Constituyente!*
> *[What are we?*
> *Popular resistance!*
> *What do we want?*
> *Constituent assembly!]*

"The power of the people," he told us, "is going to result in massive transformations in this country. We are demanding a constituent assembly that is going to transform this country into a participatory democracy. It will be a new Honduras—a country with social justice, with equality, with a new model of development in which everyone is included, and, as the Bolivians say, so that our entire country can live well." Alegría contrasts this vision with the "current situation, in which there is a privileged oligarchy, which owns and controls everything, while on the other hand there is an immense mass of impoverished people. This can't continue."

Two days earlier, in a gathering of the resistance outside the Brazilian embassy to celebrate National Women's Day in Honduras, Brenda Villacorta, of Feminists in Resistance, expressed many of the same sentiments. "Lobo's possession of office doesn't represent anything. It is the continuation, the perpetuation, of the coup d'état that took place in this country on June 28, 2009. The protagonists have changed but the scenario is exactly the same." The marchers of January 27 agreed:

> *!No existe presidente!*
> *!Si a la constituyente!*
> *[There is no president!*
> *We demand a constituent assembly!]*

"The resistance will take to the streets again and again," Villacorta said. "This is the only way we can apply pressure, or at least the most effective way of doing so." "The process to create the constituent assembly will be a long one," she estimated, but worth the struggle. "The old constitution was established under a military dictatorship, and it does not benefit the Honduran people, the authentic Honduran people. Instead, it works in the interests of the business class and the big power groups."

For the Honduran Resistance, Lobo does not signify an end of the coup but rather its consolidation under the veneer of democratic legitimacy. One day into his presidency, Lobo had already declared a financial emergency and called for new fiscal austerity measures. Together with the amnesty law for protagonists of the coup and the opening up of mining concessions, all signals pointed to the consolidation of a hard-right shift in domestic and economic policy, no doubt designed to roll back the modest reforms introduced by Zelaya. The coming socioeconomic assault on the popular classes, in the midst of a deep recession exacerbated by the coup plotters, alongside continuing repression and political intimidation, present formidable challenges to the resistance looking forward. If January 27 revealed anything, however, it was that there are two sides to Honduras. The pole of Pepe Lobo and the imperialists, on the one hand, and the sea of exploited and oppressed. If the masses have not yet gathered sufficient power to toss Lobo into the dustbin of history, they have just as clearly demonstrated that they will not be easily cowed by a tiny minority, even when it is armed to the teeth.

Conclusion

By tracing the narrative of domestic Honduran political struggles and the role of U.S. imperialism in the country since the 1980s, this chapter has sought to provide a historical context for a richer understanding of the June 2009 coup against Manuel Zelaya and the resistance that has emerged against the successive Micheletti and Lobo regimes. The chapter revealed how the Honduran Left, in both its social and its political modalities, has traditionally been much closer to the *izquierda permitida* ideal type than the lefts of its immediate neighbors, particularly in the 1980s. U.S. imperialism took advantage of the weaknesses of the Left in Honduras and transformed the country into a geopolitical base of counterinsurgent operations against the Sandinista regime and Salvadoran and Guatemalan guerrillas. In the 1990s and 2000s, as Central America transitioned toward formally democratic electoral regimes, the state terror of the 1980s metamorphosed into the silent economic weapons of neoliberal economic restructuring. The already weakened infrastructures of the Honduran Left were battered still further, as urban trade unions and peasant movements suffered under dramatic transformations in rural and urban class structures.

Out of this context, it was argued, Zelaya emerged as a president of the modest Left, instating a range of domestic reforms that fell broadly within the *izquierda permitida* policy domain. However, in foreign policy, Zelaya's pragmatic alignment with the Chávez administration in Venezuela led to heightened tensions with the Honduran ruling class and North American imperialism. Since the ouster of Zelaya was carried out through military violence, a new and dynamic social Left has arisen through the structures of the anti-coup resistance. Deviating from Honduras's past of moderate leftism, a core of the resistance is increasingly expressing radical political practices, informed by anti-imperial, anti-oppressive, anti-neoliberal, and even anti-capitalist ideologies.

Notes

1. This report also points to the rise since the mid-1990s of nontraditional exports such as shrimp, tilapia, melons, and African palm oil. In the traditional agricultural sector, it charts the renewal of high prices in coffee since 2004 and the increased production that has consequently arisen, whereas bananas have suffered from increases in tariffs in the European Union. One of the areas highlighted to be of great interest to foreign investors is the mining of zinc, silver, lead, and gold. Honduras is thought to have large unexploited mineral deposits that could become available for foreign investors if controversial environmental legislation can be passed.

2. Likewise, the Inter-American Development Bank projects that remittances flows to Latin America and the Caribbean will fall by 11 percent in 2009 to the lowest level since 2006, with El Salvador, Honduras, Haiti, and Nicaragua to be hit hardest. See Mapstone (2009).

3. It should be noted that while Honduras benefited overall from the high price of its principal export commodities in these years it also suffered from the high price of oil between 2004 and 2007 given its status as a petroleum importer.

4. Note that the 2008 figure was still an approximation at the time of writing.

5. On the Via Campesina, see Desmarais (2007).

6. Hurricane Mitch, which struck in October 1998, left more than eleven thousand dead and an astonishing two million people homeless (of a total population of 7.1 million). Among the worst hit were the rural-to-urban migrants "who had settled on the crowded hillsides surrounding Tegucigalpa, which were washed away" (Booth, Wade, and Walker, 2006: 145).

7. See also Thomson (2008).

8. "Supporters of the coup," Mark Weisbrot (2009) notes, "argue that the president violated the law by attempting to go ahead with the referendum after the Supreme Court ruled against it. This is a legal question; it may be true, or it may be that the Supreme Court had no legal basis for its ruling. But it is irrelevant to what has happened: the military is not the arbiter of a constitutional dispute between the various branches of government."

9. Vásquez, it is relevant to point out, was trained at the School of the Americas on two separate occasions, in 1976 and 1984. The commander of the air force, Javier Prince Suazo, who also played a part in the coup d'état, was trained at the school in 1996 (Brooks, 2009).

10. The composition of the 128 seats in Congress was as follows: Liberal Party (62); National Party (55); Partido de Unificación Democrática (Democratic Unification Party, PUD) (5); Partido Demócrata Cristiana (Christian Democratic Party, PDC) (4); and the Partido de Innovación Nacional y Unidad-Social Demócrata (Party of National Innovation and Social Democratic Unity). The only party that formally took a position against the coup was the PUD.

11. The former Republican administration officials include Otto Reich, Roger Noriega, and Daniel W. Fisk.

12. On the killings of journalists or activists in Aguán, consult http://hondurashumanrights.wordpress.com and www.cofadeh.org.

13. For fuller elaboration of Canada's role in the coup, see Gordon (2010) and Gordon and Webber (2010b, 2010c).

14. "Pinocheletti" refers to Augusto Pinochet, the Chilean dictator in power between 1973 and 1990. See Borón (2009); Cano (2009b, 2009c); Cuevas and Weissert (2009).

References

ALBA. 2009. "Declaration of the ALBA Political Council on Honduras." August 9. http://mrzine.monthlyreview.org/alba180809.html.

Bird, Annie. 2010. "Land Crisis and Repression in Aguán, Honduras." *Works in Progress*, May.

Booth, John A., Christine J. Wade, and Thomas W. Walker. 2006. *Understanding Central America: Global Forces, Rebellion, and Change.* 4th ed. Boulder, CO: Westview.

Borón, Atilio. 2009. "Honduras: la futilidad del golpe." *Rebelión*, June 29.

Brooks, David. 2009. "Golpe de estado en Honduras." *La Jornada*, July 1.

Cálix, Álvaro. 2010. "Honduras: de la crisis política al surgimiento de un nuevo actor social." *Nueva Sociedad*, no. 226 (March–April): 34–51.

Cano, Arturo. 2009a. "Zelayistas desafían el toque de queda; hay decenas de heridos." *La Jornada*, June 29.

———. 2009b. "Golpistas agradecen apoyo en mitin de 'autoconvencimiento.'" *La Jornada*, June 30.

———. 2009c. "Zelayistas afirman que se requieren 'nuevas estrategias de protesta popular.'" *La Jornada*, June 30.

CEPAL. 2000a. *Anuario estadístico de América Latina y el Caribe.* Santiago: Comisión Económica para América Latina y el Caribe.

———. 2000b. *Panorama social de América Latina 1999–2000.* Santiago: Comisión Económica para América Latina y el Caribe.

———. 2008. *Panorama social de América Latina 2008.* Santiago: Comisión Económica para América Latina y el Caribe.

———. 2009. *Anuario estadístico de América Latina y el Caribe 2008.* Santiago: Comisión Económica para América Latina y el Caribe.

Clinton, Hilary. 2010. Address to the Second Plenary Session of the General Assembly of the Organization of States of the Americas. June 7. http://www.oas.org/en/media_center/speech.asp?sCodigo=10-0045.

Cockburn, Alex. 2009. "Gob-smacked." *CounterPunch*, July 3–5. http://www.counter-punch.org/2009/07/03/gob-smacked/.

Cruz, José Miguel. 2010. "Estado y violencia criminal en América Latina: Reflexiones a partir del golpe en Honduras." *Nueva Sociedad*, no. 226 (March–April): 67–84.

Cuevas, Freddy, and Hill Weissert. 2009. "World Leaders Increase Pressure on Honduras." *Globe and Mail*, June 30.

Dangl, Benjamin. 2009. "Obama Set for a Summit in the Sun." *Nation*, April 16. http://www.thenation.com/article/obama-set-summit-sun.

Davis, Mike. 2006. *Planet of Slums*. London: Verso.

Desmarais, Annette. 2007. *La Vía Campesina: Globalization and the Power of Peasants*. London: Pluto Press.

Dunkerley, James. 1994. *The Pacification of Central America: Political Change in the Isthmus, 1987–1993*. London: Verso.

ECLAC. 2006. *Preliminary Overview of the Economies of Latin America and the Caribbean 2005*. Santiago: Economic Commission for Latin America and the Caribbean.

———. 2009. *Preliminary Overview of the Economies of Latin America and the Caribbean 2008*. Santiago: Economic Commission for Latin America and the Caribbean.

Economist. 2008a. "Zelaya Plays the Chávez Card." October 30.

———. 2008b. "Leaning Left: Honduras Joins a Club Promoted by Venezuela and Cuba." October 20.

EIU. 2008. *Honduras: Country Profile*. London: Economist Intelligence Unit.

———. 2009. "Honduras Politics: Mixed Report Card for Zelaya." Economist Intelligence Unit, May 10.

Fernandez, Belen. 2010. "U.S. Advises Security Apprenticeships in Colombia." *Upside Down World*, April 23. http://upsidedownworld.org/main/colombia-ar-chives-61/2463-us-advises-security-apprenticeships-in-colombia.

Flynn, Patricia. 1984. "The United States at War in Central America: Unable to Win, Unwilling to Lose." In *The Politics of Intervention: The United States in Central America*, ed. Roger Burbach and Patricia Flynn, 91–132. New York: Monthly Review Press.

Frank, Dana. 2005. *Bananeras: Women Transforming the Banana Unions of Latin America*. Cambridge, MA: South End Press.

———. 2010. "Out of the Past, a New Honduran Culture of Resistance." *NACLA.org*, May 3. https://nacla.org/node/6541.

Gill, Lesley. 2004. *The School of the Americas: Military Training and Political Violence in the Americas*. Durham, NC: Duke University Press.

Goodman, Amy. 2009. "A Coup for Lobbyists at the White House." *Rabble.ca*, August 5. www.rabble.ca/columnists/2009/08/coup-lobbyists-white-house.

Gordon, Todd. 2010. *Imperialist Canada*. Winnipeg: Arbeiter Ring.

Gordon, Todd, and Jeffery R. Webber. 2008. "Imperialism and Resistance: Canadian Mining Companies in Latin America." *Third World Quarterly* 29 (1): 63–88.

———. 2010a. "Canadian Mining and Popular Resistance in Honduras: An Interview with Carlos Danilo Amador." *Upside Down World*, February 2. http://upside-downworld.org/main/honduras-archives-46/2345-canadian-mining-and-popular-resistance-in-honduras.

———. 2010b. "Canada's Long Embrace of the Honduran Dictatorship." *Counter-Punch*, March 19–20. http://www.counterpunch.org/2010/03/19/canada-s-long-embrace-of-the-honduran-dictatorship/.

———. 2010c. "Consolidating the Coup in Honduras: Pepe Lobo, Imperialism and the Resistance." *CounterPunch*, February 5–7. http://www.counterpunch.org/2010/02/05/consolidating-the-coup-in-honduras/.

Grandin, Greg. 2006. *Empire's Workshop: Latin America, the United States, and the Rise of the New Imperialism*. New York: Owl Books.

———. 2009a. "Battle for Honduras—and the Region." *Nation*, August 31.

———. 2009b. "Waiting for Zelaya." *Nation*, July 28.

Hart-Landsberg, Martin. 2009. "Learning from ALBA and the Bank of the South: Changes and Possibilities." *Monthly Review* 61 (4): 1–18.

Hernández Navarro, Luis. 2009. "La conversión de Manuel Mel Zelaya." *La Jornada*, July 1.

Hristov, Jasmin. 2009. *Blood and Capital: The Paramilitarization of Colombia*. Athens: Ohio University Press.

Jornada, La. 2009. "Honduras: Contexto de la crisis política." June 30.

Joyce, Rosemary A. 2010. "Legitimizing the Illegitimate: The Honduran Show Elections and the Challenge Ahead." *NACLA Report on the Americas* 43 (2): 10–17.

LaFeber, Walter. 1993. *Inevitable Revolutions: The United States in Central America*. 2nd ed. New York: W. W. Norton.

Latin American Herald Tribune. 2009. "Deposed Honduran President Drops Deal in Letter to Obama." November 19. http://www.laht.com/article.asp?ArticleID=3474 20&CategoryId=23558.

Latin Business Chronicle. 2009. "Honduras Business Supports Zelaya Ouster." June 29.

Litvinsky, Marina. 2009. "Honduras: Obama Administration Restating Its Position?" *Upside Down World*, August 13. http://upsidedownworld.org/main/content/view/2051/68.

Malkin, Elisabeth. 2009. "Honduran President Is Ousted in Coup." *New York Times*, June 29.

Mapstone, Naomi. 2009. "Remittance Flows to Latin America Fall Sharply." *Financial Times*, August 12.

Mejía, Thelma. 2007. "In Tegucigalpa, the Iron Fist Fails." *NACLA Report on the Americas* 40 (4): 26–29.

———. 2009. "Honduras: Talks Stalled; Warnings of Civil War." *IPSNews.net*, July 20 http://www.ipsnews.net/news.asp?idnews=47732.

North, Liisa, Clark, Timothy David Clark, and Viviana Patroni, eds. 2006. *Community Rights and Corporate Responsibility: Canadian Mining and Oil Companies in Latin America*. Toronto: Between the Lines.

Ocampo, José Antonio. 2009. "Latin America and the Global Financial Crisis." *Cambridge Journal of Economics* 33 (4): 703–24.

Organization of American States. 2010. "Resolution on the Situation in Honduras." June 8.

Pine, Adrienne. 2010. "Message Control: Field Notes on Washington's Golpistas." *NACLA Report on the Americas* 43 (2): 18–22.

Reid, Michael. 2007. *Forgotten Continent: The Battle for Latin America's Soul.* New Haven, CT: Yale University Press.

Robinson, William I. 2003. *Transnational Conflicts: Central America, Social Change, and Globalization.* London: Verso.

———. 2004. "Global Crisis and Latin America." *Bulletin of Latin American Research* 23 (2): 134–53.

———. 2008. *Latin America and Global Capitalism: A Critical Globalization Perspective.* Baltimore: Johns Hopkins University Press.

Rogers, T. 2009. "Hugo Chávez, Daniel Ortega, and Other Leaders Met in Nicaragua Saturday Night to Offer a Response to the Ouster of President Manuel Zelaya." *Christian Science Monitor*, June 29.

Rojas Bolaños, Manuel. 2010. "Centroamérica: ¿Anomalías o realidades?" *Nueva Sociedad*, no. 226 (March–April): 100–114.

Ross, Clifton, and Marcy Rein. 2009. "Honduras, Washington and Latin America: Doctor Jekyll and Mr. Good Neighbor." *Upside Down World*, July 8. http://upsidedownworld.org/main/content/view/1978/1/.

Shannon, Tom. 2009. Interview. *CNN en Español*, November 4. http://www.youtube.com/watch?v=asbYkOMvbj8. Accessed November 30, 2009.

Thompson, Ginger. 2005a. "Race Tight after Vote for Honduran President." *New York Times*, November 28.

———. 2005b. "Honduras: Opposition Candidate Wins Election." *New York Times*, November 29.

Thompson, Ginger, and Marc Lacey. 2009. "OAS Votes to Suspend Honduras Over Coup." *New York Times*, July 4. http://www.nytimes.com/2009/07/05/world/americas/05honduras.html.

Thompson, Ginger, and Ron Nixon. 2009. "Leader Ousted, Honduras Hires U.S. Lobbyists." *New York Times*, October 8. http://www.nytimes.com/2009/10/08/world/americas/08honduras.html.

Thomson, Adam. 2008. "Pragmatic Alliances Determine Loyalties." *Financial Times*, September 18.

———. 2009. "Army Ousts Honduras President." *Financial Times*, June 28.

Torres-Rivas, Edelberto. 2010. "Las democracias malas de Centroamérica: Para entender lo de Honduras, una introducción a Centroamérica." *Nueva Sociedad*, no. 226 (March–April): 52–66.

UNDP. 2009. *Human Development Report 2009.* New York: United Nations.

Weisbrot, Mark. 2009. "Latin America Drags a Reluctant Washington into Supporting Democracy in Honduras." *Guardian*, July 1.

White House. 2009. "Statement from President on the Situation in Honduras." June 28. http://www.whitehouse.gov/the_press_office/Statement-from-the-President-on-the-situation-in-Honduras/.

Index